**A unique and thrilling picture
of one of the worst disasters
in British Imperial History**

On Sunday, May 10th, 1857, troops of the 3rd
Light Cavalry were relaxing in a brothel in
Meerut. The previous day 85 of their comrades
had been jailed for refusing to use the cartridges supplied for the new Enfield rifle,
which they believed were greased with fat
from animals that were forbidden to both
Moslems and Hindus. Taunted by prostitutes,
the Meerut troops rose in defense of their
comrades and stormed the jail, releasing the
prisoners and many other criminals as well.
Arson, looting, and murder began at once.
Cries of "Din! Din!" (For the Faith!) echoed in
the streets. A colonel was shot by his own
troops. A woman was stabbed. By 8:00 PM
Meerut was a city of terror, and the Great Indian Mutiny had begun.

> *"There was never a mutiny like it
> and there can never be another to
> compare with it. Collier's story is
> magnificent, sordid, uplifting and
> horrifying."*

—Detroit News

THE GREAT INDIAN MUTINY

A Dramatic Account of the Sepoy Rebellion

by

RICHARD COLLIER

Ballantine Books   *New York*

*To all the children of the Mutiny in
the hope of a new and deeper understanding
this book is dedicated*

If there be fuel prepared, it is hard to tell whence the spark shall come that shall set it on fire. . . . The causes and motives of seditions are, innovation in religion, taxes, alteration of laws and customs, breaking of privileges, general oppression, advancement of unworthy persons, strangers, dearths, disbanded soldiers, factions grown desperate; and whatsoever in offending people joineth and knitteth them in a common cause.

FRANCIS BACON: Of Seditions and
Troubles

CONTENTS

i CALCUTTA: *Morning 10th May*   11

ii CALCUTTA: *Afternoon 10th May*   21

iii MEERUT: *Evening 10th May*   31

iv DELHI: *Morning 11th May*   41

v DELHI: *Afternoon 11th May*   54

vi SIMLA *and* LAHORE: *11th-14th May*   60

vii CAWNPORE *and* LUCKNOW:
24th May-9th June   70

viii DELHI: *8th June*   78

ix GANGES VALLEY: *20th May-9th June*   89

x LUCKNOW: *30th May*   96

xi TILOWEE VILLAGE, LUCKNOW: *30th May*   104

xii CAWNPORE: *22nd May-6th June*   112

xiii CAWNPORE: *6th-25th June*   119

xiv CALCUTTA *and* ALLAHABAD:
17th June-7th July   130

xv CAWNPORE: *25th-27th June*   137

xvi LONDON: *26th June*   148

xvii TILOWEE VILLAGE, LUCKNOW: *July*   154

xviii BEHIND THE REBEL LINES: *September*   159

xix HAVELOCK'S COLUMN: *15th July*   162

xx CAWNPORE: *15th July*   167

xxi BEFORE CAWNPORE: *16th July*   170

xxii CAWNPORE: *17th July*   179

xxiii DELHI: *21st June-9th July*   181

xxiv DELHI: *26th July-4th August*   194

xxv DELHI: *7th August*   198

CONTENTS

xxvi	DELHI *and* GANGES VALLEY: *7th-26th August*	202
xxvii	LUCKNOW: *27th-30th June*	208
xxviii	LUCKNOW: *1st July-31st August*	220
xxix	CAWNPORE: *Afternoon 27th June*	234
xxx	BEHIND THE REBEL LINES: *July-September*	237
xxxi	LUCKNOW: THE REBEL LINES *September-November*	240
xxxii	DELHI: *11th-20th September*	243
xxxiii	DELHI: *20th-24th September*	261
xxxiv	LUCKNOW: *25th September*	268
xxxv	LUCKNOW: *26th September*	275
xxxvi	LUCKNOW: *26th September-8th November*	277
xxxvii	LUCKNOW: *9th November*	290
xxxviii	LUCKNOW: *9th-10th November*	296
xxxix	LUCKNOW: *10th-12th November*	302
xl	LUCKNOW: *14th November*	309
xli	LUCKNOW: *16th November*	312
xlii	LUCKNOW: *17th-29th November*	323
xliii	GANGES VALLEY: *After 3rd December*	334
xliv	LUCKNOW *and* CALCUTTA: *After 3rd December*	340
	Postscript	345
	Acknowledgments	348
	A Note on Sources	351
	Bibliography	355

ILLUSTRATIONS

Brigadier-General John Nicholson

Earl Canning, Governor General of India

Sir Colin Campbell

Major-General Sir Henry Havelock

Robert and Katherine Bartrum

Harriet and Robert Tytler

Henry Kavanagh

Flag Staff Battery, Delhi

Bridge of Boats, Delhi

Mohammed Bahadur Shah

Lahore Gate of the Palace, Delhi

Kashmir Gate, Delhi

General Wheeler's entrenchment, Cawnpore

British reprisals

Artist's impression of the storming of Delhi

Baillie Guard Gate, Lucknow, showing clock-tower

Road by which Havelock entered the Residency, Lucknow

Sikanderbagh, Lucknow. Interior

Sikanderbagh, Lucknow. Exterior

AUTHOR'S NOTES

This is not and was never intended to
be a definitive history of the Indian
Mutiny. Three Indian scholars, Dr.
Surendra Nath Sen, Dr. R. C. Majumdar
and Dr. S. B. Chaudhuri have in recent
years added much needed fundamental
research and shrewd interpretation to
the earlier synoptic accounts of Forrest,
Kaye and Malleson and Thomas Rice
Holmes. My purpose in writing this
book was solely to present an evocative
portrait of the time through the eyes of
a handful of people—what it looked like
to them, how it felt, how it sounded and
how it smelt.

R.C.

I. CALCUTTA

Morning 10th May

A football echoed in the marble corridor. The sepoy guards, ramrods in scarlet slashed with white crossbelts, snapped to attention. Eyes riveted ahead, they saw the handsome impassive profile of the Governor-General of India acknowledge their salute, passing on to his study. Relaxing, the bodyguard now knew the hour without need for consultation. Even on Sundays, in these weeks of crisis, Lord Canning reached his desk by 6 a.m.

Already the room lay in twilight, shuttered against the white heat of a Bengal morning. But enough light filtered through Venetian blinds to reveal the wine-coloured despatch boxes awaiting him. They loomed everywhere: on the polished mahogany desk, on side-tables, on high-backed blackwood chairs. For twelve hours now, Charles John, Viscount Canning, would be captive within the four walls of Government House, Calcutta, engrossed by the story of mounting disaster these State papers told. Sounds from the world beyond would reach him but faintly: the raucous shrieking of green parakeets in the colonnade flanking the window, the shuffle and mutter of the bodyguard, covertly busy with palm-leaf fans; the sound of St. Paul's Cathedral bells, precisely at 10 a.m. on this tenth day of May 1857, calling the citizens to worship. Still Lord Canning would not stir. The times were grave, so grave he could go but once to church this day.

It was a fantastic tale that the Governor read, set down in feathery copperplate handwriting: a tale of symbolic cakes passing from hand to hand by night, of Army barracks gutted by unknown fire-raisers, of a message passing like a wind through the bazaars: "All shall become red." For four months now reports had poured into the pigeonholes of the Honour-

11

able East India Company of a strange unrest affecting the
150,000 sepoys of its Bengal Army, whose province was not
Bengal Presidency alone but all northern India from the
mouth of the Ganges to the Himalayas and the Punjab. Along
the Grand Trunk Road, village drums had throbbed in the
night, carrying the wild rumour that the Lord Sahib sought to
destroy the caste of this Army through new cartridges
smeared with cow's fat and hog's lard—unthinkable alike to
Hindus, who held the cow as sacred, and to Moslems who
abhorred the pig as unclean. Denials, proclamations, reasoned arguments—all had proved unavailing. Already two
regiments, the 34th and 19th Native Infantry, had been disbanded for open mutiny. And now had come the stubborn
defiance of the eighty-five cavalry troopers of Meerut.

The superstitious had expected no less. It was now 100
years since an officer in the Company's service, Robert Clive,
aided by 2,100 Indian mercenaries, had vanquished the
French at the Battle of Plassey to set the seal on British rule
and an old prophecy had decreed that in this centenary year
their power would crumble to dust. They spoke, too, of the
ill-omen of Lord Canning's own coming: ascending the crim-
son-carpeted stairs of Government House to assume office
fourteen months ago he had stumbled, almost toppling, and a
shudder of apprehension had rippled through the servants
lining the roped gangway. Viewing the high domed forehead of the 45-year-old Governor, one man had noted "something tragic about his countenance . . . a look of Hamlet
distraction".

Even Lord Canning could not know that 10th May, 1857,
was to prove the most dramatic day in the Company's history:
the genesis of a mutiny that would sweep the land in a holocaust of blood and fire, laying a thousand homes in ashes,
costing tens of thousands of lives.

At this era of its history, the East India Company was a
trading concern in name only. More than 250 years ago a
small cabal of "Governors and Company of Merchants trading to the East Indies" had won a charter from Elizabeth I.
Now, a mighty feudal organism, their right to trade for profit
had long since been surrendered to the Crown. Instead, the
Company were the great landlords of India, the great tax-

collectors. Through their appointed deputy, the Governor-General, they held undisputed sway over 838,000 square miles from Cape Cormorin to the Himalayas—land which adventurers like Clive had wrested or bartered from feudal princes. Many of India's 200 potentates, Hindu and Moslem, with 48 million subjects at their command, were the Company's puppet creations.

Their power was a strange anomaly. Seventy years earlier, alarmed by the Company's growing omnipotence, the British Government had renewed their charter on less favourable terms: henceforth, a Board of Control, whose President was a Cabinet Minister, must oversee the directors' political policy. From this time on, though all business was done in the Company's name, they became the front through which the British held India in check.

Commercially its great years were past. Dividends, up to twelve-and-a-half per cent when Clive was paramount, had for sixty-four years been pegged at ten and a half. Annual profits, over £1,250,000 under Clive, had at times slumped below £275,000. Its shares now paid dividends in terms of power, not profit; directors could appoint cronies to salaried staff posts in London, these posts being illegally for sale, although by the Charter Act, 1853, the covenanted service was entered by examination.

Gone, too, was the frontier spirit of Clive's India. Then every British clerk had wielded a sabre as deftly as a pen to defend the Company's warehouses but a hundred years of dominion had wrought a subtle change upon the rulers. Their place in the sun assured, French, Dutch and Portuguese competition stifled, the East India Company had waxed fat and grown slothful. They spoke of it now as "John Company"; it conjured an irresistable image of a stout man warming his backside at a merry fire.

Among the Company's officials, few shared Canning's qualms. From the tall white belfries of a hundred churches, from Christ Church, Cawnpore, St. John's, Meerut, St. James's, Delhi, the bells now broke the Sunday silence. Gigs and curricles stood parked in neat semi-circles in pounded red-brick compounds. Within, the people sat placidly in semi-darkness, ranged for coolness in sissoo wood armchairs lined with velvet cushions; officers in undress summer uniforms, frock-coats and white overalls, civilians, as custom decreed, in black alpaca coats, their ladies in loose white muslin.

Overhead the white wings of the punkah flew tirelessly, teasing the India paper of prayer books, its flounces swooping to hide the chaplain in his pulpit, now dipping back to mask the congregation. The services were brief and as always adapted to the comforts of a conquering race. Few, because of the heat, would kneel in worship. The collection plate did not pass, for no East India Company official, any more than his Queen, deigned to carry money. After drowsing through much of the sermon, they would specify their donation on a pad, as a rich man might endow a charity. For six days thereafter many would forget God and worship Him only with their lips.

By noon their clubs would have claimed them, or the white bungalows they called Home, lining the shady malls. Thereafter, in keeping with the island life they lived, their Sunday routine would be fixed, immutable; the blistering heat of May demanded only submission. Life was so languid most families communicated through chits borne by their bearers—few knew Hindustani, the hybrid of Hindi and Urdu used for dealings with servants, well enough to send a verbal message. A housewife socially inclined might send twenty-five chits a day.

The British did not know it but they were really fighting a losing battle against the sun, a sun that caused tempers to flare murderously, that made social standards at times of rigid importance, at other times a burden not worth the shouldering. For eight months of the year the sun was a monstrous weight pressing down on all their lives, curtailing movement, hedging them in darkened rooms. The sun sent pianos out of tune, dried ink as it touched paper, melted the peaks of officers' bell-shaped shakos to a sticky black glue. It gave rise to fashionable fictions; by common consent the greatest beauty had the palest cheeks in the station. To spare his wife and children from pitiless sun a man would strive to send them to Simla or Mussoorie, hill-stations, 6,500 feet above the baking plains. Often this sacrifice meant a debt involving ruin.

Houses were designed with one purpose: to cheat the sun of victory. In military stations, called cantonments, sited mostly near the 1,500 miles of Grand Trunk Road between Calcutta and Lahore, the pattern was a stereotype, so rigid it was hard for a stranger to know whether he was in Cawnpore or Meerut. Bungalows faced west to escape the morning sun, with the sepoy lines on the east side of the parade ground. Most bungalows were thatched for coolness with raised verandahs. In the May sunlight they looked like enormous beehives perched on milestones.

Interiors were without doors, a series of interlinking rooms, screened off by turkey-red cotton cloth. Walls were covered with a pale pink or lime-green wash that left a pastel dust on the fingers of the unwary. The furnishings were standard: a round blackwood table, chintz-covered chairs, sometimes a piano. Kitchens and servants' quarters lay separately across the compound. Life could be pleasant in such homes, given an average of twenty to thirty servants, but senseless savagery was not unknown. Newspapers condoled with a Delhi subaltern who kicked his groom to death, for the shock it must have caused him. Up country, the indigo planters had a sure way to teach an Indian manners—harness him between two bullocks and plough a field with him.

The sun decreed breakfast, in the brief cool hours, to be *the* main meal of the day. Important business was clinched over breakfast, finishing with a No. 1 Manila cheroot. A good breakfast might offer a choice of devilled turkey thighs, Irish stew, pigeon pie, omelettes, fried fish, snipe and green peas in season, washed down by tea, beer or iced claret. Lunch, called "tiffin," followed at 2 p.m., dinner promptly at 7.30 p.m. To tickle palates jaded by heat, the recipe books counselled Cold Meat Sauce, a fiery compound of horseradish, garlic, mustard and red peppers.

European goods were now easy to come by, bridging the gap with an England none saw more than once in ten years. The Hall of All Nations, Calcutta, could, in May, 1857, supply "fresh York hams, cheddar cheese, red herrings, fine ox tongues, comfits, spice nuts, Moselle and Madeira wines."

In outstations the price of imported foodstuffs trebled, but the people, living on credit, shrugged this off. Hermetically sealed goods, lobsters in stone jars, preserved oysters, Portuguese sardines, were now symbols of status, of a kinship with England, and the British habitually equated a rupee with a shilling, not the two it represented.

Encouraged by this, prices mounted steadily. English Lavender Water was 8s. a pint, tinned Cambridge sausages 9s. a pound, an untrimmed linsey-woolsey dress £5. It cost 16s. to have a watch cleaned, £25 to buy a second-hand buggy.

The people were lusty, adolescent in mentality, often conscious of their own right opinions. Compared with later generations they had a morbid preoccupation with their own salvation. They were also curiously unsophisticated. A steamer tying up at Garden Reach, Calcutta, brought a stampede of residents to gawk at the new arrivals. The height of humour was the Delhi *Sketchbook* magazine and its atrocious puns. ("Question: Where might a lady best buy a fur cape? Answer: Sialkot.") Their belief in weird nostrums was unflagging; Holloway's Ointment cured everything from mosquito bites and yaws to "secondary symptoms." Their medicine was primitive; a hornet sting would be cauterised with a glowing cigar.

Theirs was a tight secure-seeming world, jealously proud of the growing amenities which helped to assuage the pangs of homesickness: bottled soda-water since 1835, ice from Boston a year earlier, lucifer matches by 1838. Above all, its security was bolstered by a great illusion which had held good only until the British brought their brides to recreate England in India: that the native army with which they held the country was tamed and content. "They experienced little trouble," a guide book boasted, "in managing the happy and tractable sepoy in cantonments." Such men as Lord Canning, who warned that "in the sky of India . . . a small cloud may arise . . . which growing bigger and bigger may at last threaten to overwhelm us with ruin," were lone voices crying in the wilderness.

Each Presidency—Bombay, Bengal, Madras—maintained its own army, with sepoys or Hindu infantrymen serving under British officers in regiments raised by the Company. Indian officers also served in these regiments, though the most senior among them was subordinate to a lower-ranking British officer, even to a British non-com. But one key factor set the Bengal Army apart from the others: three-fifths of the sepoys serving in its sixty-three infantry regiments were high born Hindus, men whose lives were ruled by the taboos of the caste system, who worshipped a plurality of gods and held the cow as sacred. Apart from these men, in their own lines, lived eleven cavalry regiments of Moslems—war-like followers of Mahomet.

Most European soldiers serving in India belonged to Queen's regiments, British-based regiments raised by and belonging to Queen Victoria, though at times hired out to serve under the Commander-in-Chief, India, for a tour of overseas duty. But despite the unrest of recent years the ratio of European troops to Indian sepoys had dwindled perilously. Many, their service done, had returned to Britain; others had been posted to Persia or Burma. The ratio which a former Governor-General had fixed at one to three, never less than one to four, was now less than one to six—45,522 European troops as against 232,224 Indians.

Among those who had grave doubts about the Bengal Army's well-being was Harriet Tytler, who had passed all her thirty years in India. A soldier's daughter, wife of a captain in the 38th Native Infantry, Harriet was already the mother of three healthy youngsters and was shortly expecting her fourth confinement. This morning, in the cool linseed-scented interior of St. James's, Delhi, the thought crossed her mind that Subadar-Major Munsoor Ali might look in on them after morning service. An Indian major in her husband's regiment, Munsoor Ali had two days earlier departed to Meerut, a military station forty-four miles north, as President of a Court Martial trying the eighty-five mutineers of the 3rd Light Cavalry who had dramatically refused to accept the new cartridges for the Enfield rifle. Robert Tytler, his wife knew, was anxious to learn the verdict.

"Sir, if I find these men guilty I will give them the severest punishment in my power," Munsoor Ali had assured Robert before he left. But somehow the Tytlers found the whole concept of mutiny, much discussed in these weeks, more disturbing than the offence itself. Meerut and Delhi had always been peaceful stations. No British troops had been stationed in Delhi for thirty years, for the old walled city and the blood-red Fort that frowned above the river were the kingdom of the 82-year-old Mogul Emperor, Bahadur Shah, now a British puppet though living on in semi-royal state. But life in the cantonments two miles beyond was pleasant for young couples like the Tytlers, with Robert devoting himself as keenly to amateur chemistry as Harriet to her sketching. Harriet Tytler's prayer was a simple one: that this idyllic life might continue undisturbed.

But the Tytlers saw that little by little standards were slipping. It was as if the British, conscious they were but sojourners and that the sun was winning, were losing heart. Gambling was the sick fever of the day and many a youngster of twenty left the green-baize table white and shaken, with i.o.u.'s totalling £10,000. Young subalterns' quarters, a visitor noted, were growing dirty and slapdash: a squalid turmoil of cheroot boxes, hunting whips, forage caps, swords and dirty soda-water bottles. Some officers' wives, tiring of the unequal battle, now received guests without corsets or stockings.

The social round, the ties of home-life—all these had seen the gulf between British officers and their men yawn wider. Sepoys, if they saluted their officers at all, often saluted with their left hands as a mark of discourtesy. To spit in the dust after a simulated coughing fit was another covert way of showing resentment. Some officers, in any case, were too idle to return even a smart salute. Beneath the spit-and-polish façade of red serge jackets, pipeclay and gleaming muskets, the discontent of the Bengal Army trembled like near-boiling water.

As recently as September, 1856, had come the bombshell of the General Service Order, decreeing that henceforth newjoined recruits must agree to serve in any overseas theatre. "Next," the older sepoys grumbled, "they'll be carrying us to London," for to cross the *Kala pani* (black water) at once reduced a Brahmin to the same caste as a lascar. What future could the army now hold for their sons and grandsons? Already, since 1805, five outbursts of mutiny had been crushed by harsh reprisals but humiliating defeats in Afghanistan and the Crimea had sent British prestige plummeting. Worse, from 1853 the sepoys saw their commanding officers as no more than a knot in a long chain of red tape: none, by Government order, had power to award greater punishment than five days' drill.

Even conscientious officers had, in the eight hot weather months, little more than an hour's duty a day. Absenteeism was rife; at any one time exactly half the officers of the Bengal Army were absent from their regiments, on furlough in the hills or transferred to the civil posts which were created following the Government's wholesale annexations of land.

These annexations were a source of discontent and anxiety to many people besides the sepoys. In eight years, Canning's predecessor, the despotic Lord Dalhousie, at 35 the youngest Governor-General India had ever known, had annexed over 250,000 square miles—an area three times the size of England and Ireland. The Punjab, Sattara, Nagpur—Dalhousie's hands had stretched out to embrace them all. "An Indian Governor-General," stormed *The Hindu Patriot*, "is chartered to destroy dynasties with a scratch of his quill." Indignities were heaped upon crowned heads: the jewels of the Royal Family of Nagpur were publicly auctioned in Calcutta.

South of Bombay the clumsy fiscal policies of Dalhousie's Inam Commission, set up to examine the tenure of rent-free lands, had spawned new enmities with every day that passed; out of 35,000 plots under review, 21,000 were confiscated. Often, due to the ravages of white ants, the owners lacked all documentary proof. In Bengal alone, ousted properties each year yielded "John Company" £5 million revenue. These ruthless sales of land not only uprooted peasants from their holdings but destroyed the land-owners to whom they had looked for protection.

If the British had brought progress by railway and telegraph they had also brought harsh laws and crippling taxes. Justice was mostly a mockery: the village police, paid a starvation wage of four shillings monthly, openly gave their allegiance to roving bands of robbers. To reduce litigation to the minimum, "John Company" ordained that even a coolie must present his plea over a shilling stamp before consulting an attorney. Torture—lighted matches between the fingers, the arms tied behind the back and screwed together with a Spanish windlass—was the recognised mode of extracting confessions.

Taxes were a cynical outrage. A man could not travel twenty miles without paying toll at a river ferry, farmed out by the Company to private speculators. Land Tax, often demanded before the crop was raised, was made in quarterly instalments; beyond sunset on a specific date the Collector could refuse to accept it. A shortage of sixpence in the amount and the defaulter's property was forfeit for auction. Salt was heavily taxed for labourers who earned three-farthings a day; also taxed were opium, saltpetre and all fermented juices. The annual rent for an acre of land was 3s., yet the produce of that acre rarely averaged 8s. in value. For two months each year most labourers—or "heathens" as official documents styled all Indians—could not purchase rice. They existed on roots or on bread made from a coarse flour of ground mango stones. Salt was grubbed from the alkali of burnt vegetable ash.

These abuses hardly troubled the majority of officials; it was still possible for a man to amass a fortune of £30,000 and retire at 45.

They basked in the shadow of "John Company" like wayfarers beneath a great tree, and the Company repaid their allegiance with brazenly preferential treatment. In the matter of public services they had spent less developing India in 14 years than Manchester city spent on piped water. Until 1853 more than 40 per cent of their appointments had been direct nepotism. With a starting salary of £300 a year, many youngsters saw India not as a responsibility but as a birthright. Of an annual revenue of £28 million, over £26 million was swallowed by official salaries.

Thus few of the élite whose words were law to 131 million native subjects were inclined to share Lord Canning's concern. There were so many other prospects to divert the mind: lunch, the afternoon siesta, promotions and precedences, the petty jealousies of the outstations. If they had seen the danger signs most chose to ignore them; "a croaker" was the universal term for a man who prophesied disaster. This morning, disaster was poised above them all as inexorably as the bright blade of a guillotine; they did not heed it. They did not know "John Company" was dying, would not know when "John Company" died.

II. CALCUTTA

Afternoon 10th May

At 3 p.m. the people slept. In loose muslin dressing-gowns, faces and necks powdered, the women lay down in darkness, verandahs curtained from the sun by plaited screens of sweet-scented grass drenched with water. Close at hand their pets, poodles, mongeese, blue Persian cats, lay sprawled inert, conserving all energy. Only the dust-devils whirled on the white shimmering roads, whipping straw, dust and dead leaves into a frenzied *danse macabre*.

Meanwhile, in Government House, Calcutta, Lord Canning worked on. His study was in the south-west wing, on the first floor, at 81 degrees the coolest room in Government House, yet one unwary move bathed the body in warm sweat. To open a window before 6 p.m. was foolhardy, letting in "a flood of hot air, as though one were passing the mouth of a foundry."

In three hours, he might, after evensong, take the day's only exercise, a furious solitary marathon round the Government House gardens. Or, as his private secretary, the Hon. Gerald Talbot knew, he might by mid-afternoon slump forward speechless with migraine. The doctors would revive him with chloroform, ice on the temples; next day he would again renew the fight to learn, to understand. Those close to him satisfied the restless probing brain only with difficulty. It was hard for a man who had spent eighteen years in the House of

Lords to grapple with the administration of a country where men moved deviously, like assassins in the night.

There was the strange affair of the chupattis and it puzzled many more versed in Indian lore than Lord Canning. The first report had come almost three months ago, on 19th February, from William Ford, the magistrate of Goorgaon district, south of Delhi. Ford had reported: "A signal has passed through a number of the villages of this district, the purport of which has not yet transpired."

Though other reports had flooded in, the basic story was always the same: in the first milky light of dawn a village watchman, who patrolled the boundaries after sunset with his long irontipped staff, would be hailed by a watchman from another village. In his right hand the newcomer clutched a bundle of chupattis. Flat discs of unleavened bread shaped like ship's biscuits, two inches in diameter, a quarter of an inch thick, these formed the daily diet of both rich and poor.

The greeting held the strange flavour of an incantation: "From the north to the south, from the east to the west. Take two and make ten more." So the cakes changed hands, unchallenged.

As the weeks passed, the mystery deepened. By 5th March, three weeks after the first report, men spoke in whispers of the cakes in all the districts south of Delhi—though never to the north—and they had passed on to Lucknow, 240 miles south and east. The watchman's bidding never varied: two cakes were to be held in safe keeping by the village elders, eight more baked by sundown, on flat iron plates over a cow-dung fire, to be passed to other village watchmen by dawn. Sometimes the messenger sought a hand-written receipt.

But who had ordered the baking of the cakes? A young indigo planter, Emery Churcher, who intercepted some, was assured by the watchmen that they had no idea what to do with them. They had baked them, they said, at the instigation of some travelling fakirs who were spreading a report that the British *raj* (rule) would soon be swept from the earth.

Many men came by them; all had their own interpretation. Messengers questioned by Sir Theo Metcalfe, Joint Magistrate of Delhi, apologised humbly; they had believed the circulation of the cakes to be by Government order. Were they, one Indian scholar wondered, a test of how quickly news could be promulgated? If so, the answer was disquieting, suggesting a chain of fleet faceless messengers. A Divisional Commissioner found traces of them one February morning at the village of Etawah. Within a day he had news of them 200 miles away at Aligarh. Forty miles a night was then the utmost one man could travel.

Were they a storm signal, a fiery cross? One District Officer, told it was an old Hindustani custom whenever a chief required special service from his people, enquired what this service might be. The answer was an enigmatic smile: "We don't know—yet." Sir John Lawrence, Chief Commissioner of the Punjab, heard the cakes were a symbol of food: their circulation warned men to hold together or lose all. The summing-up of Mainodin, head police officer of a village outside Delhi, was chilling in its implication: "I suspected it was the sign of a time of trouble. . . ."

Too many other signs had betokened a time of trouble: the passing of plantain flowers from household to household, a talisman to avert family misfortune. In Meerut, where the eighty-five had stood trial for mutiny, cabalistic red and white scrawls had appeared overnight on every European gatepost.

For years now men, both famous and unknown, had prophesied that stormy times lay ahead for India. Harriet Tytler always recalled how Robert, hearing the first rumbles of discontent, had told her: "If our native army is to rebel against us, India is lost." Only eight days earlier, Sir Henry Lawrence had written to Canning from Lucknow, "Until we treat natives, and especially native soldiers, as having much the same feelings, the same ambitions, the same perception of ability and imbecility as ourselves, we shall never be safe."

But none had prophesied the full and appalling extent of the unrest: the wave of incendiarism that had swept cantonments from Ambala in the north to Barrackpore in the south. Still less had they prophesied the sepoys' inexplicable belief that Lord Canning was bent on converting them all to Christianity, a fear no commander seemed able to allay. In Lucknow the men of the 7th Irregular Infantry had told Sir Henry

Lawrence of a rumour both current and credited: the widows of the Crimean War were to be shipped to India and betrothed to Indian princes, that their children might be brought up as Christians to inherit their estates. From mid-January, it was rumoured in Calcutta, all sepoys, by Queen Victoria's command, would be baptised.

The charges held no vestige of truth, yet for years, culminating in the rule of Lord Dalhousie, the British, with the same blindness and lack of sympathy that cost them their American colonies, had laid themselves open to such slurs. Heedless that the sepoys were no mere mercenaries like a European army but a guild in which father and son took up arms from cradle to grave, they had time and again shown high-handed disregard of the sepoys' caste customs and religion.

One thing alone had saved the Government from a major mutiny years before. In no factor could Hindu and Moslem find common cause.

On 22nd January 1857, that cause had been found. On this day Lieutenant John Wright, commanding the Rifle Instruction Depot at Dum Dum, outside Calcutta, reported a strange hysteria had seized the sepoys of the 2nd Native Infantry stationed there. Some days earlier a coolie had hailed a sepoy with a rare request: the boon of a drink of water from his lotah, the pear-shaped brass drinking vessel used by all Hindus. Outraged, the sepoys had refused. The touch of a low-caste man would defile it.

The coolie's retort was to echo round the world. "You will soon lose *your* caste—ere long you will have to bite cartridges covered with the fat of pigs and cows."

The story had a kernel of truth. A Government order had decreed that "Brown Bess," the sepoys' old heavy smoothbore musket should be replaced by the Enfield rifle, a streamlined affair weighing only 8 lb. 14 oz., as against the 14 lb. of "Brown Bess," more practicable in the field. But the Enfield needed a far closer fit of cartridge and ball. For a marksman to ram them deftly down the 39-inch barrel, the cartridge must be greased, its thin end-paper bitten off and the powder poured down the barrel. The cartridge was then withdrawn, reversed, and the bullet placed in the muzzle and rammed home. Now 150,000 men were asking what this grease might be.

At once Colonel Richard Birch, Military Secretary to the Government, called for a searching report. The Director-General of Ordnance's reply was alarming: it was entirely possible beef-fat *had* been used. Mutton-fat had originally been ordered but some contractors, to save a few shillings, had supplied pig's or bullock's fat instead. The Army had faced this potential crisis before. As long ago as 1853, Major-General Henry Tucker, Adjutant-General to the Military Secretary of Government, had urged extreme caution in making up such grease: practice cartridges containing cow's fat had just then arrived from England for climate tests. The residue had been fired by the 60th (Queen's) Rifles; not one round had been issued for practice to sepoys.

Obviously this earlier warning had gone unheeded but Colonel Birch felt that all was not lost. No cartridges had yet been issued to the rifle depot at Dum Dum; these were safely under lock and key in the arsenal. But 22,500 had been sent to the instruction depot at Ambala, 1,020 miles north, 14,000 to Sialkot nearby. Birch now instructed these depots that the cartridges, sheathed in yellow glazed paper, must henceforth be used in the dry state only.

It was too late. In station after station, the sepoys, both Hindu and Moslem, now "respectfully but firmly" refused to touch the cartridges at all. Soon a further complication ensued. Embittered by their legacy of distrust, convinced the Government was out to break their caste, the sepoys now refused to accept even the cartridges some had used for forty years.

A small-minded man, Colonel Birch sought a foolish and furtive way out. Unwilling to admit himself in the wrong, he now saw the prestige of the Government at stake. On 5th March, Lord Canning had wisely decreed that the biting of the cartridge be abolished; the cartridges could as easily be torn with the left hand. But Birch's prime concern was loss of face. In his memorandum to the depots he wrote: "This mode (tearing) the Governor-General in Council is disposed to think will be an improvement . . . early instructions may be given to the depots . . . not making any allusion whatever to the biting of the cartridge but drawn up in such a way that they may appear independent of anything laid down in previous regulations. . . ."

Now the Commander-in-Chief, India, General the Hon. George Anson, entered the fray. A handsome intolerant man of sixty, who made no secret of despising Indians, he was determined, as he saw it, to maintain discipline. At first suspending all practice pending an analysis of the old-type cartridge papers, he made no allowance for the sepoys' lingering doubts once laboratory reports proved negative. "I'll never give in to their beastly prejudices," he burst out. At Ambala, on 17th April, he decided that whatever the sepoys' misgivings the cartridges must be used.

A man shorn of his caste through pollution could be punished by death or mutilation for having intercourse with his wife. If Anson knew this he did not care.

As the distrust spread like fire in a stockyard, some officers were appalled by the ugly tension. The horrified musketry instructor at Ambala, Captain Edward Martineau, sent this impassioned plea to an officer on Anson's staff: "Good God, here are all the elements of combustion at hand . . . men sullen, distrustful, fierce—if a flare-up from any cause takes place at one station it will spread and become universal and then what means have we for putting it down? You can view the position more coolly in the Himalayas than I in the plains. . . ."

Young officers might scoff at what they called "cartridge phobia" but the dark rumours were hard to ignore. A servant came secretly by night to Major Alexander Boyd, commanding the 2nd Bengal Fusiliers at Ambala. "Bad things are being done in camp," he whispered, eyes busy for all who might betray him. "A meeting of sepoys assembles every night to plot mutiny against the Government."

The Major at once reported by letter to General Anson. This letter was never acknowledged.

"At all three depots," Anson wrote to Lord Canning, "the practice has been commenced . . . men of all grades have unhesitatingly and cheerfully used the new cartridges." But night after night a fiery orange tumult of sparks streamed from the thatched roofs of Ambala cantonment. On one night over £3,000 worth of property was destroyed.

In the third week of April the crisis was brought to a head by a man who did not so much despise Indians as cherish his own self-esteem: Brevet-Colonel George Carmichael Smyth, commanding the 3rd Light Cavalry at Meerut. On 23rd April, twelve hours after returning from leave, the Colonel ordered a parade of the regiment's skirmishers—ninety picked sepoys, the élite of the corps—to demonstrate once for all that the cartridges were harmless and could be torn. Smyth had already heard from his troop commanders that the men were likely to reject them. Still he would force the issue.

All was as predicted. Mounted on his horse, Smyth watched in growing fury as the non-coms lugged the heavy cloth bundles housing the cartridges along the ranks. Trooper after trooper shrank as if from infection. Sick at heart to refuse an order, they would not, could not, touch them. Smyth's pleasure was to be right: his vanity demanded the charade be played out to the bitter end. He drew bridle before each man, asking directly, "Will you take the cartridges?" Among the ninety, only five would accept. Eighty-five others spoke with a single tongue, shaking their heads, repeating stubbornly, "I shall get a bad name if I do so." In vain Smyth urged that the regiment, in accepting them, would win the entire Bengal Army's approval for their good sense. "There will be cries of *Wah wah*" (Bravo!), he said. Between the Colonel and his men, sullen silence lay like a wall. Abruptly Smyth ordered, "Threes about," dismissing the parade.

This same day, Smyth made his report to Major-General William Hewitt, the Divisional Commander. At 67 the General was so obese he now reviewed his troops from a buggy instead of a horse; the last thing he courted was trouble. "Oh! Why did you have a parade?" was his first plaintive reaction. "If you had only waited another month or so, all would have blown over." For now he was duty bound to convene a Court of Inquiry and pass on the findings to General Anson. Its Indian officers finding no grounds for leniency, Anson's reply was automatic; all eighty-five troopers must be court-martialled for mutiny.

On 8th May fifteen Indian officers—six Moslems, nine

Hindus—sat in solemn judgement. Forty years later, one officer of Smyth's regiment, Lieutenant Hugh Gough, could never shake off the pain of this day: the Court, presided over by Robert Tytler's brother-officer, Subadar-Major Munsoor Ali, ranged at a long scrubbed Army mess-table on trestles, the prisoners squatting cross-legged on the hard earth floor, the creak and squeal of the punkah overhead. Many of the older men, wearing medals, were "worn and anxious." A verdict of guilty would forfeit the pensions for which some had served for twenty years. No prisoner offered to cross-examine.

The unanimous verdict was guilty, two members of the Court voting for death.

Events now moved swiftly. The night of 8th May was breathless and sultry. Unable to sleep, men stirring uneasily on beds that "burned like hot bricks" came wide awake to a sound that carried a long way in the still night. *Clang! Clang! Clang!* It was the sound of cold iron ringing upon hot, borne from the regimental smithy.

That morning, when the sentence of guilty on the eighty-five men had been formally confirmed by General Anson, General Hewitt had reached a shabby decision. The troopers' shame should be as deep and lasting as he could make it; at the punishment parade that announced their sentences the rebels would be publicly fettered in irons. Later Anson was to "express his regret at this unusual procedure."

At dawn on 9th May, heavy dun-coloured clouds lay low in the sky above Meerut. Across the parade ground of the 60th Rifles a hot wind stirred. The uniforms of almost 4,000 officers and men, drawn up to form three sides of a hollow square, made vivid splashes of colour: the brass helmets, tiger-skin rolls and leather breeches of the Bengal Artillery officers, the black horsehair plumes of the 6th Dragoon Guards, the olive-green of the 60th Rifles, the silver-grey of the dismounted 3rd Cavalry, the scarlet coats and white collars of the 20th and 11th Native Infantry. The Indian troops carried arms but no ammunition. The British gripped tight to loaded rifles pointing inwards at their Indian comrades.

It was a degrading scene and all who witnessed it would carry the shame of it to the end of their days. As the sentences were read out, in English and Hindustani, a visible tremor ran through the sepoys' ranks. The price of mutiny was a costly one: each man who had put aside the cartridges would atone for his belief through ten years' hard labour on the roads. The sentences of a few of the younger men had been commuted to five by General Anson.

Barefooted, to aid the fettering, the prisoners stood in silence. Now the smiths and armourers moved to the tumbrils where the fetters lay piled. The gold buttons were ripped from their chests. Their uniforms, rent from behind by bayonets, now hung in grey-blue shreds. As the fetters were slowly hammered on their ankles, man after man cast aside restraint, calling on his comrades for help. Many, seizing up the boots they had shed, shied them towards the watching immobile form of Colonel Carmichael Smyth. As they were led away a Persian regimental tutor, Mohun Lal, saw tears streaming down their faces; some, in high broken voices, cried out, "The Government has imprisoned us without fault." In the ranks the sepoys of the 20th Native Infantry wept without shame. When at last General Hewitt gave the command "March off!" the sepoys moved brokenly, in apathy, as if a clockwork spring had ground to a halt.

Meanwhile the tutor Mohun Lal was worried. A pious Hindu, he had for months been convinced the Moslem tutors attached to other regiments were plotting an uprising. Already, he claimed, they had sent letters to every other British cantonment urging them not to touch the hated cartridges; they themselves would never do so. And on still nights a man with keen ears could hear the stealthy sound of a whetstone at work behind closed doors: the Moslems were sharpening their swords.

All these suspicions he at once confided to one of his pupils, Second-Lieutenant Minto Elliott of the Bengal Artillery. The youngster brushed them aside.

Hugh Gough, the fresh-faced fair-haired young Lieutenant of the 3rd Light Cavalry, was less inclined to scoff. He had, following the shackling parade, set out for the old hospital building that formed a temporary gaol for the eighty-five. At first the men were mulish, impassive, but as each troop officer began the final task of paying off his men the realisation came like a blow in the face. Their proud days with "John Company" had ended. Flinging themselves to the ground in a paroxysm of grief, they begged their officers to save them.

Deeply moved by what he had seen, Gough returned to his bungalow. Soon he had further cause to be troubled. As darkness fell an Indian officer from his troop stole on to the verandah. When he explained that he had come to discuss the troop's accounts, Gough was puzzled. The Bengal Army's life was a leisurely one. Dusk on a Saturday evening was no hour to be doing business.

Then, in sudden secret rushes, the truth came out. The next day, Sunday, the troops would mutiny. Both the native infantry and the cavalry would rise as one. They would free their comrades from the gaol or die in the attempt. More than this the man could not or would not say.

For the rest of his days Gough was to wonder why this man, whom he barely knew, had singled him out from all the other officers in Meerut. But this was Saturday evening, soon the mess bugle would sound; time was running out. He went at once to Colonel Carmichael Smyth, to meet only with open contempt. "You should be ashamed of listening to such idle words," was the Colonel's parting shot.

Gough made one last effort. At the Club later that evening he sought out Brigadier Archdale Wilson, the artillery officer who commanded the station. Wilson, a tall wiry man with a goatee beard and "a large feeble mouth," now showed the indecision which was to characterise his every action in the months that followed. He was frankly incredulous, and the General, he was quick to point out, was fully satisfied.

This was the crisis point that British India had reached on that hot Sunday afternoon in May, 1857, when men, women and children slept and Lord Canning toiled alone in the silent twilit room.

III. MEERUT

Evening 10th May

In the brief hour before sunset, a cool breeze hushed the trees, and the long shadows of late afternoon barred the white roads. Now the British could safely venture forth. Some were bound for evensong, some for the evening promenade to the bandstand. Small clouds of yellow dust hung motionless, churned upwards by the wheels of gigs, phaetons and buggies, by the hooves of subalterns' country ponies, their manes and tails dyed orange or purple. Around the lit arena of the bandstand the young officers cantered, fetching ices from the refreshment pavilion for the "spins," as eligible young spinsters were styled. In their wake a long procession of pale-cheeked children took the air shepherded by ayahs and red-sashed bearers. People who had bowed and smiled to one another a thousand times before now bowed and smiled again.

Soon, when the German bandmaster raised his baton, the band would strike up such current favourites as "The Last Rose of Summer" and "Come into the Garden, Maud," but long before the concert's end, the buggy-lamps would twinkle like glow-worms in the thickening darkness. Patiently the horses waited, their ears pricking up at the first strains of "God save the Queen."

The first finger on the trigger is often lost to history and the blank faces in this story belong to those troopers of the 3rd Light Cavalry who that afternoon were lounging in a prostitute's house in the Sudder (Native) Bazaar, south-west of Meerut cantonments. Old photographs show the streets as unchanged to this day; a warren of narrow red-brick alleys heavy with the scent of musk and drains and men acrid from toil. High flat-roofed houses lean close together and shut out the hard terrible light of afternoon. But if mutiny was in the

31

air that day these men were unprepared for it. Unarmed,
they wore undress uniforms of white pantaloons and white
close-fitting linen jackets open at the left side of the breast,
for these were Moslems. All later evidence collected by
Colonel George Williams, a zealous police commissioner, suggests that though the present injustice rankled bitterly the
troopers debated peaceful means. Some with a view to re-
trial had talked of hiring an advocate for the eighty-five.
Others thought the prisoners might successfully plead for a
dishonourable discharge.

There were other matters for debate. Recently, to combat
a flour shortage, the Government had sent a large consign-
ment of cheap wheaten flour to the bazaars of Cawnpore.
This news had reached every cantonment, for some of the
flour, growing musty, had led to the wild rumour that the
bones of pigs and cows had been mixed with it. "Look out for
it at Ambala," one sepoy had written to his brother from
Cawnpore, "I have not cooked for two days." Others spoke
of a Government plan to destroy caste by circulating leather
rupees.

Above all, for them, there was the stirring saga of Mangal
Pande, a heady brew to men thirsting for justice. Six Sundays
earlier, on 29th March, Mangal Pande, a sepoy of the 34th
Native Infantry at Barrackpore, Calcutta, had been egged on
by the men of his regiment to defy the state. Four hundred
men, the Indian officer of the guard among them, looked
coolly on while Pande, berserk with drugs, cut down first his
adjutant, then his sergeant-major. The divisional commander,
General Sir John Hearsey, arriving on the scene, spurred his
horse unflinchingly towards him; cautioned that Pande was
armed he bellowed only, "Damn his musket!" Unnerved, the
sepoy now swung the musket on himself. But the wound
was only surface deep; by 8th April Mangal Pande had
been tried and hanged for mutiny. From this moment all
mutineers, whatever their caste, would be known as "Pandies."

The men of the 3rd Light Cavalry were not yet a mob but
the makings of a mob were there if the war-cry shrilled or
the stones were hurled.

That the harlots began it police evidence is firm. These

women, wearing the loose jasmine-hung bodices of their trade, lips shaped into bizarre carmine curves, may have sought revenge for the cards Fate had dealt them. Or perhaps one man sought an embrace and the woman deftly eluded his grasp and the other women, maliciously, took up her cry: "We give no kisses to cowards." And seeing the anguish and discomfiture of the men they ground salt into the wound: "You lie there killing flies while your brothers are in prison! Shame on you!"

Suddenly their anger could no longer be contained. With a wild cry the troopers ran from the house. At this sunset hour the streets seethed with life; British soldiers bargaining for trinkets, merchants squatting cross-legged beside gaudy bolts of cloth, pedlars with tawny-coloured sweetmeats. Amazed, they heard the troopers' cry: "To horse, brothers! To the gaol!"

The narrow alleys boiled with shouting men and from high yellow-latticed balconies, barred like cages, came the harsh descant of the harlots' cries: "We give no kisses to cowards!" At once, as if on a signal, the riff-raff from a score of districts burst into view; in every alley, men with iron-bound clubs stood waiting. Witnesses would later recall that within an hour of the shackling parade these strangers had drifted in from outlying villages like vultures scenting a carcass.

Across the sleepy tree-shaded parallelogram, five miles long by two miles deep, that was Meerut cantonment, most were taken unawares. Brigadier Archdale Wilson was finishing his daily letter to his wife in the hills, the one person who could calm his troubled neurotic spirit. "So ends this business," he wrote. "The rascals have been given a sharp lesson." At that moment the buggy of his Major of Brigade tore like a chariot into the compound. The chaplain, the Reverend John Rotton, was leaving with his wife for evening service at St. John's, when their ayah implored them not to go; something terrible would happen. Privately the young chaplain thought this nonsense; to calm his wife he agreed the children could ride with them to church instead of staying at home. The Field Officer of the week, Colonel George Carmichael Smyth, was almost ready for church when a staccato burst of musketry caught his ears. Above all the Colonel disliked breaches of routine. "That can't be by order," he said irritably. "It's Sunday."

In fact neither the Colonel nor the Reverend Rotton got as far as St. John's. The chaplain's carriage had scarcely cleared the compound when he saw, above the feathery drifts of sugar-cane, a slender black shaft of smoke climbing to the yellow sky. Outside every gate small groups of servants were watching in silent awe. The native lines, two miles to the south near the Sudder Bazaar, were on fire.

The only member of the congregation to reach the church that night, Mrs. Dunbar Muter, wife of a captain in the 60th Rifles, heard from a passer-by that the service had been cancelled; an outbreak among the sepoys required the troops elsewhere. "A slight disturbance would not stop the service," she replied, "therefore I will wait a little."

Alone save for her groom she sat rigidly on in her carriage, facing the church; to crane round and scan the horizon to the south was an action no lady could contemplate. With growing impatience she awaited the sound of the lively march that would herald the church parade.

In his house near the native bazaar, a Jewish merchant, Mr. Abrahams, was alarmed by "a strange rolling sea-like noise." Still, determined to show the servants his unconcern, he faltered bravely through a four-course dinner: cream of almond soup, curried fowl, iced mango-fool, quail on toast. With darkness, the devil's chorus of sound came nearer; the panting of terrified cream-coloured bullocks, blundering panic-stricken through the lanes, voices that cried, *"Allah-i-Allah maro Faringhi"* (With Allah's help, let us kill the Christians). Smoke billowed, men came screaming through it.

Other sounds, unforgettable to those who heard them, smote the ears; the bugle that cried the alarm from the 60th Rifles' parade-ground to the north; the drumming of hooves; the clang of steel scabbards. Bullets snapped like fire-crackers, audible above the hissing roar of burning thatch. For the first time hundreds heard the awesome rebel yell that was to resound throughout India in the months to come: *"Din! Din! Din!"* (For the faith, for the faith!).

To many of the British, the first impact of mutiny had the

stark unreality of a nightmare. Lieutenant Alexander Mackenzie, a young 3rd Cavalry officer, was reading peacefully
in his bungalow when his bearer rushed in crying that the
sepoys had risen. Mackenzie's first instinct was partisan; his
own troopers must have set about the sepoys to avenge some
taunt prompted by the plight of the eighty-five. As he struggled into his uniform, calling for his horse, his secret hope, as
a loyal cavalryman, was that the sepoys got the drubbing they
deserved.

Vaulting into his saddle, Mackenzie galloped hard for the
regimental lines. Suddenly to his astonishment the 3rd Cavalry's British quartermaster-sergeant came fleeing through the
dusk. "Oh God, sir," he sobbed, "the troopers are coming to
cut us up."

Still, as he glimpsed a white-clad horde of cavalry troops
bearing down on him, Mackenzie felt no disquiet. What harm
could his own men possibly wish him? "Halt," he shouted,
and it seemed his first instincts had been right; the men had
reined in their Arabs a few feet away. Without warning, a
forest of blades slashed at him. Parrying, thrusting, his mind
in turmoil, Mackenzie could think only: What has happened?
Why are they attacking *me*?

What *had* happened? All later evidence suggests that the
troopers' sole concern was a desperate attempt to rescue their
comrades from the gaol. As they thundered 200 strong towards the gaol gates the sentries fled without a shot being
fired. Officers who arrived too late saw the eighty-five swarming into the night while blacksmiths worked frantically with
hammers and chisels to knock their fetters free. This was
at 6 p.m. At 7 p.m. the riff-raff and cut-throats of the bazaars
arrived to release the 720 civil prisoners housed there. These
now mingled with the sepoys, bent on plunder; the freedom-
fighters of an hour ago were now a mob ready to rend and
claw and gouge.

In the Sudder Bazaar only the thugs had scented trouble
in advance. Until the first shots were fired, the shops were
open and doing business; many friendly troopers, in the first
frenzy of riot, hustled bargain-hunting British soldiers back
to their own lines. If mutiny had been afoot, the rebels had
curiously made no provision for their wives and children; for

days after, these were forced to beg their bread where they could. Whether, as was later suggested, a rising was planned for three Sundays hence by a council of five working in each regiment like a latter-day Communist cell, may never now be known. But one thing seems certain: the sepoys as a body had no concerted plan. Their only policy had been to present a united front.

In the infantry lines, no man seemed decided whether his neighbour was friend or foe. Only a later police probe revealed one coherent story: for days the men of the 60th (Queen's) Rifles had brooded on the possibility of disarming the Indian troops, and a cook-boy with a smattering of English had overheard their conversation. At 6 p.m. as the Rifles, immaculate in white cotton drill, turned out for church parade, a feverish rumour spread south through the sepoy lines: "The Rifles and artillery are coming to disarm us!" As at every church parade, the 60th were wearing only side-arms, without rifles or ammunition, but the rumour took no account of this.

Now, as the cry redoubled, the narrow lanes between the sepoys' thatched huts surged with men bereft of reason; the men of the 20th and 11th Native Infantry were racing to defend themselves against a non-existent foe. The Colonel of the 11th N.I. (Native Infantry), Colonel John Finnis, arrived on the parade-ground to witness an appalling sight. Howling like dervishes, their minds unhinged by long weeks of humiliation, his men were pounding at the barred doors of the bells-of-arms, small circular masonry buildings sited just behind each company's lines. Here, immediately after each parade, all arms were stacked.

Somehow, with the aid of the few officers who had battled their way through, Finnis managed to check his men. In vain they pleaded they wanted arms to defend themselves against the sepoys of the 20th N.I., now ranged across their own parade-ground on the other side of the road. With more assurance than he felt Finnis stressed that the 20th would do them no harm. More than an hour had passed and still there was no sign of British troops coming to their aid. Only the Indian officers now held the gibing ranks of the 20th in check.

"Keep the men steady," Finnis told his second-in-command. "I'll go over and see what I can do."

Then, as he cantered through the gloaming, drawing bridle before the swaying shouting line of the 20th, pandemonium broke out in the rear ranks. Twenty bullets tore into the Colonel, toppling him like a sack of meal in the dust. Whatever had been in the minds of the 20th N.I. it had not included the murder of British officers. The recruit who fired the first shot was torn to pieces by the mob.

This death, above all others, set the seal on the rebellion. A thousand eyes had seen Finnis fall and in the final reckoning every man now saw himself as culpable. Many, hurling away their muskets, now fled blindly from the lines. Such men were ill-prepared to wage a holy war.

The sights that many saw now were past belief. After half-an-hour's vigil, the Captain's wife, Mrs. Dunbar Muter, unbending so far as to turn in her carriage, now caught her breath. For an unbroken mile the horizon was a sea of flame; the thousand bungalows of the sepoy lines were burning as one. The young lieutenant, Hugh Gough, rode pell-mell to the cavalry lines to see a thousand sepoys "dancing and leaping frantically about, calling and yelling to each other . . . blazing away in all directions." Lieutenant Alexander Mackenzie, who had escaped by inches from his men's attack, joined two brother officers to lead a cohort of loyal troopers. Suddenly the trailing loop of a severed telegraph wire whirled him with breath-catching force into the dust. Flat on his back he lay numb with horror as the shining hooves of forty horsemen "poured over my prostrate body."

Remounting swiftly, Mackenzie had barely caught up with his fellow officers when all glimpsed a palanquin gharry—a box-shaped Venetian carriage—rattling driverless towards them. Beside it a mounted trooper kept pace, plunging his sword again and again into the body of a dead European woman. Without hesitation, Lieutenants Henry Craigie and Melville Clarke spurred forward. As Craigie's sword sliced downwards on the trooper's neck Clarke's ploughed upward through the bowel. The first avenging blow of the Indian Mutiny had been struck.

Never in their sunlit sheltered lives had most men envisaged such horrors. Torches were hoisted high above contorted faces that shone with sweat; mounted troopers thundered by, their horses, snatched hastily from the stables, accoutred only with watering bridles and blankets. Steam rose from scarlet swords. Seeing the riff-raff of the bazaar armed with cudgels, officer after officer swerved his mount expertly; attack from this quarter was expected. Then on all sides nine-foot staves drove at them and many found their mark. Trusting minds had not numbered the blue-coated civil police among the enemy.

Incredibly, in far-flung corners of the cantonment, the peaceful Sunday round went on. At the east end of the station, sepoy guards knew nothing of the riot, punctiliously saluted every officer who passed. Mrs. Dunbar Muter, returning home, saw no signs of unrest; when her household steward advised her to flee with the remainder of the British to the quarter-guard of the 60th Rifles she was deeply mortified. Eventually she agreed with one proviso—the steward would be held personally responsible for the family silver.

By 8 p.m. on this night, Meerut was a city of terror. The last sepoys had fled the station; the mob warmed to its orgy of destruction, though risks were to be avoided. Keeping their distance from an officer's wife recovering from smallpox, they pelted her with lighted brands until her filmy muslin wrapper took fire. Others, dying from deep wounds, were heaped on pyres of broken bedroom furniture.

Some died shamefully, alone and at bay. Mrs. Charlotte Chambers, a captain's wife, fled from a screaming mob; pregnancy slowed her steps, she stumbled and fell. In a ghastly parody of a Caesarean operation, long knives delivered her. Elsewhere women lay dead, on moonlit grass wet with dew, among beds of canna lilies, stripped naked, their backs and thighs flayed repeatedly by sword cuts as with a steel whip, huge sticks and tow and burning thatch driven far into their bodies.

Strangely there were few reprisals—strange because Meerut was the one military station in all India where British troops were on near-level terms with Indians, 2,028 Europeans against 2,357 sepoys. Further, the British had twelve field guns, the sepoys lacked any artillery. Prompt action might yet have averted needless bloodshed.

Yet from the outset chaos reigned. Colonel George Carmichael Smyth spurred his horse through the blazing streets, double-barrelled pistol levelled. He sought first the Civil Commissioner, next the General, lastly the Brigadier, wisely giving his regimental lines a wide berth. He was Field Officer of the week; it was not in the scope of his duties to seek out his men.

Others showed as little initiative, as if the impact of the unforeseen crisis had paralysed their wills. Though the 60th Rifles had been mustered and ready for church parade by 6 p.m., their sergeant-major deemed white drill unsuitable for street-fighting—the men must return to barracks and change into the Rifles' dark-green. Next balled ammunition must be served out and 800 men, having dressed by the right, were taken through the roll-call. Finally, at a steady seventy-five paces to the minute, not the "double quick," the 60th set out to seek the enemy.

Brigadier Archdale Wilson, who had joined them, acquitted himself no better. Foremost in his mind loomed Section XVII of Bengal Army Regulations; a brigadier commanding a station which was also a Divisional Headquarters could give no orders if the Divisional Commander was present. The mighty bulk of Major-General William Hewitt slumped in his carriage happily relieved him of the responsibility.

And the troops available, as Wilson later pointed out, presented an extra problem. Of 475 artillery men, 200 were recruits learning foot-drill who had never handled a carbine. Of the 6th Dragoon Guards, 652 strong, half were again recruits unable to mount a horse. Despatching patrols to guard the treasury and other strongpoints, Hewitt, Wilson and more than 1,000 men set out for the sepoys' parade-ground.

No sepoys were in sight, but behind the dancing wall of flame that engulfed the bungalows there sounded a babel of voices. "Are we to load with bullets and shoot straight?" Captain Dunbar Muter of the 60th asked Wilson uncertainly. "Yes, for execution—you see the position," Wilson replied. At once the 60th, bringing their Enfields to the aim, sent a volley of bullets singing into the heart of the fire; seconds later the Horse Artillery, unlimbering, followed up with a fusillade of grapeshot. Shot rattled dryly among brushwood of

a copse nearby; no other sound was heard. It was, as a
surgeon commented sourly, a "useless and ineffectual demon-
stration."

Only one man, Captain Charles Rosser of the 6th Dra-
goons, showed a spark of enterprise. When a messenger
brought word that the mutineers had fled by the Delhi road,
Rosser at once rode up to his commanding officer. "If you, sir,
will get me two squadrons of the regiment and three or four
horse artillery guns *I* will pursue the mutineers and ride into
Delhi now."

But Brigadier Wilson would have none of this; he "did
not wish to divide the force." Dumbly the fat old General
stood by, saying nothing unless appealed to, convinced the
one prudent plan was to withdraw swiftly behind safe cover.
Later Hewitt was to make the astonishing confession: "I
gave no orders without Wilson's permission."

As the dull roar of toppling buildings shook the night,
Hewitt and Wilson led their force back to bivouac on the
race-course.

And now travellers on the roads south heard the eerie
clank of fetters in the night, the steady *kock-kock* of hooves;
in scattered parties of five and ten the rebels of Meerut
were on the march. Lacking artillery there was but one place
to hide now, the impregnable stronghold of Delhi, and one
master to serve—old Mohammed Bahadur Shah, last of the
Mogul Emperors, whose Red Fort within the city walls still
symbolised the golden years before the British reduced all to
bondage. Sometimes they paused in darkness to listen but the
British were not coming. Only fate bayed behind them, driving
150,000 men towards a common destination.

IV. DELHI

Morning 11th May

Yellow light streaked the sky to the east and Delhi city awoke. In the dark courtyards of the old city, within the blood-red walls of the Emperor's Fort, towering sixty feet above the shining river, 150,000 people stirred sleepily on string beds or thin quilts and wondered what this day would bring. For the city's Moslems, this dawn of Monday, 11th May, the sixteenth day of Ramadan, was the signal to breakfast hastily; once the sun had risen, no crumb of food or sip of water might pass the lips. Soon, from the great mosque close to the fort, the guttural rolling cry of the muezzin would ring in their ears:

"La! il-lah-il-ullaho! La! il-lah-il-ul-la-ho!" (There is no god but God!).

At the bathing place on the river bank, where the Hindus came to perform their religious ablutions, the worshippers crouched shivering in the steely water. In this dawn hour a chill wind ruffled the tall reeds. Squatting on the muddy shore, the *pujari*, the master of ceremonial, was busy with little saucers of vermilion and sandalwood and gypsum; later, when the bathers waded from the river, he must replace the caste-marks on their foreheads. It was at this moment, as he later related, that his eyes turned east and he paused, spellbound by what he saw. Others, following his glance, now watched in silent awe.

Above the broad metalled road to the north, a fine cloud of dust hovered, motionless as a bird of prey. Someone was coming from Meerut.

Slowly, as the dust-cloud seemed to take wings, all drew audible breath. Not one man but two thousand were on the march, a long straggling cavalcade of horsemen riding in-

41

exorably towards the bridge of boats. A gangway of lighters overlaid with huge planks, akin to the corduroy roads of Canada, this bridge spanned the three-quarter-mile width of the river within hailing distance of the Emperor's private quarters.

At this hour the 82-year-old Emperor, Mohammed Bahadur Shah had already breakfasted: for forty years, following his physician's instructions, his strange morning routine had begun with an emetic to freshen the stomach, an opium pill to calm the nerves, finally a heaped plate of pilaff. Hunched in a loose wadded dressing-gown, he sat as always in the cool latticed private quarters in the north-eastern face of the palace overlooking the river. In this cloistered world of marble colonnades set about by orange trees and jewelled fountains the last of the Moguls had reigned for twenty years now, supported by an East India Company stipend of £120,000 a year, still attended by a dingy retinue of 5,000 courtiers. Since the day he decreed that even a Governor-General must remove his shoes in the royal presence, he saw few Englishmen. The belief that the Company might abolish the title with his death caused him nothing but bitterness but by now he was too old to care; his only pleasure was to sit for hours composing rhymed couplets in flawless Persian. In the pale finely-chiselled features twitching uncontrollably, the nervous fingers, the muttering, irritable, incoherent speech, compassionate strangers saw the ruins of a great dynasty.

By now the rebels were streaming across the bridge, the horses' hooves beating a tattoo on the stout planking, making for the open space below the walls used by all who had a personal petition for the King. The sound of their cries rang in his old ears; leaning heavily on a stick he hobbled to the small turret that jutted out above the river bank. At the sight of the frail white-bearded figure hovering at the low marble balustrade, the troopers' yelling redoubled. Their horses reared in salute, their manes streaming in the sun.

"We have come to fight for the faith, O King!" they called, "Open the gates and let us in."

But the sight of these unruly men in their French-grey jackets and light dragoon shakos filled the old man with fear. Some, advancing with drawn swords, told how they had killed their officers rather than accept the tainted cartridge, but they spoke with bravado, like men drunk with defiance, not as subjects seeking the honour of an audience. Hastily withdrawing from the balcony the old King sent a servant speeding for the English guard commander, Captain Charles Douglas. From his quarters above the fort's Lahore gate, the captain commanded the ceremonial force of artillery and infantry 1,200 strong the Company permitted the King. This token bodyguard was a Bengal Army detachment; the King had no power to give them orders.

Already the British were learning trouble was at hand. Two miles north, in the cantonments on the Ridge, the day for Robert and Harriet Tytler had begun like any other. By 8.30 a.m. both Robert and Harriet had taken their morning baths and had settled down to breakfast. Edith, aged two, and Frank, four, too young to be at school in England with the Tytlers' eldest son Frederick, had already breakfasted with Marie, the family's French maid who invariably wore an ornate Breton head-dress. Later Harriet was to recall every moment of this last meal in vivid detail: the household tailor stitching busily on the verandah outside, the sweet orange pulp of the musk melons which made up the last course, Robert grumbling over the untoward events of the past twenty-four hours.

Above all he was still perplexed by an incident that had disturbed his siesta the previous afternoon. A bugle heralding a travelling carriage had shrilled close at hand; carriage wheels were grinding past the door. Tytler had called a servant to enquire after the guests, but the man shook his head. A carriage full of Indians was heading for the lines.

At last, thought Tytler, Munsoor Ali had returned; he could obtain positive news of the Meerut court martial. Hastily he told the servant to intercept the carriage and ask the Subadar-Major to drop in. Soon the man returned. The carriage had been full of sepoys, who had come from Meerut, but none had belonged to Tytler's regiment.

By the standards of the time the sepoys' pay was good—roughly 14s. a month—yet few could afford a travelling carriage for a forty-four mile journey. Bewildered, Tytler had retired to rest.

This Monday morning all over British India special parades had been assembled to announce the recent sentences passed on mutineers like Mangal Pande. It had fallen to Robert's lot to translate to his regiment the warning words of Lord Canning's proclamation: ". . . To no men who prefer complaints with arms in their hands will the Governor-General of India in Council ever listen . . ." To Harriet's dismay her husband had returned bitterly disappointed.

"Harriet, the men behaved infamously today," he burst out. "They hissed and shuffled with their feet when I was reading out the order."

Next instant, as Harriet would always remember, all was confusion. With a yell of terror, the tailor burst in from the verandah: "Sahib, sahib, the Army has come." At once Robert leapt to his feet. "Give me my sword and helmet. I must go and see the Brigadier." For a moment the tailor's lamentation drowned all other sound, so that Harriet, bewildered, cried out: "What is the matter?" Already Robert was buckling on his sword. "Oh, nothing—only those fellows from Meerut have come over and I suppose they are kicking up a row in the city."

To the old Emperor quaking in his riverside palace it seemed as if the whole city cried out with a single tongue. Even Captain Douglas, the guard commander, seemed powerless to stem the tide; no sooner had he joined the King at his balcony, bidding the rebels be gone, than a scream of execration arose. Douglas, undismayed, shouted back that these were the King's private apartments and no place to create a disturbance.

"Encamp somewhere on the river-bed," he ordered. "The King will afterwards listen to your complaints."

Suddenly, with deceptive compliance, the rebels wheeled their horses, striking up river towards the Rajghat Gate of the city. Douglas saw prompt action was vital. "Have the gates of the palace, as well as of the city, closed immediately," were his last words to the King, "lest these men should get in." The thought that now struck other officials hastening towards the city had already struck him: of the walled city's ten gates, the Calcutta gate, on the river side, was the one that afforded the rebels easiest access. The gate must be closed and held fast.

Douglas saw that these were desperate men but he consoled himself that General Hewitt's troops must already be in hot pursuit. He could not know what the rebels knew—that no English troops had so far left Meerut, that the telegraph wires between the stations were cut, that the sepoys at Delhi were ripe for revolt.

With Douglas's departure, the King was in a quandary. He had no cause to love the British. For fifty years, at their own leisurely pace, they had stripped the Moguls of the last trappings of power. When gossip had it that the Bengal Army would desert the British because of the cartridges the King did not mourn. A new owner in the land, he believed, would show him more respect.

Though the old man was barely aware of it, rumours of a bloody rising had been current for months. In the dark vestibules of the fort, where filthy matting contrasted oddly with sumptuous silver chairs, the King's servants and advisers had murmured of changes that would shake India like an earthquake. Russia would avenge the Crimea by invading with 400,000 troops, reestablishing the Mogul Empire. Persia was to help. Yet no direct evidence ever linked the old man with such high-flown intrigues. No spider spinning a mesh of intrigue, he lay himself a prisoner within the web of circumstance.

One hour passed, then two. Still Douglas did not return. In his private chamber, on the ornate bedstead surmounted by carved lions, the King dozed. Outside in the Hall of Audience, a massive arched one-storey building of dull red sandstone, his lawyer, Ghulam Abbas, and Ahsanullah Khan, his physician, conversed in low tones. Suddenly a thunderclap of sound tore at their eardrums. Petrified, lawyer and physician saw the mounted officers and men of the 3rd Light Cavalry gallop into the courtyard, their horses' hooves ploughing recklessly across trim green turf. Carbines and pistols levelled, they fired salvo after salvo in savage exultation, the echoes bouncing from the marble walls. Behind swarmed fully five hundred armed men. In alarm the advisers saw they wore the black jackets and red turbans of the King's infantrymen, whose duty was to guard the fort gates against all intruders.

Now Bahadur Shah himself appeared, calling feebly for his attendants. The noise must cease and he demanded, moreover, a personal explanation from the officers as to what this meant. Blood-red roses snapped and fell as the snorting line of horses spurred forward across the flower-beds. In their eagerness to be heard, to stress anew the iniquity of the cartridges, men grew fevered with excitement, shouting one another down.

"I did not call for you," the King quavered. "You have acted very wickedly."

A throng of Meerut infantrymen shouldered their way forward, 200 men in scarlet and white with their unwieldy bell-shaped shakos, pressing towards the foot of the steps.

"Unless you, the King, join us," a spokesman exhorted, "we are all dead men. We must in that case just do what we can for ourselves."

In this moment the fate of the Indian Mutiny was poised in the scales. As the King lowered his old body into an ivory chair, the rebels seized their chance. One by one officers and men stepped forward, humbly now, bowing their heads before him, craving his blessing. Did flattery stir a faint memory of forgotten grandeur within him? In any case, without demur, he laid his hand solemnly upon each man's head. The clamour was so incessant that Ghulam Abbas, the lawyer, withdrew. The rebels had won and he knew it.

Nor would this first victory be relinquished. Guards were mounted. Some, seeking no permission, calmly spread their bedding on the polished marble and settled to rest. Their horses, fed and watered, were tethered in the shade of willow-leaved ashoka trees. Overcome by weariness the King returned to his quarters.

Already Douglas and scores of other Europeans were dead. Unable to command the sepoy guards to close the gates against the rebels Douglas had fled wounded to his quarters. There the mob had found him. On the stone stairs below, the Commissioner, Simon Fraser, and John Ross Hutchinson, the Collector, were both hacked to death. The Reverend Midgly Jennings, a Delhi missionary who had been visiting Douglas, laid about him with a sword then went down beneath a tidal wave of brown bodies. Annie, his daughter, and her friend, Mary Clifford, hiding in a wardrobe, gained only two minutes' respite. The sabres flashed, the white splinters flew; panting and kicking they were dragged out.

In the city's wide tree-lined streets hundreds went to work with the fierce energy of vandals. The manager of the Delhi and London Bank, George Berresford, retreated to the roof with his wife and children; armed with clubs and matchlocks the rebels swarmed to a higher roof, hurtling into space like a boarding-party of privateers. As they leapt, Sarah Berresford lunged with a hog-spear. Her spear had claimed two before the mob tore them all to pieces. In the offices of the *Delhi Gazette* the compositors had just stamped a mutiny edition "EXTRA" when men burst in and battered them to death. Soon the type had been torn from the founts and hurled far into the river. Others stormed into St. James's Church, pounding at the monumental slabs, shivering the altar rails and armchairs to matchwood with their swords. Some, racing to the belfry, rang a jangling peal of mockery before severing the rope and the bells came ricocheting down the long funnel of the steeple. Far over Delhi they rang like a knell, heard by Harriet Tytler on the sun-baked Ridge, audible to Bahadur Shah in the confines of his palace.

On the wide thatched verandah of her bungalow, Harriet stood lost in a twilight of indecision. Within minutes of his departure Robert had returned with barely comprehensible instructions; Brigadier Harry Graves, commanding the cantonment, had sent a first detachment of the 54th Native Infantry under Colonel John Ripley, to pacify the mutineers. Robert and another officer were to take two companies and guard the river ferries.

Aloft, on the baking infinity of the Ridge, the drowsy city seemed half-buried in green foliage, white onion domes glinting under a bright and vertical sun. Yet to Harriet there were uneasy signs that all was not well: gun carriages diminished like nursery toys, rattling at speed down far-off roads; Mrs. Hutchinson, the Collector's wife, hatless with flowing hair, carrying one of her own children, as careless of appearance and status as a private soldier's wife.

Word now came that all civilians must repair to the Flag-staff Tower, two miles north along the rocky spine of the Ridge. A soaring spire 150 feet high, flanked by balconies and ascended within by winding stairs, the Tower was the traditional meeting place of the British, where the Union Jack snapped unchallenged. By noon, Harriet, Marie and the children had joined the long stumbling phalanx of women toiling along the dusty road: some in gigs or on ponies, in white muslin robes, their hair bound with blue ribbons, clutching gold-stoppered smelling bottles, more on foot, still wearing loose moccasin-like slippers, their hair flowing free, their children's heads bound with wet handkerchiefs to ward off the heat. All of them alone in spirit, their hearts crying out with apprehension, all of them beset by a hot harrying wind.

At the Tower all was confusion; the news that filtered back from the city stilled speech on the tongue. The first detachment of the 54th Native Infantry speeding to the city had met the mutineers near the main guard of the Kash-mir Gate, which commanded the approach from Delhi to the cantonments on the Ridge. Colonel John Ripley's sharp command to load had gone unheeded. Within seconds the rebels had ridden him and his officers down. As he lay squirming on the stones his own men, turning him over, bayoneted him nine times. With that the 54th had fled like madmen to swell the howling mob that already, as gate after gate yielded, packed the streets. To guard the vital Kashmir Gate there remained only two guns of a picked bat-tery, an uneasy sepoy guard of Robert Tytler's regiment and the British officers of the 54th. His voice hushed with emotion, a regimental doctor told Harriet, "Mrs. Tytler, God only knows how the day will end."

To Harriet Tytler it seemed it could end only in disaster. In the tiny upstairs room of the Tower, only eighteen feet in diameter, "a Black Hole in miniature," women, children and servants huddled together, swooning with heat and nervous excitement. When the wife of an officer in Robert's regiment thoughtfully provided a chair, Harriet sank into it gratefully; all too soon her fourth child would be born.

Cradled in her arms, two-year-old Edith whimpered fitfully, "Mama, do come home . . . me no like this place."

In every mind and on every lip the question trembled: When will the reinforcements from Meerut come?

The answer was in doubt. Still convinced they stood in deadly peril from the riff-raff of the bazaars General William Hewitt and Brigadier Archdale Wilson had barricaded themselves and their men behind a fortified entrenchment, intent on defending Meerut to the death. Ignoring the fact that the entire Meerut Division—which included Delhi—was his responsibility, Hewitt, to quote the report which six weeks later relieved him of command "thought only of the safety of the place in which he himself resided." No troops were allowed to venture beyond their pickets, and Hewitt reported that he was "defending his position successfully." Against what or whom was never made clear.

Yet military hindsight is fatally easy and it is plain that once Hewitt's Sunday-night failure to check the mutineers was accomplished fact, no force of men, mounted on half-broken Australian horses, could have stopped the Indian Mutiny. Twelve hours had given the rebels a matchless chance to consolidate. Scarcely knowing what had befallen him, Bahadur Shah had been snatched up, a banner faded by sun and rain, to rally all to a common cause.

Meanwhile Robert Tytler, deserted by all but forty of his older sepoys, had returned hastily to the Flagstaff Tower. Unaware that the lines were cut, Brigadier Graves had sent off an unavailing chain of messages to Meerut and to Agra. To Robert it seemed more than time to shape a firm policy.

His voice, steady, outspoken, carried clearly to Harriet on the second floor of the Tower: "Excuse me, sir, but what do you propose doing?"

"Stay here, Tytler, and protect the women and children."

Tytler was too disturbed to set a guard on his tongue. "It is madness, sir. Have you any food?"

"No, Tytler."

"Have you any water?" Again Graves had to confess it: there was no water.

"Then how do you propose protecting the women and

children," Robert demanded, "with those two remaining guns
ready to blow us up?"

Graves seemed at his wit's end. "I know, but what can we
do? If we expose ourselves they will shoot us down."

At Robert's confident retort, "My men will never shoot us,"
a roar of derision arose from the other officers; the tragic
end of Colonel Ripley was but too fresh in their minds. "For
God's sake, don't listen to Tytler—he has been talked over
by his men." But Robert was more than a match for them in
logic. "Gentlemen," Harriet recalled his rejoinder, "it is not
for you to say, listen or not listen to Tytler. We cannot
hold our post, therefore it is our duty to form a retreat."

To the listening women in the room above it seemed then
that Robert had won the day. "Go and ask your men, Tytler," Graves replied.

Harriet felt a stir of pride as Robert walked, empty-
handed and bare-headed, into the sunlight to meet his men.
His appeal was simple and courageous: "Listen to me, my
men. If you intend to do any harm to those within, let me be
the first to fall that they may know their fate." Then he went
on: "But if you will be true to your salt and go with us
wherever we tell you, then say so."

Without hesitation some of the older sepoys now stepped
forward, laying their hands upon Robert's hair to signify the
solemnity of their oath. "We will not harm a hair of your
head or that of any of you," one of them said quietly. "We
will go with you wherever you tell you to provided you command us yourself." And they added two further provisos:
they wanted water to drink and an assurance that the two
remaining field guns would accompany them as protection.
Hearing this, Brigadier Graves stood in a mute agony of
doubt, but again the officers cried angrily, "For God's sake
don't listen to Tytler."

His voice rising with anger, Robert Tytler still stood his
ground. "Very well, gentlemen," he told them. "Stay here
and be butchered but I will go with my family and stand my
court martial. I will not stay here any longer to see my wife
and children killed in my presence." Irresolute, Graves could
say only, "Go, Tytler, and ask the men again."

But the sepoys, like Robert, were fast losing patience. In

exasperation one man broke out: "Are you playing with us, sir? Do you know that the troopers are already at hand refreshing their horses?" Patiently he explained the rebels' probable plan of campaign: they believed that the British would linger all night at Flagstaff Tower and they could presently kill them at their leisure. "If you do not go at once," was the sepoy's parting shot, "we will not go with you."

By great good fortune, as was to happen time and again through the months that followed, one civilian with an enterprise the military commanders signally lacked, snatched the opportunity to warn the outside world of the danger. In the tiny wooden signal cabin a mile from the city walls, midway between the Flagstaff Tower and the vital Kashmir Gate, William Brendish, a young Eurasian signaller, and his fellow-operator, J. W. Pilkington, were beset by cruel anxiety; all morning news had trickled into the cabin, brought by the messengers of the *Delhi Gazette,* who normally stood by to carry telegrams from the cabin to their office. Already the two youngsters knew the 3rd Cavalry had entered the city; they knew that the 54th Native Infantry had killed their own colonel. Yet no official telegram had been passed to them for despatch that morning, though the spider's web of line that ran north to Ambala, and on to Lahore, Rawalpindi and Peshawar, was in perfect working order.

There were other causes for alarm. The day before, being Sunday, the two youngsters, following custom, had prepared to close down the office at 9 a.m. and re-open at 4 p.m. At 9 a.m. Brendish had heard from the Meerut signaller of great excitement prevailing: eighty men, it was incorrectly reported, were shortly to be executed. Though Brendish did not know it, this was the last pre-mutiny message ever to leave Meerut. By 4 p.m., when the Delhi cabin re-opened, the wires had been cut.

Neither Brendish nor Pilkington realised this, any more than Charles Todd, the Delhi postmaster. An innovation of four years' standing in India, the electric telegraph was still beset by vexing hazards; many of its 4,044 miles of wire ran across rivers too wide to span and the ever-shifting river beds caused frequent damage to the underwater cables. Often, too, the villagers would cut the wire to make bangles for their wives. Brendish and Pilkington, crossing the river later that Sunday, had found no such fault; it was plain the line was broken closer to Meerut. At 8 a.m. on this Monday, Charles Todd had set out in a pony carriage to trace it. Four hours later, he had not returned—nor was he ever seen again.

At noon, leaving the cabin to prospect, Brendish was appalled to see a stream of native carts and wagons pouring past the office, crammed with household goods, laden with Indian shop-keepers and their wives. Suddenly an officer smeared with blood, his uniform in tatters, staggered past them, heading for the Ridge. "For God's sake," he implored Brendish, "get inside and close your doors." A passing shopkeeper underlined the wisdom of this: if the sepoys were murdering even Indian merchants, what chance did a white face stand?

Brendish was only eighteen, paid a pittance of 15s. a week, but he saw the need for action; above all he must let the authorities a hundred miles north know the gravity of the disaster. Until his death in Calcutta, fifty years later, awarded a pension of £240 a year as a tribute to his presence of mind, he would hold this memory fast: the hasty settling to the keys in the instrument room as, at the maximum eighteen words per minute, he tapped out the last words from the doomed city.

"We must leave office, all the bungalows are on fire, burning down by the sepoys of Meerut. They came in this morning. Mr. C. Todd is dead, we think. He went out this morning and has not yet returned. We learn that nine Europeans were killed. We are off. Goodbye."

Thus, as it had come to Harriet and Robert Tytler, the news came hour by hour to all men and women, and their reactions were as diverse as the moulds that had shaped their lives. Some took it with bravado; at Agra, close to the marble wonder of the Taj Mahal, a straggling procession of British drove their carriages at funeral pace through the streets, defiantly flourishing double-barrelled shotguns. Only when the shopkeepers set up a barrage of gibes—"Ah! *Here* come the invincibles! No chance now for the poor sepoys"

—did their folly come home to them and they sheepishly turned tail.

Others, hearing that Delhi was doomed, recoiled with fear or resisted with ferocity. In Ambala, the officers of the 2nd Bengal Fusiliers bade the armourer sharpen their swords before engraving each blade with the name of a fallen comrade and taking a solemn oath; only when rebel blood had worn the names away would they cease from killing. A few heard the news farsightedly, with philosophy. At Lucknow, Sir Henry Lawrence sent for his private secretary and handed him a telegram outlining the tragedy of Delhi. "It will mean the rising of the whole army throughout the country," he said. The Maharajah of Kashmir, Gholab Singh, commented, "Well, it will give the English some trouble . . . but in a few months they will be all right again." The Prime Minister of Nepal, Jung Bahadur, lifted his hands in horror. Whatever, he asked, would the London *Times* say?

And despite past blindness there came now the first dim stirrings of realisation. A clergyman's wife in Gwalior, south of Agra, recalled her ayah's mounting interest in whether the tops of her scent-bottles were real silver. A merchant at Fatehgarh realised that for months Indian traders had spurned cheques, accepting only cash. A colonel in Calcutta remembered a Government official's angry outburst at a dinner party: "I shall be innocent of the blood but if you have a head on your shoulders in the month of May I shall be very much surprised."

And at Delhi, where the plight of all in the Flagstaff Tower grew hourly more desperate, they recalled other portents. Brigadier Harry Graves remembered the sepoys from his old regiment passing through in mid-April; they had loved him as a father; what had they known that they had so persistently urged him to apply for leave in England or the hills? Harriet and Robert Tytler recalled the inexplicable tears of Dabi, their bearer; he had planned to go home for his eldest daughter's wedding and they had drawn on their savings to give him a cow and an English doll for his youngest but for three days he would not start, only wept inconsolably at intervals. "I cannot bear parting with the children," he excused himself but at the last as he started out he had said a strange thing: "Sahib, if your hearth is still burning I shall hope to see you again."

At the time the Tytlers had dismissed it as had all the British dismissed such signs. They had reflected on them at idle moments then banished them from their minds only to recall them again. They had wondered and wondered.

They knew now.

V. DELHI

Afternoon 11th May

At 2 p.m. the Ridge was quiet. In the breathless heat of the Flagstaff Tower, Harriet Tytler and a score of others, armed now with loaded rifles, vainly awaited news. Apart from Brigadier Graves and his officers, there remained only the sepoys of the 74th Native Infantry, the sepoys of the 38th and some Indian Christian band boys. Of the officers trapped with a number of women in the main guard of the Kashmir Gate nothing was yet known. The sun poured a rain of fire on the crocodile of red rock that was the Ridge but nothing stirred on the road to Meerut. Only Marie, Harriet's Breton maid, remained irrepressible, flirting openly with Graves' officers.

In the city, ten men had a rendezvous with death. Since early that morning Lieutenant George Willoughby and a staff of eight had barricaded themselves inside the powder-magazine which lay 600 yards from the Kashmir Gate's main guard. To ward off a sustained assault their armament was meagre—nine six-pounder guns, double-charged with grape, and one 24-pound howitzer in front of their office building— but Willoughby, in the last resort, had planned a desperate remedy. The sooty streaks that ran straight as arrows to the heart of the arsenal from the stunted lemon-tree in the court-yard's centre were powder-trains that would, if need be, blast them all to eternity. To Willoughby and his staff of eight this was in line of duty. The tenth man, whom history has forgotten, was J. C. Ryley, a 35-year-old clerk in the judge's office. Ryley had scarcely expected this, though he too, as a report avowed, "rendered valiant service." By a strange irony he had scaled the gate simply because the magazine seemed the safest place to be.

From the bastion overlooking the bridge-of-boats, Willoughby and his lieutenants had kept anxious watch on the Meerut road, but it seemed their lives could be numbered in minutes instead of hours. Already men clad in the blue uniform of palace artillerymen were pounding at the heavy barred doors, demanding admission in the King's name. Nervously, Conductor John Buckley fingered the brim of his forage cap. At Willoughby's command the raising of this hat would be the signal to fire the train.

It was 3.30 p.m. To the ten men waiting tensely within the magazine, a new sound became audible above the howling of the mob below: the scraping of iron against stone. Now the walls above their heads came alive with scrambling men, poised on iron-jointed scaling ladders. At once Willoughby's deputy, Lieutenant George Forrest, raced with Conductor Buckley to the nearest six-pounders: eight-ounce pebbles of grape-shot, glowing red-hot, scythed great lanes in the rebel ranks. Undismayed the rebels hit back with a biting musketry fire. A ball tore into Buckley's arm above the elbow. Forest, too, recoiled, his left hand a useless red pulp where a ball had mangled it.

Their affliction was short-lived: by now hundreds of rebels were lining the walls and Lieutenant Willoughby, half turning towards Buckley, shouted, "Now, if you please!" With ironical politeness, Buckley raised his hat. Ducking beneath the shade of the lemon tree, Conductor John Scully, holding a portfire, a slow-burning fuse impregnated with saltpetre, bent to the black serpent of powder. Then with a force that shook the earth 110 miles away in Ambala, the powder-magazine went sky-high. From the Flagstaff Tower, Robert and Harriet Tytler watched bereft of speech as a cauliflower of yellow-white smoke trembled half a mile above the city, pressed slowly upward by a corona of red dust. Strangely enough, those within the magazine suffered least but as Willoughby and six of the ten, faces black and bleeding, stumbled through the broken wall a slow rain of flesh and dust and twisted metal poured on them from the sky. At least four hundred of the besiegers had perished.

It was a courageous though futile gesture—for Delhi's mutineers had ammunition and to spare for many weeks to come. The main magazine, packed with 3,000 barrels of powder, had for six years been sited three miles from the city, transferred thence by Lord Dalhousie who had shared the citizens' fears of a fatal explosion. Though Brigadier Graves had earlier attempted to secure this stronghold, a spattering fire from the native guard had driven his officers back. Thus the rebels' fighting strength was unaffected; the magazine for which Willoughby and the others risked their lives held only 50 barrels of practice ammunition.

To scores of men and women the thunderclap of the detonation was the signal for urgent flight; no help could now be expected from Meerut and once the Indian night had fallen as swiftly as a shutter, the rebels could hunt them down at leisure. At the Kashmir Gate, the surviving officers of the 54th Native Infantry escaped with their womenfolk only by fastening their sword-belts together and dangling twenty-five feet into the city ditch. As they and the women fought their way up the almost perpendicular counterscarp, a hail of sepoy bullets from the walls sent the dust spurting about them. Thereafter for five days and nights the party of ten— among them Willoughby's badly-wounded deputy, George Forrest—stumbled through thistles and stubble, waded waist-deep through rivers, until a scouting party from Meerut led by Hugh Gough and Alexander Mackenzie escorted them to safety.

The rocky terrain below the Ridge, a chequerboard of crumbling garden walls, scrub and prickly pear, was given over to a deadly game of hide-and-seek. Householders whose words a day before had been law to twenty servants now lay prone in dappled shade, their hearts beating fearfully at the clop of troopers' horses on metalled roads, scrambling into drains or jackals' lairs, as the voices of sepoys hallooed across the gardens. Many were women who had depended on their husbands' every decision, yet in these hours they showed matchless courage and resource.

Mrs. Elizabeth Wagentreiber took the reins of the phaeton that carried her family overnight to Kurnal, a military station seventy-eight miles away, leaving her husband George, a sub-editor on the *Delhi Gazette,* free to fend off the mutineers with a brace of pistols and a double-barrelled gun. Four times on this moonlight night mobs armed with spears and stones surged forward to cut the traces; four times Wagentreiber emptied the pistols at point-blank range; the phaeton wheels jolted over men dead and dying. Beside him Eliza, aged twenty-two, mechanically loaded and reloaded for her stepfather. An iron-bound stave clubbed with excruciating force on Elizabeth Wagentreiber's shoulder, temporarily paralysing the right arm; she did not cry out nor did she loose the reins.

Others, by strange quirks of providence, survived by a hair's breadth. The proud joint-magistrate of Delhi, Sir Theo Metcalfe, escaping in his shirt and under-drawers, owed his life to a unique circumstance; the peasant who sheltered him recalled Sir Theo's deciding a court case against him and respected his shrewdness. Joseph Brown, an Eurasian compositor of the *Delhi Gazette,* hiding all night beneath a washerman's boiler, escaped death only by persuading the Hindu sepoys who found him that he shared their faith. Next, seeking to ingratiate himself with some Moslem troopers, he posed as a would-be convert. He got away in the nick of time; the Moslems had plans to circumcise him. Major Francis Paterson, of the 54th, sought sanctuary in the regimental ice-pits; the association prompted him to send a friendly Indian for iced champagne but the man, a sergeant-major of his regiment, did not understand. Three times he returned from the mess bearing an enormous bottle of vinegar.

Few knew now whether any man was friend or foe. At the Flagstaff Tower, as the magazine exploded, the sepoys, with a wild cry of *"Din! Din!"* rushed to their arms and raced down the white road towards the Kashmir Gate. One, however, lingered to tell Robert Tytler bitterly. "From now on we will taste the blood of the English—this is no time for soft words. Go, sahib, save your wife and children—we won't go with you another step."

To Robert it seemed high time to escort Harriet and the

others to safety, but he accepted gratefully the offer of Subadar-Major Munsoor Ali's son to hasten to the Tytlers' bungalow and salvage some of his chemistry notes. Robert and the old Subadar had been experimenting on metals before the mutiny began. To the boy's astonishment he found the butler and the table-waiter seated implacably at the gate, each nursing one of Robert's double-barrelled shot-guns. "It is not likely the sahib will escape from the soldiers," the butler said, "but if he does he will not escape from us."

Now, as twilight cloaked the Ridge, the Tytlers set out on their weary journey. Already six were crammed into a buggy meant for two, Harriet and Marie, along with Harriet's children, sharing with Mrs. Gardner, the adjutant's wife, and their small boy. As Robert Tytler sped back toward the cantonment to find Captain Herbert Gardner, he saw flames already licking greedily at the thatch of their bungalow half-a-mile away. Cantering on he met Gardner who sprang for the rump of his horse. Then he turned his back on the fire that was consuming everything he and his wife had loved: the manuscripts and illustrations for a chemistry book he had planned to publish, all Harriet's paintings, their plate, their books, their furniture and carriages, more than £2,000 worth of property. As Robert caught up with the buggy he was distressed to see Thakur Singh, their sepoy orderly, pleading to be taken with them. In vain they reasoned that the buggy was full up; there was but one horse to carry Robert and Gardner. Despite his heavy marching order, Thakur Singh pounded after the buggy until at last he lay down exhausted like a dog in the dust.

Only three of the British remained now at the Flagstaff Tower: Brigadier Harry Graves and two of his staff officers. To the west, copper-coloured light flooded the sky; the flames of the burning bungalows were merging with the glow of the sunset. In carriages and on horseback, in buggies and on foot, the others had all gone, seeking the safety of Meerut or Kurnal; in eight short hours the power of life and death at Delhi had passed from "John Company" to the hands of the Moguls. Yet still, near the base of the tower, a few sepoys lingered, avowing their intention of retiring with the Brigadier.

Heartened, Graves decided on one last appeal to their loyalty. "Bugler," he ordered, "sound the Assembly."

Though he had not consciously provoked it, this was a symbolic moment. As the bugle cried across the darkened Ridge and a flight of cormorants shafted in arrow-head formation across the sky, only one man, a sepoy of the 74th Native Infantry, stepped forward. A black silhouette against the sunset, he stood immobile, rigidly at attention, as the bugle shrilled on.

Come—to the col-ours! Come quick, come all—come quick, come all—come quick! Quick! Come to the colours!

As the last notes died away, he stood alone, the one sepoy in Delhi whose allegiance the British could command.

Thus sadly and with blind incomprehension the British left the Ridge. Some would never understand the complex nature of the forces that had driven them from thence; others in time achieved a rare compassion and understanding. These men and women learnt to avoid such phrases as "just retribution" and seek within themselves the causes of this carnage. They would tabulate many sins of omission, many occasions when they, the rulers, had failed in their duty to understand.

This mood would come later. At midnight on the 11th May those toiling towards Ambala were too stunned and shocked by the cataclysm that had overwhelmed them to indulge in the luxury of self-analysis. For Robert and Harriet Tytler and their party the days that followed resolved themselves into a chapter of accidents so ludicrous that at times Harriet did not know whether to laugh or cry. Long before they had covered the seventy-eight moonlit miles to Kurnal, one wheel of the buggy had splintered into pieces under the unaccustomed weight, their horse was stumbling with fatigue. For the first time it dawned on them they were penniless. It was Marie who proved their savior, for the resourceful Frenchwoman had rescued not only some trinkets of Harriet's and the silver teapot that had graced the breakfast table this morning, a lifetime ago, but her own money-box. The ten shillings that purchased a fresh horse from a livery stable came from Marie's savings.

Once a passing mail-cart had helped repair their wheel the journey proceeded smoothly for a few more miles. Then, with a breath-taking jolt that set the children wailing afresh, the hind wheel rolled off its axle. This time repair proved impossible and the party trudged silently through chill early-morning mists until a bullock tumbril manned by two Indians creaked into view. Alarmed by the sight of two grime-streaked officers armed with pistols, the drivers bolted for their lives.

Luckily they did not bolt far, for Robert's confident attempts to steer the tumbril towards Kurnal proved unavailing. Stripping off his shoes he threaded the cord yoked to the bullock's tail between his toes, tweaking it imperiously as he had seen the Indians do. To Harriet's uncontrollable amusement, the bullocks now sat down and refused to budge.

Emboldened by this ineptitude the drivers returned and offered for a price to convey them to Kurnal. By a strange irony they knew nothing of the revolt, for the tumbril was carrying broken rifles to be scrapped by the arsenal at Delhi. Days later, when the party reached Ambala, the women and children crammed in a small bullock carriage, Tytler and Gardner for economy's sake were travelling on foot. By now their feet were so blistered that shoes were no longer bearable; both men covered the miles from Kurnal to Ambala with blood soaking their stockinged feet. For the first time they were able to take stock and wonder what the future held in store—for themselves and for India.

VI. SIMLA AND LAHORE

11th to 14th May

At Barnes Court, Simla, set among blood-red rhododendrons, 160 miles north of Delhi, the Commander-in-Chief, General the Hon. George Anson, had on the evening of 12th May presided as host over a dinner party of twenty-five. Anson knew the Bengal Army was in a state of tension but this had not deflected him from the time-honoured custom of spending the hot weather in the hills. Nor did he wish military matters to obtrude on good table-talk, sparkling silver and good claret. One guest would always remember that when the signaller William Brendish's telegram arrived Anson tucked it beneath his plate.

Only with the ladies withdrawn and the port circulating did Anson open the blue flimsy and rise aghast from the table. He was now over a thousand miles from Lord Canning and the seat of Government and his army was irrevocably in revolt.

The situation could scarcely have been worse. Since India's defence was geared to frontier attacks, ammunition and ordnance depots were hundreds of miles away in the north-west. To advance men and munitions on Delhi Anson needed transport, but since 1846, the end of the first Sikh War, "John Company" as an economy measure had forbidden the Army Commissariat to maintain any carriage at all. To move troops or provisions in emergencies, through a convoy of carts called a "train," the civil officers of a district must first impress bullocks to draw the carts, elephants to haul heavy guns, camels to carry the baggage. Then there were camp followers to be rounded up—grooms, water-carriers, sweepers—for a force of ten thousand troops on the march often called for thirty thousand retainers.

Two days later, leaving Simla for Ambala with a mighty retinue of six thousand souls, it seemed to Anson his worst forebodings had come true. "John Company's" parsimony was proving disastrous. From each of his departmental heads —the Commissary-General, the Army Medical Department— he heard the same story: there were no hospital stores, no carriages, no litters for the wounded, no ammunition. At least sixteen to twenty days would be needed to put a force in campaign order to advance on Delhi. Three regiments had less than twenty rounds apiece. Wagons to carry the horse artillery's ammunition were seven days' march away. The tents were not ready and the only guns to breach the walls of Delhi, in some places 12 feet thick, were 6 or 9 pounders, suitable for a mud wall of roughly four feet.

And those who might have given Anson most support seemed a long way from understanding his problems. On 17th

May Lord Canning bade him "make as short work as possible
of the rebels who have cooped themselves up (in Delhi).
Allahabad, Benares . . . and a host of other places will continue to be a source of anxiety until Delhi is disposed of."
The Chief Commissioner of the Punjab, Sir John Lawrence,
was also giving Anson no peace. "Rough, coarse . . . more like
a navvy than a gentleman," as one aide recalled him, a striking contrast to his spare ascetic brother Henry at Lucknow,
Lawrence abhorred the indolence and luxury that Anson
seemed to represent. Now, to Anson's fury, a constant
stream of advice and admonition poured in from Lawrence,
then at Rawalpindi, three hundred and twenty miles north-
west. "Delhi would open its gates at the approach of our
troops," he wrote confidently. "Pray only reflect on the whole
history of India. Where have we failed when we acted vig-
orously? Where have we succeeded when guided by timid
counsels?" As yet, Anson felt, even Lord Canning had an
imperfect grasp of the hazards confronting him; Anson, Canning wrote, must detail both cavalry and infantry to safe-
guard Cawnpore, two hundred and sixty-six miles south-east
of Delhi. How Anson was to achieve this and storm Delhi
with only 2,900 men was not made clear.

The situation Canning faced would have daunted a lesser
man. Already the rebels held Delhi, India's largest arsenal,
with its hundreds of heavy guns, tens of thousands of stands
of arms, millions of cartridges. Every principal city was without European troops. Apart from one weak regiment, the 10th
Foot, barely a thousand strong, at Dinapore, there were none
in the seven hundred miles between Calcutta and Agra, only
one other regiment in the 1,200 miles between Dinapore
and Meerut. A few gunners at Cawnpore and Benares were
the only British troops between Calcutta and Lucknow. As a
conquest of only eight years' standing, John Lawrence's Punjab, the "Land of the Five Rivers," had absorbed fully ten
thousand British troops. Its frontiers marched for eight hundred miles with those of Afghanistan and its seven million population included the men of the wild Moslem
clans who held the hill passes with shield and spear.

Though lightning-shafts of criticism were to flicker about
the Governor-General's head no evidence has ever shown

that Canning was unduly dilatory. Not until 16th May, when he was shaken from slumber by an urgent telegram, was he made fully aware of the appalling catastrophe of Delhi and Meerut. As a prudent move, the sepoys in the Calcutta area had already been disarmed; now Canning sent cables for reinforcements to every available theatre—Madras, Bombay, Ceylon, Lord Elgin's China Force speeding to avenge the seizure of members of the crew of a British trading vessel on the Canton river. If this force did not touch at Singapore for coaling, Canning stressed, a steamer must if necessary pursue it as far as Java. "The need," he told Lord Elgin frankly, "is very great and very urgent."

Events were moving fast; he saw the need for speed and firmness that further bloodshed might be checked, but the cruelty and cowardice possessing so many of his people sickened him. To these threats he would not yield. "There is a positive thirst for blood," Lady Canning lamented. "Hardly anybody can speak about natives in a tone that does not drive me wild, so I hold my tongue. It would charm the Indian-English public to hang . . . any number of people. . . . C. is terribly unpopular because he is just and firm too." Thus Canning would remain until the end, even when his rule that Europeans and Indians alike must obtain licences to carry fire-arms, his security restrictions on the European and Indian press, brought him noisier critics. In May, 1857, wisdom and mercy, Canning knew, were the unforgiveable sins.

As news of the revolt spread from north to south many lost their heads so completely as to give Canning cause to wonder: How dependable in a crisis *were* "John Company's" men? In Calcutta, six days after the mutiny, men rode to their offices with loaded revolvers on their knees; in the muddy river, ships and steamers were packed with families who had fled from their tall white mansions. The fireworks of an Indian marriage festival were the signal for scores to pack their baggage and fly. A hundred yards from Government House, where Canning, as a mark of trust, resolutely clung to his sepoy bodyguard, one householder crouched nightly on his stairs with a loaded smooth-bore and bowls of molten lead on a brazier. "We must expect all kinds of reports," growled brave old General Sir John Hearsey, "and timid and nervous people will believe them and act accordingly."

In Simla, four days later, the panic was worse. Here, too, the people were hundreds of miles from danger yet the news that a battalion of Gurkhas, the stocky little Nepalese hillmen who for thirty-nine years had served as British mercenaries, had mutinied in sympathy sent high-ranking officers running from bungalow to bungalow crying, "Fly for your lives! The Gurkhas are upon us." Chivalry was forgotten; officers fumbling with their note-cases spiritedly outbid women for baggage coolies. One officer, sighting an imaginary Gurkha, deserted his fiancée and bolted outright. For some women this headlong thirty-mile trek ended in death from heat and exhaustion.

A few days later, when the people drifted back to find the Gurkhas pacified and every house, even to the silver thimbles on ladies' work tables untouched, a Miss Clementina Bricks placed this announcement in a local paper:

> The ladies of Simla will hold a meeting . . . for the purpose of consulting about the best measures to be taken for the protection of the gentlemen. The ladies beg to inform those who sleep in the khuds (ravines) that they sincerely compassionate their sufferings, and are now preparing pillows for them stuffed with the purest white feathers. . . . Rest, warriors, rest.

At Lahore, the capital of the Punjab, over thirteen hundred miles north-west of Calcutta, there was no panic, only a relentless determination to wither trouble in the bud. The Chief Commissioner, Sir John Lawrence, was two hundred miles north in Rawalpindi, and William Brendish's telegram, arriving early on the Tuesday morning, became the sole responsibility of his deputy Robert Montgomery. A smiling, rosy-cheeked man known as "Pickwick," Montgomery at once investigated the loyalties of the four sepoy regiments stationed at Mian Mir, the military cantonment five miles from Lahore. "Sahib," reported the Brahmin spy briefed to check on them, laying a finger across his throat, "They are up to *this* in it."

But Montgomery's resources were meagre. Sepoys outnumbered British troops—the 81st Foot, who were to leave

next morning, and two troops of European horse artillery—
by roughly four to one. Seeking out the officer commanding
Mian Mir, Brigadier Stuart Corbett, Montgomery proposed
using the excuse of the greased cartridge to deprive the sepoys of their ammunition and copper percussion caps. Corbett agreed—while stressing that in deference to his native
infantry officers he could not disarm the troops. Later that day
Corbett changed his mind. He would, he wrote, "go the whole
hog" and disarm them altogether. Fearing a leak, he did not
impart this news to his native infantry officers, all of whom
would have staked their lives on their men's loyalty.

To a vital 25-year-old lieutenant of engineers, Arthur
Moffat Lang, this ruse was closely akin to treachery. The son
of a Bengal Civil Servant and his wife who had loved India
passionately, Lang, a handsome youngster, was destined to
play a leading role in the stormy saga of the Mutiny. A
prize pupil of the East India Company's Military College
at Addiscombe, his pleasures were as diverse as his engineering talents: boxing, the novels of Charles Dickens, singing
operatic duets, all played a large part in his life. But for the
chicanery so prevalent in many of "John Company's" dealings,
he had a bitter and outspoken dislike. "The sepoys are in an
awful fright of us and we apparently of them," he wrote
sourly to his mother. "They will be presently goaded by
sheer anxiety and fright to end the suspense by running
amok."

But the buzz of discontent running through the hot glaring
cantonment of Lahore this day was voiced not by the sepoys
but by the puzzled officers under Brigadier Corbett's command. At 10 p.m. that night a farewell ball to the 81st Foot
was being held in the artillery mess-house, yet Corbett had
ordered a general parade for 5 a.m., barely an hour after the
ball ended. In the entire cantonment only six officers—including Arthur Lang—knew Corbett's secret.

Many like Arthur Lang felt they lived through history that
night. Some were of opinion that for tension and suspense it
must have rivalled the Duchess of Richmond's legendary ball
at Quatre Bras, on the eve of Waterloo. When at 10 p.m. a
gong signalled the arrival of the first buggy at the gate and
torches flickered in the portico Lieutenant Lang felt in the

mood for anything but revelry by night. "There is really no telling where all this will end," he had broken off a letter home. "Goodbye, dearest mother, for the present." Then, in tight-fitting blue shell jacket, he had set off for the ball.

As always the evening began with a quadrille; above arched doorways, floral wreaths of lemon-yellow cassia and white thorn-apple trumpets stirred in the night air. Patent-leather boots and white satin shoes swirled through a graceful succession of polkas, lancers and schottisches. Waves of muslin and tarlatan, sky-blue and white, broke and re-formed against shifting strands of scarlet; the scarlet and white of the 81st, the scarlet and buff of the native infantry. Against the walls, the buff colours of the 81st were ranged beside a glittering display of bayonets and ramrods set in black velvet, that caught the light like the facets of diamonds.

Even dancing with pretty Sarah Boileau, who had granted him many dances in her programme and was soon to become his fiancée, Arthur Lang found the minutes dragged like hours. The young ladies, as one present recorded to her sister, made happy small-talk—how dashing men with whiskers looked, what a splendid dancer was First Lieutenant Alfred Light of the Artillery, how providential had been that day's thunderstorm, which cooled the air so deliciously. But tonight Lang found such normally absorbing topics "a perfect sham of smiles over tears."

Yet the sepoy pickets about the mess-house suspected nothing: security demanded that the grim gaiety should not falter. Promptly at 1 a.m. the string music died; to the shrill bugle call of "The Roast Beef of Old England," the ladies and their partners filed into supper. Made hungry by exertion many piled their plates with Hunter's Beef, salted and spiced with cloves, limes and brandy. Then more dancing until 3 a.m., when the ladies retired and the officers returned to the supper-room for hot devilled biscuits and brandy-and-water. Some launched into long choruses known as "the sentimental": "Green Leaves Come Again" or "Maggie Lauder."

But in the small hours of this May morning the officers of Lahore had grimmer affairs to occupy them. Already dim suspicions were stirring. In the barrack-rooms of the 81st, the privates were agog with curiosity; ten men per company had been summarily ordered to sleep with their clothes on. Now, at 3 a.m., as the officers escorted their partners home, the surprised ladies saw a picket of artillery drawn up on the Mall outside. Near St. Mary Magdalene's Church a half-company of the 81st dozed in their cloaks on dew-soaked grass. "Don't get up early after your late dance," Brigadier Stuart Corbett cautioned the ladies anxiously.

In his bungalow Arthur Lang scrawled: "Just back from the Ball and will finish and close this in case of accidents. . . . Three hours hence it will be over, one way or another, and God grant that there may be no bloodshed. . . ."

All in the secret echoed this prayer, but none could tell what dawn might bring. Outwardly confident, Captain Lambert Denne of the Artillery bade a lady friend, "Get up at five and have your horse saddled and come to the edge of the compound; you can see the parade from there." Then with unusual emphasis he repeated, "Be sure to have your horse saddled." Only a sergeant of the 81st, told to fall in his men at 4 a.m., remarked phlegmatically to his commander, "I suppose, sir, it's them niggers again."

At 5 a.m. Arthur Lang waited on the edge of the parade-ground; normally he loathed rising early but in this chill dawn, tension banished all thoughts of sleep. Not far away Deputy Commissioner Robert Montgomery also watched silently, keen blue eyes alert behind his spectacles. This sight was common to all: 3,500 sepoys, muskets shouldered, surging like a scarlet sea on to the dimly lit parade ground. With clockwork precision they formed up in contiguous columns to the artillery and the 81st. In silence they heard Brigadier Stuart Corbett read the order on the disbanding of the 34th Native Infantry at Barrackpore. Intent on the translation they did not notice the two troops of horse artillery breaking formation, wheeling away to command the parade-ground from the rear. They were listening to the Brigadier's second announcement.

They were, he told them, fine regiments; he loved them and longed to see them win further honours and to keep their name unsullied. Now he would ask them to show their loyalty by laying down their arms.

Even as he spoke the 81st Foot, three hundred men in

scarlet and blue, were marching steadily backwards. Orders rapped out and the sepoys, changing from front to rear by a wheel of subdivisions were puzzled to find themselves facing the 81st. Packed tightly together the British ranks curtained the sight Lang saw clearly: the gun trails rattling clear of the limbers, the gunners' ramrods thrusting home the case-shot. At this moment Major Charles Prior of the Adjutant-General's Department rode slowly towards Captain Thomas Gardiner commanding the 16th Native Infantry. His orders were final: "Captain Gardiner, order the 16th to pile arms."

A hush fell over the parade-ground as slowly Gardiner turned, his voice carrying clearly on the still morning: "Grenadiers, shoulder arms." The muskets jerked upwards. "Ground arms!" The stocks stabbed downwards as one. *"Pile arms!"*

Now, as Lang espied a wavering hesitation, two things happened. The incisive voice of Colonel Henry Renny, com-manding the 81st, rang through the silence. "81st—LOAD!" With a metallic snap, three hundred ramrods drove a ball-cartridge home. Simultaneously, the men of the 81st fell backwards and sideways, forming long chasms in the ranks. For the first time the sepoys saw what Arthur Lang had watched with sinking heart: twelve corridors, their ends blocked off by the squat black mouths of twelve cannon. At each breech stood a gunner, portfire in hand, the cold blue smoky flare like a gas-flame in the gloom. The magnitude of the ruse came home to them. They stood disgraced, humil-iated forever before the British.

Stooping they laid their muskets on the ground. The faces of their officers, weary from the night's gaiety, were now frozen in passionate unbelief. But the other three regi-ments were following suit; they collected themselves to give fresh orders.

"Stand from your arms! Right about face! Quick march!"

"Away they went unarmed," recalled Arthur Lang with compassion. "The clusters of bayonets glittering under the morning sun, marking where they had stood and showing their obedience."

Thus for the Punjab the precedent of swift bloodless dis-armament was established. At Peshawar, Amritsar, Mooltan,

Ferozepore, despite the bitter protests of native infantry officers—at Peshawar they flung their spurs and swords on the sepoys' piled arms—other commanders followed Montgomery's example. Frequently Lord Canning would question the wisdom of this—did not justice avow a man innocent until he was proven guilty? "How could we hurry on the mutiny and exasperate the whole army by declaring war against it?" Lady Canning demanded. But to Sir John Lawrence, on fire with ruthless zeal, political necessity made a right. If the British troops in the Punjab were wiped out, no mobile column could advance to storm Delhi. To achieve security in the Punjab he could—and did—disarm thirty-six thousand men, confiscate sixty-nine thousand stands of arms. Iron-bound clubs were proscribed; restrictions hedged in the sale of sulphur and saltpetre.

The people, he did not fear; for seven years, since the British conquest of the Punjab, many, tiring of bloodshed, had been converting swords into ploughshares. The majority were Sikhs, once a small religious group which had repudiated Hinduism and grown into a nation in their own right; forswearing idolatry, caste and holy pilgrimages these bearded warriors, who wore their long hair coiled round a steel dagger, had many affinities with the British. By 17th May it was plain the rebels could expect no aid from them. But to bring about the fall of Delhi within weeks the entire province, ninety-seven thousand square miles, must be stripped of British troops. John Lawrence's solution was to disarm every doubtful sepoy regiment and replace them by new forces raised in the Punjab itself, a fleet, hard-hitting, moveable column recruited from the Sikhs and the wild frontier clans.

And he saw signs that allies would not be lacking among the puppet princes. Already Gholab Singh, the Maharajah, was sending strong reinforcements southwards from Kashmir. The Rajah of Jhind himself took the field at the head of his forces. The Rajah of Patiala, in chain mail and grey Berlin-wool gloves supplied five thousand retainers to guard the Grand Trunk Road between the Punjab and Delhi. In weeks to come this would be the vital pipeline that fed men and munitions to the British on the Ridge.

All too easily, Canning knew, Delhi could become the rally-ing-point for every potential rebel in British India. If Delhi fell to the British, Lucknow, Allahabad, Cawnpore, all the stations bordering the Ganges, might remain tranquil. Suc-cess or failure here was the yardstick whereby the cause would lose or gain adherents. He knew well the truth of the time-honoured legend, "who holds the valley of the Ganges holds India."

VII. CAWNPORE AND LUCKNOW

24th May to 9th June

There are times when one small departure from cher-ished routine seems to betoken greater catastrophe than the holocaust which follows. Thus Miss Amelia Horne would always date the first shocking impact of the Indian Mutiny at Cawnpore from 24th May. On this Sunday, Queen Vic-toria's birthday, the bells in Christchurch belfry remained alarmingly mute. Tomorrow, she knew, no crackle of massed musketry, proclaiming a *feu de joie* in the Queen's honour, would splinter the echoes across the hot sandy wastes of this cantonment two hundred and sixty-six miles south-east of Delhi. Attendance at divine service, ruled General Sir Hugh Wheeler, the spare 68-year-old Irishman command-ing Cawnpore Division, was forbidden. Nor must any public celebrations mark the Queen's birthday. One shockwave of bells, like an echo in a glacier, might bury the whole station in an avalanche of rebellion.

Some months earlier Amelia's stepfather, John Hampden Cook, the agent for the North-Western Dak Company, had transferred both his family and his business from Lucknow to Cawnpore and the eighteen-year-old Amelia had revelled in every moment since. Fifty-three miles north-east of Luck-now, on a broad sandy plain, Cawnpore was a station where something was always afoot; amateur theatricals, when private soldiers donned frilled muslin dresses to play the ladies' parts, balls where the young subalterns of the 2nd Cavalry, gay in their French-grey undress jackets and orange waistcoats, proved dashing partners in a waltz or a quadrille. Life had much to offer this pretty petite Eurasian girl with dark thick hair and wheat-coloured skin, who had dress-sense and played the piano skilfully and had the daintiest hands in the cantonment.

But General Wheeler's decision, as Amelia recalled later, "frightened us not a little, for it was something so strange allowing the day to pass unnoticed." Her stepfather, John Cook, had been consumed with anger; like every merchant he had anticipated a fine profit from the celebrants. But Wheeler was adamant. Against three sepoy infantry regiments and the 2nd Native Cavalry, three thousand men in all, he could muster only sixty European artillerymen, two hundred infantrymen. Of these, fully seventy-four were invalids, a further eighty-four a detachment of the 32nd Queen's, sent post-haste from Lucknow by Sir Henry Lawrence. With this army he must keep watch over hundreds of women and children and sixty thousand camp followers.

Already the storm-clouds were massing. Marketing in the bazaar a British sergeant-major's wife was berated by a sepoy: "You will none of you come here much oftener—you will not be alive another week." The shopkeepers, fearing riots, secured their shutters. Timid servants, pleading sickness, stayed away from work; bolder ones vowed that they would serve no more. Every steamer bore more civilians, the cautious or the canny, down-river to Allahabad. The ladies were shocked that of all people, Mrs. MacDowell, the milliner, had already gone. She had four children to support and £500 worth of uncollected debts; still she had left Cawnpore.

All these people looked to General Wheeler for protection. The small spare man from County Limerick was weighed down by the responsibility. He held endless inconclusive discussions with Brigadier Alex Jack, the station commander, and Collector Charles Hillersdon. They must not fail the people—yet they must not alarm the sepoys. To their astonishment Wheeler rejected all suggestions that the people take refuge in the magazine, in the north-west corner of the military lines. A three-acre site, close to the Ganges, hedged in by stout walls, this, the others believed, was the ideal stockade to combat a sustained siege. Wheeler would have none of it. Within three weeks at most British reinforcements must arrive from Calcutta. Accordingly, he chose the closest possible site to their approach route—an arid four-acre plain six miles south-east, a mile from the river, close to the sepoy lines.

In this way, Wheeler reasoned, relieving troops would not have to battle for Cawnpore city, through unfamiliar streets so narrow that sunlight seemed an intrusion.

This was a hazardous decision. The site had only one well. The sole accommodation for a thousand men, women and children was two single-storied hospital barracks flanked by verandahs, one wholly of masonry, one with a thatched roof. Yet to demolish the bungalows and Indian dwellings surrounding them, Wheeler pledged his Government to pay fully £10,000 compensation—an entire year's salary for a lieutenant-governor. As gangs of coolies sweated in the boiling sun, heads balancing wicker baskets of rock-hard earth, younger yet wiser soldiers shook their heads. The rectangular mud wall parallelogram rising about the hospital, three feet thick at the base and two feet at the crest, was nowhere more than four feet high; a subaltern mounted on a tired hack could have scaled it with ease.

On 21st May, three days before the Queen's birthday, Wheeler had ordered Cawnpore's citizens to take refuge within this frail fortress. It now held provisions for twenty-five days, everything from champagne to game soup, but the bulk of these provisions were flour and dried peas.

One of Sir Henry Lawrence's aides, arriving from Lucknow on a quick dawn inspection, had never witnessed "so frightful a scene of confusion, fright and bad arrangement as the European barrack painted. Four guns were in position, loaded, with European artillerymen in night caps and wide-awakes and sidearms on, hanging on to the guns in groups— looking like melodramatic buccaneers. People . . . of every colour, sect and profession were crowding into the barracks . . . cargoes of writers, tradesmen . . . a miscellaneous mob of every complexion from white to tawny—all in terror of the imaginary foe; ladies sitting down at the rough mess tables in the barracks, women suckling infants, ayahs and children in all directions. . . ."

His verdict was damning: "If any insurrection took or takes place we shall have no one to thank but ourselves . . . we have now shown to the natives how very easily we can become frightened and when frightened, utterly helpless."

Amelia Horne's optimism was undiminished. About this time, 25th May, her mother, Emma Cook, wrote to a friend in Calcutta: "Fancy us sleeping in an open verandah with men, women and children all huddled together and in momentary expectation of an attack . . . we are in a sad predicament." But Amelia saw compensations. During lulls in the tension they could still slip away from the entrenchment to hear the band, which played each evening as if no emergency existed. True, they must proceed on foot, for carriages were at a premium, but there were lingering traces of the gracious cantonment life: the feathery shade of the neem trees, the scarlet buds of Syrian pomegranates overhanging beds of violets, the water-carriers in gaudy loincloths laying the roadside dust with great streams from their goatskin bags.

Amelia was not alone in her feeling that all might be well. From stations all down the Ganges, as May ended, only bulletins of buoyant confidence reached Lord Canning in Calcutta. From Agra, the Lieutenant-Governor of the North-West Provinces, John Colvin, signalled, "The worst of the storm is past." From Cawnpore, Wheeler exulted, "The plague is stayed. All well at Cawnpore!" The sepoys were "well disposed" at Allahabad, whose fort held forty thousand stands of arms. From Lucknow, Sir Henry Lawrence reported cautiously, "Time is everything just now—a firm and cheerful aspect must be maintained . . . no panic . . . everywhere the first germ of insurrection must be put down instantly."

But as Chief Commissioner of the newly-annexed kingdom of Oudh, which stretched from Nepal to Central India, Sir Henry was taking no chances. He had long anticipated trouble here, for three-fifths of the Bengal Army was recruited in the ancient kingdom. For years the East India Company's policy of ruthless annexation had been anathema to him and to others—particularly the talukdars or powerful land-holders of Oudh. For years he had seen the Company's covetous eyes appraising Oudh's eighteen million green acres, piously justifying land-hunger with high-sounding phrases. The misgovernment of the kingdom was a byword; Oudh was corrupt, Oudh was "a damned orchid house."

Nor was this without foundation. The native city of Lucknow, a dripping honeycomb of dark lanes and shaded gardens heavy with the scent of jasmine, was notorious for vice. Upwards of a hundred houses, both taxed and registered, were brothels run for homosexuals. Wandering bands of robbers, terrorising the kingdom's five million souls, burned down a hundred villages a year, committing over eighteen hundred murders. Many of the king's soldiers had worn the same tattered uniforms for fourteen years; the commissariat bullocks received only one-third of their ration. Twice Lord Dalhousie had warned Wajid Ali, King of Oudh: unless these evils were remedied the British would be forced, for the good of the people, to step in. Fifteen months before the mutiny, "John Company" was as good as its word. The then Resident, Sir James Outram, was ordered to inform Wajid Ali that since no improvement had been forthcoming, Oudh was now British territory.

In vain Henry Lawrence had urged that Oudh be governed for the benefit of the people. "John Company" should derive no profit from its revenue. "We are doubly bound to treat them kindly because they are down," he pleaded. But the Company, too greedy to resist the £1,000,000 the kingdom annually yielded, were too short-sighted to realise their one hope of retaining the kingdom was to garrison it with British troops. Feudal barons who had supported the Company's credit by investing large sums of their private fortunes in Government loans were dispossessed of their holdings, their forts dismantled, their armed retainers dispersed.

Despite Dalhousie's own warnings, the Company added insult to injury. The King and his family, he had urged, must be paid a liberal allowance, but up to March, 1857, no money was ever paid. The women of the zenana were forced to beg for their food and Lawrence's predecessor stabled his horses in the former Umbrella Palace. Thus to the people of

Oudh it mattered little that the King had been almost always drunk, an insomniac who drove out at night with naked girls to fan or massage him. He was their king, a man generous to underlings, and the British had needlessly humiliated him and exiled him to Calcutta. In the fullness of time they would remember these things.

This kingdom, roughly the size of Scotland, was dotted with a dozen or more lonely outstations, manned solely by sepoys under British officers; if the sepoys rose, Sir Henry knew, it would be Delhi all over again. On 5th June he ordered Lieutenant Hamilton Forbes, commanding the 1st Oudh Irregular Cavalry, to bring the women of Secrora and Gonda to safety.

At 4 p.m. on Sunday, 7th June, this news struck a chill through Katherine Mary Bartrum, the wife of Gonda's station surgeon. Three years ago she had been plain Kate Wright, a shy darkhaired silversmith's daughter from Bath, Somerset; the advent of Captain Robert Bartrum, the handsome young graduate of Guy's Hospital, London, had changed this almost overnight. Though Robert was but twenty-six to Katherine's twenty-three his masterful air was wonderfully comforting to the sheltered newly-wed Katherine—had he not, with all the assurance of a man-of-the-world, urged his solicitors that only £1,000 from his trust fund could see his young bride comfortably settled in this barren land? And now, fifteen months ago, their union had been blessed, as Katherine put it, by little Bobbie, who had his father's blue eyes and fair hair; "such a precocious little fellow," as Kate had written home, "when I tell him he is naughty he runs into the corner by himself."

For two weeks now since the terrible news of Meerut and Delhi the tiny outstation had received each fresh scrap of news with mounting alarm. Katherine had scarcely known what to do for the best. Five British officers and their wives would be utterly at the sepoys' mercy—but she resisted all her husband's suggestions that she and Bobbie could be ferried down river to Calcutta. Better to die with Robert than be left alone. And the belief that the sepoys thought her afraid made even Katherine, "who was never very brave," so angry she found she was not afraid at all.

The long May days went by on waves of heat and the tension mounted. The heat was trying little Bobbie sorely; Katherine prayed for the monsoon that would break in a few weeks now. It was an effort even to finish a letter to her father. Despair preyed upon her; she could no longer eat, sleep or make small talk. At times great waves of grief broke in her body; she sat silently beside the sleeping child, tears pouring down her cheeks, wondering how soon a power-drunk mob would tear him from her arms. On the morning of 7th June news of a massacre at the nearby station of Seetapore sent fear and anger surging through her. Among the slain was Mrs. Sophia Christian, beheaded as she wept over her fallen husband. All who had known tall graceful Mrs. Christian felt a thrill of horror, recalling her vivid performance in the Christmas pantomime of "Blue Beard." "And will you *really* cut off my head?" she pleaded.

"I hope not one stone of Delhi will be left standing," said Katherine, with a violence that was new to her.

Many changes had come upon her in these weeks. She who had taken only passing interest in military matters could talk of nothing but when General Anson would reach Delhi. She would lie awake with a cavalry sword unyielding beneath her pillow while Robert lay beside her with loaded revolver, "ready to start up at the slightest sound." Both had delighted in comparing notes on the baby's progress but now as he gurgled and clawed for his toys it was as if a shadow lay between them; each would catch the other's eye for a long moment, unable to speak.

"If things come to the worst I will destroy you with my own hands rather than let you fall into their power," Robert said once. Katherine clung to him; there was nothing she could say, nothing at all.

Now Sir Henry's summons had come and Katherine knew she must obey. Long and earnestly she pleaded with Robert to be allowed to stay; she was reconciled to death at his side but not to separation. But the young doctor was adamant; for the baby's sake she must seek the safety of Lucknow. "God alone knows how bitter was the struggle to feel that it was my duty to leave him," wrote Katherine later.

At 6 p.m. in company with Mrs. Elizabeth Clark, the Assistant Commissioner's wife, Katherine Bartrum started out, both women clutching their children, swaying precariously on an elephant's back. Bartrum and Clark would accompany their wives to Secrora, sixteen miles away, to join the party proceeding under Lieutenant Forbes' escort. But at 11 p.m. on this star-shrouded night they reached Secrora to find Forbes' party had left two hours previously; evidently he had thought the women of Gonda unwilling to make the journey. Now there was barely time to snatch a cup of tea at the magistrate's and give the children some milk before they set off in pursuit. In vain Katherine pleaded that Robert should travel with them to Lucknow. His duty, he said, was to remain with the regiment.

"Goodbye, dear Kate," he said in parting. "Keep up your spirits, we shall soon meet again, and take care of my little darling."

She held a swift vision of him, still standing by the magistrate's house, as the elephants, accompanied by a guard of sepoys, lumbered towards Lucknow. Then tears washed him from her view and she could only wonder, When and where will I see him again?

The memory stayed with her through much of that night; despite her uneasiness concerning the sepoys who often halted the elephant and lay down to laugh and talk, they readily brought water for the baby whenever she asked for it. Once, alarmed to see them loading their guns in the moonlight, she asked fearfully what they were about. "Oh," was the reassuring reply, "there are so many bad people about we are going to fight for you." At 8 a.m. on the Monday, fording a wide brown river in tiny craft, they caught up with Forbes' party. At 4 p.m. with four officers and a sepoy guard to protect women and children, they set out again. Only narrowly, by granting the sepoys three hours rest en route, did Forbes avert a mutiny by night. The leaping fires of burning outstations, the distant throb of tom-toms was working like alcohol in the men's blood.

At 1 p.m. on 9th June they saw the grey graceful outline of the Residency Building, built on a low hill at the far side of the native city of Lucknow, loom through the dancing heat-haze. As they came nearer, Katherine Bartrum caught her breath. The soft green lawns, the flowerbeds gay with marigolds and bougainvillæa that she recalled a year ago had all gone. Everywhere there were sandbags and cannon and the slopes beyond bristled with chevaux-de-frise and timber shoring. The compound was a bedlam of tramping soldiers, distraught women, crying children. She knew she would need all the resolution she possessed to see this through alone.

Little by little in lonely stations down the Ganges, a new spirit was becoming apparent: whatever their past shortcomings, men and women, knowing themselves about to die, summoned new resolution to face an almost unimaginable terror. At Fatehgarh, Mrs. Elizabeth Freeman, a missionary's wife from Elizabethtown, Illinois, wrote simply to her sister: "Goodbye. Pray for us. Will write next mail if we live." A young surgeon assured his family, "Death will not overtake me sneaking in a corner . . . I should make a good fight for it." The wife of a Captain of Engineers calmly composed a letter to her parents; it was the last they would ever receive from her, her quiet testament of faith.

"I am so thankful I came out to India to be a comfort to beloved John . . . ere you get this we shall be delivered one way or another . . . we are quite prepared for the worst. . . . The flesh a little revolts from cold-blooded assassination but God can make it bear up . . ."

VIII. DELHI

8th June

Early in June—at the time when Amelia Horne and her family were moving into the entrenchment at Cawnpore and Katherine Bartrum was leaving Gonda for Lucknow—Captain Robert Tytler at Ambala realised his income stood in desperate need of augmentation. One child at school in Scotland, two soon to come of school age and a wife eight months pregnant made cruel demands on a man's purse when most of his worldly goods were grey ash on the Ridge at Delhi. Thus when an old friend, Captain Frederick Maisey, of the Judge Advocate-General's Department hinted at the chance of a staff appointment, Robert was avid for details. Aside from the possibilities of promotion it offered, a staff appointment could sometimes increase an officer's income by £4,000 a year.

Maisey outlined the shape of things to come. Thanks to the driving energy of Commissioner George Barnes of Ambala, who in one week had stripped his district of five hundred carts, two thousand camels, two thousand coolies and over two million pounds of grain, the Delhi Field Force was equipped for war. From Meerut and Ambala, on 27th May, 2,900 men, one column commanded by General Sir Henry Barnard, the other by Brigadier Archdale Wilson, whose vacillation had proved so fatal at Meerut, had marched on Delhi. If Tytler was willing to join the force as Paymaster, the job was his.

Robert was only too willing. The British had now been encamped on the Ridge since 8th June, so he and his family could travel safely from Ambala to Delhi. Once there it was planned that Harriet, Marie and the children should journey via Meerut to the hill-station of Mussoorie, where the Tytlers owned a charming little house.

The one fear in Robert's mind was that the siege would be over before they reached Delhi and put paid to his staff appointment. Surely once the "Pandies" saw the British had returned they would realise that the odds were against them and open their gates in surrender?

Now the first shock of the mutiny had passed, the same confident spirit gripped everyone; they thirsted for action before it was too late. Men who had been on leave bear-hunting in the snows hastened through Simla, pausing only to grab a crust of bread and a glass of water. A major of cavalry, Henry Ouvry, was on furlough with his wife in Kashmir, three hundred and eighty miles north, when news of the mutiny came. Though Matilda Ouvry was an invalid the major did not hesitate to return at full speed, shooting foaming rapids on rafts made from inflated bullock-skins, swaying across perilous gorges on grass-rope ladders. Often their fare was of the plainest, raw onions and thick chupattis, known as "dampers," to stave off hunger; Lieutenant Hugh Gough, journeying from Meerut, choked his down only by moistening it with sardine oil. Most were too young to realise that the rebels too had a cause: they wrote lightheartedly that they were eager to "get at those devils"; "contemptible rascals," "double-barrelled traitors," were their kindest epithets for the enemy. If a few made their wills in advance, more enlivened the march by games of pitch-and-toss with "the rupees clattering . . . like hail."

They had marched through silent steaming villages of dark mud hovels where an excited jabbering broke out the second they passed. Sometimes there was an ambiguous cry of "God grant that there may be victory." Many officers travelled in pony carts covered with light awnings; the troops came on foot or in bullock carts roofed and sided with tarred canvas, often in the wicker panniers borne by camels which held the company's cooking utensils. In later years a surgeon who marched with them recalled with aching nostalgia "the stars bright in the dark deep sky and the fireflies flashing from bush to bush . . . the heavy roll of the guns, mixed with the jangling of bits and the clanking of the steel scabbards of the cavalry; the infantry marched behind with a deep dull tread . . . sutlers and camp servants toiled along for miles in the rear . . . gigantic elephants stalked over bush and stone by the side of the road . . . ."

They viewed Delhi as a prize to be taken within hours, and the boast of the rank-and-file summed up prevailing feeling: "We'll fight in the morning, we'll drink our grog in Delhi at night."

But once on the Ridge the British began to contend with a deadlier enemy than the King's troops: the sun that beat down for ten hours each day on scrub and rose-pink quartz with the concentrated glare of an arc-light. "The perils from the climate," Hugh Gough noted, "were far greater than from the invisible enemy." Against this foe they were ill-prepared. Only a few officers, since the Punjab campaign of 1848, had taken to wearing sun helmets. Most wore white drill covers and curtains over shakos or foraging caps, which gave them the raffish air of Foreign Legionnaires. On 27th

May, the Horse Artillery had left Meerut stifling in brass helmets, tiger-skin rolls, cloth dress jackets with high red collars, leather breeches and high jack-boots. Only the un-orthodoxy of Major Henry Tombs, who halted them two miles from cantonments and ordered them to rip off their collars with jack-knives saved many from death by apoplexy.

Already the heat had brought cholera in its train. Robert and Harriet Tytler arrived at the Ridge to learn that the Commander-in-Chief, the Hon. George Anson, was already dead; so swiftly had cholera claimed him at Kurnal that he was buried without military honours. Unkind voices, remembering the remorseless stream of telegraph messages and memoranda that had flowed from Rawalpindi, whispered that he had died of "an attack of John Lawrence." Thus General Sir Henry Barnard, former chief of staff to Lord Raglan in the Crimea and at fifty-eight a martyr to gout became Commander of the force. But Barnard had no intention that Harriet Tytler or any of the wives remaining on the Ridge should linger there; on 19th June he ordered that all should return to Meerut on "pad" elephants. A straw mattress took the place of a howdah and the passengers clung on as best they could. But already the child was lusty within her; try as she might Harriet was too weak to mount. Disturbed, Robert Tytler sought audience with the General.

Hearing of this additional complication, Barnard could only sigh heavily. "Poor lady! Poor lady!" he said. "Let her stay."

For Harriet the shock of knowing she must live through the siege to the bitter end at first concealed the strangeness of the situation: that she with two children and a French maid, was the only wife with the Delhi Field Force. Although a vast white city of single-poled tents fourteen feet square had sprung up at the rear of the Ridge, covering the entire length of the gutted cantonments, she was now too weak to endure the heat under canvas. In an ammunition tumbril with a thatched roof she lay on a thin quilt spread over straw awaiting the birth of her child.

For all the force's outward confidence, some men knew a deep foreboding. Of these Brevet-Major Octavius Anson is typical. A solitary introspective idealist, Anson, a thirty-nine-year-old officer in the 9th Lancers, had a nagging fear that the British would pay dearly for this false optimism. A deeply-religious man who cherished his wife and children, he hated life on the Ridge: the tossing slumber beneath his bed, a sodden towel coiled round the temples and blankets piled above to ward off the heat; the eternal fears of cholera, for their camp was pitched in the hollow of the old parade-ground, close to the canal; the lonely pangs of separation from his family.

All night the guns and mortars of the British batteries, some only a thousand yards away from the city walls, grumbled and boomed. For Anson these night assaults held a celestial beauty—"the battle raging in the dark, one could see the flash of every matchlock."' Yet he hated all that the night pickets entailed: the heavy dew that chilled his six foot two inch frame to the bone; "the devil cry of the jackals"; the tired horse stumbling on rocky ground, covering no more than one mile in every hour. Above all, doubts as to the justice of the British cause gnawed him constantly. "Our great sin in this country," he wrote to his wife Frances in the hills, "has been paying too much attention to their religion and too little to our own. . . . I look upon this business in the light of a heavy punishment for the ungodly infidel lives the greater part of us have lived in India." Though the heat glare made reading difficult, Anson was never one to neglect his Bible and the words of the psalms he read took on a terrible relevance: "My soul is among lions and I lie even among them that are set on fire . . . deliver me from mine enemies, O my God . . . save me from bloody men."

More of the British, with customary optimism, were certain that all would come right; to the rigours of this new life, they adapted themselves cheerfully. Lieutenant Edward Thackeray, a cousin of William, the novelist, noticed how soon a man grew accustomed to being under fire; after perching on a battery's parapet eight hours a day for three weeks it became second nature to shout "Down" when the swift crushing sound of shells passed overhead. A subaltern who had three fingers of his hand carried away in a skirmish, consoled his family that it was the *left* hand—he could still hold reins.

Such men were still fresh enough to war to be stirred by epic deeds: on 9th June, when the Punjab's Guide Corps marched into camp under Captain Henry Daly, the men roared a welcome as the Corps' swarthy Afghans and stocky olive-skinned Gurkhas strode by in loose dusty shirts and sunproof turbans. These men, the first of John Lawrence's many reinforcements from the Punjab, had marched three hundred and eighty miles in twenty-two days to reach the Ridge—"a feat," as Octavius Anson said, "unparalleled in the records of Indian marching."

Yet each fresh day made it plain that Barnard's greatest problem was the city of Delhi itself. If Delhi did not fall within days, the lives of thousands stood in peril. "The King is a watchword to Mohammedans," Sir Henry Lawrence urged from Lucknow. "Once Delhi is recaptured the game will again be in our hands if we play the cards with ordinary skill."

But the walls of Delhi city were a near insuperable problem. From the sixty-foot eminence of the Ridge the British peered down through yellow heat-haze on a stone-girt fortress—seven miles of walls twenty-four feet high with a ditch twenty-five feet broad and almost as deep. Well-protected gates pierced them in ten places, and these walls were knotted with bastions mounting 114 heavy guns, the bulk of them 24-pounders, firing shot which would tear through thirteen feet of rammed earth. Against this the British on the two-mile stretch of the Ridge that commanded the city's northern face could muster only 2,900 troops, armed with twenty-two light field-guns.

And while the southern end of the Ridge lay within 1,200 yards of the walls the northern end sloped gently to the river more than two miles from the city. Stray British pickets with field-guns held a series of buildings along the Ridge's horny spine—the Flagstaff Tower, the observatory, a crumbling mosque, the house of a dead Mahratta nobleman named Hindu Rao—but the main body of the British, including Robert Tytler and his family, were encamped on the reverse slope, out of sight of the city.

Thus Delhi's river front, far from being invested, could receive supplies and rebel reinforcements all through the siege: the sole triumph of the Field Force was to keep the Union Jack flying on the Ridge. One observer succinctly summed up: "We came to besiege Delhi, but . . . in reality, *we* were the besieged . . . the mutineers the besiegers."

What was to be done? Hot-blooded young sappers on Barnard's staff urged a "peep of dawn" attack on two of the city's principal gates. As yet, they pointed out, the Kabul and Lahore Gates were not bricked up, the bridges remained in perfect repair. Given a 3.30 a.m. attack with powder bags to blow in the gates, the British could harry the mutineers from the city into the last stronghold of the King's fort. Though General Barnard was severely criticised when this plan fell through, it seems likely that 2,900 men hacking their way into a city of 150,000 people courted only annihilation.

Yet such an onslaught—what Barnard and Brigadier Archdale Wilson called "the gamester's throw"—seemed the one possible gambit. "Reverse will be fatal," Barnard warned Lord Canning on 13th June, "for I can have no reserve on which to retire . . . assuredly you all greatly underestimated the difficulties of Delhi."

What of the enemy's strength within the walls? Though estimates varied from forty to sixty thousand there was as yet no reliable intelligence on this score. But one man had the job of finding out and as always he intended to do his cold clinical ruthless best.

This was William Stephen Raikes Hodson. As a man he stood alone. Behind him stretched thirty-seven years of ignoble deeds. He was 5 ft. 11 ins. tall, lithe, with yellow hair and a heavy curved moustache. What a contemporary called "hot blue unforgiving eyes" were set far apart in a white, smooth, almost bloodless face. His manner was sarcastic and fearless. He was almost always in reckless high spirits, a man who could sleep upright in the saddle and return to battle fresh as a lark within the hour. Summing up the life he craved he wrote: "I would rather cut my way to a name and poverty with the sword than write it to wealth with the pen." Four years earlier the edict which ended his command of the Punjab's Guide Corps for imprisoning a chieftain in chains stressed he should never again be employed in any civil capacity. None could impugn his physical courage; one commander wrote that he would rather have Hodson in a tight corner than five hundred others. Few would go so far as to say they liked him.

His mutiny service had begun as early as 16th May, when the late General George Anson had found every telegraph cut between Meerut and Ambala. On his own initiative Anson appointed Hodson Assistant Quarter-Master General or Intelligence Officer of the Delhi Force, for now he needed a born intriguer, a courier of daring and resource who could fight his way through from Ambala and hasten the Meerut force towards Delhi. "If it can be done," the General opined, "Hodson is the man." Nor was his faith misplaced. Despite a broken ankle that for months had kept him hobbling on crutches, Hodson spurred for three days and nights across hostile terrain, covering the 150-mile stretch unscathed to deliver the message. Then, pleased with the sensation he had caused, he posted back to Ambala. Ahead lay the task of gleaning every crumb of secret intelligence the Delhi force would need.

No man was better fitted for the mission. Though reduced to a subaltern's rank following his expulsion from the Guides, Hodson knew every shade and nuance of Indian rural life. Once, as overseer of four hundred and fifty coolies, he had constructed a building from top to bottom, absorbing every detail of carpentry and masonry. His keen unscrupulous brain had an unrivalled grasp of local dialect and idiom; whether joking with a village headman or flirting with an old peasant woman while reconnoitering troop dispositions, Hodson put no foot wrong. Now, with the aid of Rajab Ali, an elderly Indian clerk of noble birth, who had worked under John Lawrence, he began to build an espionage system destined to prove one of the Force's most valuable assets in the weeks to come. By mid-June every landholder in the Delhi district had been enlisted as a Hodson spy.

The reports now flooding in to his tent convinced Hodson that the sappers on Barnard's staff were right. So at logger-heads were the rebel commanders, one fierce onslaught on the city would see their total rout. "The mismanagement," he stormed, "is perfectly sickening. Nothing the rebels can do will equal the evils arising from incapacity and indecision."

In these first weeks of June, few men would have agreed with him more than Mohammed Bahadur Shah.

Since the tempestuous day when the rebels stormed into the Red Fort, the old King had been increasingly bewildered. A few weeks earlier, even high-ranking officers like Simon Fraser, the late Commissioner of Delhi, had courteously dismounted at the passage leading to the Hall of Audience and saluted him with all the honours due to the last of the Moguls. Now, sepoy officers galloped up to the very door and strode brashly in, their swords clanking, to the pillared alabaster hall of his ancestors. Beneath the broken mosaics, the gaudy banners so glazed with dirt they seemed like funeral serge, they sprawled nonchalantly on brocade cushions, side by side with chiefs and courtiers. Contemptuous that the King's sons needed an interpreter to understand them, they jeered openly at their courtly Persian. Often when the old man's attention wandered, they plucked at his sleeve or even his beard, crying, "Hey, you, King!" or "Here, old fellow!"

Often the Palace was besieged by a mob of howling sepoys demanding pay. The hundred-strong police force to whom the King had entrusted the city's safety could do nothing with them. The mutineers would not leave Delhi, nor would they protect it; they seemed demoralised by plunder and violence. As early as 16th May wealthy citizens had offered up prayers for the rebels' defeat and the speedy return of the British.

Nor was this surprising. "The state of the people is not to be described," a Rajah's envoy wrote from the city. "They are alive yet they despair of their lives." Already the shopkeepers at the city's Delhi Gate had found their homes requisitioned by the rebels as barracks. Gangs of sepoys still clad in tight red jackets, their shakos replaced by white linen hats, roistered half-drunk through the wide sunlit streets. They stripped the wood from door frames and wells as fuel for their fires; they plundered even poor men of beds and earthenware vessels. They rode out in vast noisy parties to ravage the sugar-cane crops of nearby villages. In vain the old King told his son, Prince Mirza Moghul, who had assumed command of the troops, "It is the business of the army to protect not to plunder." The princes themselves went on drunken forays and assaulted street watchmen. Although his reign had been proclaimed by beat of drum and he had solemnly taken his seat on the silver throne, the old man was powerless to check their excesses.

It came home painfully to Mohammed Bahadur Shah that he was now no more than a symbol that had served its purpose and he took refuge in futile pleas and threats. He sent for the rebel chiefs and charged them with destroying a kingdom that had lasted five hundred years. "This is the will of God," he said despairingly, "that I and my kingdom shall be destroyed. I wish you all to leave the town." If their oppression did not cease, he threatened, he would shame them all by taking poison.

He knew that the mutineers did not wholly trust him, despite the fulsome titles they bestowed on him. On 11th May, while the rebels were still spreading their bed-rolls in his marble halls the old King and his physician, the crafty Ahsanullah Khan, had concocted a letter to John Colvin, Lieutenant-Governor of the North-West Provinces at Agra, begging for a force of European troops. This letter, delivered by a camel-trooper, was duly received at Agra, but Colvin had no troops to send. Though the mutineers knew nothing of this they suspected both Ahsanullah and the Queen, Zeenat Mahal, of trying to come to terms with the British. They claimed Ahsanullah Khan intercepted the King's newsletters to neighbouring chiefs, or that he bribed the messengers to return, swearing they had been plundered by robbers.

Little by little a new confidence was growing within the rebels. At first they had believed they stood alone, that the one ultimate choice was death or glory. But as news filtered through that unrest was widespread they took fresh heart. In the King's name they would promise anything. They urged the disarmed sepoys of Mian Mir to hasten to Delhi; the pay was twelve rupees a month and there was abundant food and drink.

But the King's coffers were fast emptying, as Trooper Devi Din of the 3rd Light Cavalry soon discovered. A handsome swarthy figure in his French-grey uniform, with a booming laugh that seemed to begin in his boots, Devi Din was on furlough in his home-town of Bareilly when the mutiny began and had thus played no part in the massacre of Meerut. Like hundreds of others he had no burning grudge against the British and had respected such 3rd Cavalry officers as Lieutenant Hugh Gough. He and his fellow troopers agreed that for the time being they would "ride with a foot in both stirrups." "If the British are successful at Delhi," Devi Din reasoned guilelessly, "we can always say we went up there to rejoin the regiment."

But soon the excitement palled. On 1st June, some troops were complaining bitterly that their pay was three days in arrears. Such men, thought Devi Din and his comrades, were lucky; they, like many newcomers, received no pay at all. Each day, the old King held an inspection on the parade-ground outside the fort; the band crashed out such rousing British marches as "Cheer, boys, cheer" and "Every land's my home" while an elephant lumbered up and down the ranks, the King's yellow wrinkled face peering from a howdah. His quavering promise of bonuses fell sourly on the ears of men who as yet had not received a rupee. Already they suspected the true state of affairs: much of the £12,000 levy the King had imposed on the city's merchants had not been forthcoming. The fearful merchants had buried their treasure and barred their doors. Only when the King made a ceremonial round of the bazaars would they open their stalls for a few hours.

Then, when the British returned to the Ridge, the city's gates were shut and the country people brought fewer supplies. Devi Din had a shrewd suspicion that the commandants were now frightened men. Only the Rissaldar-Major of the 3rd Cavalry preserved his impeccable standards at each morning's parade as if victory hinged on the brightness of a button. "What would Colonel Carmichael Smyth say?" he chided slovenly recruits. Always Devi Din was consumed with silent laughter for Colonel Carmichael Smyth was the one officer all would have gladly killed.

Yet to the old King's distraction a steady stream of troops was pouring in each day, their bands playing "God Save the Queen," their colours borne proudly by standard bearers, marching in drill-manual precision across the bridge of boats.

How was he to pay and feed them—and above all where were they coming from? Mohammed Bahadur Shah, Shelter of the World, Nourisher of the Poor, Father of Victory, Lord of Mankind, did not know.

IX. GANGES VALLEY

20th May to 9th June

The teeming hordes of rebels who risked death rather than dishonour in this first week of June might puzzle the last of the Moguls. In Calcutta, Lord Canning felt no such perplexity: he knew from whence they came. All down the valley of the Ganges, the village war-drums were pulsing in the night, bringing news of rebellion spreading so fast it could be charted now by the uprush of flames as station after station took fire. On 20th May, Azimgarh; on 31st May, Bareilly; on 3rd June Fatehgarh; on 4th June, Benares; on 6th June, Allahabad; on 7th June, Fyzabad; on 9th June, Fatehpur. Thus mutiny had swept unchecked across an area a quarter of the size of Europe, held by less than twenty thousand British troops, but no man on earth could have halted the slaughter now.

Often there was no bloodshed, only a bizarre chivalry, as if the bond of years was too firm to be dishonoured now. At Jaipur the sepoys gave formal notice of intention to revolt but insisted on first being paid up to date. At Mullaon, near Lucknow, the sepoys exhorted a British subaltern to march them to Delhi; when he refused they swore angrily they would loot the treasury. "I cannot prevent you," he retorted, "but . . . I beg to remind you that my last month's pay is due and that amount you must hand over to me." Meekly the rebels complied. The signal for mutiny at Fyzabad was a subadar's parade-ground proclamation: "The Company's *raj* (rule) is ended. The English have been long in the country but they know little of us." Then, having arranged boats to carry the officers to safety, he politely asked permission to try on the Colonel's dress-coat. "I'm a little bigger than you," he sighed, "but I dare say the tailor will let out the seams."

In vain Lord Canning warned, "Our hold on Bengal and the Upper Provinces depends on the turn of a word—a look." Ordinary men and women still would not credit it: how *could* the tragedies of Meerut and Delhi affect *their* lives in this breathless week when a scalding wind withered the roses and the cicadas whirred all night and 4.30 a.m. was the one hour you could enjoy the garden? The magistrate of Chanderi rejected a well-wisher's warning of danger because his petition was not submitted on stamped paper. In Gwalior, one officer realised mutiny was imminent only when a sepoy failed to salute the Brigadier. In Benares, a chaplain, using a drum-head as an altar, chose a text from St. Paul for troops drawn up in hollow square armed with loaded rifles, "If God be for us, who can be against us?"

But hundreds were under no illusions. Already scores of out-stations, having failed to evacuate their women and children in due time had given precious hostages to fortune; almost every fort along the Ganges was ill-provisioned, pitifully armed. At Fatehgarh Fort, the British defenders mounted some bastions with dummy guns, school blackboards taking the place of backboards; a trail of charcoal outside an undefended bastion did service as a sham mine. Thus with desperate ingenuity they sought to lengthen their lives.

Along with this lack of foresight went the abiding trust most native infantry officers placed in their men. "Every crow thinks its own bairn the whitest," grumbled an artillery Captain, George Bourchier, who had bitter experience of the anger native infantry officers evinced if one hinted their Corps might go wrong. The same men, Bourchier noted, would willingly allow no other regiment was safe. To their officers the sepoys were "The Faithful Jacks," the *baba-log* (the dear children.) If caste had ruled out their eating together they still shared warm memories of old battles, of Sobraon and Chillianwala, of open-air parties in the lines with jugglers and the leisurely smoke rising from hookahs, the sleepy talk of crops and village-life. Critics scoffed that such officers trusted too blindly, but if a man gave his life to a regiment and did not trust his troops he trusted nothing.

Though fresh details of Meerut and Delhi filled every issue of *The Englishman* and *The Friend of India,* their faith remained unshaken. Lieutenant Colonel Arthur Spottiswoode, commanding the 37th Native Infantry at Benares, believed implicitly his subadar's assurances that "the good men of our corps are too powerful for the rascals"—had not the man brought his own wife to live at the station? From Bareilly, Brigadier Hugh Sibbald, parading his sepoys to still their doubts, assured Calcutta: "Their conduct is beyond praise." At Fatehgarh, Colonel George Smith, anxious to preserve his regiment's reputation, offered them a month's advance of pay to remain peaceful.

For this unswerving loyalty hundreds paid dearly. At Allahabad the sepoys rose four hours after Lord Canning's proclamation praising their loyalty had been read on parade; as a bugle shrilled the signal for revolt, the artillerymen holding the bridge wheeled their guns upon the British officers who came racing from the mess-house. His arm shattered by a bullet, Colonel Simpson reached the fort by a hair's breadth, his horse dying beneath him, blowing red spray. Captain Augustus Alexander was charging the guns single-handed when a sepoy rammed a musket against his side and fired; his heart was blasted from the rib-cage to hang dangling as he plunged downwards. Six young ensigns, the most junior aged sixteen, who minutes earlier had raised their glasses in the Loyal Toast were cut down like sheep as they tumbled from the mess. In the fort, garrisoned by sixty artillery pensioners, a company of sepoys and a wing of four hundred Sikhs, disaster was averted only by Lieutenant Jeremiah Brasyer, a one-time gardener who had risen from the ranks. Standing defiantly over the magazine with a red-hot iron he swore by all the Gods of the Sikhs to blow them to Hades if they did not obey his orders. Obediently the Sikhs shouldered their muskets and drove the remaining sepoys from the fort. Soon, from the wide gravelled walks that flanked the ramparts, the survivors watched small fires prick the night as Allahabad burned.

Station after station could tell the same appalling story. At

Jaunpore, Lieutenant Patrick Mara, hearing that the 37th Native Infantry had mutinied at Bernares, demanded, "What have we to fear from the 37th? Are not our own men here to defend us?" Then a sepoy fired from the ranks and he knelt down and died. At Bareilly, a bullet fired by his own orderly shattered Brigadier Sibbald's spine; he died slowly, clenched with pain, to the Sunday sound of bells, his blood welling on to the dung and straw of a camel-shed. His troops, bound for Delhi, busied themselves collecting seven hundred carts of treasure, gutting every building except the Freemason's Lodge. Strange mysteries, it was said, were transacted there; a man might forfeit his luck by laying a finger on it.

No man, woman or child was safe from the vengeance of men who sought to destroy. In Delhi the rebels laid hands on Walayat Ali, an Indian Christian; no stranger to persecution, he had long known the bitterness of being stoned through the streets, the pain of finding his dog poisoned by men who despised his faith. They seized his ankles and dragged him face down through the dust; they spat upon him and beat him with shoes, taunting him, "Now preach Christ to us." One man, seeing the mask of yellow dust coating his face, sneered, "I suppose you would like a drink of water?" Walayat Ali answered, "When my Saviour died He got vinegar mingled with gall—I don't need your water." With this a sepoy's sword struck the head from his body; Walayat Ali was suddenly a monstrous torso founting blood.

Mrs. Anna Lysaght had expected death; for twenty years she had been haunted by the nightmare that awakened her in screaming terror as a five-year-old. In dreams she was adult, worshipping with other Europeans in a church she could not identify. Outside in the sunshine harsh voices shrieked; the door shattered open and a swarm of turbanned men burst in, laying about them with swords, snarling like dogs. For years she travelled from outstation to outstation, the wife of Captain Corney Lysaght, 28th Native Infantry, looking intently at each church, before shaking her head afresh: "This is not the one." But when, in 1855, she saw the church at Shahjehanpore and cried out, "*This* is the church," her listeners were frankly incredulous. The church had been built only a year earlier—how could she have dreamed of a church that had not then existed? Did she recall it all at the blinding moment when dream became reality at Shahjehanpore on Sunday, 31st May, 1857? Her mother, Mrs. Elizabeth Sneyd, did and recorded it in her diary.

"Let not the enemies escape nor their wives and children," ran a rebel broadside. "Shut the mouths of the slanderers . . . destroy the enemy; trample down the survivors; kill the British—extinguish them."

But the shortcomings of British rule were not the only cause of this appalling wave of license. For thousands the decay of authority was a golden opportunity to wipe out old debts or to pay off old scores. "They liked the freedom they were enjoying," a magistrate noted. "Life for them was now full of anticipation." West of Delhi, village feuds flared so savagely, not even the blind and helpless were spared; the tongues of small children were crushed between hot tongs to make them reveal their father's treasure. By a strange irony thousands now fled the district seeking British protection. An old proverb of the lawless assumed a fearful meaning: "The man who holds the bludgeon owns the buffalo."

Since most Indians spent their lives in debt, the death of law and order was a unique chance to begin life anew. Under the system then prevailing, irregular cavalrymen had to provide their own horse and pay its fodder bill from their monthly wage. Often they lived their entire lives in poverty; the debts among eight regiments of irregular cavalry in the Punjab totalled £33,000, on which the troops paid interest at between 12 and 24 per cent. "The man who joined the insurrection considered that he got rid of his debts," John Lawrence wrote to Lord Canning. "He was free to commence a new career." Few men were more detested than the corn-merchants and usurers, for crops could fail and a lavish three-day marriage festival might cost the bride's family £3,000. The houses of such men were torn down brick by brick and the dusty roads beyond the out-stations were strewn with a confetti of cancelled debts. Soon the rebel ranks were swelled by more than eleven thousand felons released from gutted gaols; the countryside swarmed with homeless hungry men who robbed both sides impartially. A song that throbbed through the bazaars captured the antic mood:

> *People got shawls, large and small; my love got a*
>   *kerchief.*
> *There is a great bazaar at Meerut; my love did not*
>   *know how to plunder.*
> *People got coconuts and dates; my love got an al-*
>   *mond.*
> *There is a great bazaar at Meerut; my love did not*
>   *know how to plunder . . .*

The old idols were toppling and everywhere new hands reached out to snatch the reins of power. Near Agra, one man, hearing British rule had ended, declared himself Rajah of fourteen villages and set up his own government: nearby, five other landowners had also assumed this title. An Indian sergeant-major, given £160 to buy blankets for his troop, deserted on the strength of it and proclaimed himself "King" of the Meerut district. Even fifty years ago old men in the bazaars at Fatehgarh recalled the stutter of the drums and how children dawdling home from school in late sunlight heard the town crier's paean: "The World is God's, the country is the Emperor's, the Nawab, the ruler, is in command."

But Taffuzil Hussain, ninth and last Nawab of Farrukhabad whose rule the town-crier proclaimed, lusted less for power than for vengeance. A man £10,000 in debt, he had in vain sought the courtesy title of "Highness," but all this paled beside his hatred for Ensign Reginald Sutherland Byrne, attached to the 9th Native Infantry at Fatehgarh. A handsome dissolute youngster, the Nawab was infatuated with "Bonny" De Fountain, a fourteen-year-old Eurasian girl living with her widowed mother in a small thatched house near Fatehgarh cantonment. Each day a carriage and pair clattered from his palace down a narrow lane flanked by open drains to take Miss De Fountain for a drive. Turbanned retainers daily delivered large baskets of fruit, flowers and sweetmeats. It was known that she walked too often on the neat sanded walks of the palace grounds screened from the eyes of the world by mud walls twenty feet high. The magistrate remonstrated with the widow in vain. To pacify public opinion the authorities sent "Bonny" out of harm's way to Kidderpore Girls' School, outside Calcutta.

Such schools, in a contemporary's words, were "virtually

match-making establishments"; young officers went three times to tea and took their choice of any eligible girl. It was bitter irony Reginald Sutherland Byrne, one of the few Eurasians to hold a Bengal Army commission, should choose "Bonny" De Fountain; within months he and his bride were posted to Fatehgarh. Returning unexpectedly from parade to find "Bonny" alone with the Nawab the hot-tempered Byrne pitched him bodily from the bungalow. The Nawab warned Byrne he would pay for this in blood.

Two months later when the mutiny broke out Ensign Byrne vanished so strangely from Fatehgarh fort that Army records listed him as a deserter. This was unjust; the price of vengeance the Nawab exacted was Reginald Byrne's head. Severed by bayonets, it was spitted on a pole and borne in triumph round the palace grounds. In later years the Nawab was exiled from India for ever for this and other crimes; his palace with its ornate chandeliers and silver divans was confiscated. "Bonny" Byrne and her mother were imperturbable. They had lived in comfort through the mutiny in the Nawab's zenana.

No mortal man, it is said, may look direct at death or at the sun, but many men in these terrible weeks of vengeance had little option. On the evening of 9th June, Robert Tudor Tucker, the judge, waited quietly for death, Bible in hand, at Fatehpur. Already he had sent all other Europeans downriver to Allahabad but Tucker held strict concepts of duty; he himself must stay. Convinced his police force was loyal he had summoned his Indian deputy collector to a conference, but the man's reply left no room for doubt. "Tell the sahib to make himself happy and when I come in the evening I'll give him eternal rest."

A deeply religious man and a keen hunter, Tucker now barricaded each door and window, loading every rifle and pistol in his armoury. At last he heard the mob yelling in the compound of the court-house. He advanced to the window firing with deadly precision, reloading and firing again.

Sixteen lay dead before the mob stormed into the house to pillage it and cut him down. They surged in a tide past the pillar where Tucker had once inscribed the Ten Command-

ments in English and Hindustani for the benefit of his people; "Thou Shalt Not Steal," "Thou Shalt Not Kill," but men
must live by new rules now.

X. LUCKNOW

30th May

Despite the savagery of these fateful weeks, one feature of
the Indian Mutiny shines forth like a beacon: the courage of
countless sepoys and servants who risked their lives to preserve the British from mob violence.

At Gwalior the night wind carried the smell of burning
to three women and a man crouched in a darkened garden
behind a masonry wall; they heard the shattering of glass and
frenzied shouts of laughter and saw red light wavering on wet
grass. Their lives, Mrs. Ruth Coopland, the chaplain's wife,
recalled later, were now in the hands of Muza, the faithful
table-waiter who had hidden them there; later when the
sepoys came to search the garden, moonlight glinting on their
bayonets, it was Muza who hastened them to his hut close by
and hid them anew. Muza lied to the sepoys when they
broke into his kitchen after midnight, swearing he had no
Christians concealed, then led the fugitives stealthily through
darkness to a bearer's small mud hut, bringing other women
and children to join them. Muza's life hung in the balance
when a baby's wailing cry revealed their presence to the
sepoys but he and the women were left unharmed. A firing
party led away the Rev. George Coopland and volley after
volley split the night. Afterwards it was so still in the hut, Mrs.
Coopland remembered, a mouse crept out and looked at
them with small bright eyes.

At dawn the sepoys returned half drunk and dragged the
women to their lines; they mocked and reviled them but at
length said they might go where they pleased. Again it was

Muza who escorted them, driving the springless bullock cart that carried them with agonising slowness towards Agra, eighty miles away. It was Muza who drew the cloudy bitter water from native wells, purifying it with camphor water, to assuage their thirst; it was Muza who begged chopped cattle-food that they might not starve. He was still protecting the party of a dozen women and children three days later when the cart rumbled over the drawbridge into Agra Fort.

All who lived through the pain of the Mutiny had similar tales to recount. At Benares a Sikh chieftain showed such bravery in guarding the Mint that the British subscribed £100 to buy him a set of fire-arms. A young telegraph signaller was buried in a dungheap by a groom; two Allahabad watchmen concealed their master in a fowl-house. Another man lay packed inside a drain while his servants hurried to and from the bungalow negotiating with sepoys bent on loot. Would he furnish the key to the silver cupboard—and where were his wife's best shawls?

When it came to disguise they showed rare ingenuity. One magistrate got away masquerading as his butler's wife. The ladies of Sultanpore fled disguised as an Indian wedding party, villagers escorting them, chanting songs of nuptial bliss. A Moslem servant hid his mistress beneath a straw-stack and drove the sepoys away with mock anger, claiming the ground was sacred because his wife was buried there. Often, faced with distress, the humblest men showed true compassion. Near Sialkot, the villagers banded together to carry a pregnant woman forty miles on a litter.

Such men were scarcely prompted by self-interest for any Indian might readily have believed that British rule had ended. Shorn of their power, high officials who had worn good black broadcloth, maintained two carriages and swayed the destinies of millions, were now hunted like wild dogs through pestilential swamps and jungles. Cramped in tiny mud huts, tortured by prickly heat, men paced up and down for exercise like tigers in a den, hands calloused with the constant wielding of palm-leaf fans. Many endured this life for months on end, sleeping in their clothes in a heat that touched a hundred degrees in the shade; the sepoys, they knew, were watching every landing-place for a hundred and fifty miles down the Ganges. Some alleviated the nagging boredom by playing draughts on big squares marked in the dust. Others went mad, gobbling and gibbering in a private hell that terrified even loyal villagers. These fugitives they left alone, only setting food and water near the hut door as for a savage beast.

But many people caught in the mutiny's toils proved once again by heroism, stubborn courage and sacrifice that the human spirit is equal to life's fiercest challenges. A Eurasian clerk, George Yeoward, fleeing with his two children through the jungle, sought refuge in a stack of chopped cattle-straw. To his horror he heard rebel voices close at hand; rather than the British should make use of the straw they proposed setting fire to it. He heard a match scratch noisily, then a long silence followed by sullen curses. The straw was too damp to take fire and the rebels moved on, disappointed. Later, encountering a lone rebel on a river bank, Yeoward pounced on him, gagged him and bound him to a tree. Before nightfall, he knew, the wild pigs would have torn the man to pieces but how else could he preserve the children he loved?

Forced to live like the humblest peasants, the fugitives developed a peasant shrewdness. Each night, the magistrate of Budaon, William Edwards, a canny Scot from Inverness, who hid for three months in a buffalo hut, solved the mosquito problem by lighting a fire of dried cow-dung to windward of his sleeping-place. The acrid smoke wreathing over the bed kept the insects at bay. Others, when matches were lacking, ignited fuel by firing pistols at it. Deprived of roast mutton and spicy curries they cooked grasshoppers, chameleons and lizards, fashioning crude platters of river clay. Watch-cases became improvised feeding-bowls for men with injured jaws.

Primitive medicine was the key to life or death; many men covered the last vital miles with bleeding feet bound in cool plantain leaves. A twenty-one-year-old railway engineer, Gavin Jones, escaping with a wounded shoulder from Fatehgarh Fort, recalled that animals healed their own festering wounds by licking them. In the village that sheltered him he coaxed a small puppy to cure his wound in return for a share of his rations. A fugitive indigo planter, David Churcher, neutralised the heat of the sun for seven months by plastering his head daily with wet mud.

But it would take more than courage and individual loyalties to save British India now, as none knew better than Sir Henry Lawrence. Long before most men saw where this disquiet must lead, Sir Henry had begun to prepare for the worst. Night after night, provisions and munitions of war had been brought into the Residency at Lucknow and stored in cellars and outhouses. No longer could Lawrence's young aides enjoy a strenuous game of rackets in the cool of the evening; the court was piled to the ceiling with three months' supply of chopped cattle straw. At least £230,000 worth of rupees was buried near the northern face of the Residency, ruling out the need for a guard.

Each day at sunrise every fit man was paraded for musket drill; officers had been issued with arms to defend themselves within their own quarters. Beyond the walls three thousand coolies worked with gunpowder and pick-axes, demolishing the crumbling palaces and mud houses crowding the sloping ground. Only the mosques and temples, despite the staff-officers' protests, remain unscathed. "Spare the holy places," had been Sir Henry's irrevocable order.

This abiding respect for what others held sacred was typical of Lawrence, as Henry Kavanagh well knew. A humble clerk in Lawrence's office, this tall thirty-six-year-old Irishman, a theatrical figure at any time with his red-gold hair and beard and blazing blue eyes, had faced only eighteen months ago the grim true-life drama of the Insolvent Court. Foolishly involved with Indian moneylenders, his debts had mounted to almost £780—more than two and a half years' salary.

Ruin, dismissal from the Company's service, had stared him in the face until Canning's predecessor, Lord Dalhousie, had ruled with rare wisdom: "Were the mere fact of being in debt to disqualify him . . . I apprehend there would be a large number of vacancies in the service." Often Kavanagh, an incorrigible romantic, had railed against a fate that kept him hamstrung by his creditors, unable to buy gay bonnets for his wife or add a pillared verandah to his bungalow.

But since mid-May Kavanagh had found the days, instead of dragging interminably, had passed all too fast. The dispiriting knowledge that twelve years might pass before his debts were cleared, for he could barely repay £10 a month, had been blotted out by the need for prompt action. He had discarded a clerk's alpaca jacket for a blue uniform tunic with white cords, jack-boots and felt helmet, using every spare hour to drill the volunteers. Always he and the hundreds of others about the Residency were conscious as they worked of Sir Henry's quiet wisdom. Unwilling to disarm the three infantry regiments and one cavalry regiment quartered three miles away at Mariaon cantonments, Henry Lawrence knew that mistrust could only provoke risings elsewhere in Oudh where no British troops were stationed to resist them. Many lives were saved by his decision.

At fifty-three Sir Henry Lawrence was a striking figure—both physically and spiritually. A thin lathy figure with haggard sunken eyes and a Vandyke beard he reminded many observers of Abraham Lincoln. Lawrence, like Lincoln, was a man careless of personal finery. Clad almost always in an antiquated frock coat and old grey shepherd plaid he would as readily cloak his shoulders with a strip of matting as a coat. Since the death in 1854 of Lady Lawrence, whose miniature he wore always about his neck, he seemed to many to live more in the next world than in this. Courteous, gentle, unselfish, the oppression of Indians stirred him always to passionate anger—"the friend of the man who was down," a colleague styled him. To the six hundred men of the 32nd Foot, who formed the bulk of his European troops, he was "a right good man to soldiers" whom they would follow through fire and water. Recently they had cheered him so lustily one man had burst a blood vessel.

A born diplomat, Sir Henry had a shrewd understanding of the Indians' love of parable. About this time a high-ranking Hindu called on him with solemn advice: the chief Commissioner should have some of the lithe brown monkeys, held sacred by the Hindus, rounded up and fed by high-caste Brahmins. This would ensure the favour of the Hindu gods.

Lawrence listened courteously, then rose from his seat. "Your advice is good," he said snatching up his hat. "Come, and I will show you my monkeys." Gravely, leading the way to a battery just completed, he laid his hand on an eighteen-pounder gun. "See! Here is one of my monkeys. That," indicating a pile of shot, "is his food." His hand rested on the shoulder of a private of the 32nd who stood rigidly at attention. "And *this* is the Brahmin who feeds them. Now go and tell your friends about *my* monkeys."

At 8.30 p.m. on 30th May, Sir Henry was dining in the Residency with his staff-officers. It was, as all had come to expect, a barely-eatable dinner. As heedless of food as of money, Henry Lawrence would invite twenty guests to dine on a cold half-shoulder of mutton and forget to tell the servants; often crisis was only staved off by a friendly official diverting a chain of dishes from his own kitchen to Lawrence's. The compensation lay in the benison of Sir Henry's presence and in hours of good masculine talk that might stretch on until midnight.

But that night, as some present later recalled, conversation was fitful. Every man there knew the issues at stake—for Lucknow and for India. These Lawrence himself had outlined, and his gift of prophecy was uncanny. The entire Bengal Army would shortly be given up to mutiny—of this he was confident. The Sikhs, he thought, would stay loyal. Each Lucknow regiment harboured a core of loyal sepoys and these he would retain.

Garrison statistics alone showed the gravity of the position. Among the seven thousand sepoys and troopers stationed at Lucknow, many were doubtless mutineers. There were exactly seven hundred Europeans on whom Sir Henry could rely. Beyond lay the native city, with upwards of five hundred thousand people trembling on the brink of revolt.

If General Wheeler kept the peace at Cawnpore, if Delhi was swiftly re-taken, Lucknow might well stay peaceful. But if Cawnpore rose and the King's troops held Delhi, Lucknow would be hard pressed and no relief could reach the Residency for ten long weeks at the earliest. On 21st May, Lawrence, who had been readily granted plenary powers by Lord Canning, had telegraphed the Governor-General: "I have assumed military command. All quiet, but several reports of intended attack on us."

These reports, Sir Henry's aide, Captain Thomas Wilson affirmed, timed the attack for that night, 30th May, at nine.

Lost in thought, the men sat silent over their wine. The scent of orange blossom drifted from dark gardens beyond and the jackals whooped and howled. Insects dashed themselves recklessly against the glass shades of coconut-oil lamps, magnetised by small steady flames towering within. Precisely at 9 p.m. the boom of the time gun rolled through the darkness. In the silence which followed, all present found their ears straining.

Leaning forward, Sir Henry chaffed Captain Wilson, "Your friends are not punctual."

"Well, sir," Wilson answered, "It's all right for another evening."

Wilson had scarcely spoken before the detonation of scores of rifles tore the warm air. They heard the urgent patter of running feet, the confused alarm of a crowd.

His face expressionless, Sir Henry at once ordered that their horses, waiting ready saddled, should be brought round. Then, followed by his staff, he strode to the Residency steps to await them. Immobile in the moonlight they watched fire surge upwards at a score of points from the black mass of the cantonments.

At this moment there was a tramp of feet and a body of sepoys came doubling, swinging into line forty paces away to face the waiting officers. This was the Residency bodyguard, commanded by an Indian officer, who now saluted Captain Wilson and asked if the men should load. Wilson stood appalled. The men were known to be disaffected and before dawn were in open mutiny; should they until they had proved otherwise be treated as loyal? Quietly Wilson repeated the question to Lawrence.

Lawrence seemed lost in thought. "Yes, load by all means," the Commissioner agreed absently. Quietly the group stood watching while ramrods rang sharply in the musket-barrels and the gun-nipples were capped; the sound of ramrods striking leaden bullets was quite audible in the hush. "I believe Sir Henry was the only man of all that group," wrote Wilson later, "whose heart did not beat the quicker for it."

Yet human beings confronted by the strange and inexplicable cling closely to the normal round. The Hon. Julia Inglis, wife of a colonel in the 32nd Foot, was preparing for an early night when the Financial Commissioner, Martin Gubbins, rapped excitedly at her door. "Bring your children and come up to the top of the house immediately." Following his bidding, Mrs. Inglis found a score of men and women, quartered for the emergency in Gubbins's house, watching the cantonments burn as calmly as at a fireworks display. The Rev. Henry Polehampton, also present, was silently debating a theological point put privately by her husband; would Inglis be justified in killing his wife rather than let the rebels capture her? Polehampton's decision was affirmative since women could be dishonoured but divine law could never countenance Mrs. Inglis' destroying her children; children could only be killed. Even in the cantonments some men preserved an uncanny calm; Lieutenant Alexander Thain of the 13th Native Infantry continued his leisurely game of billiards with Lieutenant William Campbell of the 71st while the sepoys fired volley after volley at the portals of the mess. Edward Hilton, a seventeen-year-old schoolboy from La Martinière College, was chanting the "Magnificat" in the cantonment church when the bugle shrilled the alarm. Presently Hilton and the other choirboys returned to their school but not until the soaring notes of the "Magnificat" had died to a sweet hush.

Others, though seized by greater urgency, were still lighthearted, as though the onset of mutiny was a welcome release from burdensome suspense. Leopold Ruitz Rees, a Swiss wholesale grocer, was staying with his friend François Deprat, a soldier-of-fortune turned merchant; he awoke to hear Deprat call excitedly, *"Le jeu a commencé. Dépêchez-vous!"* Henry Kavanagh, cantering by after reporting to Sir Henry Lawrence that the native city at least remained calm, burst into involuntary laughter. Deprat had fortified the upper storey of his house, which lay between cantonment and residency, as if for a siege, but the lower storeys were entirely unprotected.

XI. TILOWEE VILLAGE, LUCKNOW

30th May

In this week, while the fate of Lucknow trembled in the balance, one senior member of the Bengal Army was on furlough twenty-six miles from the city in the tiny village of Tilowee, where he had been born over sixty years earlier. He was a Jemadar or Indian Infantry Lieutenant named Sita Ram Pande, one of the commonest surnames in Oudh, where most were of farming stock and where few families did not boast one member in the Bengal Army. Through his eyes we can learn much of why the virus of mutiny—"the wind of madness," he called it—worked so powerfully in men's blood.

At sixty-two, Sita Ram stood 5 feet 11 inches high with magnificent moustaches sprinkled now with grey. As a member of the highest caste of Hindu, he carried the sacred cord of the Brahmins round his neck as well as the necklace of gold beads worn by all Indian officers. On the parade-ground of the 31st Native Infantry at Jullundur he was still an imposing figure in the tight scarlet coat and blue trousers he wore over white linen jacket and drawers. For forty-five years he had served the British, ever since 10th October, 1812, and in that time he had seen grievous changes. He had seen the British, all unwitting, sow the seeds of the whirlwind now uprooting all they cherished most.

Sometimes when Sita Ram thought of those days a sigh ran through his burly frame. What prestige the army had enjoyed in the long ago—and how passionately he had yearned to enter its service! He had been seventeen when this urge first seized him, and all because his uncle Hanuman, a jemadar in an infantry regiment, had passed through at the beginning of six months' furlough to spend a few days with them. In those cool evenings, when the flutes wailed from the servants' quarters and the scent of cow-dung fires pricked the nostrils, Uncle Hanuman in his scarlet coat with gold buttons sat on the steps of his brother-in-law's house, jingling a handful of gold mohurs, talking softly of old wars and the conquering might of "John Company." Then it was that Sita Ram fell in love with a dream. To him, who had never seen a white man, it had seemed that Uncle Hanuman was equal to Saadat Ali himself, the exiled king's great-grandfather.

This was no youngster's fancy, Sita Ram knew; only the sepoy's privileged status had won him the glory of wearing scarlet and white. His mother, who had set her heart on his becoming a scholar, wept bitterly when the subject was broached. Duleep Ram, the family priest, who had taught him from the age of six to read and write and add up figures was aghast. To throw away the precious teachings of eleven years and become a soldier? He would be defiled by setting foot in the army.

Sita Ram came of a pious people and this horror of defilement was woven in and out of their lives as the warp thread runs through a soft Persian carpet. On every day, for example, in the house of Sita Ram, the whole family would cleanse themselves from head to foot. They would scrub their teeth with green astringent twigs. Their kitchen was like a private chapel; no stranger might set foot therein. Food that had held the germ of life—even eggs—was taboo. Anything from childbirth to death could desecrate this house until Duleep Ram ceremonially pronounced it pure. During menstrual periods the womenfolk were banished to an out-house. A doctor could feel a patient's pulse only through a layer of decontaminating silk.

Thus Sita Ram was reared in a world of regimented hygiene where the household gods, worshipped each day at noon, were the silent arbiters of what one could and could not touch.

But Sita Ram's father, a well-to-do landowner, had a law suit pending just then concerning his rights over a grove of four hundred mango trees. So great was a sepoy's status in

Oudh he held prior right to have a case heard in the law courts; many sepoys took three months' special leave to prosecute a suit. A son in the Company's service could turn the scales in his favour. A petition sent by a soldier through his commanding officer to the Resident at Lucknow carried far more weight in court than a bribe.

But once Oudh was British territory, the sepoys had no more legal privilege than any other civilian—a democratic move they resented bitterly. "I used to be a great man when I went home," an Oudh cavalryman had told Henry Lawrence. "The best of the village rose as I approached; now the lowest puff their pipes in my face."

For Sita Ram the months before he attained this god-like status were the longest he had ever known. Once his father had agreed to his joining, dreams of army life haunted him. His job was to help manage the estate, overseeing the coolies who harvested the crops and drew the water, but for weeks he forsook it all for wrestling and playing with sword-sticks until Gunga Din, his father, swore that if he did not come to his senses he would never see Uncle Hanuman again, mango grove or no. Sita Ram bided his time until one cool October morning, the rainy season past, he was standing with his back to the highway, cutting the purple-green sugar cane, when a man's voice called. Uncle Hanuman had come back.

Then followed days of tears and tensions with his mother convinced she would never see him again, and the family priest busy with the horoscope that would decide whether the gods looked kindly on a martial career for Sita Ram. And it seemed they did, for Duleep Ram announced that the lucky time for departure would be 6 a.m. on the fourth day from now, provided no thunder was heard, since untimely thunder rendered a journey inauspicious. For three days Sita Ram scanned the skies anxiously and prayed to Narayan and Indra, the gods of the rain and clouds. But on the fourth day with the sky clear, Duleep Ram bade him never disgrace his Brahminical thread and gave him a charm so powerful no harm could ever befall him, so long as he kept it safe; a phial of dust in which a thousand Brahmins had trodden at Allahabad. His mother gave him £10 worth of gold mohurs sewn in a cloth bag, then wept more piteously than ever. A coolie was

hired to carry his and Uncle Hanuman's baggage to Agra
where the regiment was stationed, for no sepoy any more
than an officer carried his own. Apart from the gold coins
Sita Ram now had a sepoy's standard equipment: a brass
lotah with a string to lower it down wells, three brass dishes,
an iron dish and spoon, two changes of dress, a smart turban,
a scorpion dagger and a pair of shoes. Thus had he set out to
serve "John Company."

No man could say that Sita Ram had not served them
well, for the medals of six campaigns glowed on his breast
and he had, as the sepoys put it, "eaten" seven wounds. He
had fought against the Gurkhas under General Ochterlony
in the Nepal war of 1914, against the Afghans in that terrible summer of 1839 through "a land of stones with no
green thing" and on into that searing winter in Kabul where
the snow lay as high as a man was tall and the sepoys' toes
and fingers withered from the limbs like dead sticks through
frostbite. He had seen the sepoys lose faith in the invincible
British after this bitter defeat and many times heard whispers in the lines that "a new caste of sahib now comes out to
India."

Was he so old he dreamed of a sunlit glory that had
never been? This could scarcely be, for the disillusions of his
recruiting period were as vivid as if it were yesterday: the
eight gruelling months of drill under an Indian sergeant, who
rewarded mistakes by wrenching his ears or cuffing him
senseless, eight months' probation which lacked even the
glamour of red coat or musket. That first red coat, he recalled,
was so tight it cut him beneath the arms and the musket and
knapsack seemed a coolie's load. Even his first sight of the
British had disappointed him, for he had imagined them
seven feet tall, in keeping with the legend that they were
born from eggs growing on a tree in a far away island. But
most were either young and smooth faced or red and bald.

Yet they had aspects which demanded respect. Colonel
Charles Stuart had been very old but he was a nine tiger
man, to a Hindu the zenith of bravery, and he could endure heat. His Hindustani was fluent for he, like his officers,
had an Indian mistress to keep him in touch with the sepoys'
needs and grievances. All the officers had been fluent in the

language for they attended nautches and took the men hunting; the sepoys wandered in and out of their bungalows chatting so that sometimes it seemed they were the sahib's favourite children rather than soldiers. Nowadays the British shunned hot weather and their command of the language was uncertain—not that they spoke much to the sepoys unless they were obliged to; they shut themselves away with their wives and children. One officer had explained to Sita Ram that he never knew what to say.

"The sahibs always knew what to say and how to say it when I was young," Sita Ram confided in his friends—but only in Army friends. He was blanketed with shame and this was not a thing you could talk about to civilians.

Roaming disconsolately over the sun-scorched acres he had long since inherited from his father, Sita Ram thought how well the officers of that day had understood. Caste and its jealous obligations had been a living entity to them; the British troops had understood it, too. The soldiers did not walk near their cooking places, knowing the shadow of an unbeliever must defile the sepoy's food. They did not spit in their cooking pots or snarl mongrel words of abuse like the troops of today.

Sita Ram knew too well about caste; he himself had twice lost it, once without realising it himself. That had been in the bloody Pindari campaign, four years after leaving home; a bullet tore through his left shoulder and he was left for dead in a ravine. He had lain there dumbly, believing he must die; it was two days before he crawled away, coughing up gobbets of blood, his musket serving as crutch and only the water the cowkeeper's little daughter drew for him in the jungle saved his life.

It was strange that caste could be filched from you by another, no matter how warily you walked. Sita Ram had been granted six months' sick leave after that campaign; it was five years since he had been home and he left Agra in high heart, riding on a country pony. To surprise them he had waited outside the house until almost dawn, then called softly to his mother as she came forth to draw water. The sight of the mighty whiskered twenty-two-year-old at first terrified her, then she wept as when they had parted. Her son had come home a man.

At first Sita Ram rejoiced in that homecoming. They listened open-mouthed while he told of the herd of wild elephants that ran amok amongst their tents in Nepal, of Chitra, the lecherous Pindari chief whose name caused young brides to weep softly, of the fakir who had tended his wound in the jungle with a poultice of cool mint-flavoured neem leaves. Basking in their admiration he told them of the cow-keeper's daughter, but at once a Brahmin priest among the audience recoiled in horror. The girl must have been of the Dom tribe, lower than a sweeper, and Sita Ram, having drunk the water, was forever defiled. In vain Sita Ram protested he had drunk from his own lotah. Angrily the group broke up, snuffing out their acrid native cigarettes; they would not smoke with an outcast. That night, as any Hindu father would have done, Gunga Din drove his son from the house.

Then Sita Ram revolved through the lonely limbo of a man from whom all but the lowest menials recoiled as unclean. Only his father's influence persuaded a court of five village elders to consider his case, for until he was purified he was a pariah; no man could eat with him, smoke with him or talk with him. He fasted many days and nights. The priests performed rites over him and he was lavish with feasts and gifts. He scarred his feet for life walking over a bed of red-hot charcoal. He gulped down a nauseating bowl of the five products of the cow. But at last he knew the unspeakable joy of being pronounced clean and receiving a new Brahminical cord. All his five years' savings had gone but he no longer stood lower than a leper—"and who can combat against destiny?"

Such subtleties this new breed of officer could never understand. In that cruel winter of 1839, in Afghanistan, the Hindus, too cold to observe the sacred ritual of washing before eating, were forced to receive their food from Moslem cooks. In charity the British officers doled out sheepskin coats—unaware the Hindus they led were forbidden to touch the skins of dead animals. Sita Ram himself, struck senseless by an Afghan bullet, had been taken prisoner, roped to a camel and sold as a slave in the market place at Kabul. Three hellish years had passed before he escaped with a caravan train and reached Ferozepore in October, 1843. Bugles shrilled, drumsticks rattled like dry bones as he neared the cantonment; tears of joy coursed down his cheeks.

But like all the Hindus who had come through that war, he was shunned as an outcast by his people. Only the brigade-major showed true kindness and allowed him to live in his compound. For the rest, although he rejoined the 31st at Delhi as a havildar, he could mix only with Moslems, and Indian Christians. Penniless, only his father's generosity regained his caste for the second time. Thus Sita Ram was made angry by many of "John Company's" decrees. Didn't they realise that to lose caste was to lose life? A man would slay, steal, obey the wildest promptings of the blood, to retain it.

Of course, the British faced no easy task; too often discipline ran counter to caste. More than one-third of the Bengal Army sepoys were Brahmins, before whom even Indian officers of lower caste must prostrate themselves when off parade. On sentry duty these privileged men had four others to relieve them, never performing more than six hours' guard in twenty-four. Yet many Government measures affected the caste of common people no less than the army; the introduction of mixed messing in gaols, the abolition of suttee, the grim immolation wherein a Hindu widow was pinned down on the blazing brands of her husband's funeral pyre.

Many were well-meaning much-needed reforms prompted by sincere men who sought to write a brisk fresh page in India's history but they went too far and too fast. In less than a hundred years, fifty civil rebellions had rent the countryside.

Many times Sita Ram tried to warn his officers; "they were as stone walls." Fourteen years ago, at the end of the Sind war, every regiment between Delhi and Ferozepore had been ripe for revolt; the special campaign allowance their officers had promised was never honoured by the Company. Moslem agents had been at work in every station; even then they talked of restoring Bahadur Shah to the throne of Hindustan. Sita Ram returned from Afghanistan to find the situation worse. "We could fight 'John Company' as well as the Afghans," the Moslems of Delhi boasted. "Why, we originally came from Persia and Kabul." Envoys from the old King's court were forever in the lines, sounding out the temper of the army. All this Sita Ram reported to his commanding officer, but he was still suspect after the Afghan war; there were rumours he had been forcibly made a Moslem and had eaten beef. Convinced the warnings were prompted by spite, the Colonel told Sita Ram to hold his peace.

After this Sita Ram remained silent for many years. Why say anything further if the sahibs would not listen? It would only serve to alienate the few friends he had left.

The British had acquired a deadly air for stirring animosity, Sita Ram well knew. Many Indians said openly that King Wajid Ali had been shabbily treated; if all the army acted in concert it would be so easy to restore Bahadur Shah. As for the greased cartridges—well, Sita Ram guessed that story had a kernel of truth or why did the British protest so much with their parade-ground proclamations only three sepoys in a company could understand for the interpreters gabbled so fast, often employing mandarin tongues like Persian or Arabic? Doubtless it was doltish incomprehension and no deliberate attempt to destroy caste, but the younger sepoys believed the worst. "Their real aim *is* to make us Christians," they told Sita Ram. "That's what they'd like."

Sita Ram was fearful, he did not know why; he was like a dog that scents the footsteps of disaster long before the human ear. Most definitely he had not wanted to go on furlough. Many men apart from himself would stay faithful—if he stayed he might help to turn the tide. Lieutenant-Colonel Bulstrode Bygrave would not hear of it. "You go home, Jemadar-Sahib," he soothed Sita Ram. "There's bound to be excitement but I think it'll pass off." But as the tension stretched to snapping point it was plain that it would not pass off, for the sky was black with chickens coming home to roost.

XII. CAWNPORE

22nd May to 6th June

To the British, so many of the Indians, be they Rajahs or coolies, were an enigma. They ate strange-smelling foods, clothed in as much ceremony as communion wafers; they lived in an alien world of ritual. Despite "John Company's" corruption, many of the British were honest men, seeking to do their best in a strange land. They yearned to understand the Indians. An Indian adapted to western ways would never lack for friends. In his company the British breathed a sigh of relief. He was "one of us."

Although his wife was of Indian blood, General Sir Hugh Wheeler knew this feeling well. He counted himself lucky that in this hour of crisis at Cawnpore there was one Indian more British than the British, a man you could trust with your life. This feeling lay behind the message that reached the shocked Sir Henry Lawrence on 22nd May: "Two guns and three hundred men, cavalry and infantry, furnished by the Maharajah of Bithur, came in this morning." By 3rd June, confident he could hold his own, Wheeler despatched two officers and fifty men of Her Majesty's 84th Foot to swell Lawrence's garrison at Lucknow. The Maharajah's men were staunchly guarding his treasury.

Everybody at Cawnpore knew the Maharajah of Bithur, though most knew him by his Mahratta courtesy title of Nana Sahib, meaning "maternal grandfather." This jovial corpulent man of thirty-six, with black brilliant restless eyes, was a byword for his kindness. He was cleanshaven, like all Mahrattas, his round sallow face tattooed by smallpox. The young officers pronounced him "a capital fellow."

Though he spoke no word of English his taste for western

ways was well known. A schoolmaster named Todd accompanied him everywhere, translating the English newspapers and acting as interpreter at the station balls which the Nana attended. He threw hunting parties for the officers and picnics for the ladies, pressed diamond rings on the men and Kashmir shawls on their wives. The English looked on him so benignly that when the electric telegraph reached Cawnpore he was invited to experiment with it by the engineers. When Mrs. Louisa Chalwin, wife of the newly-posted veterinary surgeon, found her piano had not yet arrived, the Nana promptly gave her one of his own.

Life at the Palace of Bithur, five miles from Cawnpore, had bizarre aspects. The dinner table was covered with a cloth but bedroom towels took the place of napkins. Soup was ladled from a tea-cup into a trifle dish bearing the crest of the 9th Lancers; other dishes followed on blue-and-gold soup plates. The Nana's personal tastes were simpler; much of his day he reclined on a string bed in a dingy apartment where a heifer roamed at will, with an attendant to dispose of its droppings. But he *was,* all agreed, a gentleman. His gun-room was stocked by Purdey, his larder by Fortnum and Mason.

At Lucknow they were less certain of Nana Sahib. In April he had visited the city with a large retinue, bringing an introduction to the Financial Commissioner, Martin Gubbins. Gubbins, who introduced him to Henry Lawrence, found him "arrogant and presuming." The Nana had entered his room with six or seven followers, demanding that all should be provided with chairs. Soon after, with no explanation, he cancelled all remaining appointments. "The Nana," Sir Henry Lawrence cautioned Wheeler, "is a Mahratta and an adept at deceit." Wheeler would not credit such a slur. Had not the Nana furnished three hundred men when asked? Was he not enthralled by the new entrenchment, visiting it time and again to note where the artillery was sited? The Nana was "one of us."

That the Nana had quarrelled with the East India Company everyone knew. But many Indian princes experienced such troubles and saw their memorials to London rejected. Six years ago the last Peshwa or king of the Mahratta dynasty, Baji Rao, had died at Bithur; the British had long since dethroned him but paid him an annual pension of £8,000 until the day of his death. For years the Peshwa pressed successive Governors-General that when he died his pension should pass to his adopted son, Nana Sahib. Always the Government was adamant. The pension was "purely personal to himself." The Nana could inherit all private property; the pension would die with Baji Rao.

The fact was, Lord Dalhousie argued, the Peshwa had been paid £2,500,000. If he had not salted away some of this, that was his affair.

Though none at Cawnpore suspected it, Nana Sahib was crippled with debt. True, the Peshwa's death brought him a fine palace, thickly carpeted, glittering with chandeliers and tall mirrors. It brought him Government stock yielding an annual £8,000. He became sole owner of £100,000 worth of jewels, £80,000 of gold ornaments, £20,000 worth of silver, £30,000 of gold coins. But to settle the Peshwa's debts the Nana was at once forced to sell £20,000 worth of coins for he had inherited, too, 15,000 of the old man's pensioners; a few were still in service but most were too old and must be nourished in the sunset of their days. To convert family jewels and plate into cash was unthinkable—a Maharajah would lose face. Shortly before the mutiny, his monthly expenditure now double his income, he had sold out £70,000 worth of Government securities.

The Nana had many times pressed his case. Attorneys drew up memorials urging that an adopted son had the same rights as a natural-born son. He invested £50,000 in sending his aide, Azimullah Khan, to petition "John Company" in England. A slim handsome youngster who had perfected his English both as clerk and school-teacher, Azimullah Khan became notorious for his prowess in the boudoirs of London and Brighton, but he found the East India Company's directors of tougher fibre.

Not always could Azimullah keep his rancour against the British in check. "What," he asked one young lieutenant with whom he chatted near the entrenchment, "do you call that place you are making out on the plain?"

The youngster was at a loss. "I am sure I don't know."

"You should call it the Fort of Despair."

"No, no," the officer retorted, perhaps with more confidence than he felt, "we will call it the Fort of Victory."

Did this intelligence ever reach Wheeler? In any case there was no turning back. He had decided not to occupy the magazine, and to blow it up while the sepoys stood guard over it would have been to "show mistrust." Instead, three hundred of the Nana's men, commanded by the chief of his bodyguard, Tantia Topee, a slightly built thirty-year-old with a bold pugnacious face, now trained their guns on the magazine and the treasury, with its £100,000 prize.

Latter-day historians poured scorn on Wheeler's blind faith—yet the letter he wrote to Sir Henry Lawrence as late as 4th June proves that whatever faith he placed in Nana Sahib, he had none in his own defences.

Trust in any of the native troops is now out of the question . . . it is now said that the 1st Native Infantry is sworn to join and they now speak of its going off this night or the next morning doing all the mischief in their power first, this to include an attack on our positions . . .

Overriding all was his knowledge that Lieutenant-General Sir Patrick Grant, Commander-in-Chief, Madras Army, had been chosen to replace the late George Anson. Old jealousies spilled from his pen:

. . . I can but serve under him but it is a poor return for above fifty-two years of zealous service to be thus superseded. My name with the Native Army has alone preserved tranquillity thus up to the present time and the difficulties that I have had to contend with can only be known by myself . . . I have performed subaltern duty in going the rounds at midnight because I felt that I gave confidence . . . I write with a crushed spirit for I had no right to expect this treatment . . . placing me under the orders of a Regimental Lieut-Colonel my junior by more than fifteen years . . . I have had thanks ad nauseam but there it stops . . .

In these last moments he harboured no false hopes about their position:

Of course we can offer protection to nothing with our entrenchments . . .

Despite the old General's qualms, Amelia Horne and her

family clung to vain shreds of hope. A few days of sleeping on the verandah of the barracks had proved such acute discomfort that once they realised a few undemolished bungalows stood empty near the barracks they abandoned the entrenchment. Even Amelia's step-brothers and sisters, ranging from Florence, aged eight, to Herbert, aged three, gladly seized the sweeper's discarded twig brooms in an attempt to clean things up. Amelia's step-father sent a servant to prospect for chairs in their own bungalow. The man returned empty-handed; already an Indian had moved in and commandeered everything.

Their bungalow was shared with the families of two other merchants, Thomas Greenway and John Schorne and the Berrill brothers, Tom and Harry, both railway engineers. Yet outside the entrenchment they could cling to an illusion of home. At night, menfolk banded together in pickets keeping watch. Rumours reached them the sepoys were moving their families from the lines to the slums of Cawnpore city. To surrender to tranquillity was still irresistible. On the night of 4th June, for the first time since moving to the bungalows, all sank on to their pallets undressed.

At midnight they came wide awake, hearts beating painfully. The earth was shaking as if with thunder; gun limbers bumped and squealed over baked earth. Peering into darkness they could see nothing, but the import of the sounds was plain. The cavalry and artillery were leaving their lines. Stumbling over rutted ground in the darkness, hugging their clothing to them, Amelia Horne and her family fled in their night attire through the darkness to the grounds of St. John's Chapel nearby. There seemed no time now to reach the gate; barking shins, grazing fingers, they scrambled breathlessly over the wall. It was a short-lived refuge. Scarcely had they reached the chapel when the dull *crump* of the alarm gun sounded from the entrenchment: the signal all Europeans had prayed for twelve days past they would never hear.

Two days of eerie silence followed, broken at times by the distant cannonade of artillery. Within the entrenchment Amelia Horne and her family could brood only on dark rumour. In the north-western suburb of Nawabgunge where the treasury and magazine were sited, dark plumes of smoke sullied blue sky but the native officers remained within their lines so surely all was still well. Once, inexplicably, the battery of nine-pounders on the north-east face of the entrenchment, under Lieutenant St. George Ashe, sent a charge of grapeshot shrieking towards the lines of the 53rd Native Infantry. The grave truth remained cloaked in uncertainty; the 2nd Cavalry and the 1st Native Infantry, after an orgy of looting, were already roistering towards Delhi. The 56th Native Infantry, at first half-hearted, had followed suit. Now, by an inexcusable blunder, Wheeler, convinced that the 53rd Native Infantry were about to attack, had ordered the gunners to open fire on their lines. At this hour the sepoys were peaceably cooking their breakfasts. They fled now in anger and terror, converted within seconds to the rebel cause.

At dawn on 6th June, Amelia Horne awoke to a tumult of excitement; half-clad, clutching a strange assortment of pith helmets, handfuls of cheroots, and sporting guns, the native infantry officers were flooding into the entrenchment. To Captain Mowbray Thomson, a cheerful, red-bearded twenty-five-year-old of the 53rd Native Infantry, they seemed "like a band of seafarers who had taken to a raft to escape their burning ship." In silence these officers now listened while Sir Hugh Wheeler read out the text of a strangely formal message he had received from the Nana Sahib. The seeming treachery left him shaken and sick: "I am about to attack you."

Even a century later Nana Sahib's actions are something of a mystery. Why had he thought it necessary to warn the British—and why had he thrown his lot in with the mutineers? No valid evidence suggests that he was behind the Cawnpore mutiny yet two days after its onset he was the rebels' acknowledged leader. Later the British were to accept this explanation: at Nawabgunge, the site of the Treasury, a deputation of Indian officers, infantry and cavalry, entreated the Nana to lead them to Delhi.

"Maharajah," one officer assured him, "a kingdom awaits you if you join our cause, but death if you side with our enemies."

The Nana's alleged reply was: "What have I to do with the British? I am altogether yours."

This is hearsay evidence, though the mutineers did march six miles on to Kullianpore, first stage on the Delhi road. Now a controversy arose, prompted, it was said, by the Nana's aide, Azimullah Khan. What profit could there be in marching to Delhi where the noonday sun of Bahadur Shah would eclipse the Nana's evening star? Better to seize Cawnpore, next Lucknow, then sweep down the valley of the Ganges and conquer all southern India. Thus won over, the Nana spurred on with his aides to Kullianpore.

"Don't go to Delhi," he is said to have urged the rebels. "Stay here and your name will be greater. Kill all the English in Cawnpore first and I will give you each a golden bracelet and unlimited plunder." Eager knots of scarlet and French grey surged about him, as pliant as ripe wheat, and the Nana made the first of many promotions. Subadar Teeka Singh of the 2nd Cavalry became a general. Jemadar Durga Singh of the 53rd Native Infantry was now a colonel.

The Nana's bodyguard, Tantia Topee, told a different story. Both he and the Nana, he later affirmed, were imprisoned in the Treasury and guarded by sepoy sentries. Then they were marched willy-nilly towards Kullianpore where the Nana persuaded the sepoys to halt for the night. Next morning the rebels urged him, "Come to Delhi," but the Nana was unwilling. Then, said they, "Come with us to Cawnpore and fight there." Menaced by a strong guard of sepoys the Nana had no choice.

Was the Nana under the sepoys' coercion from then on—and did this lie behind his last message to an ally he could no longer sustain? We know only he marched at the rebels' head as the cavalcade swept back towards Cawnpore.

Within the entrenchment, the appalling nature of their plight now came home to Amelia Horne and a thousand others. They had seen the white puffs of artillery smoke drawing closer and closer; suddenly the wide sandy plain seemed alive with mounted men, yelling and curvetting. The Nana Sahib had made his choice; with Delhi and Lucknow beleaguered they would stand or fall alone.

Precisely at 10 a.m. the bugle blared "All hands to arms"; told off under officers into parties of twenty, the defenders sprinted for their posts. At this moment a round shot tore through the crest of the mud wall and went hurtling into the masonry barrack to smash an Indian footman's leg to jelly. Above the thunder of the explosion, the war-whoop of the mutineers, one fearful cry arose as from a lost soul: terror, like a tuning fork, had struck the chord among five hundred souls, underscoring the hopeless odds. For every fighting man who crouched at the sand-bagged parapets with five loaded muskets beside him, Wheeler's entrenchment held at least two non-combatants—invalids, women or children.

XIII. CAWNPORE

6th to 25th June

Dawn, 14th June, 1857. Implacably the sun rose above Cawnpore, molten in a blue indifferent sky. On this day the thermometer would touch 138 degrees; even in other years, granted the gift of shade, such heat had driven men to lock themselves in darkened rooms and blow out their brains. On this day five, perhaps six, people within Sir Hugh Wheeler's entrenchment would die of sunstroke. A band of steel seemed to encase their temples followed by a great drowsiness; they sank vomiting to their knees, faces blackening as they died. Today some muskets would split apart like fire-crackers, touched off by the sun. From the mud walls, men would see, across the arid sandy plain, a strange chimera of forest glades and blue sparkling water. Against their wills they would suck in the unbelievable, unbreathable smell of the entrenchment, like the contents of a thousand privies rotting beneath the sun. Small children pleading for a drink of water would be told to suck on a leather strap to quench their thirst. Water was an elixir to be cherished in tiny birdlike sips; night and day the well was under fire. Water, if the privates of the 32nd Foot were in a bargaining mood, might cost 10s. for a goatskin bag.

This day was Sunday, the sixth since the mutiny began, but no man could be spared from his post. There was no place where women and children could safely gather to worship. Instead, the station chaplain, the Rev. Edward Moncrieff, hastened from post to post while the men stood at arms; at such meetings, where one or more men would be saying his prayers for the last time, the prayer "In Time of War and Tumults" sprang readily to the lips:

King of all Kings and Governor of all things, whose power no creature is able to resist . . . save and deliver us, we humbly beseech Thee, from the hands of our enemies; abate their perils, assuage their malices and confound their devices that we being armed with Thy defence may be preserved evermore from all perils . . .

On this night, at 8 p.m., General Wheeler wrote on coarse white-brown native paper, a despairing letter to Lucknow: "We have been besieged since the sixth by the Nana Sahib, joined by the whole of the native troops, who broke out on the morning of the fourth. The enemy have two twenty-four and several other guns. We have only eight nine-pounders . . . our defence has been noble and wonderful, our loss heavy and cruel." Then the heart-cry was wrung from him: "We want aid, aid, aid!"

The Indian messenger brave enough to cover the fifty-three miles to Lucknow would be paid £100 to deliver this letter, which surgeons extracted from his ear. But no aid would come.

Despite the passionate arguments of his Financial Commissioner, Martin Gubbins, a vain embittered paranoiac, Sir Henry Lawrence remained obdurate. Only a few boats were available at Lucknow and it would have been hard, if not impossible, to collect them in one spot on the river. Since Nana Sahib held the Ganges shore, the task of getting men from Lucknow into Wheeler's entrenchment could only sacrifice Lawrence's troops in vain. When Gubbins proposed sending a relief force on elephants, Lawrence was moved to confide in Lord Canning: "He is perfectly insane in what he considers energetic manly measures . . . he thinks ill of all who will not cut about the country."

Even the fifty men of the 84th that Wheeler had rashly passed on to Lucknow would have made little difference now. Within their entrenchment, the defenders faced a near-insuperable task. On every side the rebels hemmed them in. The officers who worked the eight guns behind the frail earthworks were experienced men, yet their batteries were neither marked nor fortified. The shallow ditch, two feet deep, that girdled the mud walls had never been completed. By 11th June, they were ringed in by a horseshoe of hot steel; the non-stop fire of three mortars, two 24-pounders, three 18-pounders, two 12-pounders, two 9-pounders, one 6-pounder. Some of these guns were only 700 yards from the entrenchment and by 15th June seven complete batteries were keeping up a day and night fire. At peak periods, one man calculated, shells and round shot were howling into the entrenchment at the rate of 300 an hour.

Nor was this all. On the south-western front, three hundred and fifty yards from the entrenchment, lay seven partially-erected red-brick barracks, each almost seventy yards long. From the walls of these buildings, some forty feet high, and from nearby St. John's Chapel, almost twelve thousand rebels whipped them with volleys of musketry fire.

After the first day, the women cried only when anguish tore at them. They had learned the gift of silence. To Amelia Horne it seemed only the courage of the few sustained her in these days. She marvelled at the endurance of Lieutenant Henry Delafosse, who had charge of three 9-pounder guns at the south-east angle of the entrenchment. A gun-carriage in his battery took fire: loaded with powder, it would have exploded within minutes. Spying the flames the rebels turned all their guns on the spot but Delafosse, wriggling beneath the burning carriage, clawed with his bare hands at the splinters, smothering them with earth until the fire was out. Captain John Moore of the 32nd, a champion skater, demonstrated time and again the luck of the Irish. Wounded, his arm in a sling, Moore put himself at the head of fifty men and crept from the entrenchment by night to spike five of the enemy's guns. In a hand-to-hand encounter he killed his adversary with a blow from a sponge staff used to clean the gun-barrels. "He was absent only an hour," Amelia Horne recalled, "but oh! that hour was eternity."

Already the rebels held the northern half of the avenue of unfinished barracks; the three barracks commanding the entrenchment's south-western face must, the British knew, be held at all costs. Barrack No. 4, as the defenders called it, was held for three days and nights by twelve young railway engineers under M. C. Heberden. In the tiny fortress of Barrack No. 2, sixteen unwashed smoke-blackened men under the merry red-bearded Captain Mowbray Thomson, plied their rifles in grim silence, knowing they could not afford to miss.

For Amelia Horne the first eight days were the slow attrition that shook the foundation of her faith. Too young to summon up adult philosophy, she was too old to fall back on a child's puzzled acceptance of life as it came. She saw death lose the dignity of pall bearers and waxy wreaths: girls in dirty draggled muslin lay dead in untidy rows on the verandah, alongside sheeted officers. At dusk their bodies were dragged away by the legs, their heads drumming against stone steps, to be cast down a disused well two hundred yards outside the rampart. At least two hundred and fifty would know this fate.

Once Amelia saw a round shot shear off an officer's head; he was sitting on the verandah and he did not move when the shot struck him, only sat there, his hands relaxed at his sides, though the head had gone and the blood pumped like a freshet from between his shoulders, drenching those who ran to aid him. On many nights she awoke to find a private sharing the string-bed beside her. Both were too exhausted to know the response of flesh.

She told herself, This is true. The people, the stench, the noises, they will not fade away.

More than a thousand people, all of them making sounds. The thin stretching shrieks of women who writhed in labour; the squalling of children, frightened and fractious; a small girl's whimpering, embarrassed because she must perform all natural functions in her clothes and people were watching; obscene raving spouting from the Rev. W. H. Haycock, the missionary, going mad and stripping himself stark naked; the sentry's half-hourly shouts of "All's well"; the squeal of the well-tackle and the thud of the leather bucket, inviting a shower of red-hot grapeshot through the sultry night: shells making their terrible screaming sound far off into space; a snarled altercation over water; sleepy curses from a pallet; thick hacking sounds as men dismembered dead horses and pariah dogs, stuffing the bloody hunks into a camp kettle; the clatter of a mess-tin; the cries that their Calvary tore from men whose lower bowels dripped in shreds. The sound of Cawnpore.

They could imagine no lower depths: they would learn to plumb them. On the night of 13th June, a high hot breeze was blowing. Stretched out on quilts, the sick and wounded, together with the women and children of the soldiers' families, dozed fitfully within the thatched barracks, packed like the uncomplaining dead. Precisely at 5 p.m. a carcass or fire-ball of sulphur, tallow and rosin, fired from the battery of Riaz Ali, an invalid Subadar of Artillery, struck the northern corner; the thatch was all at once a blinding canopy of flame. Rafters canted to fall toppling like tall trees; squirming under refracted light, the sick screamed hoarsely in pain and fear; thatch parted in spasms of flame to loose a roaring rain of bricks upon the milling contorted silhouettes. Many toiled to drag children frantic with terror clear of the torrent of flames, all medical niceties forgotten. Here were invalids who must, the doctors decreed, lie still because their lives depended on it; the battle for survival now demanded they must be dragged forth by their feet, even their hair, high shorn-off screams drowned by bellowing flames, shouted unprintable oaths. Still forty were charred beyond recognition. All medical stores, save a small chest of drugs, two boxes of surgical kit, burned with them. For his ingenuity in rendering the thatched barracks untenable, Subadar Riaz Ali received a reward of £9 and an embroidered shawl.

This mishap marked the turning-point of Cawnpore. Already the entrenchment's four acres were a wilderness of honey-combed bricks, blackened ruins, beams crazily tilted.

Now the only shelter for the women and children were the trenches, eighteen inches deep, on the southern corner or in the dark suffocating warehouses that adjoined the quarter-guard. Beneath boxes, cots, crude awnings of canvas they lay fainting with heat and women who had never soiled their hands before soiled them now scooping shallow setts in the rocky ground because a baby's life depended on it.

Inflexibly, the walls of the charred barracks retained their heat; for five days this heat was so great no man or woman could venture within three feet for fear of losing his reason. Amelia Horne, "the spoilt and petted child of kind parents," struggling to come of age, to shoulder burdens beyond her understanding, knew the form this took; she had become suddenly shockingly conscious of the rupture of her mother's brain. Nine days earlier, Emma Cook, seven months pregnant, had been strong in comfort and reassurance, tucking all of them in each evening with a goodnight kiss, hearing their whispered prayers. Now compassion had fled from her eyes; at times they mirrored a sly idiocy, at other times they cried out in unbearable torment. These were the times when she lamented her own mother, whom Amelia had never known, calling stridently for a carriage to take her home, a jumble of railing and high crazy laughter, then the sly secretive look; she would outwit them all. Then incongruously, as the laughter died, Amelia heard a steady scraping sound from the barracks' cooling embers, the men of the 32nd, raking the ashes with bayonets, searching for cherished campaign medals. This was the fourteenth day.

A pound of parched grain each day, such as horses relished, choked down by sweet and fiery rum, was no diet for a young fastidious girl, yet hunger allowed no choice. Secretly, "as a miser would his gold," Amelia hoarded a porridge of rice and lentils for her little sisters; she could not bring herself to touch it, even to dole it out until the last. At first they had shared all good things that were to hand so that Captain Mowbray Thomson could not resist the humour of one private "trudging away from the main guard laden with a bottle of champagne, a tin of preserved herrings and a pot of jam for his mess allowance . . . another with salmon, rum and sweetmeats for his inheritance." Within a week these supplies ended; crouched at their parapets, punishing their bodies far harder than any machine, men made do on a gill of flour, a handful of split peas, served in tin pots. Within a week, the Captain of the Well, John Mackillop, a thirty-one-year-old civil servant who protested himself "no fighting man" lay dying, his conscience troubled because a woman still had need of water. Mackillop had hauled his buckets up hand over hand for a depth of sixty feet, for the machinery had been shot away. Thereafter water came irregularly, often polluted, always high-priced. One night it came to Amelia filmed with the blood of the dying; a round shot had landed close to the well, blowing away an ayah's legs. Amelia bit her lips and grew one year older; she must learn not to ask for water. This was the fifteenth day.

Often, for hours on end, the British guns grew silent; the defenders had learned the wisdom of conserving ammunition. In any case, they could do nothing save repel attacks; such light metal as the British had, availed little against the rebels' 24-pounders. In one week fifty-nine artillerymen had died at their posts; only volunteers served the guns now. The guns themselves were in pitiful shape: the howitzer knocked completely off its carriage, some with their sides buckled by shot, some without a muzzle. The bores of others were warped and grooved; canister could not be driven home. Without protest the women had yielded up silk, net and cotton stockings to fashion some of the strangest cartridges in the history of war; once the canisters were tapped, the stockings could be packed with shot. For gun waddings they used without scruple pages from the Old Testament. Grim urgency became the keynote. Lieutenant Henry Delafosse, vexed by a small rebel gun in Barrack No. 1, crammed his worn-out 9-pounder in final despair with a monster charge of three 6-pound shots and a stockingful of grape, all rammed tightly down. The gun shuddered but did not burst. The rebel gun was heard no more.

Across the entrenchment a reddish-brown dust that stank of plaster and saltpetre hung as thick as fog: red dust from shell-torn buildings lying open to the sky, brown dust stirred from the plains by a hot booming wind. On leprous patches of plaster still remaining, men scrawled broken messages in charcoal or pencil, as if to assure themselves a tenuous hold on immortality. In a kind of wonder the postmaster, J. W. Roach, catalogued his wounds: "4th June, wounded in the thigh . . . 6th June, ditto leg, bullet . . . all this and still alive," then signed his name. Another wrote, "This is worse than the siege of Jerusalem—My God, my God, when wilt Thou deliver us?" One man strove to efface the enormity of what he had seen by setting it down in black and white: "Here a round shot came and killed young Wheeler. His brains and hair are scattered on the wall."

This was the General's son, Godfrey; the shock of it broke the old man; he lay on a mattress, all pretence at command abandoned, the tears streaming down his cheeks. On 24th June he scribbled one last fervent appeal to Sir Henry Lawrence at Lucknow: "British spirit alone remains but it cannot last forever . . . we have no instruments, no medicine, provisions for ten days at farthest; and no possibility of getting any, as all communication with the town is cut off . . . we have been cruelly deserted and left to our fate . . .

"We had not above 220 soldiers of all arms at first; the casualties have been numerous. Railway gents and merchants have swollen our ranks to what they are—small as that is, they have done excellent service; but neither they nor I can last forever." Broken by seeming betrayal, he could no longer contain himself . . . "Surely we are not to die like rats in a cage?"

The entrenchment had become a charnel house: the pillars of Cawnpore society, men and women so often with Nana Sahib at summer race meetings died one by one like stricken cattle. Charles Hillersdon, the Collector, who had negotiated the alliance with the Nana, fell at his wife's feet, clutching the coils of his own entrails. Two days later Mrs. Hillersdon, whose rendering of Mendelssohn's *"Rondo Capriccioso"* had been the talk of the cantonment, died beneath a niagara of masonry. Major William Lindsay, blinded by shell splinters, lay in a sightless agony until death took both him and his grief-stricken wife. A child died choking in the blood of its ayah. M. C. Heberden, the railway engineer, lay face-down for a week drenched in icy sweat, his coccyx shattered by grapeshot. Spreadeagled on her back, a private's wife,

Mrs. White, lay with both arms broken, suckling a twin at each breast. Death had forgotten age or precedence, rank or status; the dark angels claimed them all.

At times Captain Mowbray Thomson would spring across from Barrack No. 2 for a brief chat with brother officers; one glance at the women and children and he was glad to return swiftly to the dangers of the front line. A man could die but once here, and cleanly; within the entrenchment you felt the death of the heart.

Yet the rebel cause was not prospering. On 23rd June, the anniversary of the battle Robert Clive had fought in the mango groves of Plassey to place all Bengal under British sway, the mutineers made one titanic attempt to breach Wheeler's walls; field-guns, pulled by horses and bullocks, were unlimbered within a few hundred yards of the ramparts. From the riding school four hundred yards north-east, the cavalry troopers kicked into a hand gallop, the horses' rumps bunched in unison, one thousand hoofs drumming and booming across hard baked sand. From east and west came dense scarlet swarms of infantry, led by skirmishers crouching behind rolling bales of cotton. Tensely the British held their fire; this extended run was winding the horses badly, their gallop slackening to a breathless lunge. Suddenly, sheets of artillery fire checked them like a wall; they foundered, bucking and plunging, trampling their screaming riders. Still the infantry did not falter; a hundred yards from the fort, led by a tall powerful sergeant-major of the 1st Native Infantry, they charged from behind the cotton bales. A musket-ball whirled him to the ground; canister tore the racing ranks asunder. With two hundred dead and wounded littering the plain, the rebels fell back. At dusk a party of sepoys returned unarmed. They saluted and in the soft light were given leave to take away their dead.

Three miles north-west of the entrenchment in the gardens of a tall mansion called Salvador House, the Nana Sahib, in a tent pitched amongst silver-barked pipal trees, heard the news in grim silence. It seemed plain now that the entrenchment would never be carried by storm; each section of the rebel force had been too soundly beaten. Rumour girdled the defences with a minefield which would blast any besieger to eternity; Indian officers had debated a plan to stampede two hundred asses in an effort to explode it but the scheme had petered out. The Nana knew that a crisis point had come. Not far from his tent, beneath a grove of mango trees, the armed sepoys of his guard lolled murmuring in breathless heat; the taste of freedom was sour and their voices showed it. Close by, near the bamboo stockade which held twenty-five Indian prisoners, mostly servants who had quit the entrenchment, an old man wearing spectacles squatted on a dirty carpet taking depositions.

Name? Father's name? Caste? Occupation? Place of residence? What do you know of the entrenchment? How many fighting men are still alive? What is their store of provisions?

Always the answers were vague, contradictory; they did not know or were afraid to speak. Yet if no answer could be found the rebels' cause seemed doomed to failure. Most sepoys, resenting the defeats, spent more time in the toddy-shops than the batteries. Already bitter strife was evident between the Hindu and Moslem factions. Even Teeka Singh, whom the Nana had promoted General of the Force, had been summarily arrested, confined to his tent by insolent Moslem troopers who accused him of amassing private treasure. The Nana could do nothing to save him. His chief task was to save something from the wreckage.

How real was Nana Sahib's authority? Many local officials took their orders direct from him; while Waris Ali, the treasury keeper, collected his taxes, the local police chief, Shah Ali, worked in a vain attempt to stamp out mob violence. From the verandah of Duncan's Hotel, shielded from the sun by a red umbrella, a court made up of the Nana's brother, Baba Rao, a dark middle-aged man, and Azimullah Khan meted out summary justice. A Moslem trooper guilty of robbing a merchant was sentenced first to fifty lashes, next to be seated backwards on a donkey and drummed by tom-toms through the bazaar, lastly to three months in irons. For lesser crimes men were beaten insensible with shoes. The Nana wanted order in his city.

Many of his army told of similar measures. Jemadar Durga Misra, of the 56th Native Infantry, always recalled the Nana's first question when he reported himself, "Are your men in hand?" When the jemadar replied: "Not on the march, but they may be here," Nana Sahib was final. "If they don't obey orders here, I'll turn them out." The jemadar noted a steady stream of supplies—bullocks, horses, telegraph wire—paraded for the Nana's inspection. "His orders," Misra summed up, "were supreme".

All evidence suggests Nana Sahib did his utmost to whip the insurgents into a streamlined fighting unit. No sepoy need have money worries, for all had been paid for two months in advance. Each regiment was placed under a colonel with an adjutant to oversee munitions and stores, hold regular kit inspections, check the serviceability of muskets, notify men absent without leave. Monthly sick rosters must be rendered; every man would be paid a pension, to survive him for one generation. Men incapacitated by wounds were eligible for life pensions. Those growing old in his service would "receive pensions according to custom."

But few would grow old in the Nana's service, for the final arbiter was the mob. At first they had killed for the love of killing but mundane slaughter was no longer enough: only cruelties that outraged the living flesh would satisfy them. Natives who had crept from the entrenchment as spies were turned loose with hands, noses and ears severed, the bloody stumps staunched with boiling oil. A captured officer was crucified on the ground then served the same way, mounted troopers thundering past like Cossacks, sabres swooping until he was literally hewn to pieces. A boat-load of captured fugitives who had left Fatehgarh Fort on 3rd June were bound with ropes and marched to Cawn-pore "like French criminals in chain-gangs." When the ele-phants set to trample them lifted them gently aside with their trunks, troopers of the 2nd Cavalry advanced in a packed dangerous line with drawn sabres. "This is the Gov-ernor of Madras," they mocked the rolling dying shapes. "And this the Governor of Bombay." Memories of past servi-tude rankled: a man on the threshold of death was taunted, "How would you like your mutton chop and bread and butter now?"

Thus Nana Sahib saw that if the rebels could not storm the entrenchment, somehow the British must be persuaded to come forth before anarchy toppled him from his pinnacle. This conclusion he reached on the afternoon of the eighteenth day.

On the nineteenth day, a lone woman came in sight of the ramparts toiling painfully across the scarred earth. Aloft she held a white handkerchief, betokening a flag of truce.

XIV. CALCUTTA AND ALLAHABAD

17th June to 7th July

Eight days earlier, at dusk on 17th June, Lord Canning had waited anxiously on the landing-stage below the whitewashed barracks and green ramparts of Fort William, Calcutta. Despite the season, the Governor-General sweated profusely in a black frock coat and white silk hat for this was a momentous occasion. Since the acting Commander-in-Chief, Sir Patrick Grant, was unwilling to go campaigning without an entire regiment to guard his papers, Lord Canning had taken two radical decisions: a third moveable column would be formed to hasten the relief of Cawnpore and Lucknow and a brand new commander appointed to lead it.

In the greying light the East India Company steamer *Fire Queen,* outward bound from Madras, edged slowly towards the landing-stage, the pilot in tall hat and lavender kid gloves, a dark silhouette on the poop. Already Canning could see Sir Patrick's tall, soldierly figure loom from the saloon deck. Then as the Governor-General mounted the gangway, he saw beside Grant a prim erect officer, who carried his five foot five inches—"and five-sixteenths," he would add meticulously—like a ramrod, sporting a snow-white beard, moustache and whiskers. Sir Patrick's introduction had a fine theatrical ring: "My Lord, I have brought you the man!"

The man he had brought was Brigadier Henry Havelock, who at sixty-two had never held an independent command in his life. Baulked of promotion by poverty and lack of influence, Havelock was forty-three before reaching even captain's rank though already something of a legend in cantonment life: a strange, stiff, wiry little man who scorned balls and gaiety, veteran of more than a score of battles, whose whole life was military lore. Though once on the staff at Cawnpore, few officers of that station would have looked first to him in time of trouble. The brigadier was known primarily for his Baptist faith and his rigid principles; the schoolboy who had begged removal from one school because the headmaster was too lax had evolved naturally into the company-commander whose troops were styled "Havelock's Saints"—men never drunk, always ready for battle. Insistent on wearing his sword and a dozen campaign medals at the dinner table, he was normally so ill-at-ease that society hostesses gave him a wide berth. Only recently a saucy army wife had chaffed him, "It's no use asking you to dinner, Colonel Havelock, as you do not like champagne; but if you will come and take a cold bath with me some morning I shall be delighted."

Now Havelock awaited his finest hour, and those with perception to see beyond the martinet exterior could guess that he would seize the long-delayed chance with both hands. The shrewd Sir Henry Lawrence, meeting him once for two brief hours, had summed him up: "As good a soldier as a man, the best of both perhaps."

In the shuttered study at Government House, where the wine-coloured despatch boxes still towered in piles on every chair, Havelock listened while Canning, quiet, incisive, outlined the situation. The Governor-General's first urgent call for European troops had not gone unheeded; troops were arriving, though all too slowly. A wing of the Madras European Fusiliers' Regiment, many of them hard-drinking gentleman-rankers, arriving in Calcutta on 24th May had already posted up country to Allahabad. The 78th Highlanders and Her Majesty's 64th Foot, both regiments Havelock had known in Persia, had followed suit. Though this force had restored order in the eighty miles between Allahabad and Benares, tides of war still washed the Ganges valley where eight thousand rebels were on the march.

In whole tracts of the countryside, the situation was now so desperate, martial law had been proclaimed: a man could be hanged for so much as stealing a spoon. Yet Canning maintained his impassive calm, though the news grew daily worse; a slave to the despatch boxes, he often toiled into the small hours now, Lady Canning taking over when exhausted secretaries gave up. Outside Government House, sepoys from disbanded regiments openly hawked their scarlet coats in the gutters. Still Canning rode out with a sepoy escort, refusing a European guard.

As Havelock's high-pitched voice posed telling questions, the bare scaffolding of facts became plain. At best he could expect to operate with four European regiments, roughly two thousand eight hundred British infantry. Of these some were at Allahabad, some about to leave Calcutta, the rest would follow as soon as might be. This force, he knew, would be barely adequate—even if all of it arrived in time. His mind shrewdly sifting details, Havelock now stated his prime needs. Since the mutineers had slaughtered many transport animals at Allahabad, every draught animal on the Grand Trunk Road must be swiftly made available or the moveable column's mercy errand might be gravely imperilled. Intelligence, too, would be vital; he wanted freedom to pay spies lavishly. Readily Canning granted these requests.

From his room in the United Services Club, Havelock, writing to his wife Hannah, summed up his mission with moving simplicity: "The object (of this important command) is to relieve Cawnpore, where Sir Hugh Wheeler is threatened, and support Lucknow, where Sir Henry Lawrence is somewhat pressed. May God give me wisdom and strength to fulfil the expectations of Government and restore tranquillity . . ."

It was a task to tax a superman—and only a man of Havelock's faith, wont to pray two hours each morning even before marching at 6 a.m., would have held out much hope. On 25th June—the very day the Cawnpore defenders saw the unknown woman approaching their ramparts— the prospect facing him as he left Calcutta for Allahabad was a daunting one. Before any relief could reach Lucknow he must fight his way through almost six hundred miles of hostile country in the year's worst season, battling blinding sun and monsoon rain, hampered by lack of horses, guns and gunners. Once again a commander in the field was to find himself hamstrung by "John Company's" parsimony for in all India only two hundred and seventy-three miles of rail had been laid down. The railway carriage in which Havelock and his staff were packed would carry them only to Rani-gunge, one hundred and twenty-three miles north of Calcutta.

What did this mean? Quietly debating the problem with his staff officers—among them his twenty-seven-year-old son Harry, a dark hot-tempered youngster—Havelock saw that chances of reinforcements journeying up country in time were slim indeed. Whether officers or privates, all would travel the same way: in jolting springless four-wheeled wagons hauled by two bullocks, labouring at a snail's pace of two miles an hour. These were nightmare journeys. Carts fell behind and must be waited for; bullocks grew restive and must be unyoked; wheels flew to pieces. White floury dust, inches deep, billowed up to coat the travellers' lips and eyelids.

True, officers enjoyed more comfort, riding only two to a wagon; troops were packed in ten at a time with five more marching behind, changing places every four hours. But even the jaded bullocks must be changed every ten miles; thirty miles a day was the utmost men could travel thus. Only enough carts were in service to carry a hundred men daily; the Madras Fusiliers had taken ten days to cover the four hundred and twenty miles from Calcutta to Benares. The few river steamers available, old tubs with decks only four feet above the water's surface, took sixteen days for the same journey, for even when monsoon rains had not swollen the turbid river, the craft, battling a twelve-knot current, were lucky to cover twenty miles a day.

Not until 7 a.m. on 30th June did Havelock himself clatter into the great red fort beside the river at Allahabad. From Colonel James George Neill, commanding the Madras Fusiliers, a man destined to become his implacable foe, Havelock heard the news to date. A cruel and able Scot, with a supercilious patrician face, Neill was just then the hero of the Calcutta clubs. Reaching Calcutta he had placed the station-master under armed guard when the man objected that the Fusiliers were delaying the grain. A Calcutta jeweller, who besought silver rather than bank-notes in these troubled times, was promised the same fate for treason. "I am sure if I deserve all the praise I get it ought to do something for me," Neill exulted in his diary.

All Neill's actions were bold, violent, unstable. To restore order in Allahabad and Benares he embarked on a reign of terror that drove every villager within miles into hiding; with this factor Havelock must contend while striving to requisition transport animals. To reach these cities at speed Neill had marched his men seventy miles in three days though every fourth man was down with sunstroke and Neill himself kept alive on champagne, his men dashing buckets of water over his head and chest. When his commissariat officer raised difficulties over provisions, Neill at once threatened to hang him. Bitterly jealous that Havelock commanded the moveable column, he was unsparing in his efforts to harm him behind his back.

But the ardent little brigadier, more than a match for Neill, was pushing ahead with his plans. That very afternoon a force of four hundred Madras Fusiliers, three hundred Sikhs, a detachment of irregular cavalry and two small guns was to press towards Cawnpore, one hundred and twenty-eight miles north-west, under Major Sydenham Renaud. Another Madras Fusiliers officer, Lieutenant John Spurgin, was to take the one river steamer available and move up the Ganges in support. Meanwhile, though carts and animals were sadly lacking, Havelock busied himself briefing spies, ordering thin linen clothing for European troops, inspecting the fort's defences. This same night an urgent letter arrived from Sir Henry Lawrence at Lucknow: "You . . . will easily beat everything at Cawnpore *as long as Wheeler holds his ground; but if he* is destroyed your game will be difficult . . . it is . . . *most important* that your detachment should not lose an hour."

It was plain that Havelock must march without extra reinforcements, but still he would not budge without carts for the commissariat; a seasoned campaigner, no men of his should die of starvation before ever reaching Cawnpore. Too often, also, the baggage of each corps could not be easily identified when long marches ended. He wanted coloured flags for each one: light blue for the Madras Fusiliers, red for the 64th, tartan or green for the 78th Highlanders, white for the artillery. Within the walls of the fort, officers and men chafed irritably. What kind of commander was this, who trifled with finicking details when Cawnpore was besieged? "Havelock is not . . . a man for these times," grumbled one officer, "he already begins to calculate what would be the best measures for us to pursue under further reverses."

Yet now came disquieting news. A young subaltern of Neill's force, William Tate Groom, was first to learn it, at 2 a.m. on 3rd July. On duty at the main guard of the fort, he had seen the gate opened to an officer he did not know, haggard and wayworn, slumped on a lathered horse. Blurting the incredible intelligence his voice faltered: Cawnpore had fallen. Not one European within Wheeler's entrenchment had been left alive. So saying he galloped hard for Havelock's tent. Shortly, across the parade ground, Lieutenant Groom saw the firefly flicker of lights. Through darkness he heard the boots of hurrying men.

Was there a germ of truth in this? At Allahabad no man save Havelock could be sure. This first message had come from Major Renaud, forty miles up country, but two days later his second message cancelled out the first: the Nana Sahib having withdrawn his men, Sir Hugh Wheeler had quit the entrenchments, hoisted the Union Jack in the bazaars and now held all Cawnpore. "I think *this* story is more likely than the horrible account brought in two days ago," wrote young Lieutenant Groom to his wife, for this was what he wanted to believe. Equally sceptical was Colonel James Neill. "I don't believe this," he scrawled in his diary of the first message, "but General Havelock does and his staff also have lost nerve."

Havelock, however, had no such illusions; the two Indian spies who had brought the news to Renaud had reached Allahabad. Pressing home question after question, Havelock next bade his staff to do the same. That night he telegraphed Lord Canning: "If the report be correct, which there is too much reason to believe, we have lost Cawnpore . . . my duty is therefore to endeavour to retake [it] . . ."

At 3.30 p.m. on 7th July, though he had twelve hundred British troops at most, Havelock knew the time had come.

In a general's undress blue frock coat, a forage cap with a large white curtain draping his neck, drab-coloured water-proof leggings buttoned to the instep, the small prim figure rode out on to the parade-ground of Allahabad Fort. A disciple of Napoleon, his high-pitched voice now rang out in a brief Napoleonic oration: "Soldiers! There is work before us. We are bound on an expedition whose object is to . . . avenge the fate of British men and women . . . we have a common aspiration which knits us together as one man . . . I know the stuff you are made of; I know you will give me no cause to waver in the implicit confidence I have in you . . ." From the ranks there now burst a wild storm of cheering.

Many hazards lay ahead for the skies were angry; at 4 p.m., as the force moved off in column on route, the band of the Madras Fusiliers vying against the wild skirling of five Highland pipers, the sun swam from sight behind indigo clouds. Five hundred yards ahead rode all the volunteer cavalry Havelock could muster, twenty planters, unemployed officers, and shopkeepers, under Captain Lousada Barrow; behind straggled a ragged cavalcade of infantry, elephants loaded with tents and baggage, stately supercilious strings of camels with rope muzzles, milling flocks of sheep destined for slaughter, covered stretchers each one borne by four bearers, buffaloes slowed to a slug's pace by creaking tumbrils of ammunition. Thunder cannoned, drowning the unearthly clamour of an army on the march; a blue-white vein of lightning picked out with clear exactness the white linen hip-length jackets of the 84th, the red frizzy doublets of the 78th, who could obtain no summer issue, the sky-blue cap covers of the Fusiliers, known always as "Neill's Blue-Caps." A quarter of a mile on white lances of water were hurled from the sky; the brown earth hissed and seethed beneath them as they struggled on.

Blinding flurries of rain blotted out all visibility as Havelock, leading the smallest force that ever set out to save an empire from anarchy, moved north from Allahabad.

XV. CAWNPORE

25th to 27th June

At Cawnpore it had seemed at first that deliverance was at hand—from the very moment on 25th June when the lone woman approached their ramparts, a white flag of truce held aloft. As she came closer, Amelia Horne saw plainly that this was Mrs. Henry Jacobi, Eurasian wife of a watchmaker, who knew her family well. Barefoot, without either shoes or stockings, she carried a child at her breast. As the survivors lifted her half-fainting over the low wall, they saw that she clutched tightly to an envelope. It was inscribed with strange punctilio: "To the Subjects of Her Most Gracious Majesty, Queen Victoria."

Here a strange confusion arises. Captain Mowbray Thomson, the first to aid her, swore the messenger was Mrs. Edward Greenway, wife of a wealthy Cawnpore merchant. But Amelia Horne recalled vividly her conversation with Mrs. Jacobi; though she and others had implored her to stay, the woman had replied in anguish that she could not. For sixteen days she had been held in captivity in the Salvador House, close to the Nana's tent. The rebels still held her children as hostages. Now she awaited General Wheeler's decision with half-hysterical impatience. If the terms were not accepted her children would pay with their lives.

This discrepancy aside, the Nana's terms were undisputed. Along with Mowbray Thomson, Captain John Moore and Captain Francis Whiting, Sir Hugh Wheeler now read this message:

All those who are in no way connected with the acts of Lord Dalhousie and are willing to lay down their arms, shall receive a safe passage to Allahabad.

Though it was unsigned the officers had no difficulty in recognising the handwriting of Azimullah Khan.

Now a bitter argument arose. Though Wheeler was fast failing, he at first rejected all idea of making terms with Nana Sahib. Surely relief from Calcutta must soon come? Angrily Captain John Moore disagreed. There were but three days' rations left and already the plight of the women and children tore at the hardest heart. Within days the rains would break and what shelter would there be for them then? To some it seemed that Wheeler was too tired to think. Wearily he ordered Moore to do whatever seemed best.

All day the guns were silent; like a vast mattress heat and silence pressed down on the entrenchment. At dusk the woman returned to the Salvador House to plead that Wheeler was still in conference. At his picket in Barrack No. 2, Captain Mowbray Thomson waited, listening to silence. Suddenly Captain Moore loomed from the darkness. "We are about to treat with the enemy," he breathed.

Peering through darkness Thomson saw now that Azimullah Khan had appeared together with Jwala Pershad, brigadier of the Nana's cavalry, and a guard of troopers. Watching, he saw Captains Moore and Whiting, accompanied by the postmaster, J. W. Roach, leave the entrenchment and cover the two hundred yards to where the Indians waited. When Azimullah greeted them in English, the troopers broke into angry protest. Negotiations would be conducted in Hindi or not at all.

At first the British terms seemed foolproof. They would surrender the barracks but they wanted free exit under arms, with sixty rounds of ammunition per man. They wanted carriages to convey their wounded and women and children. Boats with provision of flour must be moored at the riverside. "We will give you sheep and goats also," was Azimullah's generous offer.

These proposals, set down in writing, were returned by Azimullah Khan to the Nana. Then came the bombshell. At late afternoon a trooper returned. The Nana Sahib agreed to all conditions. And the entrenchment must be vacated that very night.

Stung by this cavalier treatment, Wheeler, pressed by Captain Moore, rejected the treaty. They could not move five hundred people from the entrenchment before dawn at the earliest. When the trooper next returned, Captains Francis Whiting and Mowbray Thomson went resolutely to meet him. The man was sullen; the Nana would not change his mind. Their guns were riven metal, their provisions coolies' fare. If they did not evacuate the rebel guns would break silence to annihilate them all. Whiting showed a flash of temper. For three weeks the Nana's soldiers had tried to carry the entrenchments—let them try again now. "If pushed to the last extremity," Whiting blazed, "we have powder enough in the magazine to blow both armies into the Ganges."

Half an hour passed; the trooper came back. The Nana had sympathy with their problems. Departure might be delayed until dawn.

Men came and went on strange errands, grave, tight-lipped. A committee of three, including young Lieutenant Henry Delafosse, had ridden with a guard of troopers to inspect the boats at the riverside and what they had seen angered them. Forty large up-country boats had been provided, their sterns high above the bow, ninety feet long by twelve across the thwarts, manned by crews of nine. In the evening light they looked, with their heavy thatched roofs, like floating hayricks. But as yet not all the boats were roofed, most were unvictualled, their decks bare. Later, the city magistrate, Hoolass Singh, testified he had been hard put to it to find craft at all; perhaps the boat-owners were eager to see the colour of the Nana's money. As Delafosse and the others returned to the entrenchment, four hundred coolies were set to work to re-roof the boats before dawn.

Women that night asked Captain Mowbray Thomson, "Do you think it will be all right tomorrow?" "Will they *really* let us go down to Allahabad in safety?" said others dubiously. It seemed that only the old and middle-aged snatched at straws. They gulped down whole pannikins of mortar-clouded water from the well, they ate greedily of chupattis and lentil stew. Tomorrow they would live again. The young hugged disillusion as a newfound friend. The soldiers of the 32nd Foot found drumsticks and an empty cask; the sticks rattled, a fife fluted; a private capered into a jig. This was to amuse the children. Filthy, as skinny as spiders, the children watched with grave politeness. They had come of age in three weeks, but perhaps this amused the adults.

Yet the British officers were reassuring and the officers would surely know? Jwala Pershad himself and two aides were spending the night within the entrenchment as an earnest of the Nana's good faith. These were not native infantry officers but men of Nana Sahib's own bodyguard, long in service at the Palace of Bithur. Jwala Pershad had even sought out General Wheeler to express his sorrow at the turn events had taken. It was a shocking thing, he said, that Sir Hugh, commander of sepoy regiments these long years, should find their arms turned against him. So why—if all was not well?

At sunset the shattered British guns were formally made over to Nana Sahib. All night a company of his artillery would stand guard over them. Amelia Horne lay uneasily, courting sleep, conscious of the broken whimpering of small stepbrothers and sisters, jarred by her mother's sudden railing from the darkness. She felt the pangs of a curious presage. A young Eurasian girl can be quick to sense slights; the sepoys who had entered the entrenchment seemed too watchful, too conscious of power. Captain Mowbray Thomson, drifting to sleep with bricks piled as a pillow, was more fatalistic. Wet glutted sounds came from beyond the walls; in time of truce the birds and beasts of prey could do their work. The jackals and the vultures, Thomson thought, who has profited from this but them?

The entrenchment came awake early at dawn on 27th June. Through broken brickwork, under harsh white light, people bent on small private errands. From hiding places in the ruins they dug iron boxes of plate and silver. Turquoises, silver spoons, gold sovereigns, slid secretively into pocket and fold of dresses. Others hugged Bibles, locks of hair, notes scribbled on the fly-leaves of orderly books; the able-bodied, like Mowbray Thomson, stuffed hats and pockets with ball cartridges "till they were walking magazines." Amelia Horne watched it all with misery darkening her soul: she and her family had salvaged their lives, no more. Their tin boxes had long been taken to strengthen the barricades; round shot and grape had pounded them like a blacksmith's hammer. Only the bodice of her dress remained; the frilled skirt, so fash-

ionable that year, was now bloody bandages round the heads
of the wounded. The old passed before her eyes, hobbling on
skeletal limbs, babbling or staring, children drooling, their
eyes grown imbecile, men and women without shoes, haggard, crusted with dried excrement. Why should there be a
strange reluctance to leave this place? Subalterns stood silent
at broken loopholes, where they had fought till their shoulders were blue, rifles clogged with lead. Beyond lay the
undiscovered country.

Across the sandy plain a cavalcade now wound into view:
sixteen elephants, foreheads painted in gaudy patterns, tusks
adorned with brass rings, followed by a swaying phalanx of
eighty palanquins. Thus more than two hundred of the sick
and wounded would be conveyed to the riverside, under an
advance guard headed by Captain Moore.

As the sepoys thronged into the entrenchment, one of them,
approaching Captain George Kempland, who was armed, demanded, "Give me that musket." "You shall have its contents, if you please, but not the gun," was Kempland's cool
reply.

"This," wrote Mowbray Thomson later, "was the only . . .
interruption to our departure." But Amelia Horne saw yet
another; into one barracks where no officers were present the
sepoys burst to wrench bundles and jewelry away from the
terrified women. At this moment, undeterred by the sepoys'
muskets, Captain John Moore burst upon the scene. "Your
triumph will be short," he told them fiercely, "and each man
will pay dearly for his deeds." A snarl of foul abuse "that
made the ears of all tingle" volleyed back. One of the sepoys,
gathering saliva, spat deliberately in Moore's face. The
thought flashed through Amelia Horne's mind: We are walking into a trap.

Outside, Mowbray Thomson and others worked to load the
wounded on to palanquins. Of these many should have lain
still for months or should never have moved again. Aloft, on
the garishly-painted elephants, the mahouts stared down
with eyes empty of mercy; they would not use their irontipped goads to make the elephants "bite" or slump to their
knees. Those who rode did so only by grasping the beast's
tail like a bell-rope, and hauling themselves up.

The first detachment moved off. It was now 7 a.m.

From the entrenchment to the stretch of riverside called Sati Chaora Ghat, or landing place, was a full mile. At the head of the long column strode Moore and the men of the 33nd. Behind them a throng of loin-clothed bearers groaned under the weight of palanquins, sliding panels open to show the wounded lying listless, heads and limbs swathed tight in soiled bandages. Bullock-carts jolted and creaked over land now lion-coloured beneath brassy sun. Elephants padded ponderously in their rear, followed by all who could still walk, muskets sloped, revolvers in belts. They wore no facings and kept no martial pace; they marched mutely in dirty flannel and draggled nankeen. Their thoughts marched with the dead.

Three hundred yards from the river, the main road spans a wide gorge. Then, as now, the gorge was dry before the rains, with rocks and brown soil steeped sharply above the barren funnel of the watercourse, fringed by feathery neem trees and the twisted silver trunks of pipals. It is a valley where the old trees throw long shadows, approached across a small white-painted bridge. On that far-away morning the meaning of this terrain escaped the survivors. Once at the river they clustered on dusty open ground one hundred and fifty yards long by a hundred deep. To the rear is the high ground, dotted with prickly pear; ahead lies the Ganges. On a mound to the left lies a small white temple; to the right the ruined village of Sati Chaora. From this temple, steps run sheer to the coffee-coloured Ganges water. Without wading no man can command a view either up or down river. From this point there is no going back. They were committed.

Among the officers, few saw cause for alarm. Captain Mowbray Thomson chatted with some of his sepoys as informally as at a party in the lines. Had it not been for lack of food, he told them, they would have held out to the last man. Cordially the sepoys enquired after Surgeon Nathaniel Collyer and Captain John Reynolds; tears sprang to their eyes on hearing they had died during the siege. The 53rd, they said, had lost almost a thousand men. "Are we to go to Allahabad without molestation?" Thomson asked. Warmly the sepoys assented. Memories of old camaraderie stirred.

Major Edward Vibart, 2nd Cavalry, was escorted by his former troopers, who insisted on piling his family's property into a bullock cart. General Sir Hugh Wheeler, anxious to make no fuss, rode in a palanquin, consigning his wife and daughters to the elephant with the state howdah the Nana had sent for his personal use.

It seemed the embarkation could never end. No planks were provided to serve as gangways and all, wounded, women and children were hoisted or were wading knee-deep through muddy water to board the boats. The Hindu boatmen and bearers stood by, saying nothing, offering no help. By 8.30 a.m., the boats were over-crowded with freight, flat down on the sandbanks, two feet of water rippling about them. Beyond, the river stretched four hundred yards to the mud flats of the Lucknow shore, dazzling now in the white light of morning. In tall trees overhanging the water, palm squirrels with bottle-brush tails scuttled with bright eyes.

Aboard the boats, the heat was torrid. Each boat was designed to ferry four persons at most but now ten or more were packed aboard each, shutting their ears to the taunting that came from the shore. Guarding her little step-sister Florence, whose broken leg was crudely splinted, Amelia Horne squatted on the baking foredeck with two grimy privates of the 32nd Foot. Beneath the thatched awning her stepfather, John Hampden Cook, was jammed in with four of her step-brothers and sisters. In the confusion her mother had been carried aboard another boat.

Three hundred yards west, sepoys now formed a double line beside the white-painted wooden bridge, denying access to the river. Confronted by levelled muskets, scores of curious bystanders fell back. The sepoys were inflexible: none could approach the landing place while embarkation proceeded.

On the river bank, up to this moment, there had been little sign of the Nana's army.

One of the few sepoys idling there told another, "They know not what is before them. Now let them repent of their misdeeds and ask pardon of God."

The time was 9 a.m. From the stony slopes of the gorge there now ricocheted the shrill battle cry of a bugle. At once, as if on cue, the crews of each boat, coxswain and eight oarsmen, dived overboard, close to four hundred men thrashing like lemmings for the shore.

Without hesitation Mowbray Thomson and his brother officers opened fire. Tiny fountains of brown water leapt about the heads of the swimmers.

From the bank, sixteen mounted troopers of the 2nd Cavalry, carbines levelled, sent an answering fire blasting back at them.

Startled, a flock of yellow-beaked mynah birds rose raucously from overhanging branches, taking wing.

From down-river and from the high tawny reeds on the Lucknow shore, the withering blast of five cannon swept the tight-packed straw-roofed boats.

A large, a very large, rebel force had been waiting.

Through blazing carcasses and glowing balls of charcoal secreted by the boatmen, the thatch of boat after boat was taking fire. Panic-stricken, scores piled headlong into the muddy water.

A round shot no bigger than an orange burst on the foredeck of Amelia Horne's boat, killing one soldier outright. The other sagged forward, modesty forgotten, fumbling at the blood that soaked his fly.

Close to the river's edge, General Sir Hugh Wheeler was beseeching his palanquin bearers, "Carry me a little farther towards the boat." A trooper said roughly, "No, get out here." A sabre struck him face forward into the water.

Crawling beneath overhanging prows, women waded up to their chins along the river's shelving bottom, seeking shelter from bullets that pattered like hail on the water.

Sobbing with exhaustion, men braced their shoulders against the boats' planking, struggling to launch them into mid-current. The keels of all but three stuck fast in soft silting sand.

Spurring their Arabs, the cavalry troopers came plunging down the sheer banks, their horses' hooves churning the water to coffee-coloured froth.

Sunlight dazzled like a flash of heliographs as a score of sabres rose and fell rhythmically.

Crouched in terror, Amelia Horne saw John Kirkpatrick, the trader, wallowing to his waist, throw up both arms to protect his face. Sabres fell like twin guillotines, chopping the arms from the trunk.

An hour later he was still alive bobbing helplessly like jetsam in the shallows.

A captain of Native Infantry, Athill Turner, recalled too late inspecting the boats the previous evening. Sepoys standing by had used the word *"kuttle."* Translated this means "massacre."

Farther up the shore, a boat-builder named Dabi Din swiftly reckoned up his compensation fees; forty boats would cost the rebels upwards of £400 and the boat crews between them must share a further £50.

Smoke from the burning thatch of these boats now furled in a black and acrid banner across the water.

A child screamed, "Oh, why are they firing upon us? . . . Didn't they promise to leave off?"

Crackle of burning thatch was swallowed by the cries of the dying, the frantic trumpeting of elephants, the crash of musketry. Crazed horses reared and plunged, screaming like terrified women as bullets ploughed home.

Sepoy Govind Singh, who had fought alongside the British in the entrenchment, was dragged clear. His world was turned to blood beneath pounding musket butts.

A colonel's daughter beseeched a sepoy with fixed bayonet, "My father was always kind to sepoys." The man had scarcely turned away when a villager dashed her brains out with a club.

Outside his tent in the compound of the Salvador House, the Nana Sahib rose suddenly from a chair, pacing to and fro. He did not speak; he seemed to be listening for something. The pacing never ceased.

Curtained by reeds on the Lucknow shore, a sixty-seven-year-old subadar, Bhondu Singh, mechanically corrected his gun crew's aim, fingering what he believed to be a personal letter from Nana Sahib: "We have sworn to kill the Europeans. You are desired to fire on them from your side of the river . . ."

If the Nana was responsible for this massacre—and later he was to aver passionately that the rebels had gone far beyond his control—he at all events now sent word that the slaughter of women and children must stop.

Before this happened time would elapse. On Amelia Horne's boat sepoys swarming aboard for plunder trampled her two-year-old step-sister Mary to death beneath brass-buckled sandals.

From down-river, from behind the fisherman's temple and the ruined village of Sati Chaora, solid sheets of musketry fire erupted from sepoys in hiding.

Floundering frantically to force a boat from a sand-bar, Captain John Moore fell with a bullet in his heart.

Casting his mother's portrait and a medal of his father's into the Ganges, Captain Mowbray Thomson, clad in a pink Thresher and Glenny shirt for which Madame Tussaud's waxworks later made a spirited bid, leapt overboard, striking out for one boat that had freed itself and was retreating downstream.

Taking aim, a vigilant sepoy sent a bullet ploughing through his scalp exposing the brain, a wound so deep an index finger later fitted snugly inside the scar. Swooning with loss of blood Thomson swam on and was hauled aboard.

Manned by Major Edward Vibart, Captain Whiting, Lieutenant Delafosse and more than twenty others, this boat now drifted downstream over shallow summer waters. Stranded on sandbanks, it was time and again cleared only by men gasping from the pain of broken arms or collar bones, working under a storm of bullets from sepoys keeping pace on the bank. After two days, when only twenty were able to move, Vibart ordered his juniors to die fighting. Bursting on to the bank, Thomson, Delafosse and twelve private soldiers saw the rebels flee before them until fresh insurgents trapped them in a Hindu shrine. Six men who could not swim now saved the lives of seven who could; charging like furies against their pursuers, they went down before a forest of bayonets while Mowbray Thomson and his party plunged stark naked into the river. Four of these, Thomson, included, reached, after a three-hour swim, the village of a friendly Rajah.

Back at Sati Chaora Ghat, the Lucknow shore was now

alive with crouching men, picking off swimmers like men at target practice.

Over the water like a miasma lay the heavy stench of blood, sulphur, sweat and charring straw.

On some boats children in tam o'shanters and sailor suits still crouched petrified, lips moving in voiceless prayer.

Immobile, Amelia Horne watched the boat her mother had boarded vanish in a curtain of flame.

Clutching double-barrelled guns, bags of rupees, Skye terriers, gold watches, sepoys laden with loot were struggling ashore.

Up to their saddle girths in water, the cavalry rode from boat to boat, firing the clothes of screaming children with lighted brands.

Musket levelled, one trooper bellowed to Amelia to jump from the boat. Conscious only of her small step-sister Florence clutching her, the child's moans of "Amy, don't leave me," she was powerless to move.

Incensed, the trooper screamed above the din to a looting sepoy still aboard. As the sepoy's musket caught her an agonising welt across the skull, Amelia fell heavily into shallow water.

Her hand clutched by the trooper's, she found herself, half-walking, half-floundering against the horse's flank, hauled ashore. The children were still screaming, a note now pitched almost beyond the human ear.

Abruptly, a messenger having arrived with the Nana's orders, the massacre ceased. Shivering with terror, plastered in grey-brown mud, approximately one hundred and twenty-five women and children were dragged ashore by grinning sepoys.

Pierced by compassion, passing water-carriers halted to give them drink.

Noonday sun beat on a river suffused to a dull rust-red. The charred shells of boats and swollen bodies nudged gently together beneath overhanging branches. Like floating islands, others drifted with the tide, buried beneath the grey heaving wings of vultures.

Amelia Horne was spared these sights. Drenched with

Ganges water, clinging to the crupper of the trooper's horse, she found herself on a dusty road, leading she knew not where, one of thousands whose life was now caught up in the vortex of a mutiny hourly gaining fresh adherents.

XVI. LONDON

26th June

At this time the British Empire was over two centuries old and its day was not done yet. It symbolised a pomp and circumstance that other nations had small desire to rival. The waters of many seas washed its lands from Gibraltar to Singapore and it included many peoples whose skins ranged from lemon to darkest ebony. The Union Jack streamed in the breeze above the harbours of Valetta, Port of Spain and Halifax, Nova Scotia; in Dublin, Rangoon, Kingston, Jamaica, Hong Kong and over much of the world between.

Its Queen, Victoria, was still a devoted wife and mother; four years would pass before she entered her long twilight of mourning for Albert the Good. But of all her territories, none was more prized by the Queen and her subjects than India, "the brightest gem in the British crown." "India," as she wrote to the King of the Belgians, was "*the* place where everyone was anxious to place a son."

Thus the first news of the Indian Mutiny, reaching London on 26th June, the eve of the Cawnpore massacre, struck the people like a lightning bolt. It flawed the foundations of their faith; if all was not right with India all was not right with their world. At first their reaction was pure disbelief, for ahead of them stretched a brilliant London season and many fascinating topics of discussion: the birth of Princess Beatrice, the launching of the liner *Leviathan*, Mr. Gladstone's bill to make divorce possible for the poor.

On 29th June, when Parliament debated the news of Meerut

and the capture of Delhi—the sole intelligence that had so far reached them—the President of the Board of Control, Mr. Vernon Smith, was blandly optimistic. Searching questions from a dark sardonic Jewish member for the constituency of Buckingham were pooh-poohed as alarmist. Reinforcements would be sent to India—but as a matter of precaution only. The Indian Empire was not imperilled for this mutiny would soon be quashed. There *could* be no danger for the troops in India were equal to any emergency. The mutiny had flared through military grievances only and these would be investigated.

When Vernon Smith's solution to the problem of Delhi —surround it and starve the mutineers into submission— reached the men on the Ridge, it was greeted by an angry chorus of boos.

Mr. Benjamin Disraeli, member for Buckingham County, held strong views on India; they were lonely views. A bitter opponent of Dalhousie's annexations, he sensed that revolt, at first military, might soon become national. Long anxious to abolish the system which used "John Company" to govern India, his voice rang out across the Commons's green leather-padded benches: "The rise and fall of empires is not an affair of greased cartridges." Yet, lacking up-to-date facts, even Disraeli could not fully grasp how far events had gone. Meeting Mrs. Anson, wife of the Commander-in-Chief at the Duchess of Manchester's town house he announced he had supreme confidence in George Anson. "He has seen the Great Mogul so often on the ace of spades," he quipped, "that he will know how to deal with him." The jest was unwittingly tasteless; Anson had been dead six weeks.

Swiftly the pendulum swung. From scoffing unbelief the public veered to conviction—often in things that had never been. They spoke of an officer's wife boiled alive in butter at Delhi, of children tossed on the points of bayonets, of rapes which, for reasons of caste alone, had never taken place. Almost before the first troops—a hundred and twenty-four men of the 3rd Battalion Rifle Brigade—had left Portsmouth in the sailing ship *Barham* on 2nd July they clamoured for vengeance. Passions ran high in the tall white houses on London's Bayswater Road. Letter writers signed themselves

"Spartacus" and "Fiat Justitia"; in a letter to *The Times* "Anglo-Bengali" declared: "Not one stone in Delhi should be left standing upon another . . . every sepoy should be a pauper, his house in flames, himself fleeing from man who hunts like a wolf." In the smoke-room of the House of Lords, a former Governor-General, Lord Ellenborough, raged that every man in Delhi should be castrated after the fall, the city named "Eunuchabad." A pamphleteer penned this fine example of nineteenth-century bombast:

> *When clergymen or pious laymen speak of mercy . . . in the presence of those writhing under the remembrance of their sisters' shame, it needs little observation to see in the flashing eye and tightened lips how entirely the ill-timed advocacy defeats its own cause. . . .*

"This blind and indiscriminate exasperation," *The Times* lamented, "is resolving itself into the mere hatred of a dark skin."

The stock-market, that barometer of Victorian England, trembled: "John Company," they said, must soon go to the Stock Exchange as a borrower. Consols had lost their shine; in four weeks bank-notes in circulation decreased by £1,000,-000. Officers were hastening to the Horse Guards to rejoin their regiments. Wiser than Lord Palmerston, her Prime Minister, who saw sailing-vessels rather than the new twin-screw steamers as adequate ferries for troops, Queen Victoria urged: "Reinforcements awaiting to go to India ought not to be delayed. The moment . . . is a very critical one." The Bishop of London drew up a prayer of intercession for all in the East—"Thou knowest how far by the neglect of privileges and of the duties we owe to those over whom Thou has given us dominion, we have provoked this judgment."

World reaction was no less vigorous. The newspaper *Washington Union* opined: "All Christendom except the slave-holders of America will suffer alike." From Rome, Pope Pius IX urged a world-fund be set up for the sufferers. In Damascus a merchant's son, named White, invested part of a £2 million fortune in raising a private army of Britons, Greeks and Italians armed with fowling-pieces to fight the rebels. To speed relief forces on their way the Emperor Napoleon III agreed that India-bound troops should use the overland route through France to Marseilles, from whence they could sail to Alexandria, go by barge to Cairo, and take the desert railway to Suez before again boarding a boat.

Aside from the main fighting units, many in India had little concept of what lay ahead. Most civilians, summoned from outstations to main cantonments by prudent Commissioners, saw it as a panic measure. At Mozufferpore, where pretty girls abounded, all guard duty before 11 p.m. had to be done by non-dancers. At Patna, close by, young subalterns and their lady friends passed the nights playing I-spy amongst the pomegranate trees. In the visitors' books of travellers' bungalows, petty grumbles still took pride of place: "No table-cloth for dinner"—"I could not get a napkin."

But often, due to one resolute soul, thousands of square miles remained free from bloodshed, which went some way to justify the presence of the British in this alien land. The Commissioner of Jubblepore, Major William Erskine, in sole charge of 42,000 square miles of terrain, was determined to keep the economy stable. For a year, to ensure his sepoys were paid up to date, he printed his own banknotes. The magistrate of Aligarh, William Watson, refusing to quit, set up headquarters in a ruined indigo factory with eleven Europeans; once they scattered a rebel force of five hundred with one charge. Many magistrates with no police establishment raised irregulars as occasion dictated: war brought them strange bedfellows. At Saharanpur, seventy miles from Meerut, Deputy Magistrate Dundas Robertson recruited a geology professor and some engineering students to strengthen his Indian levies. For five months these men ranged the district like Wild West sheriffs, restoring law and order. "It was," said Robertson later, "like a game of brag—who held the worst hand might yet win."

Often keeping the peace demanded all a man's ingenuity. A young indigo planter, Emery Churcher, was astonished to be appointed Deputy Magistrate of the Etah district seventy miles north-east of Agra; his task was to raise a small irregular force and police the district. Convinced he was riding to his death, Churcher bade farewell to his sweetheart in Agra Fort, kneeling as tradition demanded on one knee. In token of her affection she gave him a small box of chocolates;

he must eat one when danger threatened for she had prayed over them long and fervently. And Churcher bore a charmed life: his first move in Etah was to enlist every highway robber—one hundred footmen, sixty-five troopers—under his own banner.

To subdue the Rajah of Omeghur, who had plundered the poor, and proclaimed himself Bahadur Shah's agent, Churcher next enlisted twenty rebel Sikhs, offering them £10 a head and a curry dinner for one night's work. By midnight, replete with food, the Sikhs had fashioned crude ladders from mango branches and horses' heel-ropes. At 3 a.m., followed by Churcher and his men, they swarmed as silently as spectres into the fort, captured the Rajah and spiked his guns. Since Churcher divided up the Rajah's stolen treasure on a white sheet, each man drew a £3 bonus. Next the fort gates were thrown open and the peasants flooded in to claim their property. For four months, until the storm was past, Churcher and his faithful rascals kept Etah district tranquil, setting them to man police posts, draw up reports, collect revenue. In November, he saw the tender green of autumn crops prick the rich soil; it would be a fine harvest and his people were content.

Some regiments remained loyal guided by one man's shrewd insight. At Mirzapore, the 47th Native Infantry stayed staunch to a man: prompted by wise old Colonel David Pott, all had become usurers, loaning their pay at high rates of interest. They wanted no part of anarchy. Colonel George Moyle Sherer, commanding the 73rd Native Infantry at Jalpaiguri, south of Mount Everest, showed equal judgment: until the mutiny's end his was virtually the only Bengal Army regiment to retain its arms. When rumour had it that two hundred Europeans were coming from Calcutta to disarm them, Sherer, against the advice of his adjutant, Captain James Tickell, paraded the regiment fully armed to deny the report. This was providential, since the men, suspecting a ruse, had cached their muskets the previous night.

"When I disarm you," Sherer averred frankly, "*I* shall give up my own sword." To his officers at mess dinner he made his position crystal-clear: "Even an order from the General won't budge me on the score."

But no such order came—and as the weeks went by, astonished officials realised Sherer's policy was paying off. Touched that their colonel had built them a hospital surrounded by cool gardens his sepoys now repaid his kindness by building him a better bungalow. Discovering that he relished goats' milk they brought him a goat. Within an hour of his pony dying four native officers bade him make his choice from their own.

"You, Colonel, have done everything for us," one told him, "more than any other officer who ever commanded us before. *We* want for nothing and only desire *you* should be as comfortable as we are." Then, as a supreme mark of respect, they one by one laid their heads on his feet.

His officers, more wary, carried a brace of loaded pistols; Sherer himself refused to carry any weapons. A magistrate who deplored this foolhardiness at length visited the station to see if all had been cut down. He found Sherer and his sepoys peacefully playing cricket.

Such psychologists had golden value in these hazardous weeks, for vast numbers of sepoys were caught up by destiny like straws in a millrace. Time and again, profiting by the tragedy of Colonel John Finnis, at Meerut, the mutiny's ring-leaders deliberately murdered senior officers. The rank-and-file, at once implicated, had little choice but to embrace the cause.

What went to make a mutineer? Some, like Bhondu Singh, who manned the Nana's guns at Cawnpore, had been at odds with authority all their lives. In thirty-two years of service he had received two reprimands at divisional level. An expert swordsman, all the rag, tag and bobtail from life's seamy side were his bosom friends. More had affinity with the men of the 53rd Native Infantry who told their Captain, William Alexander: "Sahib, we *dare* not stay loyal, we are forced to go to Cawnpore."

At Nimach, three hundred and seventy miles from Delhi, a sepoy named Koodru, on sentry duty at the Brigade Major's house, heard an Indian corporal's soft challenge from the darkness: "One faith or two faiths?" "One faith," was Koodru's prompt response: the words seemed gibberish but days earlier a friendly peon had warned him; when this challenge came, any other reply meant death. That night the sepoys at Nimach arose in an orgy of slaughter; laden with treasure they set off to join the forces of Bahadur Shah. Koodru marched with them, an unwilling captive; soon, on the pretext of seeking water, he bolted into the jungle to seek the British. For him there was no attraction in the life so many sepoys now savoured—living on in cantonments as the sahibs had done, cutting a dash in abandoned buggies, having the band play each evening at sundown.

In a tiny mud village near Bombay the heart-cry of one deserter, taken prisoner by the British, summed up the dilemma of bewildered thousands: "Where was I to go? All the world said the English *raj* had come to an end and so, being a quiet man, I thought the best place to take refuge in was my own home."

XVII. TILOWEE VILLAGE, LUCKNOW

July

July wore on, many sepoys sought such peaceful refuge, and the heart of Jemadar Sita Ram Pande was sorely troubled. For his son, Sepoy Anunti Ram had not come home; since the great cholera epidemic had seized Scind in 1844 he had sent no word. Better, the old man prayed, that his son was dead, rather than a rebel. Gnawed by secret grief, he found it hard to ponder the problems that should engage all good landowners. Soon the rains would pass, the wells would be full. Before the slow black tide of oxen flowed before the plough, seed must be purchased; wheat, oats, barley, potatoes and carrots must be sown for the March harvest. The familiar pattern of sixty-two summers passed before his eyes unseeing. Skies were lead-grey with infinite heat; stifling air drove birds to the shade of thick trees. The maddening metallic note of the coppersmith bird drilled through conscious thought. Torrents of rain cleared the air; the brown earth steamed in the sun. Other sons had come home to Tilowee village, having no heart for mutiny, but not Anunti Ram.

It was now thirty-seven years since Anunti Ram had been born at Meerut, the very first station to feel the breath of "the wind of madness." "A joy of the world has been born to us," Sita Ram had written home in ecstasy, for never in his life had he loved a woman as he loved his wife, Mokkan Singh. The chain of fate that bound them together had been as inexorable as the leaping events of these last weeks.

Now in his mind's eye, he saw again the burning village of Ahunpoora, through wreathing scarves of smoke and the howling parrying mercenaries of the border chieftain, Appa Sahib. Surely they had been the bravest fighters in the world? They had contested that village bloodily from street to street, as pugnaciously as the man Sita Ram surprised in a wide compound, his sword poised above a kneeling girl. But Sita Ram was a foe of worthier steel. *"Arlun,"* (not now), the Arab had cried as Sita Ram ducked into view. With that he charged screaming like a rogue elephant, the impetus spitting him on the sepoy's bayonet. As if by reflex, Sita Ram fired; the thin gash in the diaphragm was now a monstrous welling hole. The man's death blow almost severed his arm at the tendon.

Sita Ram never forgot that moment: how he looked for the first time on the girl, Mokkan Singh, through choking acrid smoke that pained his eyes. Stooping, he unravelled the turban of the dead bandit to bind his wound, retrieving the man's sword as proof of having slain him. Mokkan Singh, too, bent embracing his legs, weeping, "You are my lord, my only protector now." At this bloody and improbable moment, Sita Ram fell in love, a love that would endure beyond the grave and he knew it. "More men are entangled in the wiles of a woman than fish in the net of the most skilful fisherman. The arrows from their eyes wound more than poisoned arrows. Never before or since had I seen any woman like her —even at Delhi."

Their true love had been chequered from the first. Campaign life was not cantonment life; in cantonments he could have taken her as his common-law wife, listing her as a relative. The officers as always would have turned a blind eye. This was war; it made no difference that the girl came from miles to the south; that she had been carried off by Pindari marauders and sold to the Arab as a harlot. "Leave her," Uncle Hanuman urged, "She can do you no good." "Give her up!" the Adjutant commanded. Sita Ram grew wilful and stubborn; for killing the Arab he had become an acting-corporal with no extra pay but a stripe and the command of four men. He would not give her up. "Every day my heart became inflamed with love."

Somehow he had staved off the separation while the regiment trudged through barren lands, laying siege to a chain of rebel forts; at one a mine exploded like a black uprushing spring beneath Sita Ram's feet. Forty-seven men, among them Uncle Hanuman, died among the ruins but the will to live flowed through Sita Ram like a river of fire. He lay semi-paralysed in an officer's tent with Mokkan Singh tending his wounds; later it was she who kept pace beside the litter, sponging his brow, preparing his food. Sita Ram firmly refused sick leave for this would mean going home, away from Mokkan Singh. Convalescent, he lived apart with her in a small hut while the shy and lovely girl nursed him back to life. "I was more happy then than ever I had been in my own home."

Anunti Ram had been their first-born; always he had loved him most. By 1837, he had become a fine young man, enlisted in his father's corps, though a laggard correspondent; often years elapsed between each letter. Was the boy alive—and had his regiment stayed loyal? Here in Tilowee village it was hard to sift truth from rumour.

But each day the rumours gathered strength: to assuage his doubts he rode through torrents of rain to the house of the local Deputy Commissioner. To visit his office, as in other days, would have been too perilous: many office messengers were rebel spies, watching keenly all who came and went. At first the servants were unshakeable: no petitions except in office hours. High and angry words passed before a dripping Sita Ram shouldered his way past them into the Commissioner's presence.

It was a sorely frustrating interview—frustrating because the Commissioner, chary of all Indians now, would confirm or deny nothing. Each question of Sita Ram's was shrewdly parried. How were people reacting to such rumours in Tilowee? Were they excited or merely apathetic? So these *were* purely rumours? Sita Ram was relieved to hear it. No, the Commissioner would not go so far as to call them rumours. There had been disturbances but where and of what kind was very vague. The English were pastmasters of the non-committal, thought Sita Ram. An Indian officer would have denied these reports so vehemently that it would have been obvious the rumours were true.

In the tiny bazaar of Tilowee where the shop-keepers squatted before flat wicker baskets of cummin and turmeric and green peppers and kindling wood the talk was all of mutiny now, growing daily more insistent, rising above the tinkle of bullock cart bells, the bleating of lambs and goats. Even in the cool of the evening, Sita Ram could no longer sleep. In desperation he rode back to see the Commissioner. Would it not have a fine effect on morale if he, Sita Ram, collected all the loyal men now on furlough and any army pensioners capable of bearing arms?

"Thank you, Jemadar Sahib," was the Commissioner's circumspect rejoinder, "I promise I'll let you know if they are required.'"

Each day plodding pilgrims and camel trains brought fresh rumours to the village folk at the well and beneath the banyan trees. Lucknow had gone, Seetapore had gone, all Oudh was fast going. But Sita Ram noticed they no longer brought news to him. His journeys had not gone unobserved. No one wanted truck with a spy of "John Company."

It was morning when the rebels passed through Tilowee, close to the very steps where in the long ago Sita Ram had listened to Uncle Hanuman's tales of the glory of "John Company's" army. As to the shock of cold spring water his mind raced at the sight of them. They came in a swaggering motley throng, tunics unbuttoned, the sour perfume of undigested palm liquor on their breaths. Bullock carts piled with looted rupees, gold and silver, raised dust in their wake. They moved like men concussed; appalled, the old man saw them draw closer. Was this how Anunti might look now, his eyes a stranger's eyes?

Sita Ram might have held his peace but the thought of his son drove out all caution. A lone symbol of loyalty, he marched to meet them.

"Brothers, I implore you," he begged them. "Go quietly to your homes. To fight thus against the Government is most grievous folly."

Staggered, he recoiled before the violence of their hatred. Snarling like beasts they pressed round him, fingers clamped tight about his biceps. He stared down the long dark barrel of a musket. Was the old man mad or the blackest of traitors? Go quietly to their homes when Bahadur Shah had personally called on every one of them? There was loot to be had beyond the dreams of avarice.

Sita Ram's heart contracted with pain. The minds of these men were in thrall to Kali, the destroyer-goddess; he could not reach them. "Never did I see men so crazed, even in the Holi Festival," he wrote later, for in this spring festival when revellers drenched each other with red powder and water symbolising the rites of love, passions could run insatiably high.

For now they seized and buffeted him; heavy six-pound irons weighted his legs. A man berserk with rage looped a chain like a dancing bear's about his neck. He was powerless to resist. As the cavalcade surged onward his fate was made plain. In Lucknow, their first port of call, he would die the death reserved for all who sang the praises of the British: molten lead would be ladled down his throat.

XVIII. BEHIND THE REBEL LINES

September

By September, Jemadar Sita Ram Pande realised sadly that the faith which had held him fast to the British cause was a small dry kernel deep inside him shrunken by time and doubt. Now he had been four weeks a rebel prisoner, but the heavy irons that clamped his legs, the chain about his neck, burdened him less sorely than the knowledge that the mutineers had spoken the truth. Their claim that Mohammed Bahadur Shah, King of Delhi, sought their allegiance he had at first dismissed as boasting; later his confidence began to ebb. The sepoy who led this column across flooded fields and through bird-haunted jungle wanted no truck with traitors but two subadars in the party had talked with Sita Ram as brother officers—and who could doubt their iron belief in this cause? One, from the pocket of his tunic, had fished a proclamation printed on yellow paper, thrusting it on Sita Ram. If the old man did not believe the King had called them, let him read then eat his words.

So Sita Ram read, sceptically at first, but then with mounting conviction for this proclamation bore the King's own seal. Many such proclamations had been issued of which Bahadur Shah had scant knowledge, but this Sita Ram could not know. For here the King called on all sepoys to rise and destroy the British, promising immense rewards for every officer slain. Had not the British sworn that all Brahmins like Sita Ram would be forcibly converted to Christianity? With this aim one hundred chaplains were posting to Oudh: hemmed in by British riflemen the sepoys would be coerced into eating beef and pork. Already the British, to violate caste, were urinating down the wells.

To annihilate them now would be easy for apart from the

few regiments stationed in India no more British soldiers existed anywhere in the world. The Sultan of Turkey had sent word that all had been wiped out by the Russians.

"My mind was filled with doubts," Sita Ram confessed with shame; he had seen no overt proof that the British sought to tamper with men's faith but he remembered the broken promises of other years. Then there were the missionaries; many times he had loitered in the city streets to hear them denounce the passers-by as worshippers of false gods. Over the years, their numbers had multiplied, for by 1857 over four hundred and forty missionaries, the emissaries of twenty-two societies, were established in British India. Sita Ram and his fellows knew these men for what they were— the secret agents of the Government. Of course, they claimed to be independent; the sepoys knew better. Missionaries converted less than one man in fifty thousand to their beliefs —so why else should they linger here?

The rebels' threat to pour molten lead down his throat troubled him less than the thought that for forty-five years he had served an unworthy cause. As a good soldier he had served it proudly but now, with all its guns and arsenals taken, the might of "John Company" was gone—"extinguished like hot ashes by a goatskin."

Yet how invincible the British had seemed in the flower of their reign—and how proud he had been to serve them! He would have seen no shame to die in their service then, under commanders like those who fought at Sobraon less than twelve years ago. That was the day when the British artillery laid the Sikh ranks in bloody windrows until at last they turned and fled pellmell, struggling in wild confusion across the bridge that spanned the Sutlej River. Fate had given the British unsparing victory, for in that instant the bridge had broken; thousands of Sikhs had plummeted towards the roaring river. This victory Sita Ram could never forget: the river choked with struggling masses of men, long dark hair streaming in the white water, clutching frantically at each other until the current sucked them under, "to rise no more alive."

That had been a bitter battle, like all the British battles, with no quarter sought or given; when General Ochterlony's troops, Sita Ram amongst them, stormed the Fort of Bharatpur its defenders had packed the breached walls like tigers until one of their own giant guns came toppling from above "to crush them beneath it like Juggernaut." To fight such adversaries was a proud contest for "all these men had died at their guns. What better death could they have wished?" And remembering, Sita Ram was rent by conflict, for whatever conspiracies the British had planned it was in this tradition he would wish his son Anunti to die.

Then one morning, to Sita Ram's bewilderment, there was confusion in the rebel ranks. No longer was Lucknow their goal. To fight for Bahadur Shah in Delhi was also a thing of the past. Word passed that their destination now was the jungle near Cawnpore. There a new leader, Nana Sahib, claimed their allegiance.

Sita Ram had heard only dimly of the Nana and was never destined to see him face to face, for suddenly, as the column rounded a bend in the trail, a long cantering line of British horsemen spurred into view. Sabres flashed, a fusillade of musketry exploded, the triumphant yells of the cavalry were almost drowned by the frantic thrashing of branches as the mutineers bolted for the jungle. Sita Ram sat bolt upright in the tumbril where he had been riding, hearing the click of a cocked revolver as an officer who had not spied his chains squeezed on the trigger. In the nick of time another with keener eyesight knocked the weapon aside.

Then came an armourer to free Sita Ram of his shackles, and a colonel who noted down his long statement and many officers barely able to contain their excitement as he answered their many questions. What was the state of the jungle hereabouts? Had he seen Englishmen or women in hiding? Then he was handed a certificate of recapture, so that his loyalty should be unquestioned, and the colonel and a captain gravely discussed his future. Sita Ram confessed himself a very indifferent rider but his Persian was fluent so for the time being he was appointed interpreter to the troop. They were glad to make use of his services.

Was all this an omen? Sita Ram wondered. Was the British star in the ascendant now after long darkness? For after months of doubt, calling no man his friend, he was again an

officer to "John Company"; his brothers who had seemed
his enemies were his brothers once more. Had all that long
estrangement been a dream—and would the bloodshed and
hatred pass away?

XIX. HAVELOCK'S COLUMN

15th July

For the men of Havelock's tattered column trudging to
the relief of Cawnpore, each hour on the march had become
a day, each leaden day a century. On the late afternoon of
15th July Havelock and his men had been eight days on the
march. Unrelenting sun hurled itself against them; they
"waded in a sea of slush, knee-deep now and now breast-
high . . . as far to right and left as eye could pierce extended
one vast morass." In a world like this, Havelock had known,
his men could march at best ten miles a day. This pace he
must accept.

This was the line of the Grand Trunk Road they followed,
by the standards of the time a fine road, ten feet wide,
macadamised with *kunkur,* watered tamped-down nodules
of carbonate of lime, in the dry season well-kept and almost
level. Beneath mud and slime this was now barely visible.
Its course instead was marked at twelve mile intervals by
gutted travellers' bungalows, in other places by shrines, their
white plaster defaced by rain and mould, by uprooted milestones and telegraph posts and by the bitter-smelling neem,
like giant pepper trees, which line this road even today. On
this march, men recorded, there were few sounds of human
life, only the hum of a thousand winged insects, the croaking
of frogs, the cicadas' shrill piping. And from almost every one
of the trees that lined the road hung a dead sepoy, whose
torso, below the navel, tapered into thin dark strips for thus
far the wild boars could reach.

In the last three days Havelock's force had acquitted themselves well. Not until 2 a.m. on 12th July had his Allahabad column, its pipers skirling "The Campbells are Coming," met up with the advance force under Major Sydenham Renaud. At dawn on this same day, arms had been piled on an open plain near Batinda, four miles from Fatehpur; the welcome shrilling of the breakfast bugle now smote the ears of weary men. At the Headquarters tent Havelock was briskly questioning two spies sent in by Sir Henry Lawrence. At this precise moment a 24-pound round shot crashed with unholy clangour amongst the copper camp-kettles of the 64th Foot, only two hundred yards from where he stood. Believing only Renaud's tiny force lay ahead, the rebels were about to attack.

Anxious that his main force should have breakfast, Havelock had at first held back, posting a rampart of three hundred Enfield riflemen in an outlying copse. But soon it was plain that battle must be joined; half a mile away a white-clad torrent of rebels, Sir Hugh Wheeler's defeat moving like fire in their blood, swept irresistibly towards them. To delay now would be to imperil seriously the morale of his untried force. They must stand and they must fight.

But Havelock had not hastened to attack. These bone-tired men, he knew, needed respite before the fighting was on them. Thus, as the troops had fallen in and moved forward, orders rapped and the infantry, gratefully, heard the order that men should lie down in rank. Soon the rebel cavalry had wheeled aside to reveal a long line of infantry with batteries of artillery. Puzzled, they had found themselves confronting a crouching motionless British front.

In this blinding moment, when only victory could save India from anarchy, Havelock had struck hard and fast. As a bugle shrilled, the artillery bullocks' drivers thrashed forward, forming a line to the right on the leading gun of the artillery commander, Captain Francis Maude. At a run, the eight guns had bounced forward, wheeling within eight hundred yards of the enemy's front, to open fire. Shielded by a fan of skirmishers, a hundred Enfield riflemen, firing steadily, then moved forward. On the flanks had galloped Captain Lousada Barrow's volunteer cavalry; reining at four hundred yards they opened fire to see three rebel troopers slump from their saddles. Fire tore into the rebels from all sides, bearing them backwards like a sea to their second line of guns. This was their first acquaintance with the new and deadly Enfield rifle, four feet six inches in length, longer when capped by a gleaming seventeen-and-a-half-inch bayonet, capable of snatching the life from a man at a thousand yards. Yet no rebel could fathom how rifles reached them at this range and amongst the mêlée of screaming dying men they were stripped of comfort and afraid. So they had fallen back, but still the artillery wrestled on through swampy field, at six hundred and fifty yards firing again until all the cavalry had bolted, leaving only infantry, two heavy guns and two elephants to stem the fearful toll of Havelock's advance.

"Knock over that chap on the elephant," Major Stuart Beatson, Havelock's Deputy Adjutant-General, had yelled to Captain Maude, and the gunner, not knowing that this was Tantia Topee, the commander of the Nana's bodyguard at whom he aimed, laid a nine-pounder at "line of metal"—seven hundred yards—seeing the shot plough in a gout of blood beneath the beast's tail, tearing through the vitals to the chest. Screaming, the elephant had crashed like timber; badly shaken the rebel leader had hobbled away. With the town of Fatehpur taken and the rebels routed for a third time a mile beyond, Havelock gave the order to halt. All this had been fought in the sun until 3 p.m. He could not press his fainting men further. It was time to celebrate with a chicken dinner.

For the British there had been much to celebrate. At long last the tide was turning; for the first time since that ignominious Sunday at Meerut the rebels had been routed in the open field by an army half the size, and only fifty miles ahead lay Cawnpore. Afterwards many men who had known Havelock would ponder this irony: the victor was a man once so sickly the doctors had prescribed eight pounds of grapes a day, so gentle that an Irish servant-girl had lamented, "Oh, Misther, dear, you're not fit for a soldier, it's too tinder-hearted you are . . . a praist it is you ought to be." This Havelock belonged to the past; the new man was the commander

who had spurred his horse towards the rebel ranks of the
56th Native Infantry, his old regiment, crying, "There's some
of you that have beheld me fighting! Now try upon yourselves what you have seen in me." Almost before the smoke
of battle had cleared this man, jubilant, had written to his
wife Hannah on the Rhine at Bonn: "One of the prayers oft
repeated throughout my life since my schooldays has been
answered and I have lived to command in a successful action.
. . . Thanks to Almighty God, who gave me the victory . . . I
now march to retake Cawnpore. . . ."

Yet more astonishing was the way in which he had welded
his motley force together. Many of Neill's Fusiliers were
teenage Eurasians from the Madras Military Orphanage,
quaking under their first baptism of fire. At every halt they
were forced to rub their scarified feet with melted fat. Few
of his cavalry volunteers had ever spurred their horses against
more lethal foes than wild boar. The Sikhs, "Six," as Havelock called them, marching with their whiskers tied on top of
their heads to avoid contamination from dust, were still an
uncertain quantity. These men vested their loyalty in the
sinewy white-bearded Lieutenant Jeremiah Brasyer, the ex-
gardener who had threatened to blow all of them to Hades
if they defected at Allahabad. During lulls in the fighting
Brasyer would gravely grant their formal petition to get
drunk. Among the Europeans, most were hard-bitten vete-
rans, but the 78th Highlanders sweltered cruelly in their red
doublets. Nor, despite the rebels' awe, was the Enfield rifle an
insuperable force in the hands of those who had them. "Kill
all those men in the dirty shirts and blue caps," the Nana
Sahib had stormed when the casualties of Fatehpur were reported. "They kill all my men before they fire." The real
truth was known to Havelock and his officers: the troops
understood the Enfield so little that fully three thousand rifles
had been left at Allahabad. Often in these early models the
bullets jammed so tightly the armourers were forced to bore
them out. In the hurly-burly of action and for want of
habit men forgot constantly to reverse the cartridge. The high
numbers on the back-sights were taken to indicate velocity
instead of range. The result was an elevation that made
much fire ineffective.

On this force Havelock imposed an iron discipline. All Government property looted from the mutineers must be handed to the corps commanders. No officer or soldier could leave camp without permission; no firing was allowed within three miles of camp. Officers who shrugged off the order, seeking snipe in the marshes, found themselves in close arrest. Determined Captain Francis Maude's guns should wing into action with least delay, Havelock persisted in timing him. Following Fatehpur one officer received this stinging note: "I wish to have within an hour a return of killed and wounded . . . of the force in the action of yesterday. . . . If I cannot have these without further reference I shall not form a favourable impression of things in your department." To another he fumed: "I will not permit the mischievous delays which occur in getting this small column in motion."

Hand in hand with Havelock's mastery of men, went their knowledge of how he had led them to victory. On 13th July, when he granted his camp a day's rest, a ribald song was already going the rounds:

> With our shot and shell
> We made them smell hell
> That day at Fatehpur . . .

And by 4 p.m. on 15th July Havelock's force, now only thirty-three miles from Cawnpore, had again acquitted themselves with valour, for on this day they had fought two grim actions at a cost of only twenty-five killed and wounded. Not long after dawn they had stormed the rebel village of Aong, and this had been the sternest test of their mettle to date. One artillery lieutenant commanded his battery doggedly throughout the action: only later did his men discover that the wheel of a 24-pounder gun, passing over his foot, had crushed it to pulp. A young bombardier of Maude's team, cracked into a parade-ground salute: "If you please, sir, may I fall out?" Only then Maude realised that a round shot had mangled the lad's arm from fingers to elbow.

This was but a foretaste of what lay ahead. To Havelock the most coveted prize was the Panda Nudi river, a few miles ahead, for this, swollen by rains to a width of seventy yards, was the one major natural obstacle lying between him and Cawnpore. Lacking boats and pontoons, much had depended on seizing the new stone bridge which carried the Grand Trunk Road. On the battlefield at Aong, men were still dying when scouts brought word that the enemy were now mining this bridge. At once Havelock cancelled breakfast. They must carry the bridge before it was too late.

This was no easy task even for a thousand men. The river banks were steep and shelving; from the bridge and its approach two rebel guns hosed them with a rain of fire. The one solution, as Captain Francis Maude saw it, was to envelop the rebel battery with fire from right, left and centre. So men had hugged the earth, their ears pounded by the thunderous concert of the guns duelling at six hundred yards range, until the miraculous moment when Maude's shot broke both the sponge-staves of the rebel guns. Lacking these the gunners were now powerless for unless a gun was sponged after each discharge sparks remaining within the chamber could ignite the fresh charge of powder and blow the gunner to pieces. At once Havelock's voice had rung out: "Soldiers and comrades, we *must* cross that bridge!" Then the mine went up and his words were lost in the snapping crack of stonework as the parapet crumbled. The earth rocked, a fine rain of stone sparks went skywards, but as the reverberation died the rebels saw the day was lost. The bridge had held and the sun, through wreathing smoke, struck white fire from serried bayonets as the fusiliers came on.

XX. CAWNPORE

15th July

At this precise moment it was 2 p.m. on 15th July but to two hundred and six women and children the hour and the day and the month were immaterial. For eighteen days now, since a convoy of country carts had carried them drenched and shivering from Sati Chaora Ghat to swell two captured boatloads of fugitives from nearby Fatehgarh, they had been confined in the Bibigarh, or the House of the Women, Cawnpore, a flat-roofed one-storey adobe building on the west side of the Ganges Canal. Here, in two rooms, twenty by ten feet, flanking a courtyard fifteen feet square, they had remained as captives, sleeping on coarse bamboo matting, tearing with their hands at cakes of unleavened dough, using their fingers to spoon up lentil porridge. Whether they were held as hostages by Nana Sahib or whether only death lay in store for them they did not know and no one now will ever know.

They knew only from the thunder of guns that Nana Sahib was all powerful. At 5 p.m. on 28th June when he had held the state review of his army all the air had shuddered with the concussion of cannon. Two days later, when the Nana was proclaimed Peshwa or King of the Mahrattas, and the sacred consecration mark was affixed to his forehead, they heard the guns roar again. In this week also the Nana had moved his headquarters to the yellow-painted Old Cawnpore Hotel, only thirty yards from the Bibigarh. At dusk, through slatted venetian blinds, the captives saw festival lights sparkle all over Cawnpore. The hotel was given over to music and dancing; the pulsing of drums, the wail of conches and the thick slurred male laughter reached their ears night after night.

During all this time they had remained the charges of Hosainee Khanum, a tall fair-skinned girl of twenty-eight, greying prematurely at the temples, a waiting-maid of the Nana's reigning courtesan, Adala. It was she who supervised the staff of sweepers who brought the captives' food. This was the situation when word came, late on the afternoon of 15th July, that Havelock's little army had crossed the Panda Nudi bridge and was advancing on Cawnpore.

Half-an-hour after this news reached the city, Hosainee Khanum told the captives the Nana was determined to kill them all. But when one of the women repeated this story to the Indian officer commanding the guard, he denied it. If such was the case orders would have been transmitted to him. The women had no cause to be afraid. Then one of the sepoys, seeing Hosainee Khanum close at hand, taunted her: "Your orders will not be obeyed. Who are you that you give orders?" When she heard this the waiting-maid hurried away.

At 5 p.m. Hosainee Khanum returned. Now five men were striding beside her—though some eye-witnesses counted seven—and each man carried a sabre with a razor-edge. Two were Hindu peasants, one a tall flat-faced man with a wall-eye, the second short and sallow. Two more were Moslems, butchers by trade, portly strapping men in late middle-age. These four men were clad in soiled white garments. The fifth was Hosainee Khanum's lover, Sarvur Khan, a man whose hands were thickly matted with hair. He wore the red uniform of the Nana's bodyguard.

At the word of command, the sepoys fell in on the Bibigarh's verandah. At Sarvur Khan's order a few levelled their muskets through the venetian blinds, but they fired deliberately high, at the ceiling. They could not bring themselves to kill. Now Sarvur Khan and the four men entered the Bibigarh. The doors were barred behind them. This was the hour of the evening drive, the promenade, when the band played softly in the gloom. In many peaceful stations of India this gracious custom was still observed.

Presently Sarvur Khan re-emerged. His sabre was shattered at the hilt. Shortly he returned with another. This too broke at the hilt though the stump of blade remaining was seen to retain fragments of bone and bloodstained hair. Seeking a third blade of firmer temper, Sarvur Khan returned to the Bibigarh.

Until almost sunset the doors were barred.

XXI. BEFORE CAWNPORE

16th July

In Havelock's camp the outcome was in doubt until the last. Not until 3 a.m. on 16th July did a friendly spy, conducted to the Brigadier's tent, confirm what had hitherto been rumour: fully two hundred women and children, prisoners of the Nana, were alive in Cawnpore. Minutes later the bugle sounded reveille, the pipes of the Highlanders cried their lively quick-step, "Hey, Johnnie Cope, are ye. waking yet?" In the moon-light the men hastened into line. Bareheaded, his hand on his sword, Havelock's voice announcing the news, seemed shaken by a sob: "By God's help, men, we shall save them or every man die in the attempt." Three wild cheers split the night as a thousand men, anticipating the word of command, went "fours right" and stepped off. Twenty-three miles ahead lay Cawnpore and fully eight thousand men of the Nana's army.

The column marched at bullock's pace, two and a half miles an hour at best. By 10 a.m. they neared the village of Maharajpore, seven miles from Cawnpore. Sun came through low haze to punish them, turning the sandy track to a bone-white streak that pained the eyes. Once at the village arms were piled. Animals were picketed and given fodder. Troops ate but sparingly. Because of the mined bridge the commissariat had been unable to get ration bullocks across and slaughtered until late the night before. By then men were too weary to eat and in the sultry night the meat grew putrid. They breakfasted now on great draughts of porter and hard biscuits from their haversacks. On this diet they would strive for a contested city.

Relaxed in shade, Havelock sifted the reports of two spies escorted in by Barrow's scouting party. One of these was Anjoor Tewaree, a sepoy who had marched with the Nana's

170

army from Cawnpore, risking death or worse to note his defensive positions. This man outlined the terrain. The Nana's
defences lay in depth three miles ahead, a half-moon a mile
and a quarter long screened by mango groves and mud-
villages. Massed infantry was posted between and around the
heavy guns, many of them 24-pounder howitzers. Cavalry lay
to the rear.

Smiling, unhurried, Havelock called his commanders together to map out his plan of attack. Squatting, these spies
now traced in the dust a sketch of rebel positions, Havelock's scabbard hovering above them like a blackboard pointer,
pinpointing details. Still smiling, he asked for questions, receiving none. To most he seemed in rare spirits—"when
he was being shot at," one officer noted, "he was as blithe as a
schoolboy out for a holiday." To Captain Eugene Currie,
commanding the detachments of the 84th Foot, he enthused:
"Young as you are, sir, if you come out of today's affair with
credit I promise you your promotion to major." Bowing,
Currie thanked the brigadier; neither in this moment of
warmth could know that within hours a round shot was to
blast away all Currie's body below the navel.

It was 1.30 p.m. The force moved off. Sick, wounded
and baggage remained to the rear. This was now a unit geared
to war. There was no talk, only the squeal of gun limbers,
the muffled pad of marching feet, the sound of many
animals breathing hard. The sun was hoisted as high as a
flambeau. Through thick leather cavalry boots stirrups glowed
like grid-irons; anything of metal blistered the fingers. The
heat was a living thing. Soon the choking red woollen doublets of the Highlanders, the heady fumes of porter, combined
to send men toppling from the ranks. The sky, the trees, the
faces of their commanders first blurred like an image in
water then spun like a top beyond control until they crashed
senseless at the roadside.

Battling heat, the remainder marched on. The country was
as flat as English fenland, arid and featureless. Random
clumps of palms, as lonely as sentinels, broke the landscape. Earth was the colour of freshly-ground oatmeal
dotted, after the rains, with pools that held the hard clarity
of steel mirrors. In these, water buffalo wallowed, immune

from heat, leeches hanging like fine threads of black silk
from their nostrils. This is a land of great distances, dotted
by rice-fields, scrub and cone-shaped stacks of dried cow-
dung. In any direction a man can see for three miles. A
desolate land, forsaken beneath the enormous bowl of the
sky.

This was the battlefield. Already against great odds they
had fought three battles and acquitted themselves with valour.
The last, the greatest battle, awaited them.

Cawnpore was fought in the afternoon. The Allahabad Movable Column, Brigadier-General Henry Havelock commanding,
was three miles from Maharajpore when, a mile beyond a
forked road, they sighted the enemy in force, earthworks
shearing like a broadsword across the line of both roads.
Field-glasses brought seven guns jumping into focus, two
light, five of siege calibre, and the tight line of native villages
that marked the rebel strongpoints: high mud walls rimmed
by ditches, accessible only through stout wooden gates, a
legacy of the Mahratta raids.

Rock-steady, Havelock rifled the pigeonholes of memory for
the right manoeuvre. From Allahabad on he had been a
stickler for the text-book; four days earlier, when Captain
Francis Maude had rejoiced in the anniversary of the Battle
of the Boyne, Havelock had references at hand to correct
him—battle had been joined this day at the Aughrim, not
the Boyne. Now, in the archives of his mind, an old memory
stirred: a hundred years ago at Leuthen, in Silesia, Frederick
the Great of Prussia had faced this problem against the
Austrians. A frontal attack, Havelock reckoned, would cost
him a third of his force—three hundred men. But to his
right, a grove of tall mango trees gave cover for marching
men who could seize the Nana's left flank and coil like a
striking snake to command the rebel line from the rear.

Half a mile from where the road forked to Cawnpore cantonments, rifle skirmishers of the Blue Caps struck warily off
to left and right, spaced six yards apart. With a swirl of the
coloured silk handkerchief that secured their hilts in lieu of
sword knots, Major Barrow's cavalry, eighteen sabres strong,
trotted steadily towards the enemy's centre. These men,
riding into what they saw as a second Balaclava, were

expendable and they knew it. To divert the attention of the rebel gunners from the marching column, cavalry would draw fire. An infantryman can turn and flee. Mounted, a man stands twenty-four hands high and weighs a thousand pounds. The sheer momentum of a charge, if ordered, would strip them of conscious will.

At the head of the main column, Havelock, taking out an old-fashioned turnip-watch, handed it to his personal bugler, Drummer Dick Pearson of the 78th, bidding him check the hour. The time was 2 p.m. and all the years of his life had pointed to this moment. It is 2 p.m., he noted, and this is the afternoon of 16th July, 1857.

Now a silence fell upon the battlefield. Seventy years later old men would recall that as the guns and the Highlanders, drenched in sweat, moved cautiously through the mango groves an eerie hush fell. Only these sounds broke total silence: the summer mockery of a cuckoo, heard rarely in those parts, the fitful scream of a bursting shell, white smoke beautiful against the porcelain-blue of sky, the harsh cries of the bullock-drivers as the guns lumbered forward.

But the Nana's gunners were alert. Seeing the vivid red of Highland tunics bobbing beneath the dark lacquer of mango leaves, they swung the trails of their guns; so lethal was the fire that burst about the 78th that the order passed along the line: "Lie down!" For a space men hugged the steaming earth as hot bulbs of grapeshot shredded green snow from the branches above. It was time for Maude's artillery to silence the four deadly 24-pounders behind the earthwork of the left flank.

At nine hundred yards range Maude's 12-pounder howitzers sent a crashing wave of gunfire against the village. Two rebel guns presently grew silent but the others roared defiance, well sheltered by mud walls. Grimly Havelock recognised the truth: no guns the British could muster would silence heavy guns manned by well-trained mutineers. This feat only men might do.

"The line will advance, Colonel!"

Havelock had spoken and in seconds his order was echoing down the ranks. "The line—will—ADVANCE—Ross-shire Buffs wheel into line! Forward!" From the Highland ranks there came a muffled cheer like the growl of a slowly-wakening tiger. To win or lose the day Havelock was pinning all his faith on a strangely-mixed quantity: the infantryman of the line.

Not a man alive today would serve his country under the terms laid down for Queen Victoria's army. Rated as cannon-fodder, most soldiers in sheer self-defence became brutalised automatons. In barrack-room brawls, foot soldiers slashed with belt-buckles, troopers drove home their spurs. Stark necessity drove at least sixty-five per cent of them to enlist, as Florence Nightingale said, "to death in the barracks."

Theirs was a snarling animal world where married men shared the same barracks as single; only a thin linen sheet curtaining the bed-space afforded privacy from thirty others. A man kneeling to pray risked a shower of heavy boots and dishes aimed at his head. Sheets, made of canvas, were changed once a month. One blackened tin pot served for both eating and ablutions.

All had but one thing in common: the lust for liquor. To obtain raw spirit men would break ranks on the march to storm liquor shops. An average intake was a bottle a day spiked with chopped capsicum; hog-drunk, such men lay sprawled on the washroom floor while white ants ate the skin from their backs. Only liquor could help a man forget, for most of them had run away from something. But on the battle-field they did not run.

Like a red juggernaut the Highland line came on: three hundred and five men moving steadily, a surging wall, each man weighed down by sixty pounds of kit. Already that day they had marched twenty miles; now they must march, arms at the slope, for almost fifteen minutes exposed to a fire they could not return, every man knowing he must pass the spot where he had seen others fall. The hungry guns devoured them, scattering blood and flesh and sodden hair, but still they came, not running, not cheering, bodies slightly bent, a steady springy step learned only on heather. Shells burst close at hand, deluging them with glistening yellow-brown spray; far to the rear, like a taunt, the rebel band struck up "Auld Lang Syne." Now they were only eighty yards from the guns, close enough to see, through darting red-hot splinters, the black ear-to-ear moustachioes of the rebel gunners. Already, unnerved, these men were firing too high. "CHARGE!" they heard Colonel Walter Hamilton cry as his horse floundered beneath him and at that moment Pipe-Major Alexander M'Kellar's bagpipes, a wild hawk note to make the spine tingle, keened above the noise of battle. It joined with the awesome Highland yell as the 78th went forward as if impelled by a catapult.

And then the Highlanders were in and over the guns, whose barrels were striped in gaudy rainbow colours; barely had the gunners time to drop their linstocks before the bayonets skewered through them. Few Highlanders had undergone bayonet instruction and as they stabbed with ferocity unmatched many blades bent like reaping hooks beneath the strain. As in a mist they heard Havelock's cry, "Well done, 78th, you shall be my own regiment! Another charge like that wins the day."

A torrent of orders, gabbled, screamed, shouted, swept the battlefield: "Fire! Load! Rod! Home! Return! Cap! Fire a volley at one hundred yards only! Present! Fire! Load! Rod! Fire! Fire! Fire!"

To take these guns had been the work of minutes. In confusion the sepoys now struggled back towards the Nana's centre, white-clad figures against a panorama of orange fire. Sheltered by a causeway which carried the Cawnpore road up to a small bridge spanning a stream, the Highlanders reformed. A storm of shell burst upon them from the Nana's centre. Defiantly Havelock brandished his sword at the howitzer. "Another charge like that wins the day," he cried again, then he had spurred his Arab into the glittering arc of fire. The momentum of this charge carried the Highlanders into the howitzer's emplacement and out onto the Trunk Road. They saw the dun-coloured earth dotted with white-clad men, bleeding their lives away; trumpets called, wild and sweet; the wake of shells flung men aside like branches in a millrace. The sepoy force was falling back now, covered by their cavalry. In vain Major Lousada Barrow beseeched Havelock: his volunteers could charge the native horse. The brigadier shook his head, spurring on towards the 64th.

Major Stuart Beatson, Havelock's Deputy Adjutant-General, thought this a waste of fighting spirit: he was lying on a tumbril dying of cholera, and could excusably have thought of other things but still he urged his driver towards Barrow's horsemen. Faintly his voice rallied them: "What are you doing? *There* are the enemy!"

"March!" called Barrow promptly and now the line kicked forward, as one, riding knee to knee, each man gripping his sabre, thumbs pressing on the back of the handle in line with the blade, alert to grip more tightly still before the terrible moment of impact. The hoofbeats struck up a steady rhythm. Fresh orders spurred them to a brisk trot. These men in their civilian broadcloth and wideawake hats were amateurs each one; their greatest skill was to face death with unrivalled courage. Two hundred and fifty yards from the rebel cavalry, massed and menacing in their silver and grey, the pace quickened. As one they kicked into a gallop, reins loosened now, riding neck and neck, the horses' rumps bunched in unison until each man rose from his saddle from the knees, right shoulder lunging forward with the point, crashing like a shock-wave amongst the cavalry. "Give points, lads," Barrow cried. "Damn cuts and guards," for against these odds only the "straight arm engage" might carry a man through alive, the sword held rock-steady like a rifle, the sheer momentum of the horse's run plunging the blade home. Only when four horses had fallen beneath them did these panting, bloody men relinquish the fight. "Gentlemen volunteers," called Havelock as he rode towards them, his face wreathed in smiles, "I am proud to command you."

The battle was not over. Half a mile away across waterlogged ploughland, the rebels had rallied in the village of Suktipore and now Captain Maude's exhausted gun bullocks, beaten by two miles of cruel country, sank snorting to their knees. They could be coerced no further. Again the infantry must save the day; driving themselves with the desperation of lunatics, flagging men re-formed. Under iron-grey light, through the yellow paste of mud, they stumbled towards Suktipore, shell crashing amongst them, breaking their strong lines, but still the colours surged ahead; the white of the 84th and 64th, the buff of the Highlanders. "Come," Havelock besought them as the mud walls loomed in sight. "Who'll take this village? The Highlanders or the 64th?"

The question was rhetorical. Both regiments went forward like wolves, closing their ranks as men fell dying; at this moment Havelock's horse, struck in the pastern by a bullet, crashed dead beneath him. Hastily he scrambled up unwounded.

Most now prayed that fighting was done, for the sky to the west was streaked with rose-pink light and these men had marched and fought since midnight on biscuits and porter. Only the thought that women and children were alive in Cawnpore sustained their dragging feet. Moving ahead across the skyline, the skirmishers expected to see nothing but the scattered hordes of enemy dead, broken abandoned tumbrils, dying animals. Then they stopped appalled.

Three-quarters of a mile ahead a mighty howitzer, a 24-pounder, blocked the Cawnpore road. To right and left of this gun swarmed almost ten thousand sepoys. They heard the urgent pulsing of tom-toms and the shrilling of fifes. Behind the packed ranks of sepoys a stout man with restless black eyes moved on an elephant, exhorting the troops. This was Nana Sahib's last stand.

At this moment Havelock faced only annihilation. He had barely eight hundred men in line, lying down behind a ridge; guns and cavalry were far to the rear. Worse, a shrapnel shell from the giant gun had killed and mutilated six men of the 64th Foot. Many had broken ranks and were only with difficulty rousted from hiding; their commander, Major Thomas Stirling, his nerves shattered, was close to breaking point. Yet to yield one inch of ground would be fatal. Not one hundred men would have lived to fall back on Allahabad.

Mounted on a borrowed hack, Havelock rode steadily towards the crouching men, reining with his back to the swelling roar of artillery. He faced the line. He said firmly, still smiling, with no trace of excitement, "The longer you look at it, men, the less you will like it. Rise up. The Brigade will advance, left battalion leading."

As if galvanised the column struggled up, the 64th leading on the left, head on to the howitzer and taking the full blast of the sharp orange flame streaking from the muzzles. Havelock rode steadily at the head of the Highlanders. Angered that the field-officers of the 64th had all dismounted and were virtually invisible to their men, the Brigadier's hot-tempered son, Harry, now rode to their front to rally them.

They had sprinted within a thousand yards of the gun, near enough to see the slow match of the sepoy gunner poised above the vent: at once each man hugged the earth, the grapeshot passing with a rushing shriek above their heads. Then they were up and running for dear life; at eight hundred yards they fell again but the shot was reaching them more swiftly now, scything ugly gaps in their ranks. The brain of Ensign Hugh Pearson, who charged with them, mirrored broken snatched cameos: the fearful crunch of a ball tearing at bone, men's faces "red as turkey cocks' combs" with the fierce sun, the fusillade of grape that shredded his blue drill regimental trousers below the knee. One hundred yards from the gun the last round screamed over them; up they leapt to fire one shattering volley. Then, from the ranks of the 84th, there burst a strange and appalling cry, a shriek so unearthly as to chill the blood of all who heard it. Clawing their way into the entrenchment, they wrought a fearful slaughter.

Thus the flame of battle flickered and died for now four of Maude's guns had caught up with the infantry and under their last annihilating fire the rebels fled. In the falling light the cheers for Havelock rose in a wild yelling to the sky. "Don't cheer me," he told them calmly. "You did it all yourselves."

They knew now they could rescue no women and children this day; the long Indian night had fallen and troops could not manoeuvre in the darkened streets of a native city. They were still two miles from Cawnpore; Havelock could only despatch two Indian spies forward to reconnoitre. Behind him, in the gathering darkness he heard thin cries of "Don't shoot . . . the General's in front."

For all of them this night, material rewards were small. So breathtaking had been their advance that the baggage lay five miles to the rear; there was little to eat, little save dirty water to drink. Wrapped in his waterproof cloak, Havelock settled to rest on the damp ground, sharing the one biscuit his son Harry could produce, quenching his thirst with a glass of porter brought by a staff officer. Others slept with bayonets and muskets for pillows; cavalry lay down in darkness, fingers looped round their bridles. All night men would stir fitfully, hearing the rumble of carts and gun-carriages as the Nana's army streamed from Cawnpore city. The dead too laid claim on their attention. Some went late to rest, after digging graves with bayonets, and in the soft night the pibroch sounded.

And Havelock, before he slept, looked at the watch which Drummer Pearson had returned to him. The elapsed time of the battle had been two hours forty-five minutes. This in truth had been his hour and no one could now take this away from him. Press and public had mocked him and derided his faith; "a fossil general fit only to be turned into pipeclay" they had called him, "as sour as if he had swallowed a pint of vinegar." But the last laugh was with Havelock.

XXII. CAWNPORE

17th July

Early on the morning of 17th July the streets of Cawnpore came alive with the tramp of feet. One hundred dusty, filthy men, an advance detachment of Her Majesty's 84th Foot under Captain Henry Ayton, were marching towards the city's centre. Their eyes were red-rimmed, their leathery skins veneered with dirt, they tramped in grim silence. Many, swathed in bloody bandages, used rifles as makeshift crutches. Hot dust, stirred by their feet, swirled in the silence. Timidly native vendors crept from their houses, pressing milk and sweetmeats and cigars on the victors, pathetically grateful when these were accepted, happier when payment was made. Shortly this detachment reached the low white adobe building called The House of the Women. They were here joined by a mixed detachment of Highlanders and 64th Foot under Lieutenant Richard Charles M'Crea. The door was forced and history has recorded that M'Crea was the first man to enter the building. After a moment he came out. His face was sheet-white, his jaws worked like a cretin's. He could not speak. Within six months he would have the blessed fortune to be dead. He would blot out for ever the sights which now revealed to one hundred men that they had come too late.

The flimsy door was festooned with rags with which the women had sought to secure it against the invaders, and facing this door were two pillars. Mrs. Henry Jacobi, who had taken the message to the entrenchment, and Mrs. William Probett, widow of the postal agent, had been lashed to these. Both were squarely built women, gunners' daughters, and the throats of both had been cut from ear to ear. Higher up on the wall, between the pillars, a child had been impaled by its chin from a hook.

This room and the room beyond were two inches deep in fast congealing blood, sonorous with the first flies of morning. To one eye-witness it was "as if a hundred bullocks had been killed there." The walls bore a fresco of bloody hand-prints, the lintels scarred deeply with sabre-cuts as if women and small children had crouched low to avoid the blows.

These were objects that could be identified with a minimum of difficulty: a row of children's shoes, the length of a man's index finger, the feet severed at the ankle, boys' trousers and children's toys, leaves torn from Bibles, hair a yard long wrenched from the living tissue, a poster marked "Cawnpore Summer Race Meeting," back-combs, frocks, frills, bloody bonnets, ladies' boots, broken earthenware, leaves from the *Illustrated London News,* a copy of Homer's "Iliad," many daguerreotypes, a locket marked "Ned's hair, with love"; and, as if a macabre property master had set this stage, a book, Drenlincourt's "Preparation for Death," a song "Non giova il sospirar" (It helps not to sigh).

Beyond in the courtyard, the long grass shone with crimson dew: close at hand a withered tree seemed to have sprouted leaves—a thousand tiny shreds of fine linen. High up on the bark of the tree were grey glutinous patches where the brains of children had been strewn the previous morning, after a long night of terror beneath their mothers' skirts.

It was fifty feet east of this courtyard that the well lay. The first men who approached it turned vomiting away and even those who had breakfasted meagrely could vomit and vomit again. The long brick shaft was crammed with severed heads, the raw stumps of limbs, sightless eyes, all pressed together in an obscene arabesque, so that one man could write, "I have faced death in every form but I could not look down that well again."

Another picked up a prayer-book whose fly-leaf was inscribed, "Read Psalm 18:41." Turning he read, "They cried, but there was none to save: even unto the Lord, but He answered them not."

The well was fifty feet deep. The bodies filled the well to within six feet of the top.

XXIII. DELHI

21st June to 9th July

Frank and Edith Tytler stirred sleepily. It was 2 a.m. on 21st June, though both were too young to take count of dates and times. But something was happening within the tumbril that they did not understand. Marie was there with many brass bowls of steaming water and a man with a black bag they did not know; light from a horn lantern rippled like phantoms on the tumbril's thatched roof. They wondered why Mama was lying on her left side, her thighs bent, a pillow between her knees. They wondered, then went to sleep, and in the wavering light a child was born.

Outside, the rocky slopes of the Ridge gleamed with the golden tapers of dying camp fires. In these still hours before the dawn the only sounds were the clank of a patrolling sentry's steel scabbard, a loyal sepoy's soft murmur of "*Sab Achcha*" (All's well). From within the tumbril there came now a faint wailing cry. The doctor, bending closer, shook his head. The baby seemed frail and underweight for a male child and, as was too common in this pitiless climate, had been born with dysentery. He took Robert Tytler aside and whispered the news that had to be spoken. It was unlikely that his son could live a week.

In a warm and tranquil ecstasy Harriet in the straw was drifting off to sleep. The baby lay near the opening of the tumbril "with only a small square of flannel thrown over him, the setting moon shining brightly on his little face."

Somehow, he did not know why, Robert Tytler thought his son would live. The need to tell someone, anyone, swelled within him; a British private of his own treasury guard was the first to hear the news burst from his lips. He was unprepared for the warmth of the reaction; for thirteen weary days these rough unlettered men had looked for a sign and now it had come they were strangely comforted. "Now," the word ran through the lines at dawn, "*now* we'll be all right. We've had our first reinforcement."

Yet inexorably the changes of command continued. Postponing "the gamester's throw" to the last, General Sir Henry Barnard died of cholera on 5th July—"a happy release for him," commented Octavius Anson. Stricken with ague and diarrhoea, his successor, tired old General Thomas Reed, held command for twelve days, issuing all orders from his bed. Sick leave despatched him to the hills; sole command of the force passed to Colonel (now Brigadier) Archdale Wilson, the vacillator of Meerut.

Wilson faced no easy task. He took over a force whose morale was fast waning, which counted suicides commonplace. On some days at noon, with the sun at its zenith within six degrees of the vertical, officers stared at the thermometers in their tents in silent unbelief: the mercury stood at 131 degrees. All were allowed extra rum—"the fighting dram" —when they had been under fire, but indiscipline was so rife many refused to fight at all. On 23rd June, Plassey Day, when twenty thousand sepoys poured from the Mori and Kashmir Gates of the city, British troops lay supine on rocky ground, cursing their officers, refusing to face such odds. For the first time in the history of the siege, officers themselves loaded guns with grape and shot, firing volley after volley until the mutineers, leaving a thousand dead behind them, fell back.

Such unrest was not surprising. Always the British in India had chosen their campaign weather like men who plan a shooting party; a people rooted in conservatism were now forced to adapt. No longer was it possible to distinguish one regiment from another; following the camouflage principles of the Punjab Guide Corps, officers and men dyed their quilted cap-covers and flannel shirts with mud, even curry powder—the first universal use of khaki. Light blue wooden canteens gave place to leather-covered lemonade bottles slung from a strap. Non-coms were picked out only by white worsted chevrons; officers by their small gilt buttons.

Above all, a deep-rooted sense of permanence weighed this force down. Newcomers gaped at a camp like a vast canvas city, whose focal points, the brigadier's tent and the headquarters mess tent, formed the base of a three-sided rectangle. Beyond lay the supply line of this army: thatched hovels of native servants, bazaars where merchants who had fled the city now chaffered over fruit, milk and vegetables, thousands of bullocks, camels and horses. Amongst them sauntered private soldiers in slate-grey, puffing on short cutty pipes of clay, tall blue-turbanned Sikhs with black swept-back beards, mounted Afghans with scarlet saddle-cloths, olive-skinned Gurkhas with black worsted caps.

To all in these sweltering senseless weeks, the horrors of the Ridge assumed a different guise. To an artillery captain, George Bourchier, it was the desolate stunted trees, scabrous patches of bark chawed clean by camels. To others it was the ever-present rebel dead that lay in the Ridge's rocky hollows, blood soaking their white cotton robes, their bodies nibbled by jackal bites. Where ground was like granite, men had no strength to cover their bones; "their tombs," one man wrote "were the throats of the beasts of the field." This above all plagued the sensitive Octavius Anson, whose nose was keenly attuned to strong odours. He inhaled cologne to drive away the stench; the stench seemed to creep to the pit of the stomach.

He took to wearing a fine veil over his face on picket duty.

It saved him from fever, so he believed; it could not save him from other horrors; black scorpions "like young lobsters"; the smell of damp jack-boots, yap-yapping of pariah dogs, coffee that tasted of liquorice. Prickly heat clothed him like a garment: his expenses gave him no peace. One month's messing had cost him £14 for even in mud and slime the 9th Lancers dined well, at long tables lit by silver candelabra, each with his own silver salt and pepper boxes. Would he screw it down to £10 a month, by eating in mess less often? Such campaigns could strip an officer naked for he must pay his own servants as well as the cost of baggage transport. "You seem to do wonders with your money," he wrote wistfully to Frances. "You have set me such a noble example of economy that the oftener I save the two rupees for mess wine the better." Then the thought of Frances brought the words from his heart because he loved her so: "God grant that we may meet again . . . I often fancy I see you walking into the dining-room just before prayers with your arms full of the day's work." He could no longer bear to see the water-carrier outside the tent playing with his children; how strange to envy a water-carrier because his wife and children were with him this night? "But it makes my heart long so . . ."

For Harriet Tytler, the problems of parenthood were proving almost insuperable. Since the long-awaited moment that her baby was born, she had known no moment free from anxiety. No sooner had the child's dysentery abated than the monsoon rains broke; the thatched roof of the tumbril proved a perfect colander of holes. Luckily, a company's bell-of-arms, where muskets had been stored, stood empty close at hand. Taking no time to ask permission, the Tytlers moved in.

No frontierswoman of the American west battled more strongly for survival than did Harriet now. At first she, Marie and the children lay on thin quilts spread upon straw; until Robert Tytler bid for sheets at an auction this was their only bedding. At night their clothes were rolled in tight bundles to serve as pillows. Even clothing was pitifully short; Harriet herself had but two cotton petticoats. When the children's clothes were washed and dried they crouched within the bell-of-arms wrapped in sheets.

Daily the sun beat down on their tiny masonry dwelling; even after Robert had knocked air-holes four feet by two feet in the walls, the heat was so fearful that two-year-old Edith fainted twice daily, often while taking a bath, and Harriet must clutch the swooning child from the water. Until Jamalka, their servant, stole a milch goat which gave them two full quarts a day, they drank only the canal water where the clothes of the camp-followers were washed, the elephants and bullocks watered. "But for the flavour it might have passed for pea-soup," recalled Harriet later. To choke it down she closed her eyes, kept tight hold of her nose and gulped.

By modern standards of tropical medicine, it is astonishing any man of Wilson's army left the Ridge alive. Even in cantonments, kitchens were sited alongside cesspits: often tanks into which bazaar sewage flowed were used for both drinking and bathing. Medical officers' reports on water supply were limited to "smells good" or "smells bad"; rare stations had lavatories but these lavatories lacked fittings. On campaign a lump of alum was the one specific for purifying ditch water. Cholera, which servants called "the sickness that begins in death," stalked the Ridge. Each night, Harriet charted its progress through darkness by a series of strangled cries; man after man fell at his picket post, rice-water stools streaming uncontrollably from their haunches, racked by cramps excruciating enough to rupture stomach muscles. Unaware that their enemy was a deadly comma-shaped bacillus thriving in humid air, teeming in filthy water and infected fruit, surgeons prescribed an amazing variety of remedies: laudanum, raw brandy, mercury, opium blended with chalk, castor-oil, hot bricks clamped to the chest, stomach and feet, total immersion in near-boiling water.

All were unavailing. Faces grew blue, wrinkled "like a washerwoman's hands"; in rare moments of silence their dry retching became hideous. Orderly officers moved amongst them, not varying daily custom, asking, "Any complaints?"

With no provision made for a field hospital, regimental surgeons treated men in their tents or whatever shelter could be found. Since the commissariat-agent refused to honour his promise of double pay to the stretcher bearers most had run away; only Her Majesty's 8th Foot, honouring this prom-

ise, saved its men. Men from other regiments, lacking
stretcher bearers, saw their comrades, sick and sun-stricken,
left to die by inches below the Ridge.

Flies swarmed everywhere, a metallic brassy horde, louder
than a hive in swarm. Against the flies, Harriet Tytler was
powerless. Old receipts were no longer feasible; "to destroy
flies or drive them from a room, infuse quassia chips in
water well sweetened with sugar and place in plates and
saucers." All this belonged to another life, a world of peace
and power. At the mess-table officers laid trails of sugar and
gunpowder, blowing the questing flies to perdition. In this first
soaking week of July, it seemed sometimes the flies had con-
quered the Ridge. Men awoke from sleep to find flies had
squeezed between their lips: fat black flies darkened the air,
growing swollen on putrid corpses. Flies covered a dish of
soup as if it were a bowl of peppercorns; they battled with
humans for every mouthful. They crawled down the Chaplain's neck as he read the sacraments; never again would one
man open his Bible, specked with their blood, without recalling this nightmare summer. Flies burrowed into the ears
and nostrils of the unwary; they laid their eggs in men's
rectums.

Such malaise, mental and physical, disturbed Brigadier
Archdale Wilson profoundly; in his hesitant way he struggled to combat it. Slovenly dress mirrored slovenly discipline;
no longer must men turn out to fight in shirtsleeves but wear
some kind of uniform. Officers must visit sentries and vedettes
frequently and submit written daily reports to the duty field
officer. Buglers would be attached to each picket to sound a
speedy alarm; picket supports would at night sleep fully accoutred. Regimental bands would play each morning to
lighten the hearts of weary men.

Yet Wilson's own shortcomings as a commander were as
palpable as at Meerut. Grave, silent, retiring, this mild-
mannered son of a Norfolk minister found greatness violently thrust upon him. Such was his passion for artillery he
could pass no gun without testing with his thumb whether it
was breached or empty—finally, as one observer wrote, "giving them an affectionate pat, in parental farewell, as if

to say, 'Now be a good gun and behave properly until I see you again'." The keynote of all his policy was delay.

"I must own that I dread success on entering (Delhi) almost as much as failure," he wrote as early as 16th June. "The insurgents have shown . . . how well they can and will fight from behind cover, such as they will have in street-fighting." To his staff-officers chafing for action it seemed that the chances of taking Delhi, of releasing a force to succour Lucknow and Cawnpore, grew daily more remote.

For the problem of the Delhi force was much more than cracking a mighty bastion seven miles in circumference. Chief Engineer Richard Baird-Smith, who had arrived in camp on 3rd July, the day the rains broke, was stunned to find artillery and engineering material so lacking the British stood little chance of either shortening the siege or cutting down fatalities —often one hundred and fifty after a bloody rebel sortie. To feed the seventeen siege guns in position the British had exactly 11,600 pounds of ordnance powder—barely enough for one day's active firing. Musketry powder had dwindled to a scant 12,900 pounds. The nearest magazines to remedy these deficits were at Phillur and Ferozepore in the Punjab, both more than two hundred miles away along rain-sodden roads.

A portly aloof Scot of thirty-eight, Baird-Smith took all meals apart in his tent, brooding on Delhi as a problem of pure engineering. But on one score he was adamant: to withdraw from the Ridge would be madness for "all India would at once believe that we retreated because we were beaten." Already Brigadier Wilson had written urgently to John Lawrence in Lahore: if one English regiment and two of Sikhs did not march from the Punjab now he must retire to Kurnal, seventy-eight miles north, to avoid further casualties.

Armed with bitter protests Baird-Smith sought audience with the General. To withdraw from Delhi, severing all contact with the Punjab and leaving the city as a focal point for every rebel between the Ridge and Agra? It was insanity to think of it.

Wanly Wilson agreed. For the time being at least they would stay put.

What of the enemy? Already, Baird-Smith calculated, they

could bring from twenty-five to thirty guns into action on any part of the city open to attack. They had as many mortars as they had men to use them. Thus, on 18th July, the day after Wilson took over the force, Baird-Smith outlined his needs: at least six 24-pounders, capable of tearing through thirteen feet of well-rammed earth, as well as eight 18-pounders, four 8-inch howitzers and four 10-inch mortars. But all these must come from Ferozepore; it would be three weeks at least before they could reach the Ridge. Baird-Smith must bide his time.

In these July weeks, while grey soaking clouds pressed low over the Ridge and the earth was like gum beneath the feet, few men were making more progress than William Hodson. Both as intelligence agent and leader of a newly-formed private army of five hundred fearless hard-riding Sikhs, he seemed, to this listless force, a soaring tower of strength. To the rebels, Hodson's Horse, whose scarlet turbans and sashes earned them the nickname of the Flamingoes or Ring-Tailed Roarers, were the embodiment of all they feared: time and again rebel patrols, cantering through dank undergrowth, felt the breath of death fan their cheeks as Hodson spurred insanely towards them, followed by a band of yelling Sikhs. Always his cry of elation was the same: "Come along, lads, the fun's begun." Sabres clashed and jarred; still Hodson kept up his ceaseless icy banter: "Call yourself a swordsman? Try again! Make me sweat for it!" The lips parted in laughter beneath the heavy curved moustache, the blue eyes never smiled. The joy of winning was an anodyne, blotting out the known shame of the past, the certain shame of the future.

There were darker sides to him, not known to all, hinted mostly in veiled half-sentences. Tales of shabby conduct were current; he was a man "fit only to lead Italian banditti," snorted Surgeon Edward Hare of the Bengal European Fusiliers. Almost four years after he left the Guide Corps, Hodson's misuse of regimental funds was still under investigation; here on the Ridge a bulky sheaf of depositions was locked in the adjutant's desk. Graver charges were pending: at Khurkunda, near Delhi, Rissaldar Bisharat Ali, a known money-lender, had been pistolled like a dog, pleading for a fair trial. He was, he protested truly, no mutineer; his commander had sent him home on sick-leave. Shot, too, was a boy of twelve who clung weeping to the old man's body. How much money he had owed Bisharat Ali only Hodson knew and it would never matter now.

Once Hodson captured a rebel elephant: by evening its silver howdah bubbled within his private melting pot. A man like Hodson, walking a tightrope of debt, set much store by loot; already a quarter of his salary was mortgaged on insurance premiums.

But his intelligence service thrived. Spies came and went daily, spurred by Hodson's promise of £100 reward to the first saboteur to blow up the rebels' powder magazine; he had bridged the arid miles between the Ridge and the walled city. Most brought news from friends of Rajab Ali who were still close to the old King; their messages were set down on tiny scrolls, two and a quarter inches long by one and a half broad, finer than finest tissue. Each day the cunning Rajab Ali wrote back, often fulsome letters to men who wished no dealings with him. Their receipt became known; no matter how much a courtier protested his innocence, his unswerving devotion to the rebels, he had received the letters—that was enough. Hodson's aim was the death of trust; he would set them at loggerheads, implicate them all. Once Rajab Ali taunted Ahsanullah Khan, the King's physician, with a Persian poem deriding puppet monarchs:

> *A fly was seated on a piece of straw*
> *Floating in the urine of an ass*
> *And thought himself captain of a ship . . .*

The sepoys who intercepted this were so incensed they tore down the physician's house.

Already one message had come, it seemed, direct from Bahadur Shah himself. In the first week of July, Futteh Mohammed, an opium agent who had escaped from the city, brought an astounding story to the British camp. Earlier he had been summoned to a secret rendezvous with Ahsanullah Khan "at the top of a high building." The physician had sworn he was empowered to speak for the King, now desperate to negotiate with the British. He wanted assurance his pension would be continued, payment of £10,000 a month, confirmation of his old title. If all was agreed, a document would be drawn up affixed with the Royal seal, commanding the British be given all aid. The gate giving private access to the palace on the city's river face would be left open, or any other gate the British might choose. Hodson and Rajab Ali placed no more faith in this than Brigadier Wilson. The river side of the city was inaccessible to the British. And the old man ruled in name only; who would open gates to his order when even the sepoys, ran current reports, slouched in to see him without their turbans, and wore their shoes in the Hall of Audience? It was said they had even stolen the Royal seal.

More and more, as Trooper Devi Din knew, the old man had become the helpless tool of his captors. Only on 1st July, when Subadar Bukht Khan crossed the swollen river and entered the city at the head of five thousand mutineers, the band blaring "The Rogues' March" did the old man snatch at one last straw. A stout shrewd artillery officer from Bareilly, Bukht Khan was virtually self-supporting; the treasuries at Delhi were long since emptied but Bukht Khan had brought with him £40,000 worth of treasure. He asked the King for orders but the only order the old man could give him was not to plunder the city or distress its people. The town crier made his rounds demanding police tax be promptly paid yet the police were powerless against sepoys who turned citizens onto the streets and converted their houses into shot-shelters.

The leading merchants urged that they, not the army, should raise what money was needed, for the army was bleeding them white. In later years, Devi Din's mighty frame shook with laugher, recalling those days; the sepoys had surer ways of raising cash than by endless wordy council. A merchant with hooks driven through the fleshy parts of his shoulder-blades, lowered up and down a well by ropes, was soon ashamed of bilking brave men fighting for the cause. Some merchants' memories were unbelievably bad, but a burrowing beetle imprisoned in a walnut shell, strapped over a merchant's navel with a tight turban, was a fine cure for amnesia.

On an impulse Bukht Khan now offered himself as Commander-in-Chief, then stared in unbelief as the hapless old man seized his hand in gratitude. Both could scarcely believe their good fortune. "A greater man than the General does not exist," the King quavered.

Bukht Khan stressed that he wanted proper quarters for his men and full obedience from everyone under his control, the princes included.

"You have full authority. Do whatever seems good to you," the King bade him. Bukht Khan left the Royal presence with a sword, a shield and the title of Lord Governor-General.

Following the identical measures Wilson was soon to undertake, Bukht Khan made a determined drive to bolster the rebels' failing fortunes. He warned the police chief that for further plundering he himself would be held responsible and hanged. All shopkeepers must keep weapons; those who had no weapons could apply for them free at headquarters. Sepoys caught looting would have their arms severed at the shoulders.

Next he issued stringent orders to the troops. No man would qualify for a day's pay until he had done battle with the British. All too many quit the fray by shamming lameness, returning groaning to the city, a rag tied round their leg. Others pleaded "the air outside the city did not agree with them." Bukht Khan now decreed that no man who left the city to fight in the morning could return within the walls until 4 p.m. To each went the stern ultimatum *"Jao laro"* (Go and fight).

For all this, the sepoys fought bravely; more than once their valour filled the British with dismay. Often so many swarmed from the city it took an hour for the force to assemble; to the British peering from the Ridge it seemed as if a vast anthill had been horribly overturned. Doctors were an unknown luxury; often the wounded would be buried with the dead; they did not falter. At 10 a.m. on 9th July, the whole Ridge, with shattering impact, was made aware of their mettle.

Harriet Tytler never forgot the blazing excitement of that morning. So stealthily did a hundred cavalry approach the camp through driving curtains of rain that the alarm had not even sounded from Brigadier Wilson's tent; this was standard procedure, ensuring that in fifteen minutes all officers and men were at their posts. Harriet's first intimation of alarm was an urgent cannonade of hoofs past the bell-of-arms. Outside, horses from the artillery battery thundered by, traces clattering beside them; harsh cries of *"Dugha hai"* (There is treachery) came through the weeping morning. Though Harriet could not know it, the cavalry had first approached the sepoy gunners and urged them to join the cause; finding no support they had put them to the sword before unlimbering the guns to send the battery horses racing through the camp.

The bugle shrilled; petrified with astonishment Harriet saw men in shirt-sleeves double through pelting rain, muskets at the ready, some without shoes or socks, officers still drugged with sleep, buckling on revolvers and belts. Most, a few seconds earlier had lain inert beneath their beds, wet towels coiled round their temples, thin screen blinds of finely-split bamboo called chicks warding off flies. One officer was so excited he tore by armed with a quill pen; another had seized the regimental roasting spit; the mess-sergeant of the 9th Lancers had only a corkscrew.

At the Horse Artillery picket Lieutenant James Hills, a slightly built young gunner, was breakfasting out of the rain, when a trooper of the 9th Irregulars galloped up with electrifying news—enemy cavalry were in sight. He did not add that faith in the British cause was waning; the 9th had made no attempt to check the enemy farther up the road. To Hills's horror the twenty blue-uniformed carabineers of the 6th Dragoon Guards, despite the rich oaths of their commander, Captain James Stillman, abandoned their horses and fled before a shot was fired. Hills was now quite alone but without hesitation he spurred towards the rebels. If he could but delay them for vital seconds the guns might swing into action.

Once, twice, Hills' sabre jarred through bone and flesh, then with a thud that drove breath from the body he himself was unhorsed. His sword had gone; desperately he struggled for a handhold; the rain-slicked coat of the plunging whinnying horse denied his fingers. The rain had saved his life; he felt the heavy waterproof cape falling in shreds beneath the sabres but somehow it cushioned the blows. Then the troopers had gone speeding after the fleeing carabineers.

Brigadier-General John
Nicholson

Earl Canning,
Governor General of India

Sir Colin Campbell

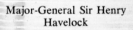

Major-General Sir Henry
Havelock

Robert and Katherine Bartrum

Harriet and Robert Tytler

Henry Kavanagh

Flag Staff Battery, Delhi

Bridge of Boats, Delhi

Mohammed Bahadur Shah

Lahore Gate of the Palace, Delhi

Kashmir Gate, Delhi, stormed by troops under
Major-Gen. John Nicholson

General Wheeler's entrenchment, Cawnpore

Artist's impression of the storming of Delhi

British reprisals. Hanging of two rebels

Bailie Guard Gate, Lucknow, showing clock-tower

Road by which General Havelock entered the Residency, Lucknow

Sikanderbagh, Lucknow. Interior after capture by the 93rd High-landers and 4th Punjab Regiment under Sir Colin Campbell

Sikanderbagh, Lucknow. Exterior showing breach and gateway

The perils of Lieutenant James Hills had only now begun. Barely had he seized up his fallen sword than three other cavalrymen, two of them still mounted, came driving at him. Feinting, parrying, Hills now changed weapons with the desperate speed of a juggler, first a lunge with his sword, next a blast from his pistol. There was no time to reload: as one of the rebels spurred at him again, Hills dashed the weapon into his face.

The third trooper would not give up; he drove at the breathless youngster with his eight-foot bamboo lance, and Hills, his fingers gaining the shaft just behind the seven-inch blade, toppled him with a crash into the mud. In a silence broken only by the sobbing of breath they grappled fiercely. To his horror Hills found that the waterproof cloak had snagged round his throat and was choking the life from him. Now the rebel had seized the sword, twisting it from his grasp; in desperation, Hills hit out, feeling the fist crunch with stunning force against the jawbone. Next instant the sabre struck a glancing blow across his forehead; his face was suddenly a blinding red mask of blood. Slumping to his knees in the rain he knew that at any moment the sabre would hew him apart like meat beneath a cleaver.

Intent on his victim, the trooper did not see that Hills's commander, Major Henry Tombs, alerted to danger by the sight of the carabineers fleeing past his tent, had come racing to the scene. Thirty yards away he saw Hills's slight form squirming in the mud, a rebel sabre poised above him. Halting, he raised his revolver and fired. Blood welled through the white tunic: the mutineer spun away dead.

But as Tombs helped his shaken subaltern to his feet they saw a few yards away the trooper whom Hills had temporarily stunned walking coolly away with Hills's revolver. Without hesitation they closed in on him but the trooper was young and active. Hills, too, was young and active and lived on to become a general, yet the rebel's third blow clove his skull to the brain. Again, like an axe, the flailing sabre cut at the turban Tombs wore coiled about his head. So skilled were the rebel armourers that these curved Damascus blades, forged with arsenic in the steel, were never passed for service unless they could slice through two plump fish at the thickest part; in battle such blades could cleave through five folds of thick leather or sever a man's leg at the thigh. Only the thick wicker helmet Tombs wore beneath the turban saved his life though the dripping blade sheared a lock of hair from his scalp. Then he drove his sword clean through the rebel's body.

For Tombs and Hills this joint exploit won them the coveted award of the newly-created Victoria Cross, yet in the days that followed the British saw courage as their sole compensation. What chance had they of ever breaching the vast red fort when the rebel strength seemed inexhaustible? Their ammunition, it was said, would last all the rebels in India a year. Early allies like the Maharajah of Patiala were wavering; frankly he confided his doubts to Commissioner George Barnes of Ambala, who had worked like a fury to equip the Delhi Field Force for action. "Barnes Sahib, can your Government *ever* survive their present difficulties?"

Commissioner Barnes knew that if his eye blinked or his lip quivered the Maharajah's five thousand men guarding the trunk road between Delhi and Lahore would be lost to them. Already, though Barnes did not then know it, the Maharajah had opened tentative negotiations with old Bahadur Shah. Confidently he replied, "Yes, Rajah Sahib, we are in a little difficulty just now but we have shiploads of troops coming from England." If it convinced the Maharajah it did not hoodwink Barnes himself or the men on the Ridge. This was the rebels' war, a war of guerilla ambushes fought under blinding sun, from behind clumps of spear grass and old stone walls.

XXIV. DELHI

26th July to 4th August

Odds at times seemed unsurmountable, but what, Harriet Tytler would ask herself, could a woman do? By the end of

July she and three thousand others had been seven weeks on the Ridge at Delhi, and the sensation affecting them above all was indescribable boredom. All day the children were whimpering and listless; with only Jamalka to do the work, Harriet was busy from morning to night, for Marie, the Breton maid, was "no hand at looking after babies." Worse, Harriet's brother, Lieutenant Edward Earle of the artillery, had been wounded by a shell; they had rescued him close to death and carried him to Robert Tytler's office tent. Now he would allow none but his cherished sister to dress his wounds. "Harrie, when will you come to me?" he hailed the bell-of-arms each dawn and Harriet, busy trying to bathe three children in a small brass basin, felt the weight of life press down on her. This worried her for surely one should be conscious of being privy to history; even a housewife should not find one of the world's greatest sieges resolving itself into an endless dismal round of mince, curry, hash and rissoles. Yet had it not been for working harder than ever in her life before, she would have been unutterably bored.

Along the Ridge's two rocky miles, every fighting man felt this oppression. Some flew kites, played quoits or cricket or crouched on camp stools fishing, with bottled beer as a prize for the first catch. To while away the tedium a cornet of the 9th Lancers lay up to his breast in the river trying to seize alligators by their snouts. From the Flagstaff Tower, on fine evenings, it became the fashion for the British to train their telescopes on the city that defied them. Often their numbers included elegant Mr. Allen, the provision merchant, who watched the battles in a frock coat, a tall hat and white kid gloves. "I dare say war is an exciting thing at first," he conceded, "but I imagine it would soon pall upon the senses." There would be few more wars like this one.

For the actions they had fought, it seemed, availed them nothing. By 26th July, the sum total of their triumph had been to repulse the enemy twenty-four times. One newcomer, touring the batteries, found them crammed with prone panting men, sapped of all will by the searing wind; in the routine skirmish which followed the exhausted British lost one hundred and sixty killed and wounded. Such casualties were commonplace and men in their letters home revealed a new and hard-eyed indifference to sudden death. Twenty artillery officers had been killed since the siege began, one gunner noted gleefully; he was getting very close to promotion. "Gun wheels went over men's heads, *crack!* just like squashing a turnip"; how much it would have upset one in England, a private admitted, but here it did not touch the heart. "In a battle you're doing what the officers tell you." One officer did not blench when a round shot crashed into the tent where he was playing écarté, taking off his opponent's head. Exclaiming, "O pilot, 'tis a fearful night," he adjusted his monocle, swept up cards and kitty and departed to seek another game.

To his fellow surgeons Dr. Campbell Mackinnon confided the disquieting truth: he found Brigadier Wilson so depressed as to be unfit to command. The General had written to his wife in the hills instructing her whence to flee once the British retreated from Delhi. The wells of self-pity overflowed within Wilson; he rounded on the one woman who understood his manic-depressive spirit: "You are getting as unreasonable as the other know-nothings who . . . think a force under two thousand bayonets can . . . hop over the walls of Delhi . . . as easy as toasting cheese." For by August, Lord Canning was complaining bitterly that Delhi should have fallen long ago, and Wilson must draft memoranda full of shrill self-justifications: even twenty-five thousand men would not be too many for the task that faced him. Worse, he knew that on this score Chief Engineer Richard Baird-Smith was his most bitter opponent. Near-crippled by a shell-splinter and gripped by diarrhoea, his gums puffed with scurvy, Baird-Smith fought on to the last, dulling his pain with port and as much opium "with as little effect as would have done credit to my father-in-law." His father-in-law was Thomas De Quincey, author of *Confessions of an Opium Eater*.

The risk would be there, Baird-Smith agreed, even when heavy guns arrived, but this risk Wilson must take.

More than any factor, this lack of leadership cast a gloom on the men of the Ridge. Few suffered true hardship. Men who had scooped up cold stew with their hands in the Punjab Campaign, now revelled in porridge and a pound of boiled beef for breakfast each morning. At lunchtime, on duty in the batteries, gunner officers were heartened to see even under a storm of fire, a solemn procession wend its way towards them: a cook-boy with a brazier to keep the sahib's food hot, a water carrier, bearing bottles in a porous pot, a steward leading the way with the mint sauce for the lamb or the mustard for the beefsteak. At night, bemused by the wax lights and sparkling silver of the mess-tents, they heard William Hodson, his glass brimming, offer the toast "To the bright eyes we have left behind." Yet, bewildered by their lack of success, they knew a feeling dangerous to professional soldiers; they were growing tired of war.

Daily, Brevet-Major Octavius Anson felt his yearning for his wife grown keener. As Mess President he must, for the benefit of his fellows, order in fifty dozen bottles of beer, twelve dozen of claret, nine dozen of brandy; he himself took solitary snacks in his tent, for if Frances on what he allowed her could still save money to send him stamps and eau-de-cologne he felt ashamed of the three shillings that dinner in the mess-tent cost—a man paid no more in the Bengal Club, Calcutta. Often he made do on bread and butter with sherry and water or tea and mango-fool and at these times he could think of Frances undisturbed. "I shall be glad to leave this filthy camp," he wrote from the heart. "May God be your rock and refuge forever."

Then one blistering morning a man who was impervious to heat cantered into the camp at Delhi; a tall man riding alone because all his life he had been alone; a bearded man with black luminous eyes and a deep sonorous voice, who held his head abnormally and smiled only at little children. A man who knew he was unpopular and could do nothing about it, yet who to his everlasting distress was worshipped by a sect of Indians wearing saffron-coloured robes and round black hats who believed him to be a god. And from this moment on, all doubt and boredom would vanish from the camp on the Ridge like river-mist scorched by the sun.

Brigadier-General John Nicholson was on time for an appointment with destiny.

XXV. DELHI

7th to 10th August

John Nicholson stepped inside the brigadier's tent, lowering his six foot two inches into a chair. He saw a soldierly man with sad pensive eyes and a small ramlike beard sitting with a bandaged head. Plagued by dyspepsia, the brigadier had grown frail and wan living on arrow-root.

Wilson saw a man aged thirty-four but looking ten years older, deep-chested, broad-shouldered. From a smooth pale face stared dark-grey eyes with black pupils. This was a man who in the presence of more than three people became shy, a withdrawal which took the form of cold curt sarcasm. When deeply moved this man could bite through an ivory paper-knife. He could hang a rebel and then weep bitter tears that this had been necessary.

Though commander of John Lawrence's Punjab Movable Column, 4,200 strong, now seconded to the Delhi Force, Nicholson had seen little soldiering. Primarily a political officer, his promotion over the heads of his seniors had earned him the nickname *"Mr*. Nicholson"; wise men levelled such gibes behind his back. Always beside him strode his Pathan orderly, the huge whiskered Mohammed Ayat Khan, who at meal-times handed Nicholson all dishes with his own hands.

What Nicholson wanted, since the general had summoned him in advance of his main force for consultation, was a chance to inspect the posts and defences of the Ridge. What Nicholson wanted he almost always got.

On 7th August his tour carried him along the Ridge's full two miles. Following him from picket to picket went heated debate, much murmured speculation. Few men in the Delhi camp had seen Nicholson; all had heard of the strange silent

man who had lived more than half his life among wild tribesmen. Such was his fame as an adversary in the second Sikh
War the Sikhs christened him *"Nikal Seyn"*; even twelve
years later one would say, "Our women wake at night trembling and saying they hear the tramp of Nikal Seyn's war-
horse." This man, the story went, relaxed by hunting tigers
on horse-back with a sword, whirling round the beast like a
teetotum until it crouched dazed and stupefied. These details
were learned by observation for Nicholson was grudging with
words. In the headquarters mess-tent he was so chill and
aloof one political officer grumbled, "If we had all been as
solemn and as taciturn during the last two months I do not
think we should have survived."

Nicholson's currency was deeds, not words. In seven weeks,
as all knew, his Movable Column had struck terror into
the rebels' hearts. Briefed to intercept a rebel regiment en
route from Sialkot to join Bahadur Shah, Nicholson had made
a forced march of forty-six miles in one day. When his men
craved respite in the shade of trees, Nicholson granted it—he
himself remaining bolt upright on his horse, under the full
glare of the July sun, awaiting their readiness. Later at
Timmu Ghat on the Ravi river he led the charge on the guns
that routed a thousand men.

A protégé of the wise Sir Henry Lawrence, who had sought
in vain to transfer him to Lucknow, Nicholson had the same
razor-edged perception of the Indian mind. On 14th August,
when his column marched into camp, the full impact of this
came home, for the wild Multani tribesmen, sitting their
ponies like men born to the saddle, had ventured thus far not
for pay but for love of "Nikal Seyn." More was heard now of
his sagacity at Peshawar in the Punjab, when the native infantry officers there had protested to the garrison commander
that to disarm their loyal troops would be rank perfidy. At
once Nicholson had risen to hand each colonel a packet of
papers. "Perhaps these letters will interest you." Without
authority, Nicholson, appointing himself postmaster-general,
had unearthed proof of treasonable correspondence. An hour
later the troops were disarmed.

At Phillur, on 25th June, Nicholson had faced this same
crisis: learning that one regiment of his mobile column was

on the point of mutiny he stood between the crossfire of two thousand men while his British troops disarmed them. Half an hour later, when the 33rd Native Infantry rode into the fort to join the column, their colonel, an old grey-haired man, sought a favour: "General Nicholson, we have made a double march this morning in our anxiety to go down to Delhi with you and have left our baggage behind. I must therefore ask you to let us halt a day to enable it to come up."

The bombshell came with Nicholson's cool reply: "Colonel Sandeman, I regret extremely to say that I must request you to return to your regiment and ask them to lay down their arms." The old man had started as if he had been shot; for a second it seemed as if he would topple from his horse. Then, after one long look at Nicholson, he rode slowly back to his men. Returning to his tent, Nicholson had confided in his brigade-major, Seymour Blane, "I shall lose the command of the column for this. The last telegram I received from Sir John Lawrence last night forbade my disarming these regiments but I know I am right."

But Nicholson had not lost command and the days that followed saw a true sense of purpose infusing the men on the Ridge. Nothing escaped Nicholson's notice for he became the unauthorised supervisor of all men's efforts; combining the duties of artilleryman, engineer, and orderly officer, he yet found time to check on the commissariat and Hodson's intelligence service. Later military experts would declare that no major operation in World War I was more thoroughly planned than the assault on Delhi. With Chief Engineer Richard Baird-Smith, Nicholson rehearsed every detail of the struggle to come. Routes and assembly-points were taped on the ground itself. In the engineers' camp, every move from loading camels to scaling imitation bastions was gone over time and again. By 20th August, only six days after Nicholson's column arrived in camp, final plans had been laid before General Archdale Wilson.

And now Wilson was racked by apprehension, for he faced that which he dreaded most in life: an irrevocable decision. Even calumny was preferable to action; to his aides it seemed that nothing less than the entire British Army would have satisfied him and even then he would have preferred someone else to order their advance. "For God's sake don't drive me quite so," he pleaded with Baird-Smith. "The old General at first took violent exception to my plans as involving fearful loss of life," Baird-Smith wrote to his wife, "if he had apprehended them clearly he would have seen they were really the safest of the series." So reluctantly Wilson had agreed.

To Lieutenant Arthur Lang, who had fretted through his daily duties at Mian Mir Cantonment, Lahore, ever since the morning of the historic disarming, it was a matter of life and death that he should be a party to these plans. "I hope I may be in time," he had chafed as early as 23rd June; already he had volunteered for Delhi and impetuously packed the forty pounds of kit permitted. But his seniors had deferred decision and soon the young engineer was lamenting: "I shall be late for the fighting, only in time for fever and cholera."

But not until a month later did the red-letter day dawn: on 23rd July he was to leave at once for the Ridge as a member of Baird-Smith's staff.

"Tomorrow I will be Field Engineer, Avenging Army, Camp before Delhi, the doomed city of the Moguls," he exulted to his parents, for now even his feelings for pretty Sarah Boileau, his fiancée, were eclipsed by his passion to test himself under fire. Much of his early sympathy for the sepoys had gone, swept aside by the tidal wave of rumours. "One month of India now would change your opinion of a lifetime," he assured his mother, "we . . . hear of nothing every day but deceit and fiendish cruelty . . . I hope no quarter will be the cry when we have the upper hand."

Lang's anxieties were premature. On 10th August the siege train had left Ferozepore but this was not due until the first week in September: 653 bullock carts laden with twenty thousand sandbags and heavy powder-barrels could not, in the height of the rains, cover the two hundred miles in less than twenty-six days. Each one of the fifty heavy guns en route was drawn by a single elephant, but often, when a gun sank deep in mud, a second elephant must free the wheels with titanic pressure from its forehead. Only when this six-mile cavalcade drew near the Ridge could the great assault be launched.

XXVI. DELHI AND GANGES VALLEY

7th to 26th August

In these August weeks while Nicholson strode the Ridge like an avenging angel it seemed to Mohammed Bahadur Shah that the mutiny now lacked all forward impetus, that it was no more than a whirlpool sucking unto itself all the inchoate forces of disaffection and discontent of the continent. As often when sorely troubled he dipped a goose-feather quill in an ink-pot of rose-pink cornelian to purge his troubles in verse:

> Heaven and the blue have surrounded us
> Sleep has vanished and comfort, too,
> Only the peace of heart remains
> That may depart by the morning, too.

At Delhi the rebel cause was all but dead. Despite his avowals that discipline would be restored, the obese Bukht Khan, the new commander-in-chief, was powerless to control the sepoys. Seduced by the prospects of plunder they would dig no entrenchments, obey no commands. The artillery were disheartened: from 9th August on, as Trooper Devi Din would always recall, the news of Nicholson's arrival cast a profound gloom over the insurgents. A deputation of officers sought out the King complaining the troops still left were starving. In despair the King convened a council to examine ways and means. Yet two days later came news that three thousand had fled.

Within the red sandstone colonnades voices were shrill in accusation and counter-accusation; no man would shoulder blame, let alone responsibilities. The artillery commander complained that unless eighty extra horses were supplied he could not make daily attacks. The princes, it was charged, had embezzled all the army's money; certainly £400,000 worth of silver, plundered from three stations alone, had mysteriously vanished. Sepoys avenged old scores by denouncing their enemies as British spies; such men died in mortal agony with red-hot ramrods driven up their rectums. Though a few districts still refused to pay revenue to any authority but the King, these were notable exceptions.

More and more the hapless old man took refuge in sudden senile tantrums. Once, when the sepoys besought him for money, he flew into such a passion he cast his velvet cushion in their faces, crying "There, take all I have, you'll rob me of my clothes soon." If they did not heed his commands, he threatened he would swallow a diamond and pierce his vitals; their conduct was worse than that of Genghis Khan. But soon he suffered a change of heart, offering them jewelry to swell their funds, though he sought only troops who would fight for two months without pay. A regiment that arrived with a troupe of dancing girls was sent packing.

Yet day by day his troops lacked heart to fight at all. Early on the morning of 26th August came the worst news to date: thirty-six miles from Delhi, in the mud and slime of the village of Najafgarh, eight thousand rebels who had set out under Bukht Khan to intercept the siege train from Ferozepore had been routed by a bare two thousand men. Prominent in the thick of the fighting had been the man they feared as much as death itself: the invincible "Nikal Seyn."

Gravely the superstitious shook their heads, for only eleven days earlier at a council of war every Indian officer had in turn cast a pinch of salt into a brass lotah, pledging thereby that should the salt dissolve so might each man who proved faithless or a coward. And the salt had dissolved.

In vast tracts of the countryside, the spirit of mutiny approached this same stage of dissolution. If law and order could be maintained without the British, well and good, but the British, it seemed, were essential to peace and the villagers craved their return. Vast forces were on the march, plundering and pillaging; the army of Khan Bahadur Khan, fanning out from Bareilly, numbered almost thirty thousand men and somehow their monthly expenses of £26,000 must be met. Often such swaggering bands, after looting villages, pressed inhabitants into service as coolies, demanding they should be carried for miles on string beds. To resist them, villagers banded together in strength, armed with axes, spears and scythes, demanding tolls of up to £20,000 before the rebels passed.

To Lord Canning, a sick blanched man, after three unrelenting months, it seemed blood enough had been spilt to prove that given mercy and understanding the people would disclaim the rebel cause. In his twilit shuttered room he sought to quench the steady flame of hatred. "The Governor-General," he wrote, "is anxious to prevent measures of extreme severity being resorted to . . . utmost severity will have the effect of exasperating the people and will probably influence them to band together in large numbers for the protection of their lives and with a view to retaliation . . ." To guide his civil officers he ordained new canons of judgment: free pardons must be granted to any who could show claim to mercy. Men who had dispersed to their villages when their regiments mutinied deserved only leniency. No man should be punished as a deserter unless he was taken armed. The laying waste of villages must cease.

Such injunctions earned the Governor-General the scoffing nickname he would carry to his grave—"Clemency Canning." No longer did men raise their hats to him when he rode abroad. Within months the European population of Bengal would urge his instant recall. Still Canning did not falter. The editor of *The Bengal Hurkaru*, Alexander Forbes, charged him with treason because he took no pride in hanging more sepoys than any other Governor-General. This paper could be and was suppressed; never the hatred that powered it. Men lacking the lust to kill were styled "white niggers." *The Englishman* described a patent gallows which could "accommodate sixteen of the largest size without inconveniencing each other." To scowl was high fashion: all Calcutta praised Thacker and Spink's art gallery for a portrait of an officer whose stern features promised "no undue lenity . . . to the murderers of women and children." Editor Walter Brett of *The Englishman* conceived a new masthead: "It is right to be taught by the enemy."

"I will not govern in anger," Canning wrote, for he saw the British viewpoint also. No man could chart their losses statistically; one could chart them less still in terms of human deprivation. The cool hill stations above the plains were crammed with penniless refugees living on credit; all banknotes were stamped with a crest-press now, a precaution against forgery. Typical of hundreds was an officer writing from the gutted station of Sialkot: "I have nothing in the world now but a night-shirt, pair of trousers, hat, one pair of socks . . . my rings, watch, studs, all gone . . . pray send me clothes of any sort."

Everywhere the British saw all life as a hazard: in Calcutta women did daily target practice with revolvers, now costing £12 apiece. For civil servants all furloughs had ceased. From September on, no unemployed civil officer could draw any allowance at all. The three presidencies, Canning stressed, must pare their expenses to the bone; already the mutiny had sent administration costs soaring by £10,000 a month. Gold mohurs, normally valued at £1 12s. Od., now fetched £2 8s. Od. for these offered the simplest way of carrying large sums. Government securities were not to be cashed at any price, no store would take a cheque and for fear of sabotage no night trains could run.

These were material hardships. Worse by far were the nails of anguish driven through the heart with each news of a death: friends, relations, beloved children. Each Sunday, at divine service, a few more black-clad forms filed quietly to their seats; for a long time black would be the fashionable colour for women. The London General Mourning House offered widows' weeds on credit and with reason: history records that this cataclysm robbed one man alone, Charles Staines of Hissar, of thirty-two relatives. Magistrates spent patient hours poring over pathetic claims for "succour money," for many women were left with five children to support on a pension of £120 a year. Each week in the churchyards below the hushing tamarisks, the marble monuments rose like mushrooms—"leaving a wife and disconsolate child to lament his loss"—"Suffer little children to come unto me, for of such are the Kingdom of Heaven."

Already in the name of justice many Britons had perpetrated cruelties as fearful as the Spanish Inquisition. Such reprisals, men argued, were prompted by Cawnpore, yet at Allahabad, three weeks earlier, the hard-swearing Colonel James Neill had restored order by a wave of stark terrorism. The hangman, Neill vowed, should never lack "acorns"; he and Commissioner Charles Chester sat in judgment day and night. One man was hanged for picking up a bag of copper coins dropped by fleeing sepoys. Six who plied a ferry for the rebels under duress met the same fate. A water drawer was hanged because his martial moustache resembled a mutineer's. Often such men were a long time dying; soldiers bribed the hangmen to make the execution slow and satisfying, with the victim dancing "a pandy's hornpipe." Hundreds were condemned by Queen's officers speaking no word of the language, understanding neither evidence nor defence.

Hindus to destroy their caste first had their faces smeared with bullock's blood; Moslems had their mouths crammed with pork fat or were sewn into hog-skins. Others gyrated from trees by their heels, charring to death over slow fires; the soldiers tore the green leaves from these "hanging trees," pressing them and posting them home as souvenirs. Even old and toothless crones were not immune. "Them's them as breeds the beggars," one soldier snarled when a subaltern checked his upraised sword.

North of Allahabad the commander of Neill's advance guard, Major Sydenham Renaud, hanged forty-two men, including twelve who "disrespectfully" averted their glances from his column. Along the Grand Trunk Road, village after village was fired; the old, the bedridden, children at the breast died in these infernos. In twelve months the population of Mauritius, an island in the Indian Ocean, swelled by a hundred and thirty thousand souls. Many fled to escape the vengeance of men like Deputy Commissioner Frederick Cooper of Amritsar in the Punjab, who executed two hundred and thirty-seven mutineers of the 26th native Infantry by firing-squad without a trial. Forty-five others died of heat and suffocation during the night. "England," Cooper claimed, "expected every man to do his duty."

At Cawnpore, where he had assumed command after Havelock's victory, James Neill sought to ensure the rebels' everlasting damnation. He could not hang the Nana Sahib for the Nana had fled across the river at midnight on 17th July; the devout had seen the flickering oil-lights on his boat snuff out in midstream and in the darkness a great cry arose. This, the Nana had told them, would herald his suicide in atonement for his defeat. Only later did they discover the Nana had tricked them and was alive, at the head of twelve thousand men, in the trackless jungles of Oudh. But over two hundred and seventy of the Nana's troops were now Neill's prisoners and for them he devised a unique form of punishment. Before his execution each man was dragged to the House of the Women and set to cleanse with his mouth a yard of the bloodstained floor. "All the Brahmins will be buried and the Mohammedans burned," Neill vowed, for no mutineer in his hands could hope for redemption in an after-life. Nicknamed "the Butcher" by his troops, he himself dragged many through the blood. "I cannot," he concluded, "help seeing that God's finger is in all this."

Elsewhere men made an ugly pageant of death, adopting the time-honoured Mogul custom of blowing men from guns. At these parades, before the ceremony, the band struck up a lively march; as the doomed sepoys, escorted by the provost marshal, walked with nonchalant unconcern to the guns, a shadow seemed to darken the sun. Motionless, like a thunder-head, a thousand vultures hovered. Jauntily the victim eased the small of his back against the muzzle of the six-pounder, standing perhaps three feet from the ground, loaded with a two-pound service charge of powder. Presently, as music died, the crowd fell back. The gunners stood with smouldering portfires and even at this moment some of the sepoys, strapped tightly to the muzzle, were looking unconcernedly over their shoulders. Then the fire was clapped to the touch-hole.

The air shivered and seemed to split apart. The whole frame, one eye-witness recorded, went skywards "in a hideous red cloud"; the head was driven thirty feet into the air.

As the body burst like a goatskin the vacuum of the blast sucked blood and bone and entrails backwards, spattering the gunners from head to foot; from above the birds fell like falcons, snatching hot gobbets of flesh. Once at Barrackpore, two English women, eager for vengeance, clad all in white, on white Arabs, spurred deliberately forward at this moment; then rode away, robed in scarlet, mounted on red roans. And again the band struck up.

Peace they would have but peace with guns and gallows. Those proud Brahmin heads must come to dust.

XXVII. LUCKNOW

27th to 30th June

Within the Residency, Lucknow, Katherine Mary Bartrum huddled disconsolately in the two-storey plaster building known as the Begum Kothi (the Queen's House), scarcely knowing what to do or where to turn. All about her were the dawn sounds of the Residency coming to life: the rolling boom of the time gun, the clash of arms that marked the changing of the guard, the tramp of marching feet, the fretting and cooing of purple pigeons, yellow hornets buzzing, children crying, the lowing of Henry Kavanagh's cows—for the adroit Irishman, with rare prudence, had taken care his family should not lack for milk. But this morning another and unwonted sound was plainly audible: the imperious cries of master and mistress calling in vain for their servants. Soon, as the realisation came home, the cries fused into a clamour of angry protest. Save for the hardy few like the Kavanaghs' loyal staff of ten, the servants, sensing only disaster at hand, had fled.

"Our trials have begun in earnest," Katherine noted in her diary, for this was the greatest problem the sheltered Lucknow ladies had so far faced. It was 8 a.m. on 27th June and this was the morning of the river-bank massacre at Cawnpore.

No weakling, the shy serious-minded Katherine was more than willing to try and adapt herself but after almost three years of marriage it was an uphill task. Her marriage with Robert had been based on the desperate need of soul for soul, both so deeply in love they knew a perfect union beyond the reach of flesh, yet Katherine, like every Victorian girl, had been dependent on her husband for the most trivial decisions. To console herself she read again the short note that Robert, on 9th June, had written to say that all was still well at Gonda: already it had become a tissue through constant re-reading.

My dearest K . . . Oh! that I may be spared to see you and my sweet little boy, but having done our best we must rest our hope on Him who is alone able to serve . . . I am not fit to die, but do, my dearest wife, as you love me, pray that a new heart may be given me . . . that I may be a more fitting companion to you in the road that leads to life . . . You must not mind the discomforts about you! only do not be too anxious and so become ill, as our little baby will suffer for it . . . I have nothing more to add, my beloved, but to ask you to pray for me, as I do for you, Your attached husband . . .

It was the strangeness of this new life that most perplexed Katherine Bartrum now. The Begum Kothi was "a most uninviting looking place, so dirty, having neither a punkah to cool the air nor a scrap of furniture to set it off but we had to make the best of it." As in a barracks, their long white-washed room was divided into fifteen portions, where each woman stowed her string bed and scanty linen as best she might. By night, when the punkah was rigged, this privacy was forsaken. Greedy for warm swirling air, women and children crowded together in the room's centre, "like the pieces in a jigsaw puzzle," plagued by a whining venomous orchestra of mosquitoes. True, little Bobbie was still fat and bonny but Katherine watched him with foreboding; how long could he remain healthy if the siege went on? As her first independent gesture she had laid in a store of candles and soap; the servants had prophesied the Residency might soon be infested in earnest. Already many women were too sick in mind or body to combat the squalor; it was Katherine Bartrum, hating dirt and disorder, who set to work unaided with a sweeper's twig broom to scour their quarters clean—"the servant of all work," she called herself wryly. At evening, when the children slept, these refugees from the out-stations had their one touch of consolation. Perched on the edge of their beds they drank weak tea by the wavering light of a candle in a bottle, recreating a world of English fields, family prayers and the cry of the muffin man.

So perhaps it was best, Katherine soon consoled herself, that the servants *had* gone; certainly it gave her far less time to grieve over Robert's absence.

On this high diamond-shaped island site of thirty-three acres there stood, besides the Residency proper, sixteen build-ings now called garrisons. Some, like the Begum Kothi, Katherine Bartrum's billet, huddled close to the Residency itself, fully five hundred yards from the mud-walled ramparts. Others, like the house of Financial Commissioner Martin Gubbins, a lofty white mansion masked by yellow creeper, were outposts set like bastions in the very line of these defences. Among the three thousand members of this crowded cosmos—927 British officers, privates and civilians, and 700 loyal sepoys who were the defenders, 700 coolies, and 600 women and children—there would in the weeks to come emerge a sense of immolation greater than any deed of individual courage: the spirit of the siege of Lucknow.

Much of this lay in the future. Such men and women needed time to readjust. Pretty, frivolous Maria Germon was typical of those unwilling to bow to the inevitable. The smallest challenge to the carefree past became a landmark in her daily journal. The impertinence of the officious Captain Green, at the main gate, known as the Baillie Guard! When they had vacated the burning cantonments after the night of 30th May, Maria had arranged for the transport of her piano to Dr. Fayrer's house, yet Captain Green had refused to let it pass the gate. Maria had to appeal to that sympathetic Major John Anderson before it could pass through.

Yet Maria, a good wife, always saw to it that "dear old Charlie" had proper rations sent each day to his garrison, the Judicial Commissioner's house: mango-fool, quail, bread and butter, fresh vegetables. Still she clung to the vestiges of better days: tea and ices in the garden each evening, pleasant mornings sewing on the verandah while Dr. Samuel Partridge read the ladies extracts from Sir Walter Scott's novel *Guy Mannering*. In this week of a wide white moon she slept on the flat roof of her garrison, Dr. Joseph Fayrer's house, an umbrella over her head to ward off the moon's baneful influence.

It was the same all over the Residency grounds—a feverish preparation for grim action, the social round continuing unabated. The chief engineer, Major John Anderson, and Captain Fulton, his second-in-command, had been unable to prepare a ground-plan of the defences. Never knowing how soon assault might come they had settled for an unbroken enceinte, or fortification, which when possible embraced existing walls. Trenches were dug, palisades rose. Beyond the ramparts the trampled slopes bristled now with cheveaux-de-frise (iron spikes set in timber to repel cavalry), entanglements of branches known as abattis, crow's feet or four-pointed iron spikes, pits filled with sharp stakes which engineers called trous-de-loup. Such obstacles, checking the enemy's storming parties, might grant the defenders time to bring a withering fire-power to bear before the inner defences were breached. The four faces of this diamond-shaped fortress were thus roughly four hundred yards long, though in places the defences bulged and jutted, to form a total perimeter of two thousand yards.

The night hours now echoed to the grating of spades, the steady clink of picks. Yet gay dinner parties, even at the current hour of 4 p.m. were still the vogue. Brimming glasses of claret and champagne held high, their favourite toast held a poignant irony: the health of General Wheeler and the defenders of Cawnpore.

Ahead of them, though they did not know it, stretched a hundred and forty days of a like ordeal.

For despite Sir Henry Lawrence's emphasis only a third of the buildings on the perimeter's gentle slopes had been demolished. Many buildings commanding the Residency were still intact on 27th June: others had only their upper storeys destroyed or their parapets thrown down. On the eastern face skirted by the Cawnpore Road, crumbling plaster buildings crowded only twenty-five yards from the Residency walls. These could readily be loop-holed for rebel musketry or used as bases for mining operations. On the western face, one of the main defence posts was Martin Gubbins's house, on which the Finance Commissioner had spent over £400 of public money, paying his coolies double wages: though his barricades incorporated sideboards, even Government records, his private amenities included a newly-constructed swimming bath. To the south, the outlook was bleak: the palisades skirting it were almost the only defence against undemolished buildings sited thirteen yards from the walls. Strongest outpost in the defence works was the Redan Battery (named after The Great Redan at Sebastopol), mounting two 18-pounder guns and one 9-pounder, jutting from the curtain of the north face. Beyond these northern defences, open ground sloped to the river, the bank crowned by a parapet seven feet high, revetted with gabions, wicker baskets filled with earth, and long faggots called fascines. This, Sir Henry knew, was the one high and wide terrain on which the rebels could mass a column of assault.

A motley crowd Sir Henry had pressed into service, as strange a bunch of mercenaries as ever took up arms under one banner. Cynical kindly François Deprat, the French merchant, knew the calling well; long ago he had served as a soldier-of-fortune in Africa. Wherever he went the Swiss merchant Leopold Ruitz Rees would surely follow. Signor Salvatore Barsotelli, the Italian porcelain dealer, a man of rare spirit, did guard duty with a musket, a double-barrelled rifle and a huge cavalry sword, an ammunition pouch resembling an Italian hand-organ strapped over his breast. A cheerful and self-confessed amateur, Barsotelli consoled one distracted volunteer who could not present arms, "Never mind, sir, make a *lettle* noise—who's to see in the dark?" For the first time in history Britain had called on schoolboys to fight her battles; under headmaster George Schilling, young Edward Hilton and fifteen senior boys of La Martinière School stood to arms each time their position on the hard-pressed south-eastern face was attacked. When the servants deserted they forsook Latin and vulgar fractions to pull punkahs, grind corn and tend the sick. Then there was twenty-two-year-old Private Henry Metcalfe of the 32nd Foot, inseparable from the Rev. James Harris's white terrier, Bustle. Fearing that rations for his family would be imperilled, Harris had sadly asked a soldier to shoot the dog, but Metcalfe, intervening, had volunteered as a single man to take the risk. Now Bustle did guard-duty side by side with his new-found master; if Metcalfe dozed off through sheer fatigue, Bustle would seize his trouser bottoms and tug till he awoke.

Along with these men served Henry Kavanagh. Unsparing in his efforts to bring volunteers up to scratch, Kavanagh took true pride in this close association with Sir Henry Lawrence. It was sixteen years since he had first served as a clerk under Lawrence, then a tense abrupt man in his thirties, and he loved Sir Henry now as a man grown mellow and reflective with the years. On 26th June, as Lawrence's orderly for the day, Kavanagh had ridden out with him on a tour of the defences, admiring his lynx-eyed inspection of each loophole, his keen interest in the volunteers' drill. No man who had a point to put to Lawrence went without a hearing. But he was weak and careworn, Kavanagh could see, and the susceptible Irishman was touched to the quick to see "the deep and drooping furrows of his face"—how would he bear up under the stresses to come? Nor was Kavanagh's concern misplaced, though one who saw Lawrence that day wrote: "Grief becomes him like the scars of battle."

Kavanagh, too, found his stamina fast waning. Anxious that the civil volunteers should be a credit to their garrisons he denied himself sleep for nights on end, inspecting sentries who were changed hourly. From the instep to the hip his left leg grew hot and stiff. Soon a bright red rash pocked with blisters, blanketed it. The doctors diagnosed erysipelas; weak and light-headed with fever Kavanagh collapsed on his bed in the Post Office garrison, racked by fears that his share in the defence was past. Lest she infect their children, even Agnes, his wife, dared not approach too closely.

Along with the virus in his bloodstream, a new resolution was stirring in Kavanagh. He had served "John Company" for twenty years now, joining them as a boy clerk of fourteen;

apart from a two-year spell in a merchant's office in the hill station of Mussoorie he had given them his whole adult life. Why? Kavanagh asked himself. The Superintendent Engineer's office, the Political Agent's Department, the Judicial Commissioner's Office—he had served them all, and it had brought him precisely what? Kavanagh like many a man nourished fierce and unfulfilled dreams of destiny; he saw his service now as twenty years of underpaid drudgery. Each month the Company squandered more tending the Residency gardens than they paid him as salary. Morosely, Kavanagh thought it all too easy to explain why revolutions thrived. Men endured years of being pressed down, stifling resentment, then the mould of power was shattered into a thousand new fragments and who knew then which would assume the most imposing shape? Clerking was not his destiny; his destiny was to lead, to do great deeds, to bend events to his will for he had tired of being bent. A line from Shakespeare's *Julius Caesar* flashed through his brain —"I love the name of honour more than I fear death"—and he reached the decision which was to change the whole course of his life. As he himself later wrote frankly: "I resolved to die in the struggle rather than survive it with no better fame than I took into it."

All the defenders, save the rancorous Martin Gubbins, shared Kavanagh's implicit faith in Lawrence. "Sir Henry is no longer firm nor his mental vision clear," Gubbins had written to Lord Canning with characteristic disloyalty on 2nd June, for Gubbins stood next in line of succession. This was untrue; Lawrence's vision was clear to the end but he had punished his body cruelly in the first weeks. As early as 9th June, his medical adviser, Dr. Joseph Fayrer, had issued a blunt ultimatum: if Lawrence did not slacken off, his life would be in danger. Accordingly, Lawrence had transferred command to a provisional council: Financial Commissioner, Martin Gubbins; Manaton Ommaney, the Judicial Commissioner; Major John Banks, Commissioner of the Lucknow Division; Colonel John Inglis, of the 32nd Foot; the Chief Engineer, Major John Anderson. Of this council, Gubbins had been president.

"He sees only through his own vision," was Sir Henry's

verdict on his deputy, "and is therefore sometimes trouble-some." What Gubbins's vision showed him now was that even armed loyal sepoys were a potential menace. In vain did the council point out that the 30th May, when Sir Henry and his staff stood on the Residency steps to watch the cantonments burn, was the testing time: these men had then stood fast. Gubbins, who as a company official of twenty-five years' standing ranked in status with a major-general, would have none of it. The men would be disarmed, dismissed. On 11th June, after granting them two months' furlough and a month's pay, he had driven them from Lucknow. "What an end to the Bengal Army!" lamented one subaltern. "After a hundred years, paid to leave us quietly, without cutting our throats."

Angrily, Lawrence tore himself from his sickbed and re-sumed command. His envoys were sent to intercept the re-treating sepoys and many, moved by this mark of trust, now returned. Convinced many old soldiers of the Oudh Army would re-enlist to restore law and order, Sir Henry summoned them by circular to Lucknow. The response was overwhelm-ing. Five hundred pensioned sepoys—men gone grey, men on crutches, some blind—toiled across the countryside and flooded into the Residency compound. Of these Sir Henry selected a hundred and seventy fit for frontline duty. Thus his Indian brigade—Sikhs, pensioners, loyal sepoys—had been swelled to almost eight hundred.

Gubbins would not rest. Charged by a former Resident, Sir James Outram, with showing "a habitual and reckless dis-obedience of superior authority," Gubbins had also, to quote Outram, "a disregard of strict veracity in his official cor-respondence." This scorn for truth cost almost three hundred lives. Incensed that Sir Henry would not lead forth a force to trounce the enemy, Gubbins at 10 a.m. on 29th June pressed on Sir Henry depositions from two spies: a rebel force of five hundred foot, five hundred horse "and one wretched gun" had reached the village of Chinhat, eight miles from Lucknow. A third report, which put their strength at upwards of six thousand, was deliberately suppressed.

"Well, Sir Henry," Gubbins sneered when Lawrence hesitated, "we shall all be branded at the bar of history as cowards."

Thus at 6 a.m. on 30th June Lawrence moved out to seek the enemy with a force of seven hundred men.

There were other factors, besides Gubbins' gibe, to spur Sir Henry on. On 26th June, while he inspected the defences, a messenger had hastened up with a despatch; as Lawrence opened it, Henry Kavanagh saw his mobile features quicken as he read the stirring—and counterfeit—news, that Delhi had fallen thirteen days previously. Next day came further tidings: though Sir Hugh Wheeler was treating with Nana Sahib, Major Renaud's force, moving in advance of Havelock, was speeding to save Cawnpore. At Lucknow, Lawrence knew, his own preparations for a siege were far from complete. With reinforcements promised and the rebels of Chinhat so ill-equipped, there seemed good reason to reconnoitre.

This, as Lawrence's secretary, George Couper later stressed, was a reconnaissance expedition, a show of strength to impress the native city. Never at any time was Sir Henry minded to engage the rebels.

What followed was unbroken tragedy. By a cruel oversight almost half the force—three hundred men of the 32nd Foot—had not breakfasted; many had been drinking the previous night. Now, suffocating in scarlet tunics and forage caps covered in white drill, they must stumble four-and-a-half miles through loose sandy soil until they rounded a bend in the Chinhat road. In silence and perfect battle-order a white-clad force, six thousand strong, now came in sight. Their range and gunnery were lethal. At the first shot a British gunner fell dead. This was the six-gun battery of Fyzabad, for which Lawrence, unavailing, had weeks earlier offered £20,000. Firing as they came, the rebels now advanced.

Though history dignifies it as a battle, Chinhat was, in truth, a headlong rout. From the first, swamped by the rebels' superior numbers, Lawrence was helplessly outflanked. Swooning with hunger, the men of the 32nd were stricken to find their muskets, long loaded without discharge, had grown foul and would not fire. Faced with odds of almost ten to one, many Indian artillery-men now overturned their guns and lashed their wagon teams forward to join the rebels. Bending to their saddle bows, on lathered horses, the Sikh cavalry rode hard for Lucknow. Of the wounded some found a perch on retreating gun limbers but more fell, their blood dyeing the hot sand, to be sabred by rebel cavalry. Only Sir Henry's presence of mind checked the infantry's pursuit at the last. Bareheaded, on his white horse, he ordered Captain Alfred Simons to execute a monstrous bluff on the last bridge spanning the river before Lucknow. Though ammunition was exhausted, Simons massed his gunners with lighted port-fires in a grim inflexible line behind the vents. Faced by the blank black muzzles of cannon, the rebels fell back. Watching the men stream past, dark wet places spreading on forearms and groins, Sir Henry wrung his hands. Tears streamed down his furrowed cheeks.

"My God! My God!" the cry burst from him, "and I brought them to this."

Many men now reached Lucknow only through the sympathy of Lawrence's loyal sepoys; anxious to prove not all were mutineers they gave European wounded priority. Other Britons lived to bless the Indian women who revived them with water and fresh milk as they stumbled towards the Residency. Yet the losses were appalling. Apart from five guns, including a mighty eight-inch howitzer towed by an elephant, Lawrence had lost 293 men killed and missing, while a further 78 were sick and wounded. He must now man a two-thousand yard perimeter with 1,720 men.

What did this mean? It meant Lawrence could no longer afford the luxury of a separate garrison to overawe the native city: the Machhi Bhawan Fort a mile up the river, where 240 barrels of gunpowder, 594,000 rounds of ammunition, lay stored. This fortress must be blown up and the defenders evacuated to swell the Residency's forces. Hemmed in on all sides, as Wheeler had been at Cawnpore, Lawrence sent a stark outline of their plight to Havelock at Allahabad: "I look on our position now as ten times as bad as it was yesterday; indeed, it is very critical . . . unless we are relieved quickly, say in ten or fifteen days, we shall hardly be able to maintain our position. . . ."

At this, even James Neill of the Madras Fusiliers commented in his diary: "God help them! Whence can come relief?"

Within the Residency all were stunned at the debacle. Mrs. Julia Inglis, recuperating from smallpox, had dozed throughout the battle: she awoke announcing, "Oh, I have dreamed our troops have been signally defeated." Peering from the window she saw her dream transmuted to reality: a straggling mass of men, plastered with dust and blood, were slumping exhausted on to creeper-fringed verandahs. Mrs. Geraldine Harris, dressing for breakfast in Dr. Fayrer's house, felt the air tremble as the enemy's guns opened on Lucknow: stentorian voices were bidding everyone run for the cellars. Her toilette only half-completed, resourceful Mrs. Harris seized her hair from the hands of her ayah and sliced it off at the plaits. With a wail of lamentation the ayah ran from the room, never to be seen again; to lose one's hair, the Hindus believed, was an omen that all was lost. Dr. George Ogilvie, Inspector of Oudh gaols, saw Henry Lawrence, hatless and wild-eyed, dismounting from his horse. "Well, Mr. Gubbins has at last had his way and I hope he has had enough of it," were Lawrence's first words.

On all sides, chaos reigned. Barricades were being thrown up, guns dragged into position, men ran shouting to their posts. Already hundreds of coolies and tally clerks had decamped, taking their tools and stores with them; such defences as awaited completion would be crowned by the labour of the besieged. Mothers sought frantically for the safest places to hide their children; it seemed that every child in the Residency screamed with a single tongue.

Among the women, even long-standing residents were now reduced to a life penned in damp cellars twenty feet below ground. None knew how to cook, for that was not a lady's province; most would subsist on a thick stew of meat, peas, flour, rice and sea-biscuits simmered in water. In a siege, copper saucepans cannot be re-lined; often their food would be blue-green with verdigris. Always it would be so dark that so long as candles lasted they would breakfast by this light.

In these first moments, their chances seemed hopeless,

their hard-wrought defences pitiful. At some points the ramparts were only firewood covered with earth. Crawling from his bed, weak with fever, Henry Kavanagh suddenly slumped on a cot near the Post Office garrison and buried his face in his hands. How could a thin wall five feet high be termed a defensive position? Aside from the cook-boys who served the meals, few really knew their way about this trodden rain-soaked no-man's-land; the neat parterres flanked by low walls, encasing green lawns, were blotted out beneath guns and piles of round shot. No garrison mustered more than fifty men but few of these could venture forth except at night when ways were dim. Here they must fight, live, or more likely, die.

This was momentary mass self-pity: hard on its heels trod philosophy, humour, rare courage. As an ear-splitting cannonade opened from the far side of the river, Mrs. Julia Inglis sought peace of mind in reading the Litany with Mrs. Adelaide Case, whose husband commanding the 32nd had died that morning. Soon an ironic cheer greeted the news that a well-aimed shell had put paid to Martin Gubbins's swimming bath—every man in the Residency had found "Buggin's Bath" rankling. And at Captain Robert Anderson's post, on the east face of the defences, one incident stood out diamond-clear: with a snapping crack a round shot tore away a pillar of the verandah, burying a Deputy Commissioner, William Capper, beneath a roaring lava of masonry. Racing to the scene, Anderson and Corporal William Oxenham of the 32nd Foot at first saw through a yellow vortex of plaster dust only a vast dune of broken bricks. Then, as from the depths of a vault, they heard Capper's voice:

"I'm alive! Get me out! Give me air, for God's sake!"

"It's impossible to save him," one man protested.

"It *is* possible—if you try!" they heard Capper call back.

Panting, scrabbling, almost rupturing themselves, they heaved at vast boulders of masonry. Only six inches of wall now protected them as they lay prone on their bellies, grubbing with lacerated fingers while enemy bullets whiplashed about their heads. After three-quarters of an hour Capper's trunk was free; an hour and Corporal Oxenham, working with total disregard for danger, had disengaged his legs. Bruised, shaken, yet uninjured, Capper had unconsciously set the key-note for the whole siege of Lucknow: "It *is* possible—if you try!"

XXVIII. LUCKNOW

1st July to 31st August

As August wore on, one fear was paramount in Lord Canning's mind: a full-scale peasants' revolt, a true war of independence, would render reconquest impossible. Military commentators in England who sneered, "The utmost extent of the rebels' cohesion is that of marbles in a bag," could not see that men like Colonel Neill were fast imposing true cohesion on them. By August's end the British held with safety only the line of the Grand Trunk Road; the area of revolt was a thousand miles broad, five hundred miles long. In Oudh, powerful feudal barons like Rajah Maun Sing had seized the reins, appointing their own police, collecting their own revenue, and behind them, recruited by repression, was a formidable army of freedom fighters—priests, servants, boatmen, shopkeepers, agricultural workers.

To many it seemed that relief would never come to the hardpressed garrison of Lucknow. "They say that we are forgotten and that reinforcements will never appear," Katherine Bartrum noted sadly in her diary. "Indeed it looks very like it . . . this hope deferred does indeed make the heart sick." She found novelty only in the infinite ingenuity which this new life inspired. After the steady bathing of rain, wood was too wet to serve as fuel; a kindly soldier split some railings for her but to kindle it in the little brick fireplace she had built for cooking on the Begum Kothi's verandah Katherine needed her dinner-knife to chop it finer still. The candles were done; a cotton wick placed in oil was the sole substitute she could devise. Soap was at a premium; it took Katherine's fast-developing mother-wit to realise that lentils ground between two stones produced a mucilage that would serve. But only brute strength could tenderise their meat ration of tough stringy gun-bullock; she would thrash it with a heavy stick, shredding it finely with nail-scissors before stewing it. The result was barely edible but somehow her anxiety for Bobbie growing daily weaker on arrowroot and semolina drove everything else from her mind; now they had only three ounces of sugar a week, scarcely enough to make the child's food palatable. "I am so stupid my cooking is generally a failure," she recorded despairingly in her diary. But soon she would summon fresh resolution, declaring, "We cannot starve just because my fingers are bad."

Small portents assumed absurd significance. "Where is Papa?" she would ask the baby each day when he awoke, and each day her heart grew more fearful for it seemed the child's tiny fingers were pointing upwards to the sky "as though his Papa was there." She yearned with apprehension, wondering, "Is it *there* we are next to meet?"

At times lethargy seized her. Boils made her knuckles swollen and painful; twice Dr. Edmund Darby visited the Begum Kothi to lance them, yet from morning to night Katherine's "stupid" fingers must labour, lighting fires, cooking, washing clothes.

At one post within the Residency—Martin Gubbins's garrison—life was still pleasant; he and his guests had ample means. At the Begum Kothi, Katherine Bartrum and her sisters sat up by night to pull their own punkah; the ladies of Gubbins's household paid a coolie two shillings a night. Defying orders, Gubbins cheerfully risked the lives of natives to smuggle private messages to relations in Calcutta. This ceased only when he was threatened with close arrest. To the end Gubbins's circle maintained its rigid code of snobbery: there were certain people to whom one did not speak, even under shell-fire. Their supplies were ample: bottled beer was reserved for nursing mothers, but no luncheon party passed without a glass of sauterne. At dinner gentlemen enjoyed a glass of sherry followed by two of champagne. Milky rice puddings were a daily luxury. At tea-time the English maid, Chivers, in cap-and-ribbons presided at the tea-table. To entertain dinner guests there was Private Matthews of the 32nd Foot, Gubbins's minstrel, with his guitar rendering of "The Old Folks at Home."

Yet often when Katherine Bartrum lay down at night she was so sick in mind and body her love for Robert had no power to comfort. Had it not been for the boy's sake she could have wished never to wake again. Somehow she achieved the miracle of nursing Bobbie through cholera, bathing him in hot water, dosing him every ten minutes with opium and brandy. Each morning the child's eyes were glazed with fever: languid with opium he could scarcely lift his head from the pillow. "What is to be the end of all this?" Katherine cried. "Will we *ever* struggle through this dreadful siege?"

There was reason to despair. In the first days of July, one early casualty had stripped the garrison of conscious thought. From post to post the news was whispered with shocked incredulity: Sir Henry Lawrence was dying.

For twenty-four hours following the disaster of Chinhat Sir Henry had kept a firm grip on the situation, accepting that the men and women of Lucknow looked for leadership to him alone. Scorning danger he had made light of it when, on 1st July, a shell struck his upper-storey room. Next day, he promised his aides, he would change quarters, if only to please them—but it would take a good gunner to lob a shell into the same place twice running.

The rebels had fine gunners and fine guns besides. One was the eight-inch howitzer of the Fyzabad battery, for which Lawrence had bid in vain. This was sited in the King's garden, a thousand yards from the Residency, a high-walled rectangle of neat gravel walks and fragrant orange trees.

At 8 a.m. on 2nd July, Henry Lawrence climbed the steep stone stairs to his private apartment. Exhausted, he lay fully clothed on the white coverlet masking his bed. To Captain Thomas Wilson, his aide, he outlined the salient points of a memorandum on ration distribution. Wilson agreed, at the same time reminding Lawrence of his promise to go below. But Sir Henry begged respite. The heat was so enervating that first he must rest. Then a servant should move his possessions.

After half an hour Wilson returned. He saw that Lawrence

had now been joined by his nephew George, lying on a bed a few feet from his uncle's. Close at hand a coolie squatted, a rope looped round his big toe, coaxing soft warm air like a mistral from the punkah.

Standing to the right of Sir Henry's bed, Wilson read out the draft memorandum. Eyes closed, Lawrence heard him through in silence. Quietly, he began to tabulate amendments.

Without warning, the air parted and clapped together. A rain of bricks hurled Wilson to the floor. There was a blinding flash like the blast from a coke-oven; a vortex of yellow choking dust blotted out the sun. Stunned, Wilson staggered to his feet; the room was in total darkness and out of this darkness there came no sound. "Sir Henry," he called, "are you hurt?" then called again, his voice high with alarm.

From the gloom Lawrence's voice came scored with pain: "I am killed."

Then smoke and dust stirred dimly and now Wilson stood aghast at what he saw: the coolie twisted in anguish, his foot torn away by a fragment of shell; young George Lawrence stunned but unhurt. His uncle lay very still upon the bed. In the darkness the punkah had all come down and the white coverlet was crimson with his blood.

Dr. Joseph Fayrer, to whose bungalow Lawrence was carried, was shocked by what he saw. Sir Henry's face had the pallor of moulded wax, his voice was low "and semi-collapsed," pitched in a hurried excited whisper. "How long have I got to live?" he pressed Fayrer repeatedly and at first the doctor reassured him. "Many hours yet, sir."

But under chloroform, Sir Henry could be easily examined and Fayrer saw there was no hope. Hæmorrhage was slight but the shell, lacerating the upper part of the left thigh, had fragmented the head of the thighbone, blasting away much of the pelvis. Amputation would prove impossible. "How long?" Lawrence pressed again and Fayrer could not find it in him to lie. "About forty-eight hours," he admitted then.

At times they had to bend low to Lawrence's ghostly face to hear him speak; "Poor fellows . . . poor fellows," he would mutter and they knew that his mind dwelt not in present pain but with the garrison in the weeks that stretched ahead. Sometimes, refreshed by great draughts of champagne, his conscious brain was resurrected; he dictated clear concise instructions, the architecture of defence: "Reserve fire . . . check all wall-firing . . . entrench, entrench, entrench . . . turn every horse out of the entrenchment except enough for four guns . . . enrol every servant as carrier of earth . . . pay liberally—double—quadruple." Always he took thought of others: "Spare the precious health of Europeans in every possible way from shot and sun . . . Sir Henry Lawrence's servants to receive one year's pay."

Then mortal anguish ruptured the skein of thought and he screamed like a trapped animal. "He is dying," an officer told Mrs. Hamilton Forbes, "as only such a good man could die, most peacefully." This was a smug Victorian fiction; all her life Mrs. Geraldine Harris, the chaplain's wife, who nursed him, would recall Lawrence's day-long screams of agony. But soon he lacked strength even to scream; only broken sentences escaped his lips under chloroform: "Let there be no fuss about me . . . let me be buried with the men . . . no nonsense . . . here lies Sir Henry Lawrence who tried to do his duty."

Towards 8 a.m. on 4th July his eyes opened. His last lucid words recalled the lesson of Cawnpore: "Let every man die at his post but never surrender. God help the poor women and children." These words men would remember long after that night, when the privates of the 32nd lowered his body into a communal plot. This the Rev. James Parker Harris had scooped with his own hands, for the night was lit by bursting shells and the grave-diggers would not venture near the cemetery.

Financial Commissioner Martin Gubbins was unmoved by Sir Henry's end. He saw Lawrence's dying wish that he should serve under Major John Banks, the acting Chief Commissioner, and John Inglis (now Brigadier) as a personal slight. Banks convened only one council in Gubbins's house following Lawrence's death; sulkily Gubbins refused any opinions on points at issue then slammed noisily from the room. Thereafter, Inglis reported later, "Mr. Gubbins was an amateur soldier who did as much or as little duty as he liked." Yet already, in the true spirit of Lucknow, all civilians had placed themselves under Inglis's command, pledged to perform any fatigue duty with the privates of the 32nd Foot.

Most would remember Lucknow for the harshest reasons. They would recall it as the siege where no man, following Chinhat, knew the luxury of a night in bed; they slept at their posts, their rifles beside them. They writhed with body lice; the ladies, in modesty, spoke of "light infantry." A man counted himself lucky who did less than twenty hours duty a day; of these, five might be passed in pouring rain on a pitch-black night, manhandling powder barrels from the magazine. When an exhausted private at the Post Office garrison threw down his musket, refusing sentry-duty, Captain Bernard M'Cabe, of the 32nd, contemptuously ordered the sergeant of the guard: "Put him to bed!" Faced by this humiliation, M'Cabe, a shrewd ex-ranker, knew the man would goad his body further still.

If the rebels' early fire had been galling it was worse by far in the weeks following Sir Henry's death. Now they had twenty-five heavy calibre guns commanding the entrenchment. Some were only fifty yards away; all were so near shells could not silence them. Ingenious barricades screened them from musketry fire. The gunners crouched in narrow trenches eight feet deep; a man watching from the Residency parapets had the eerie sensation of seeing only disembodied brown hands deftly plying linstock or sponge-staff.

To Dr. Joseph Fayrer, the civil surgeon, it was a miracle any one survived. By 22nd July, the upper storey of the Residency's banqueting hall, which had served as a hospital, was no longer tenable; sick and wounded huddled together on the ground floor. The children, living on barley porridge, seemed like "wizened little old men." Ice and vegetables were non-existent; between lulls in the firing men risked their lives darting from the ramparts to pluck green cruciferous herbs. Scurvy, now called "garrison disease," took its daily toll. The gums grew puffed and blistered then turned black; at length men spat out wads of rotted membrane. One officer, jumping from a low wall, was appalled to find his legs had turned black and blue. Grimly Fayrer diagnosed ecchymosis: a lack of antiscorbutics could lead one slight contusion to rupture a thousand tiny blood-vessels. Young Edward Hilton, of La

Martinière School, diving from a bursting shell, grazed his knee on a sharp stone: within days the wound was an angry suppurating sore. The surgeon gave only one choice: if Hilton did not lie still and rest he would be forced to amputate. For two months Hilton lay very still.

By 26th August rations were reduced; men must make do with twelve instead of sixteen ounces of meat, women were reduced from twelve to six. Gingerly the defenders cast about for substitutes, gulping down a black bitter coffee called "buck buck" made from ground wheat, which induced dysentery in most. Twenty-five handmills ground the wheat to produce the Residency's daily quota of two thousand pounds of flour.

Others would recall the siege simply in terms of its stench: the massive ancient evil smell that was the dead rotting in shallow graves, when lime and charcoal were scarce, bullocks putrefying to mounds of stinking jelly in moist tainted air. The slaughterhouse was Veterinary Surgeon Forbes Hely's post; often he begged Brigadier John Inglis to relieve him. Inglis refused; only a vet., he swore, with grim humour, could endure such a smell. In the churchyard it was worse. On one day alone—8th August—the Rev. James Parker Harris conducted no funeral service. On other days he returned from the churchyard sheet-white with nausea, drenched in icy sweat. Then he lay vomiting for two hours at a time.

In the midst of death and squalor, small acts of humanity were long remembered. At Captain Robert Anderson's post, a peacock alighted on the parapet, preening its gorgeous feathers. Though the men were anxious to kill it for the pot Anderson forbade it; to needlessly destroy such beauty was wanton cruelty. Yet shortages grew daily more acute and the devil-may-care François Deprat, the French merchant, lavished truffled sausages, cigars and wine on all who would carry them away. When Deprat found he had given away so much he had left nothing for himself, he shrugged philosophically. At least he made the gifts of his own free will. The drunken soldiers of the 32nd who plundered his cellar had left him no such choice. Champagne and brandy were all spirited away; the claret and sauterne were left untouched.

More highly priced than food was up-to-date intelligence. To the defenders of Lucknow it seemed that contact with Brigadier-General Havelock's relieving army was the very key to life. Thus, from 22nd July on, Angad, an Indian pensioner, became one of the highest-paid spies in the history of espionage, receiving £500 apiece for three subsequent trips. Despatched over three weeks earlier by Henry Lawrence to spy on the movements of Nana Sahib, Angad at length reached Cawnpore—to return with the glad tidings that the little general was preparing to cross the river and relieve Lucknow. At once Brigadier Inglis wrote urgently to Havelock: "I write to inform you the enemy have pushed up to some of the walls of our defences and keep up a heavy musketry fire day and night from loopholes . . . I trust you will lose no time in pushing on to assist us. . . ."

This despatch, like others Angad carried, was written partly in Greek characters in case it fell into rebel hands, a ruse dating from the Afghan war. Sometimes Angad secreted the message in his staff or the stem of a hubble-bubble. At other times in his hair, his nostrils, or his rectum.

On the night of 22nd July he slipped out to carry this message through driving rain, returning by 11 p.m. on 25th July with Havelock's reply: "We have two-thirds of our force across the river, and eight guns in position already . . . we have ample force to destroy all who oppose us . . . in five or six days we shall meet."

Afterwards it seemed to Martin Gubbins that no tableau more characterised these breathless weeks than Angad's stealthy night arrivals at his post: "the low room on the ground floor, with a single light carefully screened on the outer side, lest it should attract the bullets of the enemy; the anxious faces of the men who crowded round and listened with breathless attention to question and answer; the exclamations of joy . . . and laughter at some of Angad's jeers upon the enemy . . . the indistinct faces of the women in their night attire who had been attracted from their rooms . . . the animated face of our messenger as he assured us of the near approach of help. . . ."

In fact, help was very far distant. On 27th July, after one day's rest, Angad set out once more to contact Havelock with the bulkiest packet he had so far carried: an engineer's detailed plan of the Residency and its approaches and a covering letter from Inglis:

> . . . *The distance from the entrance to the city to our position is about a mile and a half. We can assist you by shelling your flanks for the last 1,500 yards or more . . . the road, however, will be very heavy and difficult for guns and is likewise lined with houses . . . Ignorant of the strength of your force and its formation I can only offer . . . the assurance that the utmost of which our weak and harassed garrison is capable shall be done to cause a diversion in your favour. . . .*

Each night at 8 p.m. officers and men anxiously scanned the southern sky for the fiery trail of rockets—these Inglis had suggested as Havelock's warning signal the night before entering the city, that the defenders' guns might hammer the rebel strongpoints. But no rockets were seen and not until 15th August did another note—brief and disquieting, written eleven days earlier—arrive from Havelock: "We march tomorrow morning for Lucknow, having been reinforced . . . we hope to reach you in four days at furthest. You must aid us in every way, even to cutting your way out, if we can't force our way in. We are only a small Force."

To Inglis it seemed Havelock was nowhere near appreciating their plight. To cut their way out of the Residency, Inglis replied patiently, was utterly beyond their power—"it is quite impossible with my weak and shattered Force that I can leave my defences." In three grim lines he summed up the desperate plight of Lucknow: "You must bear in mind how I am hampered, that I have upwards of 120 sick and wounded, and at least 220 women and about 130 children and no carriage of any description. . . ."

Until Havelock sent further news the defenders must subsist on half-rations—and even these could not last beyond 10th September.

Not until twelve days later, at midnight on the 28th August, did Angad melt from the darkness with Havelock's dumbfounding reply: "I have your letter of the 16th instant. I can only say do not negotiate, but rather perish sword in hand. . . . Reinforcements may reach me in from twenty to twenty-five days, and I will prepare everything for a march on Lucknow."

Thus many believed succour would never come, for now, when the siege was sixty days old, Havelock could offer nothing but another twenty-five days of misery.

To Lucknow's defenders it seemed incredible that Havelock needed nine entire weeks to cover the fifty-three miles between Cawnpore and Lucknow, yet the little general faced insuperable odds. With barely fifteen hundred men, ten small field-pieces and a troop of sixty horsemen, he must cross a vast river, carry a dozen strongpoints and fight his way through a city swarming with rebels. On 25th July, three days after Angad first slipped into the Residency, Havelock had crossed the Ganges in driving rain to make his first forlorn attempt but fifteen miles and two battles later he knew the task was too great. Already he had expended one-third of his ammunition: cholera and rebel bullets had wiped out a sixth of his force. Both officers and men had slept night after night on flooded ground while huge black-and-orange toads hopped in and out of their tents. At this rate of progress, Havelock knew, he would reach Lucknow with powderless guns and six hundred bayonets—and only three hundred men had been left behind under Neill. Sadly Havelock fell back on Cawnpore. He could not, he telegraphed Lord Canning, resume his march until he had been reinforced by at least a thousand infantry and a complete battery.

Already in Cawnpore Havelock had become a familiar lone figure, standing binoculars in hand on the banks of the Ganges, looking always towards Lucknow. Still his men dubbed him "the fighting General" but his staff sensed that the old fire had gone; staring gloomily at an engineer's plan of Lucknow he announced sombrely that ten thousand men might carry the city, no less. His relations with the hot-tempered James Neill (now Brigadier) were at snapping-point; advised of Havelock's retreat, Neill, who credited a false report that the Gurkhas had already relieved Lucknow, had at once sent an incredible letter to his chief: "You ought not to remain a day where you are . . . you ought to advance again, and not halt until you have rescued, if possible, the garrison of Lucknow." To this Havelock had made a brief savage reply: only possible injury to the public service prevented his clapping Neill in close arrest. "You now stand warned," he ended tersely. "Attempt no further dictation."

Worse was to follow. By mid-August Havelock had learned he no longer held an independent command, responsible only to the Commander-in-Chief. The first senior general available, Major-General Sir James Outram, had been appointed to head the Dinapore and Cawnpore divisions, which were to be merged in one command. As former Resident at the time of Oudh's annexation, Outram was also Henry Lawrence's successor as Chief Commissioner. Though Havelock would command one wing of the task force, the glory of relieving Lucknow would be Outram's alone.

But Outram had no such intention: he had for days pondered how Havelock could be given the lion's share of the credit. But not until 21st August, en route for Benares, did the solution strike him. "I know what I will do," he told his military secretary, Colonel Robert Napier. "I will go in my political capacity."

Thus on 28th August Outram routed to Havelock one of the strangest telegrams ever sent by a general in the field to a subordinate: "I shall join you with the reinforcement, but to you shall be left the glory of relieving Lucknow, for which you have already so nobly struggled. I shall accompany you only in my civil capacity as Commissioner, placing my military services at your disposal should you please to make use of me—serving under you as volunteer."

This was typical of Outram. Short, stout and florid with dark grizzled hair he was a man so scrupulous in his dealings with mankind he would climb four flights of stairs, gasping with asthma, to return the call of an obscure subaltern. An incurable chain-smoker, he handed out cheroots to his troops more readily than commands. As a civilian volunteer, he would now surrender the commander's share of prize money —an estimated total of £320,000—to Havelock.

By 15th September, it was expected, Outram would reach Cawnpore with 1,268 men. All would then be ready for the succour of Lucknow.

The rebels, too, were anticipating Havelock's advance. Already their leader, the Begum of Oudh, a shrivelled old woman who had begun life as a courtesan of ex-King Wajid Ali, had seized the reins of government, donating £50,000 towards building an impregnable wall round the city. A clever determined woman, who often led her troops into battle on an elephant, the Begum knew that only men of spirit could hope to check the British onslaught. To one faint-hearted chief she sent a pair of women's trousers with curt instructions: better he should put them on and retire to his proper place—a harem.

Appalled at the prospect of waiting twenty-five days further for Havelock, Brigadier Inglis had already attempted to make terms with the rebels. He would, he stipulated, be willing to evacuate the entire Residency if the garrison were allowed safe passage, women and children to travel first, the men to follow once their families had reached Cawnpore. But the rebels had refused.

On 31st August Lord Canning's telegraphed instructions to Outram were final: "You may let the rebels and their leaders know that if there is a repetition at Lucknow of the horrors of Cawnpore the government will never sleep till retaliation has been enacted . . . if the conduct of the Nana is imitated at Lucknow not a man who can be traced as being amongst the besiegers . . . shall have mercy."

At Lucknow they were always conscious that the enemy was very close. Between 1st and 20th July, unbroken sleep was impossible; day and night eight thousand sepoys kept up a white-hot rain of fire. Later 280 round shot were recovered from one roof alone. At times, screened by rank grass tangling the slopes following heavy rain, they crawled so close to the walls not a musket could be fired; an indignant private of the 32nd complained: "It's not the way of Englishmen to fight behind stone walls!" The chief dead-shot, an African eunuch from the ex-King of Oudh's household, earned the nickname "Bob the Nailer" since his double-barrelled rifle nailed a victim every time. With grim humour the defenders fashioned an unflattering effigy with rolling eyes and frizzy hair; Bob retaliated by shooting out both eyes.

On 7th July a surprise storming party of fifty men stole through an improvised sallyport to the Nailer's strongpoint and delivered their death blow.

As early as 20th July, a major's wife heard an uncanny scraping far below the stone floor of a cellar: the rebels' mining operations had begun in earnest. This news was heard with sinking hearts, for with large-scale mining the garrison's safety would be truly imperilled. The perimeter was upwards of a mile; it would be hard if not impossible to set up enough check-points.

The first three mines—at the foot of the Redan, beneath the walls of La Martinière post, below Martin Gubbins's stockade—were swiftly detected, the miners driven back by grenades and musketry. But the rebels were not giving up. On 10th August, fully sixteen hundred sepoys launched an all-out seven-hour attack on the Residency, unmatched in its ferocity. Against Anderson's post and Gubbins's stockade, legions of sepoys came doubling with scaling ladders. At Captain John Sanders's post, a howling sepoy seized a soldier's bayonet, striving to wrench it through the loophole. At La Martiniere post a mine burst to tear away sixty feet of the defences. Bitterly the defenders fought back, choking and retching as the howitzers unleashed a rain of shrapnel shells and "Stink Pots"—vile-smelling canvas pouches crammed with flax, resin, twisted iron and dry powder. To fight at all they needed the physique of athletes for they mustered thirty guns, only twenty-four gunners. These men sprinted from battery to battery according to the need of the moment.

Yet the keynote of Lucknow was still grim gaiety: the lighthearted fatalism of those so close to death, the true values of life had become an open book. This they maintained to the end, even though losses spiralled daily: by 1st September, the sixty-fourth day of the siege, upwards of three hundred Europeans had succumbed to sickness or mortal wounds. In one mine shaft rebels and defenders launched into a schoolboy game, playfully pelting one another with clods of earth. It was tacitly understood that everyone must put a brave face on things; to keep the women of his garrison in good heart, Dr. Fayrer hustled them all out of his cellar to sing part-songs in the portico. Oblivious to the rushing shriek of grape, the whistle of musket balls, Maria Germon and the others sang grimly on.

Some found a new zest for life in unfamiliar routines.

Assistant Surgeon Samuel Partridge spent all his leisure hours experimenting with a galvanic battery designed to blow up rebel strongpoints. At one post, eight sepoys anxious to prove their own loyalty, built their own gun and manned it between them. Others took comfort in harmless nostalgia. Maria Germon, who had procured some milk-punch to toast her mother's birthday, was touched to find that Charlie, her husband, had remembered too; from his post at the ramparts he sent her a fragrant bouquet of roses, myrtle and tuberoses. Contentedly she settled down to mend Charlie's trousers— "unmentionables," as she always called them—with a piece of the Rev. Harris's habit. A few men took time to ponder the verities. When cholera claimed the Rev. Henry Polehampton, the junior chaplain, the hard-living François Deprat exclaimed bitterly: "Just see the justice of your Providence! Here is a good man like Polehampton dead, and a rascal like myself still living."

A month later when he died in agony, his jawbone shattered by a bullet, Deprat learned that none was immune.

Only Katherine Bartrum, growing daily more fearful for the safety of her husband and child, felt at times overwhelmed by a sadness she could not contain. At evening she would sometimes stare for hours from an upper window across a vista of surpassing beauty: the curving river gleaming in the dusk, a stardust of orange-blossom among ruined gardens, minarets like tall chess-men against the sky. "I peep through the shutters, far away across the fields and trees, looking out like a caged bird."

XXIX. CAWNPORE

Afternoon 27th June

A horse was stumbling along a rutted dirt road outside Cawnpore. Beside it, for the rider kept tight hold of her hand, Amelia Horne, drenched and shivering, stumbled bare-foot, bare-headed. Stealing fearful side-long glances at the cavalry trooper, it was as if a cold hand had clutched at her heart; though he was young, perhaps not more than twenty-eight, his black piercing eyes were baleful and the black beard divided in the centre, the sallow complexion, badly pockmarked, only accentuated this. He wore a white *chupkan* or coat reaching to the knees, white pyjama trousers, close and tight-fitting at the ankles, baggy at the thighs, and a tall white turban crowned his head. This, though Amelia Horne did not know it, was Mohammed Ismail Khan of the 2nd Cavalry, but his identity aroused less curiosity than the man's constant mutter of *"maulvi sahib."* This password, repeated to every straggling group of the Nana's men who challenged their progress had a magical effect; at once they were passed on without hindrance. A *maulvi*, Amelia knew, was a Moslem scholar or teacher, usually of religion, yet what power could a priest's name exercise over these wild drunken men?

This had been the early afternoon of 27th June, three weeks before the Bibigarh massacre, and Amelia had calculated they were now some three miles from Sati Chaora Ghat. Soon they approached a thatched mud-hut; here, without a word, the man had left her. Her heart was beating like a trip-hammer, her temples throbbed with pain; only through a conscious effort of will could she fight back hysteria.

It was two hours before the trooper returned: his curt gesture bade her follow him. Still clutching her hand tightly he led her through a cluster of mud huts to a wide airy tent, perhaps thirty feet by sixteen. This, she guessed, had once served as an officers' mess tent. A patterned carpet covered the ground; canvas chairs were scattered here and there. At one end of the tent, on a wooden dais, sat two *maulvis* in white flowing robes. They were "as still as black marble effigies," their eyes cast upon the ground, and a drawn sword lay at each man's side. Scarcely daring to breathe, Amelia Horne squatted on the carpet at their feet.

Suddenly she looked up. A third man was behind her, his sword drawn, the razor-edge poised only a few feet above her dark tumbling hair. From the dais, the senior of the two began to speak.

This was Mohammed Liaquat Ali, whose chequered career had already embraced soldiering, leading the prayers in the mosque and teaching a harlot's son to read for a fee of a shilling a month—on the strength of this he called himself a schoolmaster. A violent demagogue, whose favourite slogan was "The true Paradise lies beneath the sword-stroke," this was the man who had organised the Allahabad rising of 6th June, fleeing the city to join the Nana's forces when Neill's fusiliers marched in. Though the men of forty villages acknowledged him their leader, wealthy Moslems eschewed him. What Liaquat Ali proclaimed as a holy war they saw as an orgy of licence and plunder.

None of this was known to Amelia Horne until long afterwards but as the *maulvi* spoke the impact of his words was nakedly plain. The sword now poised above her represented no idle threat. The trooper sought her as his own but first she must be converted to Islam. Her religion or her life must be forfeit.

Outside, in glaring sunlight, a horde of wild-eyed men thronged the tent-flap, some sullen, some curious, some seized by frenzy. Every instinct she possessed bade her keep a tight clutch on life. In silent assent she bowed her head.

Dazed, she watched Liaquat Ali solemnly divide a pomegranate; this fruit, he instructed her, was blessed and she must partake of it as the first stage of her conversion. Biting into the red sweet pulp she was handed next the dregs of a glass of sherbet. Listening with downcast head she heard the *maulvi's* voice rise and fall in an ecstasy of prayer. Then a female attendant led her by the hand to an improvised bathing tank. Yielding up her mud-stained bodice and petticoat, the stays and spine-pad which every woman then wore as a matter of course, she sank gratefully into the tepid water for this compulsory purification. When she again returned to the tent, she was for all the world a Moslem woman, dressed in a long-sleeved *coorta* or jacket which reached to her knees, and loose-fitting pyjamas, a shawl of white muslin draped about her head and shoulders. Bareheaded, she stood to face Liaquat Ali, reciting as she was bidden:

In the name of God, the Compassionate, the Merciful,
I betake me for refuge to the Lord of the Daybreak
Against the mischiefs of His creation;
Against the mischiefs of the night when it overtaketh
    me . . .

Bemused and degraded, she stumbled through the bizarre ceremony, her heart giving the passionate lie to this denial of her God, yet conscious always of the sabre's razor-edge trembling behind the muscles of her neck. Now she was irrevocably a bride of Islam, in duty bound to worship five times each day facing Mecca, to fast through Ramadan, to bear witness that there was but one God, to shun wine and pork. Then an attendant led her back to the mud hut.

A long time passed. Outside she could hear the sepoys discussing the massacre and it seemed that some, now the orgasm of cruelty was spent, felt a stirring of shame and regret. It had been wrong, said one, to put to the sword such fair and tender creatures. Why, one, with her dark hair and petal skin, had been like a rose.

Then her heart leapt painfully for a shadow had fallen like a black bar across the white light flooding the open doorway. The trooper had come back.

XXX. BEHIND THE REBEL LINES

July to September

Far in the recesses of Amelia Horne's mind, screened only by an effort of will, was that one blinding moment of horror: the moment when Trooper Mohammed Ismail Khan returned to the hut. After the choking shame and pain of this time her thoughts were not complex for a curious numbness possessed her and each day was as another. There was the sour spicy twilight of the hut which she left only under escort. There was the one scanty meal a day—lentils, chupattis, sometimes a mess of curry. There was the shifting shadow of the guard outside the door, pacing with drawn sabre. Sometimes there was the seashore rumble of distant guns, the scream of a late last victim.

But even in the midst of horror there is always the knowledge of a worse time and for Amelia Horne this came each day at sunset with the trooper's return.

Not all the rebels were anxious to serve Nana Sahib. To the followers of Liaquat Ali, the *maulvi* who had converted Amelia, the longed-for prize was the red sandstone fort of Allahabad whose seizure had been foiled by Neill's fusiliers. Some time in the first week of July these men left Cawnpore bent on its capture: three thousand men, many marching for comfort in linen drawers, fakirs in orange and salmon linen, loping behind gun carriages and tumbrils crowded with women and naked children, behind carts piled with rifles, bedding rolls, and brass cooking pots. With them, on a curvetting Arab, rode Mohammed Ismail Khan. Beside him, in a tumbril, her face veiled by the white muslin shawl, rode Amelia.

Now, for the first time, she allowed herself the luxury of hope. Her great-uncle, Francis P. Floriest, an indigo planter,

still lived in Allahabad. Surely there must come some chance
to escape? She had explained her knowledge of the city to
Liaquat Ali and the *maulvi* had seemed well pleased. When
the time arrived, she should be their guide to the fort's easiest
approaches. Readily Amelia agreed. She would mislead them
by every means within her power; in the resultant chaos her
chance would come.

But Liaquat Ali's men were not destined to reach Allahabad. Early on 12th July Amelia heard the dull concussion of
artillery and a bugle's wild urging; a long way off, amongst
tree-trunks she glimpsed the red doublets of advancing
Highlanders. At once Liaquat Ali and a portion of his force
swerved west and north for Delhi. They had no wish to try
conclusions with General Havelock at Fatehpur.

Then the landscape hardened and from a flat world of
stagnant pools whose depths mirrored motionless scarlet-
headed cranes, they toiled into a hell serene and beautiful.
Amethyst haze shielded far mountains; tumbling blue-grey
rocks were fissured with heat; villagers lay like the dead in
noonday shade. Again, without warning, plans were changed.
By mid-July, it was rumoured and believed, the British had
stormed the walls of Delhi; like men in shock the rebels
moved eastward. Her face a mask of subservience, Amelia
felt a gleeful hatred. With their proud army vanquished,
they were sick at heart.

Then they came to a wide river where the washermen
pounded sheets and saris on worn stones above the yellow-
grey water. Into this river wound the long phalanx of men
and bullock carts and now, to her everlasting humiliation,
Amelia was forced to dismount. Clinging to the tail of Ismail
Khan's horse she stumbled ashore through the shallows, the
mud daubing her embroidered jacket. Thus the disheartened
army came to Farrukhabad.

If ever she walked in a world at peace again, she would
tell that world what war did to men. At Farrukhabad, it
was said, the Nawab's retainers had massacred twenty-one
Europeans. Of this bloodstained sport Amelia saw the cli-
max. One, a girl no older than herself, had been kept alive
a day longer that the sepoys might dawdle over the butchery.
Amelia saw this girl stumbling and crying on the gravelled

walks before the Nawab's palace. A drunken sweating mob of men harried her steps. At close range they fired blank cartridges, staining her face with blood and smuts. With a wisp of pocket handkerchief she would dab away tears and blood; jeering a soldier fired again. Others fired small shot at her heels and toes, forcing her into a frenzied *pas seul*. At some unpredictable moment, tiring of the game, they cut her throat like a sheep's.

In an instant, because fresh victims were scarce, a whirlpool of feeling surged about Amelia Horne. Baleful faces pressed close to hers; the *maulvi's* feeble protests were drowned by high angry shouts. Her acceptance of Islam was just a trick, that her life might be spared. Rough hands bundled her to a tumbril; a tide of screaming men bore it forward until it stood level with the muzzle of a cannon. At least, she thought, death is the ultimate mercy.

But even as she crouched trembling, her lips moving in prayer, Liaquat Ali stepped forward to harangue the mob. Afterwards Amelia thought his eleventh-hour intervention was prompted less by humanity than by the urge to reassert his power; a *maulvi* alone could judge a convert's sincere acceptance of Islam. He and his brother *maulvi* must have time to re-examine the girl afresh. In the midst of snarled and noisy altercation the *maulvis* hastened her from the tumbril.

It was dark when Mohammed Ismail Khan came furtively to the outhouse where they had hidden her. Outside in the moonlight, bearers hovered by a covered litter; beyond, cowled in a shawl, an Indian woman waited motionless. Hastily the trooper bade both women climb in. The *maulvi* had devised an ingenious escape.

The litter swayed off. For a long time Amelia heard only the sharp hissing intake of the bearers' breath, the *clop-clop* of the trooper's horse keeping pace. But every checkpoint they reached that night proved the *maulvi's* ruse was working. As if on cue the Indian woman thrust a dusky hand through the curtains of the litter. Each time Amelia heard the trooper's voice proclaim proudly: "These are the women of my zenana. Before dawn we reach Lucknow."

XXXI. LUCKNOW, THE REBEL LINES

September to November

The memory which Amelia Horne held fast was of her mother's face. In memory the face was not benign, as in Amelia's infancy. The eyes, as in the Cawnpore entrenchment, held the glint of madness. Nor was it random fancy that conjured, day after day, this vision Amelia sought to blot out. Only an iron effort of will, she knew, preserved her from the dark night of dementia.

For her new prison was in Lucknow city and only two miles distant the beleaguered British still held out in the Residency. To Amelia the rumours of their bitter lot, their meagre fare, suggested paradise, for there she could have suffered in company, amongst her own kind.

It had been still dark when the palanquin, Trooper Mohammed Ismail Khan riding abreast, swayed into the native city. And Amelia's heart had sunk. True, she had been glad months earlier when John Hampden Cook, her stepfather, transferred his business from Lucknow for night after night the city had pulsed with drums; the cannonade of fireworks, the lumbering processions of richly-caparisoned elephants passing the wide windows made sleep impossible. But the hovel to which the trooper led her now boasted no windows at all. It was a hut used by dyers, furnished only with a string bed, and the fetid waves of stench brought her close to vomiting.

A new refuge soon became imperative. The bazaar women, like the sepoys of Farrukhabad, pronounced her conversion a sham; ugly rumours of reprisal were in the air. Hastily the trooper spirited her from the hut to the Tara Kothi (Star Mansion), a one-time observatory, now a rebel strongpoint, near the banks of the canal. Once, for two days and nights, the rebels deserted this house. The air trembled with the sound of guns and Amelia Horne, crouched in the observatory's darkened kitchen, prayed as she had never done before that succour was at hand.

At length the rebels returned and the wells of fear, which Amelia had believed to be dry, were all at once flowing again. Heavy losses had made these men savage. Her heart contracting with fear and horror, Amelia remained rooted behind a pillar for all one day, afraid to eat, afraid to sit down lest the slightest movement recalled her presence to them. She watched the whites of men's eyes grow red and inflamed from drink and opium. Men naked save for thin cotton drawers rolled in snarling contest on the dirt floor, clawing and stabbing. The screaming and the yelling never stopped.

For Amelia Horne the weeks that followed blurred into a nightmare of hasty dusk arrivals and dawn departures. In the course of time all the houses where the trooper lodged her blended into one: the flat balustraded roofs, the green jalousies, a catacomb of dark rooms lit by tiny saucers of flickering oil. Always it was the same story. At first the household was willing to shelter her; within days her presence spawned distrust. The girl was a Kaffir (infidel), her conversion was make-believe, it was monstrous she should be left alive. In despair the trooper led Amelia to the one man whose word the rebels heard as law—Ahmad Ullah, *maulvi* of Fyzabad.

Long afterwards Amelia Horne acknowledged that the trooper's eleventh-hour decision saved her life. A native of Arcot, Madras Presidency, Ahmad Ullah was one of the few great organisers to be thrown up by the mutiny. As adviser to the Begum of Oudh, his inspired authority directed every detail of the rebels' strategy. With his high beaked nose, beetling brows and faded green turban he was a familiar sight in the rebel trenches before attacks were launched. To Amelia Horne the one hope of salvation lay in claiming this man's protection.

A mile west of the Residency, close to the shining river, Ahmad Ullah had made his headquarters in the fine white palace of Oudh's former prime minister, Ali Naqui Khan. In silence he heard Amelia's halting profession of faith, his deep-set eyes boring into her. Abruptly he nodded. If Trooper Mohammed Ismail Khan spoke truly, her claim was undeniable. First, though, Amelia must take an immediate oath to comply with their religious sacraments. Deftly his lean brown fingers broke a sweetmeat in half—this they would share and so sharing she would become his *murid*, or disciple. Sensing that this was to test her sincerity, Amelia ate readily. Now she was in duty bound to follow everywhere in the *maulvi's* footsteps, to observe every festival and fast.

At first Amelia found compensations. For days at a time now she did not see the trooper or submit to his will. She was allowed a room to herself and a light at night and two meals a day—saffron rice, meat, onions and green ginger skewered on reeds. The *maulvi* would readily address her in English, for he, unlike Amelia, had visited that country. Sometimes, he complained bitterly that his forefathers had owned Bombay—by rights he should be the Sultan of that city. At other times with cold clear dedication he spoke of his faith. Nothing, he said, would compel him to sheathe his sword for this was war to the death. There would be reverses, perhaps for six years or more—but after that, triumph. One day, with Russian help, his standard would fly over London.

Secretly Amelia bitterly resented the *maulvi's* disparaging remarks about the British. How could he swear he would never deign to take Queen Victoria as a wife—merely as one of his nearest bond-slaves? Of all "John Company's" officials, the one man to command his respect was Sir Henry Lawrence—"the right man in the right place." When the Residency fell, the *maulvi* assured her, Lawrence's life would be spared. When news of Lawrence's death at last filtered through, Amelia noted, the rebels saw victory as a matter of time. All, while Lawrence lived, had feared to build their hopes too high.

Even the Nana Sahib, who paid a fleeting visit to the palace, spoke in the same vein. The £10,000 price that Lord Canning had placed on his head he saw as not one whit too high—but Canning's "brainless" one would be dear at any price.

But as October passed to November, it came home to Amelia Horne that her life was a living lie; five times each day, before sunrise, early and late in the afternoon,

after sunset and before bed-time, the stones were cold beneath her knees as she knelt to worship and worship again as
the price of staying alive. *"Allahu akbar! Allahu akbar!
Allahu akbar!"* she cried that all might hear. What her heart
said was, O God, please God, have mercy and let me die.

XXXII. DELHI

11th to 20th September

The mutiny was four months old and only a hair's breadth
divided truth from rumour. By mid-September with thirty
main mail routes in British India still inoperative, men and
women kept track of events only through devious ways—a
cookboy's gossip, an innuendo, significant sights and sounds.

From the red spine of the Ridge at Delhi, thousands of
eye-witnesses watched in silent awe the truth the rumours
had suggested: slate-blue smoke drifting above scrub and
lemon groves; more than fifty guns and mortars belching fire
at Delhi's northern walls from the water bastion on the east
to the Mori bastion on the west. All men knew that the assault must come soon, for each day the hatchets rose and
fell in the lemon thickets; the air was heady with the smell of
bruised citron. All night, working by the light of large horn
lanterns the Punjabi canal-diggers constructing the great
batteries, some only a hundred and sixty yards from the
walls of Delhi, had plied their curved native spades. Yet at
8 a.m. on 11th September, when these guns first opened fire,
many were bereft of speech. Only yesterday these walls had
seemed as impregnable as an ogre's castle. Now as they
watched, eight-inch shells burst as they touched the parapets;
vast blocks of masonry toppled in a slow rending roaring
avalanche. Within ten minutes the rebel guns on the Kashmir bastion were silenced.

By 12th September the rebels were meeting trouble with

trouble. Outside the walls the advanced trenches were lined with sharp-shooters; crowds of skirmishers posted in jungle and broken ground swept the batteries with a non-stop volley of musketry. Now no gunner officer dared even peep above the parapets; to douse the smouldering wicker of the gabions masking the batteries, earthenware jars of water were kept handy. At times when the hornet-whine of bullets drove them to frenzy the gunners substituted grape for round shot and harassed the ground with teeth of iron. "Officers leave the batteries quite shrivelled up and as black as your shoes," Octavius Anson noted; they drank jorums of claret too, for a man survived only as long as he could sweat.

"Even now the walls of Delhi begin to look like those of Jericho," wrote Richard Baird-Smith exultantly to the symphony of the guns. "The enemy will be still more busy soon."

In the city, as Trooper Devi Din saw clearly, each salvo brought tensions closer to the surface. The younger sepoys said sourly that in a pitched battle with the British their own leaders would be useless: their subadar-majors were old and doddering, only they, the unpaid rank-and-file, would see this guerilla warfare through. Devi Din himself was appalled at the necessity of spilling British blood; like many others he had never believed they would come to the Ridge. Would they never go away? These warning signs were well known to old Bahadur Shah; as early as 2nd September, by way of a sop, he had doled out three rupees—roughly 6s. 8d.— to every trooper, a rupee apiece to the sepoys. This taxed his resources sorely; five days later he announced all his tenants must pay three months rent in advance. Embittered civilians raged that, willy nilly, this had become their war too; the town-crier made his rounds, urging them to bring in wood to repair the crumbling northern walls. Others, impressed as forced labour, dug clay to cram the breaches. From the 11th, three hundred troopers patrolled ceaselessly near the Kashmir Gate, waiting.

To Lieutenant Arthur Lang, his duties, now he had reached Delhi, seemed unending. From the glorious moment on the 4th September when the six-mile siege train from Ferozepore, escorted by Octavius Anson, wound into camp, "it was plain that our work must begin in good earnest." Now every day saw the 4.30 a.m. risings which Lang so loathed, for it took weary hours to instruct the 8th and 61st Regiments on the mysteries of escalading—ascending and descending the sides of a ditch by means of ladders. "They hate the thought of it," the young engineer noted sadly. Still he must take thought of the future: "Excalibur," his favourite sword, must be sharpened until it had "an edge like a razor and a surface like a mirror." And each night a letter must go to Lahore to tell Sarah that he was still alive before he fell into fevered sleep—"again in dreams to set parties to work under hot fire, howl at them, urge them on, grape pouring in, and loud guns drowning one's voice."

At 3 p.m. on 13th September the dream came close to reality. Crouched in No. 2 Battery, Lang watched transfixed as the mighty 24-pounders tore vast chunks of pinkish-grey stone from the walls to right and left of the Kashmir bastion. At this moment Brigadier John Nicholson and Lieutenant Alex Taylor, Baird-Smith's deputy, arrived with momentous orders. When darkness fell, young Lieutenant Lang must creep to the very edge of the walls to see if those breaches were practicable.

Lang thought swiftly. To work under cover of night would make for security—but how much detail would he miss? In the dark he found it hard to see at all. As to the value of this mission, the engineer had no illusions; the entire success of the assault would hinge on his report. Were the sepoys bringing up guns to defend the breach? Could the counterscarp, the steep side of the ditch farthest from the defenders, be descended with ladders? Was the breach practicable for immediate assault?

Until General Archdale Wilson knew the answer to these and other questions no man in the force could know whether the storming of Delhi was sheer suicide. He must, Lang pleaded, work by day.

Nicholson, who constantly preached caution to young officers while recklessly exposing himself, gave only grudging assent. But Lang allowed no time for a change of heart. Swiftly he passed word for the batteries to cease firing. Then, conscripting a covering party of four riflemen, he slipped noiselessly through the orange gardens towards the city ditch, worming his slight form through sharp patches of sunlight until he lay level with the mighty breach the guns had torn in the Kashmir bastion. Then, posting his men in thick shade, he drew a deep breath and broke cover. For one frozen moment of unbelief the rebels on the walls watched his haring form then a storm of bullets burst about him. Bent double, running for his life, Lang somehow scaled the sixty yards stretch of the glacis, collapsing headlong at the crest.

Now, prone on his belly, his keen eye took in every detail of the breach. British fire had ceased only minutes earlier; it was quite without wire or defences. With dismay he noticed that the berm, the flat stretch of earth between the parapet and the escarp was now so choked with debris as to make a dangerously narrow space for scaling ladders. But the ditch was open and the breach looked practicable—perhaps fifty feet across. Now only one problem remained. Lying flat at the crest of the glacis he was almost invisible to mutineers sniping in vain from the ramparts and from the flanking breastworks outside the Kashmir bastion. Suddenly he realised the firing had died and he knew why. Sooner or later, if he was ever to report to Baird-Smith he must break cover. For this moment the snipers were waiting like a cat at a mousehole.

So there was, thought Lang, but one solution—he must take them by surprise. They would expect him to break cover bent double as he had come—but one instant of shock tactics might give him a head start. Abruptly, as the silence yawned, he leapt to his feet. He rose to his full height. In the instant the astonished snipers held their fire he ran like the wind, back down the glacis, bullets clipping the red earth about his heels. He reached the orange grove and his supports miraculously alive.

Arriving back at Number 2 Battery he found to his dismay that Major Baird-Smith had detailed a brother engineer, Lieutenant "Jules" Medley, to carry out the same mission after dark. Though Lang had now gleaned all the salient facts, Medley thought it wise to measure the lower escarp. Would Lang, who now knew the way, take him down that night? Lang would, for now at last he could atone for those long sterile months at Lahore.

The evening crawled. At their picket the young officers ate a silent dinner. At last, as pre-arranged with the battery commanders, the thunder of the guns died. The copper gongs that on the Ridge now replaced the bugle for all but emergencies boomed over the darkened hillside. It was the signal for them to move. The time was 10 p.m.

Swords drawn, revolvers ready, they trod lightly through brushwood. Behind filed an officer and a support party of twenty-six riflemen. Soon Lang and Medley halted. Thirty yards away to the right the rebels' musket flashes "lit up the air as if they had been fireflies." Suddenly they froze motionless; overhead an enemy shell screamed above them to turn the night to day. Then the sound died: only silence and darkness reigned.

Hearts pounding, they tiptoed on. Within five minutes they had reached the edge of the ditch. Again they paused. Dead ahead lay the sombre shadowed mass of the Kashmir bastion. No man's silhouette broke the pale chasm of the breach.

For the second time within hours it fell to Arthur Lang's lot to tempt the fates. In sweating silence he scrambled down the steep sixteen feet of the counterscarp. He stood now on the base of the city ditch. Next, passing down a light bamboo ladder, Medley and an escort of two riflemen joined him. In two minutes, Lang calculated, they would reach and examine the top of the breach. At this moment, through darkness, they heard the sound of running men. Sepoys—and on the ramparts above their heads.

Cautiously, with infinite patience, Lang and the others inched back up the counterscarp. Prone on the grass they awaited the next turn of events. Against the stars, only twenty yards distant, the black silhouettes of rebel sepoys craned from the breach, conversing in low tones. They heard the steely ring of ramrods. Patiently Lang waited. He was game for yet a third attempt if the sepoys went away. But this second sortie had made doubly plain that the breach was a good one, its flanks lacking guns, and the slope easy to ascend.

Should they wait until the sentries departed—or risk an armed rush to the top to take final measurements? But after a hasty whispered consultation both officers decided against it.

For all practical purposes, troops could carry the breach. They must make their report now.

Abruptly, as Medley signalled retreat, they bounded as one, racing for cover. At once bullets whiplashed about them, but amongst the tangled scrub their racing forms were lost to sight. As they reached the nearest outpost, Medley, commandeering a horse, galloped for Baird-Smith's tent. The sudden roar and flash of the batteries lighted his way. Already Arthur Lang had passed the word that fire could recommence.

And now, faced with the hasty plan Medley sketched by a lantern's wavering light, Baird-Smith could reach only one decision. Already the British artillerymen neared exhaustion —while a second scouting party of engineers had reported the water bastion breach practicable, too. If attack were deferred one day more, who knew what extra defences the rebels might throw up? The Delhi Force must assault at dawn.

Within his tent General Archdale Wilson trembled on the brink of tears. Beset by a growing fear that his brain was giving way, he had, in the ten days before the siege-train arrived, bombarded Baird-Smith with fully sixty letters. Doubts, frenzied recriminations, poured from his pen. "It is evident to me the results of the proposed operations will be thrown on the hazard of a die. . . . The chances of success . . . are anything but favourable. I yield, however, to the judgment of the Chief Engineer . . ." And in shriller mood: "I should say the assault on the Water Bastion is *hopeless*, there is no approach to it apparently. What do *you* propose? . . . You are determined I shall not have a moment's sleep tonight." Only at the last, haggard with vacillation, did he yield again to Baird-Smith's judgment.

"We are at one and indivisible," he assured the engineer dryly, "like the French Republic."

It was well for Wilson that they were—for Brigadier-General John Nicholson had felt the iron enter into his soul. From the moment on 18th July when Wilson accepted Baird-Smith's view that reinforcements and heavy artillery would carry Delhi by storm, it was Nicholson who had battled to make both possible. He himself had headed the main column of those reinforcements—and at Najafgarh had foiled the rebels' one attempt to storm the siege-train. To postpone attack, Nicholson knew, meant certain ruin. Time had run out for the besiegers.

To some it seemed Nicholson viewed the general's wavering with sardonic forbearance. On this very day, 13th September, Nicholson was handed a blunt despatch from Sir John Lawrence in Lahore: "Unless Delhi falls within twenty-four hours I cannot guarantee the Punjab . . ." "You will, of course, sir, show this to the General?" Nicholson's major of brigade, Seymour Blane, asked sarcastically. "Show it to Wilson? Show it to Wilson?" retorted Nicholson's deep voice, in mockery. "Why, it would kill him!"

Yet Nicholson's pressure had already prevailed with Wilson and perhaps both men knew it. Days earlier, prior to attending a council of war, Nicholson had dropped this bombshell before twenty-four-year-old Frederick Roberts, a stocky red-haired lieutenant later to become Field-Marshal Earl Roberts of Kandahar: "If Wilson hesitates longer I intend to propose at today's meeting that he should be superseded." Roberts, incredulous, pointed out that this would leave Nicholson as the force's senior officer. Nicholson demurred. He would, he stressed, make plain that he could accept no such command. To rebut all accusations of personal ambition he would propose Colonel George Campbell of the 52nd Light Infantry took over.

At midnight on 13th September Wilson gave his reluctant assent. The assault was on.

Events now moved swiftly. Young Arthur Lang, dozing at No. 2 Battery, was shaken from sleep at 2 a.m.: urgent instructions awaited him at the engineers' camp. Hastening through darkness to the mess, Lang at once scented the strange suppressed tension that in memory he would always associate with this night: men buckling on revolvers, storing haversacks with flasks and bread, snatching a few mouthfuls of supper by candlelight. A few, giggling, their spirits at fever-pitch, were pretending to sharpen their swords on a small knife-grinder. Others pored over a vast map of Delhi, working now against time to memorise the route *their* column would follow.

The first column, one thousand men commanded by Brigadier-General John Nicholson, was to storm the breach near the Kashmir bastion and to escalade the face of this same bastion. The second column, eight hundred and fifty men under Colonel William Jones of Her Majesty's 61st, was assigned to the water bastion breach. The third column, nine hundred and fifty men, Colonel George Campbell commanding, was to assault the Kashmir Gate when an engineer's exploding party had blown it in. The fourth column, eight hundred and sixty men led by Major Charles Reid, supported by twelve hundred Sikhs of the Maharajah of Kashmir, was to fight its way through the eastern suburbs, entering the city by the Kabul Gate, once Nicholson's men had opened it from the inside. A fifth column, thirteen hundred strong, would be held in reserve. Arthur Lang was one of three engineer officers attached to Nicholson's column.

Lang at least had half suspected what Fate had in store for him. But so closely had the "big dogs," as senior officers were known, kept their counsel, many on Baird-Smith's staff knew nothing of the assault; in the chill small hours of this Monday scores were taken completely by surprise. A captain of the 52nd L.I., John Bayley, was roused from sleep at midnight to learn that he was commanding the third column's fifty-strong storming party at 3 a.m. Knuckling the sleep from his eyes, Bayley stared bemusedly at the plan hatched in pink and blue whose dotted lines showed the routes of each column: dark blue for the first and second, dark red for the third, green for the fourth. He never saw the plan again.

Ironically, few men, after their three-month vigil, were truly prepared; in these last moments they thought in dismay of many things left undone. The adjutant of the 75th Foot, Captain Richard Barter, suddenly conscious of danger, wound two turbans round his old forage cap, then tucked his wife's last letter in the top. A subaltern of the 52nd, Reginald Wilberforce, recalled hastily that he had neglected the castor-oil and opium drops prescribed as a dysentery preventive. Gulping them down he next pulled on a clean flannel shirt; if death was imminent, an officer should look his best. Surgeon James Fairweather, convinced he would run short of bandages, slipped away to slice up a night-shirt. A captain of artillery read once again the inscription he had engraved on his sword: its equation of piety and patriotism crystallised the dedication many felt this night:

> *To Queen, to Country, but oh! most to Thee,*
> *My life to give, who gav'st Thy life for me.*

With a warmth few had suspected, John Nicholson, recalling a pressing debt, hastened to each battery to thank the gunners: "I must shake hands with you fellows for you have done your best to make my work easy tomorrow." Then, back in his own tent, he rehearsed again each detail of the assault to come with his column officers. "Don't press the enemy too hard," were his last words. "Let them have a golden bridge to retire by."

It was now past midnight. The men fell in. By the flickering light of a lantern, commanding officers read final orders for the assault. The men's faces were waxy, expressionless, for these made stark reading. Wounded officers and men must be left where they fell; no man could be spared from the ranks to succour his comrades. If the assault was successful, litters would carry the stricken to the rear. If it failed, they must be prepared to face the worst. Plundering was forbidden; all prize was to be placed in a common store for fair division. No prisoners should be taken for there were none to guard them but no women or children must be injured. "No fear, sir," growled the men promptly; each officer kissed the hilt of his sword as a pledge that he would obey these orders.

Then, as Her Majesty's 75th Foot, forming part of Nicholson's column, prepared to march off, the black soutane of Father Bertrand, the Roman Catholic chaplain, melted from the darkness. Pleading with their colonel for permission to bless the regiment he urged: "We may differ, some of us, in matters of religion but the blessing of an old man and a clergyman can do nothing but good."

When Lieutenant-Colonel Charles Herbert readily assented, the old priest raised his hands to Heaven. Drymouthed they heard his prayers for their success, his plea for mercy for the souls about to die.

In strained silence the leading column moved off. It was now 3.30 a.m., at any time in India the darkest, stillest hour before the dawn. But this dawn would see history in the making and so all the air was alive with a terrifying cacophony: the bursting, hissing rushing of shells, rockets and round-shot tracing livid flashes on the steel-grey sky, the silent steady tramp of marching men. Nicholson, one man noted, looked "quiet but anxious." This was not surprising, for on the road near Ludlow Castle, the home of the dead commissioner, Simon Fraser, Column One was now halted motionless behind the trenches of No. 2 Battery. To the left, in the shelter of No. 3 Battery, Column Two had halted close to the river. At any moment the assault should begin, daybreak was at hand, yet these two columns, together with the third, a mile back on the road towards the Ridge, had been checked and none knew why. Only the gunner officers had spied that in the hours since Lang's inspection the mutineers had crammed the breaches of the Kashmir and water bastions with sandbags on which they were mounting guns. So men lay pressed to the red earth, watching with dismay as silver streaks of light invaded the sky and the artillery duel rent the air.

"What is the delay, sahib? Are we afraid?" a Sikh officer whispered to a British adjutant. "It was not by timid soldiers like these that our country was taken!"

It was now 5.45 a.m. The sun pushed higher in liquid clarity, freeing its surface from the dull red escarpment. Above on the Ridge, six hundred cavalrymen under Colonel Hope Grant readied themselves to guard the flank of the assault, opposite the Kabul Gate. To their rear lay three thousand men, too sick to quit the hospital; further back still, the silent rearguard of graves. Before the city, 4,960 men—more than half of them Indians—faced the half-mile of the northern wall that was their target.

At No. 3 Battery, General Archdale Wilson now broke the aching silence. He asked John Nicholson: "How soon can you be ready?"

"In less than five minutes," Nicholson replied.

Wilson nodded. "You will advance whenever you hear the Rifles open fire," he ordered then.

With one spontaneous gesture Nicholson clapped his arm round the shoulders of Colonel William Jones, who led Column Two, then hastened back to the head of his column. He had barely reached it before Wilson, inclining over the battery's epaulement, said quietly, "Now, Colonel Jones."

At the head of Column One, Nicholson for one fleeting moment raised his hand. Howling like banshees the skirmishers of the 60th Rifles advanced at the double, screening the heads of the advancing columns, pelting for the glacis, halting to rake the ramparts with fire. The order passed through the storming parties: "Shoulder ladders!" For the 1,850 men of Columns One and Two the assault was just two minutes away.

To Arthur Lang, striding at Nicholson's side, his sword waving to guide the storming party, the bullets seemed to pass over them "like a hissing sheet of lead." But now the storming party, outrunning the engineers, stood nakedly exposed on the face of the glacis, flayed by rebel fire. From this moment men began to die: a hundred fell within ten minutes, fighting to place the ladders that their comrades might cross the ditch. But as the ladder-men died, men from the storming-parties took over, seizing the ladders, steadying them on piled rocks and the bodies of the dead and dying, clawing their way towards the heights. To climb with ease they slung their muskets behind them; they could fire no shot in self-defence.

"To the right, sir, keep to the right," Lang was hailing Nicholson breathlessly as they hared up the glacis to the right face of the Kashmir bastion.

But Nicholson, too impatient to wait for ladders, was swerving to the left, to join the second wing of his column; there was nothing for it now, Lang thought but to follow him. Catlike, he swung himself to the berm, eight feet above—noting gleefully that it *was* too narrow to support ladders, just as he had reported. Then, gritting his teeth, he began his crawl up the crumbling face.

But now, to his horror, he felt the stones give beneath his bleeding fingers; his body was arcing backwards over a forest of glittering bayonets. Then iron fingers clamped his thighs, grinding him inwards against the wall until the world had ceased to spin and he had recovered his balance. Onwards Lang scrambled with his saviours, two small Gurkhas, pressing closely behind him; at the crest of the breach a sepoy's musket jarred against his breast-bone. At once Lang rammed it aside, lunging with his sword; to his horror "Excalibur," dismally failing to pierce the rebel's cummerbund, doubled back until it almost described a loop. Then, across Lang's shoulders, the Gurkha's *kukri* flashed like fire, a pound and three quarters of razor-edged steel chopping downwards below the man's windpipe. Warm blood bathed them all like rain; the head lolled obscenely from the trunk.

Twice, within seconds, the Gurkhas had saved his life. Only later did Lang discover that both belonged to the covering parties of the fourth column and had no business there at all.

And now the war became so personal that Lang and a thousand others lost all sense of time and direction. He never afterwards knew whether Nicholson had ascended the Kashmir breach with him or had mounted the water bastion breach close by. Somehow Nicholson and a few others had contrived to take the wrong turning and were forging southwards into the city. Lang, following the instructions on his map, turned sharp right, borne onwards by a howling press of men, the reddish-grey ramparts looming seven feet above them, the mud walls and thatched roofs of native shanties to their left. On they stampeded, firing and cheering, struggling over the writhing shapes of the wounded, the sepoys swinging from the narrow eyelets to blast them until the bayonets lunged upwards and they toppled to carpet the city ditch with white threshing forms. Tower after tower was cleared and its guns seized until at last, with the Mori bastion taken, the hot-headed Lang urged all to leap on the parapet to give three cheers for victory.

"Bad advice," he noted succinctly, for at once the British batteries commanding the city roared into life. Hastily, tearing strips of red, white and blue from the clothes of dead sepoys they ran on beneath their improvised Union Jack.

As they raced from the shelter of rose bushes to storm the water bastion the men of Column Two met grimmer resistance still: a wave of fire so lethal that of thirty-nine ladder men all but ten fell wounded or dying beneath the walls. To one officer the main force, cresting the breach seemed "like the horses of the sun all abreast." Many were drunk with blood-lust: "if every man felt as I did they felt nothing," confessed one lieutenant, Kendal Coghill. "A species of madness came over me." Biting on a bullet to keep the saliva flowing, Coghill did not even recoil when a colour sergeant fell spitted on his sword; dragging it clear he and hundreds of others hacked their way on towards the Mori bastion. "The sepoys didn't seem to care for their lives," recalled one private in awe. "They went back slow, shooting and stabbing and screeching to the last."

But upwards of fifteen hundred men had now gained the city.

To the men of Column Three, crouched tensely on the road, the Kashmir Gate seemed a visionary's goal. Once the exploding party, eight sappers led by Engineer Lieutenants Duncan Home and Philip Salkeld, had doubled for its massive wooden framework, tension had mounted to fever-pitch. Each engineer carried a bag of ordinary cotton hose crammed with twenty-five pounds of powder—but had they placed the charge? The gate was screened from sight: the column could not know.

With the party had gone Bugler Robert Hawthorne, of the 52nd L.I., who was to sound the regimental call when the sappers' work was done. But the roar of the bombardment swallowed up all sound. Even the explosion—if it ever took place—would be inaudible.

There was then no way of knowing that everything had gone wrong from the first.

Running under a hail of bullets, as men seek shelter from a storm, Home's party had reached the gate safely—teetering across the three wooden beams which were all that were left of the drawbridge, the city ditch yawning beneath. To their amazement, they saw the wicket gate lay open—yet from this gate, from the ramparts, there came no burst of fire. As they planted their powder bags beside the timber gate, then hurtled for cover in the ditch, the sepoys stood stunned by their temerity.

But Salkeld's firing party bringing up the rear saw that the element of surprise was lost. From all sides fire hammered at them. By the time Salkeld, grasping the portfire of lighted sulphur, had snaked close under cover of the wall only two men of his party, Sergeants John Smith and Frank Burgess, were still alive. Slow match extended, the lieutenant craned forward to light the fuse, as a sepoy bullet shattered his thigh.

Reeling with agony he lost balance. One second before he plunged mortally wounded to the ditch, he thrust the portfire, like a runner in a Greek torch race, into Burgess's grasp.

As Burgess, in turn, bent forward a cry escaped him: the match had gone out. Now Sergeant Smith was pressing luci-fers towards him but the rebels' aim was true. Shot, Bur-gess crashed lifeless to the city ditch. Cuddling the gate for safety, Smith, stooping, struck a light; at that instant the port-fire of the fuse went up in his face. Singed and half-blind he dived for the ditch, amazingly alive, as the gate went skywards.

Only the clawing spiral of smoke warned Colonel Camp-bell the time had come; from the canyon of the ditch the shrilling of Robert Hawthorne's bugle went unheard. Across the heaving drawbridge stormed Column Three, through a breach so narrow only one man at a time could pass through. Save for the littered dead, the open square of the main guard was now empty—and now more than two thousand men were in the city.

Despite the mounting totals a wild confusion reigned. A stickler for obeying orders to the letter, Colonel William Jones, leading Column Two, realised he had completely lost his bearings. His men had long since passed the Mori bastion and were surging along the city's western ramparts. Now, hastening up to Lieutenant Arthur Lang, Jones demanded, "Where are we?"

When Lang, consulting his map, estimated that they were close to the Lahore bastion, Jones was horrified. If this was so then they had overshot the Kabul Gate, where he had been ordered to halt, by fully three hundred yards. The Lahore Gate was Nicholson's goal. Column Two must retreat to the Kabul Gate at once.

"We were all shouting for advance," Lang recalled later. "But not a bit! All we could then obtain was permission to hold our ground."

It was a fatal decision. Kindled by their first bloody victo-ries, the men had been ready for any odds that came. Now, crouched behind buttresses, they watched snipers hidden on roofs and ramparts pick off comrade after comrade like targets in a shooting gallery. Soon the first seeds of panic and bewilderment were sprouting and then, as Arthur Lang recalled with pain, it was hard to keep them in check at all. "One by one they tried to get back . . . we staved off the flight for half an hour but out they all came at last, and, sweeping past the officers, made for the Kabul Gate."

At this news John Nicholson arrived in a towering rage. A stranger to fear, Nicholson saw only that the Lahore bastion must be taken. In the first place it commanded Delhi's main street, the eighty-yard-broad Chadni Chowk, which cut eastwards through the heart of the city. Secondly, Colonel Hope Grant's cavalry mustered six hundred strong close to its ramparts had sat their horses for two hours under a saturating fire from its turrets. Time and again Grant had been forced to move his line forward, clear of the disabled horses that had floundered to crush their riders. By now, Nicholson guessed, Column Three had penetrated the city through the Kashmir Gate and was awaiting Column Four's promised support from the Kabul Gate, already overdue. Only now did Nicholson learn that this column, whose artillery support never arrived, had retreated in disorder down the Grand Trunk Road, harried by yelling sepoys.

With mounting anger he told Brevet-Lieutenant-Colonel Edward Greathed, commanding Her Majesty's 8th Foot: "Your men are not in hand."

Greathed at once took umbrage. "What do you want done?" he flashed back. "Tell me and I will soon show you whether they are in hand."

What Nicholson wanted was more than flesh and blood could humanly achieve. Under his command both columns must rush and carry the lane ahead connecting the Kabul and the Lahore Gates. Then as now this was a stifling bottleneck flanked by flat-roofed houses, by parapeted turrets seven feet wide which compressed its width to a bare three feet. These turrets and the mudwalled houses teemed with sharp-shooters; two brass guns raked the passage. And already Nicholson's battle-shocked troops had cleared more than a mile of rampart under fire on empty stomachs.

Within seconds tragedy overtook them. As they inched up the lane, so cramped only two could stand abreast, a terrible fire-power struck devastation through their ranks. The wreckage of war strewed the stones: bandoliers, leather water-bottles, forage-caps, men burned, blaspheming, glazed with vomit, as the life ebbed from them. Again as they charged, the fire checked them. Then panic, animal and uncontrollable, swept every man. Eyes dilated, breath sobbing from their lungs, they surged like frightened cattle in headlong retreat.

It was too much for Nicholson. All his life he had subdued both mind and body to his iron will; now it was inconceivable he could not spur other men on the path to glory. His mighty frame fought through the press, until he towered at their head. Eyes blazing, he turned to face them, flourishing the weapon the Sikh nation had long ago presented to him—a sword straight as a rapier, grooved within, augmented with quicksilver to increase the force of a direct blow. His words seared like vitriol:

"Come on, men! Come on, you fools! I never should have thought that Europeans would quail before heathens. Come on, you . . ."

On the left of the alley, shadowed by the overhanging bough of a pipal tree, the rebel sepoy Kaleh Khan craned from a first floor window. At point-blank range he fired. The ball, slamming into Nicholson's body below the left rib-cage, tore on to shred the liver. As if whirled by an invisible wire, Nicholson crashed headlong into the arms of his major of brigade, Seymour Blane.

"Keep my face to them," he grated, "I am hurt."

"You are hit, sir," cried Blane, in dismay.

"Yes, yes," came Nicholson's impatient snarl, then slowly, his body buckling beneath him, he propped himself against a wall, his teeth gritting in fine fury as he sank slowly to the earth. Hastily a column officer revived him with brandy, but Nicholson refused all suggestions that he be removed to safety. "The men who would not follow me shall not lift me from the ground," he blazed. "I will remain here till Delhi is taken."

But the risk that the rebels might re-take the alley was

too great. By early afternoon he had been carried to the hospital: the doctors bent their heads and their eyes met in silence above the swift shallow breathing. No surgeon on earth could check those soaking hæmorrhages. That evening, in the tent of Captain Henry Daly of the Guide Corps, Nicholson with rare patience lay waiting for death.

Day after day, the bloody task of recapturing Delhi went forward. The song of war has diverse notes; there were many ludicrous moments. Captain Dunbar Muter's butler, secure behind a barricade, spread a serviette as a table-cloth and broiled a juicy steak for his master's dinner; the sepoys regained the street and the dinner was lost. In one building Lieutenant Reginald Wilberforce's storming party found no rebels, only what seemed like a hospital ward, its beds filled with women. Urging his men up the next flight of stairs, Wilberforce recoiled angrily; one incorrigible had lingered to steal a kiss. His curt command was lost in a yell of surprise; beneath the girl the private had made sharp contact with a bristling moustache. Swiftly the rebels were routed from bed after bed; the fight to the death went on.

There were bitter delays. In a desperate endeavour to win time the rebels had packed the streets with vats and crates of liquor. Soon the splintering of wood and glass eclipsed the whine of British bullets; drunken howling men, as loath to fight as in the weeks on the Ridge, choked the alleys. "So many troops," cried the harassed General Wilson, "are making beasts of themselves and incapable of doing their duty." Lieutenant William Hodson was forced to agree. "For the first time in my life I have had to see English soldiers refuse to follow their officers," he wrote. Despairing, Wilson diverted much-needed troops into bottle-smashing columns. Soon a blood-slicked river of Exshaw's No. 1 brandy gurgled through the deep conduits of the old city.

In St. John's Church, impressed as a hospital, the severed limbs lay piled as in a charnel-house; in one day's fighting 66 officers, 1,104 men had been killed or wounded. Six days later, the totals had mounted: 992 officers and men were dead, a further 2,843 were wounded or missing. The artillery alone had lost a quarter of their strength; the Guide Corps, 550 strong, more than half. The 52nd L.I., mustering 600 men a month earlier, had only 242 fit for duty on the day of the assault.

In the bloodstained streets the siege guns lay abandoned like nursery toys, and sunlight winked and sparkled on the gilt cross of the church.

Day after day, these scraps of intelligence filtered to John Nicholson in his tent on the Ridge. His cheeks were leaden and the white tapering fingers composed upon the sheet; it was as if he lingered only to achieve one last act of will. Once, hearing that Archdale Wilson, appalled by the losses, argued in favour of an immediate retreat, he gasped, "Thank God I have strength yet to shoot him, if necessary!" The threat was not idle; when his Multani horsemen jabbered anxiously outside his tent, Nicholson sent word begging for quiet. Twenty minutes later, concern broke through and the clatter redoubled; a shot ploughed through the tent from within. Nicholson's pistol hand was steady to the last.

On 20th September, all firing died. One by one the chief points had been secured—the Lahore Gate, the wrecked magazine, the Great Mosque, the fort. An orderly on a lathered horse came posting to General Wilson with a laconic message: "Blown open the gates! Got the Palace!" A curious silence fell on the charred smoking city and in her bell-of-arms, Harriet Tytler, the one woman to see the siege through, knelt "to offer up prayers and thanksgiving for God's mercy to our brave men."

The men of the Delhi force shared a secret: this was Nicholson's triumph, not theirs. When five thousand men captured a walled city defended by forty thousand armed troops, force of arms had not prevailed; one resolute soul had bound their minds in a kind of bloody mesmerism. "My Lord, you may rely upon this," a senior official had once assured Lord Canning. "If ever there is a desperate deed to be done in India, John Nicholson is the man to do it." By midnight on 22nd September, this deed was done. On the 23rd, at 9.30 a.m., John Nicholson died.

XXXIII. DELHI

20th to 24th September

Delhi had toppled, and with the red walls had fallen 3,835 troops, British and Indian, 378 horses—a heavier toll than in any other mutiny campaign. But the tide was turning.

"I have the gratification of announcing to your Highness that Delhi, focus of treason and revolt . . . has been wrested from the rebels," ran Lord Canning's proclamation to the forty Indian princes who had pressed troops and treasure on "John Company," and he was careful to stress that this much had been achieved without reinforcements from England.

For by 24th September, fully 2,790 men, a column ten miles long, could be spared from the city. The second decisive relief of Lucknow could be but a matter of weeks.

By now it was plain that destiny, like a skilled director, had allotted many men key roles in this drama. Some, like John Nicholson, had played roles so brief and dramatic the audience gasped when death rang down the curtain. At his funeral all were silent as the gun-carriage neared the grave; only when the clods of dry red earth struck the coffin-lid did his wild Multani horsemen, who believed a man in tears deserved only whipping by women, break down in a torrent of weeping. So was Nicholson's end tempered with irony; his followers were no longer immune. These men went north to seek the missionaries, announcing, "Let us learn to worship Nikal Seyn's God."

For William Stephen Raikes Hodson it had been an uneasy role from the first: all along he had striven to conceal the flaws in his rendition of a *beau sabreur*. For one brief moment, when Captain Henry Daly fell wounded, on 19th June, fortune dimmed the lights in Hodson's favour for as temporary commander of the Guide Corps that had expelled him, he had access to the adjutant's desk. In its secret drawer lay the file Daly was studying at Lord Canning's request: a bulky sheaf of fresh evidence concerning Hodson's mulcting of the regimental chest. Had he convinced his audience when Daly resumed command on 14th September and Hodson swore on his oath as a gentleman that he had not touched the file, now missing? He did not know and the tempo was quickening; his whole life had become a race against time.

Young Lieutenant John Turnbull, the general's aide, was openly curious for Hodson sought audience with Wilson at all hours. Mohammed Bahadur Shah, fleeing the palace, was hidden with his retinue at the tomb of Emperor Humayon, a white cluster of milk-bubble domes, four miles from the city among ruined gardens. The British, Hodson urged, must capture him, even at the cost of guaranteeing his life "for his name would have been a tocsin for the whole of Hindustan." Angrily Wilson later denied giving Hodson such authority: his brief was to take a troop of horsemen and capture the King without terms. Only Hodson knew the real urgency. His trunk held £700 of Queen Zeenat Mahal's money; even corrupt men must earn their bribes. If Bahadur Shah died, then the Queen would produce the paper Hodson had signed already, in the general's name, promising both their lives.

On 21st September Hodson, Rajab Ali, and fifty horsemen, a grim hard-riding cavalcade, approached Humayon's tomb. In silence Hodson dismounted, thousands of the King's retainers seething furiously about him. Screened by a crumbling wall he watched Rajab Ali walk alone into the labyrinth of the tomb to parley with Zeenat Mahal. Three sweltering hours became infinity. One false step, Hodson knew, and all was lost. If the general grew angry that the King's life had been guaranteed, it would be easy to throw the blame on Rajab Ali but first he must secure the King.

At length the spy emerged with heartening news. The King was coming—but he must hear from Hodson's own lips that his life would be spared. Sword in hand, Hodson remounted, spurring through the still-menacing throng to the gateway of the vast mausoleum. In a ringing voice, for the benefit of the crowd, he let his pledge be heard: the Government would

spare the King's life. Tortuously two palanquins swayed into
view down the dank stone corridors, the King's sickly aquiline
profile peering from curtains. His sword, cased in a dingy red
scabbard, now passed to Hodson. Adroitly Hodson closed his
horsemen in; they were now a solid phalanx, blocking off
the King's retainers. With Rajab Ali riding beside them, the
palanquin bearers set out. Immobile, Hodson and his horsemen sat tight, their gleaming groomed mounts straddling the
shouting throng of retainers. "Shoot the first man who
moves," ordered Hodson coolly. He saw the palanquins re-
ceding into the distance: the troops spurred after them, out-
distancing the crowd.

Mohammed Bahadur Shah saw now that Fate had miscast
him: the language of power had tripped strangely from his
tongue. One private who watched his discomfited return to
Delhi never forgot it: the clattering cavalcade of scarlet-
sashed Afghan horsemen, the King's old frightened face,
Hodson, blue eyes aglow above curved defiant nostrils. "The
officer of the guard calls out, careless, 'What you got there,
Hodson?' and Hodson, just as quiet as if he was going to
church, says 'Only the King of Delhi,' says he." Bahadur
Shah was but a spectator at this downfall: reality had died
in the moment the troops began deserting and he had upbraided them shrilly, "You have turned the whole country
upside down and now you are running off!" Angrily he had
refused to accompany Bukht Khan's retreat; he would trust
to the mercy of the conquerors.

Now he lived as in a dream. Why had they confined him
in a small house within a railing where the people could re-
gard him like a beast in a cage? Decrepit and quivering, he
crouched on his low string bed, toothless gums sucking at
the stem of a hookah. At times nausea gripped him; he
retched so violently as to fill twelve basins. Peace was denied
him for in the next cell, screened by a blanket, alert to
monitor his speech, was Zeenat Mahal, screaming like a
mewed falcon if the King spoke imprudently. "Hush!" he
would adjure his visitors, finger to lips. "Don't let the woman
hear us." Rumour armed him with the intent to swallow
powdered diamonds but suicide presupposed a reality he
could not feel. "They gave themselves up to the devil," he

shrugged whenever visitors sought for the mutiny's causes. From now until January, 1858, the moment of his trial, he would wonder how he had come to speak his lines at all.

"Well, I'm glad you have got him, but I never expected to see either you or him again," was General Wilson's sole comment on this capture. But Hodson was not content. The three princes were hiding in the tomb also and he thirsted to seek them out. He badgered Wilson until the general agreed: next day with a hundred horsemen, Hodson rode back to Humayon's tomb, demanding the princes' unconditional surrender. Perhaps they expected the luxury of a trial; at length they agreed. Close to the city, hemmed in by a snarling mob of retainers, Hodson, halting his troop, bade the princes dismount from the bullock cart in which they rode. To make degradation complete he ordered them to strip to their loin cloths before climbing back into the cart. Then, taking a carbine, he shot them at point blank range.

For William Hodson after this there was nothing left for good or evil. Six months would pass before he died as violently as the princes, a rebel bullet smashing through him as he charged sword in hand. "Oh, my mother," he cried, then blood choked all further speech. Later his trunk would be opened and the loot come to light and the file of which he had sworn ignorance and the whole tarnished story became one to be whispered. But only the simulacrum of Hodson died that day. All that was redeemable died near the walls of Delhi, on the spot where the princes died.

Shame marked the aftermath of Delhi. Emotionally only the compassionate, like Octavius Anson, profited from the sights they saw. He walked stumbling over shattered mirrors and brass lotahs and broken barricades of furniture, a handkerchief soaked in cologne pressed to his nostrils. The stench of Delhi fought back: burnt-out fires, jasmine attar, the sick-sweet stench of death. Old mumbling women squatting by vast mountains of dirty rags peopled silent streets. Mangy cats prowled fearfully through acrid smoke. Bird cages, many bird cages, hung in windows, housing only frail skeletons. Harriet Tytler saw the horrors of victory; a fear of plague beset the city and General Wilson decreed the people must be driven from the walls. For one week Harriet watched old men, women and children stream from the Kashmir and Mori gates, a ragged cavalcade smelling of sweat, spice and poverty, heading for the unknown. No Hindus were allowed re-entry before the end of November: Moslems must prove their loyalty before returning at all. And Harriet wondered. No one would harry these people as when the British had left the Ridge, their children would be safe—yet still the sense of pity was a thorn in the heart.

Not all could feel so keenly. In the Hall of Audience, now the headquarters mess, officers contentedly puffed after-dinner cheroots, sprawled on the Mogul's gilded chairs. Above the marble walls, inlaid with roses of cornelian, ran an inscription tallying with their content: "If there is a Paradise on earth it is this, it is this, it is this!" Reclining on looted cloth-of-gold elephant trappings, rankers sang a ribald victory paean:

> Come fill, fill up a bumper,
> Our trial at length is done,
> Since the Pandies are defeated,
> And Delhi has been won.

In lulls between the choruses the marble halls rang to a steady *chip, chip, chip*: the bayonets of busy men, prising stones from the mosaics.

For hundreds, all humanity paled beside the lust for loot. Eager for bounty, the British ravaged Delhi: mosques, bazaars, ten thousand houses went down before the scramble for gold. No man's house was immune; with anger Lord Canning learnt one British partisan had forfeited £20,000 worth of gold and jewels. From Lahore Sir John Lawrence begged to serve in Delhi under Wilson's orders in an effort to control the pillage.

All was in vain; avarice had bred much cunning. A house-owner's religion could be traced through his books—so in a Moslem house dig beneath the floor, in a Hindu house behind the walls. Or sprinkle water on an earth floor and watch where it dried quickest—below would lie the cash. And not only cash but diamonds and pearls; one subaltern, Charles John Griffiths, his cummerbund stuffed with £7,000 worth, still regretted he had not taken more. Others toiled back to their quarters laden with Persian carpets, Kashmir shawls, mother-of-pearl boxes, carved necklaces of sandalwood.

To the provosts' retaliation many turned a blind eye. Of 3,306 citizens arrested, the British admitted hanging only 392, but one Persian scholar reckoned the deaths in thousands. When a friend remonstrated with Sir Theo Metcalfe for hanging men on a Sunday, the joint magistrate retorted: "Why should they eat the Government rations for one extra day?" "I think I must have seen some forty or fifty defenceless people shot down before me," wrote Lieutenant Edward Vibart after one organised round-up. "It was literally *murder*, and the women's screams on seeing their husbands and sons butchered were most frightful . . . please God I may never see such a bloody and awful sight again."

But at last, on 24th September, the Delhi flying column, 2,790 strong with sixteen guns, filed through the city's Lahore Gate, across the same bridge of boats that four months ago had carried the Meerut mutineers to Bahadur Shah. "Not a sound was heard save the deep rumble of our gun wheels," one officer recalled, "or the hoarse challenge of a sentry on the ramparts . . . here might be seen . . . a jackal feeding on a half-demolished body of a sepoy; arms, carts, shot . . . lay about in the wildest manner." South-eastwards they marched through Bulandshahr, past Aligarh and Akbarabad, on a mission of "vindicatory justice" that turned men like Octavius Anson sick. For now he saw justice perverted into cruelty: the men of Her Majesty's 8th Foot smashing the skulls of sick villagers like eggshells, two women raped to death, spread-eagled beneath the heaving lust of private after private, servants half-blinded by blows, the noses of bound prisoners pounded to jelly. "Expect to see me return without a heart," he wrote despairingly to Frances as the column swept on towards Agra and Cawnpore. "Expect to see me a fiend!"

For some the mutiny was all but over. Trooper Devi Din and his comrades rode away from Delhi on the third day following the assault; it was a pity the war had come to nothing but how could men underfed and underpaid have stomach for fighting? At Lucknow, they said, there was a really successful war; fighting men would be appreciated there. But forty miles outside Delhi, Devi Din and one of his cousins changed their minds. When all was said and done who wanted to fight the British? Stooping, they buried in the moist earth all that could ever link them with the 3rd Cavalry—carbines, sabres, shakos, French-grey tunics. So they rode back to their homes and out of this story; their hearts were content and they were villagers again.

Harriet and Robert Tytler settled to live in the cool white palace of Kamuran Shah, the old King's uncle, within the city walls; here they would remain until the following year, when it was time for furlough in the hills. Slowly, it seemed, they were taking up the threads of their old life, for Harriet had begun work on a cyclorama of the fort's interior, eighteen feet by six feet, which she hoped to sell to Phineas T. Barnum. And Robert, who had bought Bahadur Shah's crown at an auction, sold it to Queen Victoria for £500, which was some compensation for the loss of their property.

And now it was time their new baby was christened, but Harriet had to exert all her will-power to resist Robert's brother officers, who yearned to christen him "Battlefield" Tytler. This Harriet resisted stoutly, but it seemed fitting to commemorate his unique birth, so Stanley Delhi-Force Tytler he became. This day Harriet never forgot: Marie was there with her Breton cap, on the arm of her fiancé, a sergeant of the 60th Rifles, the faithful Jamalka had baked a cake, and all the staff officers from General Wilson downwards gathered in the marble hall to drink the health of Stanley Delhi-Force, "the first reinforcement"—forerunner of the thousands massing to rescue almost seven thousand men and women at Lucknow.

XXXIV. LUCKNOW

25th September

By Friday, 25th September, the eighty-eighth day of the Siege of Lucknow, the garrison's combatants had shrunk from 1,720 to 979. Yet Katherine Bartrum's thoughts were as calm and ordered as in the far-off days at Gonda, for today she knew Robert *must* come. She had prayed, of course, as early as 23rd September, "Be Thou his shield in the day of battle"; only when Robert Bartrum was at her side again would their little boy regain his health and strength. But now there were duties less passive than prayer. A friendly private's gift of some bullock meat had sown the seed of a small loving deception; she could prepare a savoury stew for their reunion dinner and Robert would think they had fared thus well all through the siege. Then she would clothe Bobbie in the one clean dress she had preserved in honour of this moment.

Hour after hour a steady downpour of rain thrummed on red satiated earth and crumbling brick; small gleaming creeks puddled the ground dividing the garrisons. But Katherine was too busy to heed. Hour after hour a steady thunder that was not thunder grumbled to the east. Havelock was coming.

Within the Residency a breathless elation reigned. Later the Poet Laureate, Alfred, Lord Tennyson, would celebrate in verse the torn smut-streaked Union Jack that, as legend had it, flew throughout the siege from the Residency roof. In truth the banner for days at a time lay crumpled at the flagstaff's base, for the rebels shot it down too often. But today in honour of Havelock it was flying again. To Mrs. Julia Inglis, it seemed the distant guns repeated one message over and over, like a litany. "We are coming to save you. We are coming to save you." With each concussion Angad, the spy, danced and snapped his fingers, demanding of the Sikh cohorts, who had grown sceptical of his tales of deliverance: "Who is the liar now? Who has been inventing tales . . . about Havelock Sahib?" Three days earlier he had wormed back inside the Residency bearing Outram's last message: the army had crossed the Ganges and succour was at hand. Now Angad nobly told Brigadier Inglis, "I have got back three times, I will go no more, but live or die with you."

By 5 p.m. the firing seemed closer, an angry cannonade no less than three miles away. A tense hour passed. Within the Begum Kothi garrison the shadows were lengthening when a wild storm of shouting and hallooing rent the air. Through the open door a passer-by called, "Mrs. Bartrum, here is an officer inquiring for you. Your husband has come." "Oh, is it *really* true?" were the first words that burst from Katherine's lips.

Her next impulse was to breathe a silent prayer of thanksgiving that she and Robert had been spared to meet again. Then, unable to bear the suspense, she seized the child in her arms and sped out to mingle with the gathering crowds. She saw rough bearded Highlanders shivering in red rain-soaked doublets, others in once-white drill stained by blood and slime. She saw men weeping, men drunk, men blanched with pain; women who laughed and embraced them and wrung their hands. Of Robert she saw no sign.

"Mrs. Bartrum?" came a voice at her elbow. "Your husband *is* come . . . he and I shared the same litter last night." Then the newcomer, who introduced himself as Captain Walter Freeling of the Commissariat-General's department tenderly took the child from her, soothing him: "Baby, Papa is come." At once—as if he understood every word, thought Katherine, like any fond mother—Bobbie laid his head on the captain's shoulder and fell asleep.

To the scores of Havelock's men crowding into the Residency it seemed providence alone had brought them this far. Many were now so weak through hunger and exposure they had lacked strength even to load their muskets. In the long weeks at Cawnpore, while Havelock and Neill, still bitterly at loggerheads, awaited Outram's arrival with reinforcements, the starker realities of war had receded. They had revelled in "glorious muddy football scrimmages," bobbing for apples in treacle, chasing the pig with the greasy tail. On the night of 20th September, all this had changed. Above the Ganges a pale moon struggled through driving rain to reveal three thousand men on the march, the Colours, with their dark cloth coverings rising above the glistening bayonets "like yew trees in a garden." They moved now across a bridge that was a triumph of military engineering—seventy-four flat-bottomed flats, laid on a foundation of wooden platforms, tamped with solid earth and brushwood, topped with planking, lashed tight by stout grass cable. In forty-two hours Indian boatmen and labourers, battling against 6 m.p.h. floods, had fashioned this 2,090-foot causeway.

But in the five days following, the monsoon rains harassed them as savagely as any enemy. "Went to bed drenched to the skin for the third night in succession," one officer recorded. "The roads were ankle deep in mud and filth which we had to wade through before we could get to the mud huts where we slept . . . I dined off the wing of a chicken." One young lieutenant, William Moorsom, bedded down in a hut, with Charlie, his horse, that both might keep dry. On the third night, dismayed by the drenching rain, the baggage coolies deserted.

For the staff there had been the added vexation of a divided command. Something of this General Neill foresaw as early as mid-August, refusing Havelock's invitation to come up-country and share in hoped-for victories. "There is a farce in two Generals being together with a handful of men and one of them allowed to do nothing," he retorted. Now the tragic farce lay in the split of command between Havelock and Outram. Nominally, Sir James had ceded all command to Havelock; in practice, habit proved too strong. "General Outram's advice," Lieutenant Moorsom of Havelock's staff noted dryly, "*is* a command." Since the weather was cooler, Havelock had decided against carrying tents. Outram overruled him. At the walled garden near Lucknow called Alumbagh, Outram proposed leaving behind not only the holding force, 531 strong, but all the heavy guns. Havelock, who pinned much faith in heavy artillery, dissented strongly. This time Outram gave in.

The result was dire confusion. Few officers had any clear idea as to who was in command. The terse inflexible decisions that had swept Havelock triumphantly from Allahabad to Cawnpore were gone. "You had better go to Sir James first," was his invariable reply to all requests for orders. Outram, on the other hand, had ordered his own staff to attach themselves to Havelock. Thus, recalled one of them, Captain David Dodgson, irritably, "we acted on the staff of both and galloped all over the field, first with orders from one and then the other."

At dusk on 25th September, while Katherine Bartrum anxiously awaited Robert's arrival, the crisis came. Only five hundred yards away from where Outram, mounted on a stout Australian waler, conferred with Havelock, lay the main or Baillie-Guard Gate of the Residency, at the crest of a narrow street. Yet already wounded and stragglers dotted the entire length of their four-mile march, checked by the hail of fire that had burst from rice grass and prickly pear. Behind, too, lay much of Havelock's prized heavy artillery, eighteen-pounder siege guns hauled by twenty bullocks apiece, bogged down in the soft wet sand of narrow lanes. Now Outram urged a halt: the rearguard must close up.

But Havelock was obdurate. If the Residency was not reinforced before dark, the rebels might launch a surprise attack on the beleaguered garrison. He was, he said later, convinced Outram proposed an all-night halt. Outram, in fact, sought only a brief respite, but in this long heated conference, staff officers loitering discreetly out of earshot, the finer shades of meaning were lost.

Now Havelock urged: "There is the street. We see the worst—we shall be slated, but we can push through and get it over." At this, Outram admitted later, anger overcame all logic. He replied hotly, "Let us go on then, in God's name!"

It was a tragic decision—tragic because every foot of the street before them bristled watchfully with muskets and field guns. As the column, led by Havelock and Outram, closely followed by Highlanders and Sikhs, defiled slowly through an archway the narrow canyon of the street came alive with

plunging fire. From loopholes no larger than oranges, a whining shattering fusillade flayed them. The high mud walls were
like a sounding-box, magnifying the reports to barrage-
strength; deafened, men rose in the saddle as horses reared
to the shock. Gasping, cursing, the infantry stumbled on,
hurdling trenches lined with rebels scored deep in the road's
surface. From the Residency walls crashing salvoes of fire
from the hastily-alerted defenders harassed the rebel positions.

At this moment, legend claimed later, a soldier's wife
named Jessie Brown came bolt upright in a darkened cellar
below the Residency, crying, "Dinna ye hear the slogan?"
Her ears, she swore, had caught the distant skirl of Havelock's
pipers. As a ballad, as a poem by John Greenleaf Whittier,
as a box-office draw at Wallack's Theatre, New York,
"Jessie's Dream" echoed round the world, yet the truth was
more prosaic. The romance, composed by a French governess
to divert her pupils, reached the Calcutta papers even before word had come of Lucknow's first relief. Accredited by
Parisian papers, it was featured by the London *Times* on
14th December. But the pipes, Pipe-Major Alexander M'Kellar
later affirmed, were silent until Havelock reached the Residency. And Jessie Brown, allegedly a 78th Highlander's wife,
could never have been present to hear them. The womenfolk of the 78th were then eight hundred miles away in
Poona, enjoying free beer and rations in token of their husbands' service.

Many survived this nightmare gauntlet of fire only by a
hair's breadth. One Highland piper, lacking scope to use
either rifle or bayonet, levelled his pipes at a rebel trooper
and let forth a shrill blast of sound. Unnerved by the "in-
fernal machine" the insurgent bolted. Private O'Donagh of the
78th, his leg shattered by a bullet, owed his life to his old
chum Private Glandell who hoisted him like a sack and
carried him all the way. If a lucky pot-shot presented itself,
Glandell propped his comrade against a wall, fired—then
shouldered his burden anew. Disdaining to draw his sword,
Sir James Outram thwacked his way through with a gold-
topped malacca cane. Lieutenant William Moorsom, nearing
the Baillie Guard gate, preserved his life by one mighty

shout: in the thickening dusk he had seen the glowing port-fires of the Residency gunners hovering above their touch-holes. "May I never see such another bloody day," was his heartfelt reaction. Others owed their lives to Major Lousada Barrow's cavalrymen; at least one wounded man was slumped across the cruppers of every horse. So close were the rebels who lined the flat roofs that the Highlanders felt flints hail upon them and the cold impact of spittle.

Many were deserted by fortune. Of the two thousand men who made part of this lost last charge, over 535 were num-bered as casualties. In the howling confusion, the charging 78th ran full tilt into a dozen sepoys of the Residency garri-son, clawing at the earthwork of the Baillie Guard with picks and shovels. So unprepared were the defenders for Have-lock's headlong advance the blockade had remained in place. Before the guard commander could intervene the Highland-ers, convinced the sepoys were rebels, had bayonetted them. "It was fated," sobbed one as he fell. "Victory to the Baillie Guard." So closely was the rebel attack pressed home two hundred wounded men, cut off from the column's vanguard, were burned to death in their covered litters. Among the many dead was Brigadier James Neill, who fell like a riven tree from his horse. Men recalled later that in death "The Butcher of Cawnpore's" face had been placid as it had never been in life. By paradox he was the one senior officer to ar-range supplies of arrowroot for the garrison's women, sugar plums for the children.

The Residency's twilit compound was given over now to carnival gaiety. Tears streaming down their cheeks, the bearded Highlanders, prepared for a second Cawnpore, moved from group to group, shaking the ladies' hands, em-bracing the children. Time and again they exclaimed in wonder, "Are you one of them? God bless you! We thought to have found only your bones." To Maria Germon, the sight of them pouring into Dr. Fayrer's compound was "the most exciting scene I ever witnessed." A piper, rushing up to Cap-tain Anderson's wife, asked her where she came from. "So do I," he whooped, when she had told him Edinburgh, "and from the Castle Hill!" At once, in honour of the lady from Edinburgh, the pipes were skirling anew. Overjoyed, Leopold

Ruitz Rees, the Swiss merchant, launched into a wild horn-pipe. It was 3 a.m. before he and many like him retired to bed.

For senior officers there were initial formalities. Brigadier John Inglis approached Outram for orders, but Outram, bowing, replied: "General Havelock commands today." Hugging Julia, his wife, Inglis kissed her joyously, repeating "Thank God for his mercies." But Inglis's aide, Lieutenant Frederick MacDonald Birch, shamed by the unusual sight of officers in uniforms, at once despatched an orderly for the brigadier's sword. Inglis wore only a brace of pistols and looked, thought Birch censoriously, more like a pirate than a soldier.

In truth both generals had small heart for ceremony. A bullet wound in his upper arm, Outram was pacing distractedly, coat in hand, outside Dr. Fayrer's house looking for a lady to mend his sleeve. Havelock wept unashamedly, lamenting "My brave soldiers! My brave soldiers!" It was with difficulty Inglis persuaded him to come to dinner. The reliever of Lucknow dined by candle-light off mock turtle soup, beef cutlets and champagne. Goats padded uneasily through the flickering shadows; a colonel lay dying on a string bed in one corner.

Above the riddled shell of the Residency building, abandoned as a dwelling this month past, the moon was rising. Hour after hour small knots of stragglers gained the safety of the Baillie Guard, too late now to join in the celebrations of earlier hours. Some arrived so late they bedded down in the roadway within the garrison. Three sleepy cheers were the only proof each force had of one another's existence.

And now the night was cold and though Katherine Bartrum, still pacing, had scanned face after face, Robert had not come. Quietly she carried her baby back to bed.

XXXV. LUCKNOW

26th September

A mile east of the Residency, set in a lazy loop of the river, the graceful pearl-shaped dome of the Moti Mahal, the Pearl Palace, loomed above green trees. Here, at 4 p.m. on 25th September, a section of Havelock's rearguard realised that one of the heavy guns they escorted, jamming across a narrow passage, had effectively trapped them. Among them was Assistant Surgeon Robert Bartrum.

Since the moonlit night fifteen weeks ago when he had parted from Katherine at Secrora one thought had been paramount in the young doctor's mind: somehow he must attach himself to the force that would relieve Lucknow. Early in September his chance had come; ordered from Allahabad to Cawnpore, Bartrum had been seconded to an artillery battery forming part of Outram's column. By 20th September he was one of the three thousand men advancing across the Ganges.

"It will be almost with fear and trembling that I shall enter Lucknow," he had written to his mother a week earlier. "Should we not be successful, few of us will be heard of more; but that I do not think of . . . only of the pleasure of entering the city and rescuing my beloved wife and child."

These were almost the last words he ever wrote. By dawn of 26th September the rebel gunners had the range of the Moti Mahal to perfection. Already as Bartrum moved with cheerful purpose among the wounded, shining chunks of marble crashed from the palace's walls. "You had better keep behind and out of danger," one officer warned, but Robert only shook his head. "Oh, no," he said, "My wife and child are there and I *must* go to them."

By 10 a.m. the fire was devastating; still Bartrum did not falter. Calmly he sought the help of Surgeon William Bradshaw, 90th Foot, in an emergency operation. Bradshaw agreed, but as they crossed the courtyard he added a further caution: "I wish I could see my way out of this . . . Bartrum, you are exposing yourself too much!"

"Oh," he heard Robert reply, "there is no danger." The sniper's sights must have held him fast at this moment; next instant the surgeon felt the breath-jolting impact as Bartrum spun heavily against him. "Bradshaw, it is all up with me," he choked and the surgeon, kneeling beside him, noted almost clinically that his lips were working as if the splintered brain sought to assemble one last message. For this message, for the next breath, Bradshaw waited some two minutes. They did not come.

Back at the Residency, Katherine Bartrum still felt no cause for alarm. She knew now that Robert was with the rearguard, that he laboured tirelessly among the sick and wounded: mingled with disappointment was a warm pride that Robert Bartrum, *her* husband, should have put his duty to his men above all. Once, as she paced up and down the scarred walks, patiently nursing the baby, she passed Captain Freeling, who again had cheerful news. The rearguards would be in within half an hour.

No one had told her that by 2 p.m. General Outram, growing anxious as to the rearguard's fate, had despatched almost five hundred men under Captain Dodgson and Lieutenant Moorsom, guided by the intrepid Henry Kavanagh, to fight their way through and escort the rearguard and the heavy guns to safety. Twenty-four hours would elapse before this mission was accomplished.

"Not a thought of danger crossed my mind," as Katherine freely admitted, even at close of day on 26th September. Then, with Bobbie in her arms, she climbed as she had so often done to the top storey of the Residency, watching the crumbling red bastion of the Baillie Guard. Dusk was falling to mask the trees and minarets as Katherine prayed for their swift reunion and Robert was lying dead with a bullet in his temple.

XXXVI. LUCKNOW

26th September to 8th November

They tortured Katherine Bartrum when at last they spoke the truth; she had begged for truth but the words, when spoken, outraged her into silence. To jest on a matter so sacred was blasphemy, a vile counterfeit. It took one long moment for her world to shiver into fragments: Robert was dead. Then she screamed.

Through the screams a wild railing at length became audible: "Oh, God have mercy on me! Do not tell it me, I'll not believe it! Say he has been wounded but don't tell me he is dead . . . bring him to me, bring him to me—*then* I may believe it!"

Yet in her heart she did believe it; for twenty-four hours now she had sensed a strange conspiracy. Perhaps, too, she had sensed a subtle emanation of pity—"it was a heart-breaking sight," Mrs. Hamilton Forbes noted in her diary. "I saw Mrs. Bartrum come out of her room with her boy who was so nicely dressed, and look wistfully up and down the road for him she would see no more. . . ." Pity was in Dr. Edmund Darby's eyes when he called for a routine check-up. "How strange it is my husband is not come in!" Katherine exclaimed and Darby replied only, "Yes, it *is* strange" before departing in haste. For the first time the thought struck Katherine: something has happened which they do not like to tell me. It was Mrs. Emily Polehampton, the chaplain's widow, who in gentle halting phrases had broken the news.

That night the Rev. James Parker Harris officiated at twenty-five funerals; Robert's was not among them. His body was never recovered.

Then Katherine Bartrum passed into a timeless mindless void, where each return to conscious thought was a pain so stabbing-sharp it seemed an opiate had worn away. The cruel irony that Robert had reached the very gates of Lucknow obsessed her—this and the manner of his death. "Shot through his beautiful head," she wrote from the depths of her grief. "God bless you my baby and spare you to me and I shall have something still to love," was her diary entry for this day, for now Bobbie was all that made life endurable.

As General Sir James Outram made the rounds of the hospital no word of complaint came even from the mortally wounded; man after man, smiling with rare content, announced, "We've saved them, sir." The bleak truth was known only to Outram, Havelock and their staff officers: the relieving force had done little more than swell the garrison by over a thousand men, many of them dangerously wounded. On 17th September, Outram had telegraphed Lord Canning for an urgent briefing: how serious would be the moral effect of abandoning Lucknow altogether once the garrison was evacuated? Within a day Canning had replied: "The permanent object is the rescue of the garrison . . . if (their) safety can be more thoroughly secured by retiring, pray do not hesitate to do so." Now, one week later, Outram saw his earlier concern as all too sanguine. "The insurgents are too strong to admit of withdrawing from this garrison," he wrote. "The sick, wounded, women and children amount to upwards of 1,000 . . . two additional Brigades with powerful field artillery will be required to withdraw."

Thus, as Outram saw it, the one hope at Lucknow was to hold out until the forces now pouring in from England surged up country for a final rescue. On 2nd October even this had seemed impossible for the commissariat believed that food supplies could last a month at most: in the wild confusion following Chinhat, a wounded commissariat officer had omitted to report that fully 160,000 pounds of wheat and flour lay stored beneath the Residency. Two days later, though still unaware of these supplies, Outram judged they could last out. His task now was to ensure an unbreachable fortress for the men and women of Lucknow.

Already the Residency's outer and inner defence rings were secure, a near continuous chain of earthworks and barricaded houses. Now, by a series of local forays, Outram extended the defence area to the south and east to almost three times its original size, securing two palaces, the houses and gardens beyond and a length of the river bank. Command of this extended terrain, a two-mile perimeter, passed to Henry Havelock. The old garrison remained under Brigadier John Inglis.

Often, Outram had prefaced all discussions on morality, "For a religious man—which I am ashamed to say I am not *very* . . ." Now, in the small hours, his aides would see the thick stocky figure kneeling by candlelight in Dr. Fayrer's house, praying for guidance. For if basic rations were secure, the garrison still faced what the Swiss merchant Leopold Ruitz Rees styled "a perfect great Sahara of wants." On 2nd October, the ninety-fifth day of the siege, rations were once more scaled down: from now on the daily weight of meat allotted—12 ounces for a man, 6 for a woman—must include bone as well.

All dreams of food held the lethal quality of a sniper's bullet. Thus dreamed one young ensign: "Visions of fresh butter, milk and eggs have been floating before me for the last three months. What would I give for a dish of Devonshire cream!" Ensign Hugh Pearson planned a celebration dinner, proper to an eighteen-year-old, sausages and iced champagne; he survived to eat it at Wilson's Hotel, Calcutta.

Grimly, the defenders came to terms with privation like a widow forced to fill the breadwinner's shoes. Major Charles Napier North watched his three candles like a hawk; if he burned them only ten minutes a day, he calculated, they would last a month. When a smiling orderly presented Mrs. Hamilton Forbes with two glittering cubes of rock-salt, tears sprang to her eyes; these were infinitely more precious than the diamonds they resembled. Camp-followers, reduced to a pound of wheat and two ounces of grain daily, begged even bullock hides to broil over their fires. Slowly men forgot the luxury of pride. Leopold Ruitz Rees, paying a social call at one post, found his friend out, and the breakfast dishes unwashed. Guiltily he snatched up a well-picked chop bone and gnawed it clean. At the Martinière post, young Edward Hilton and his fellow scholars were lining up for dinner when a screaming shell-splinter blew the pot to pieces, spattering them from head to foot with stew. Rather than waste a morsel they scraped it unashamedly from their shirts and hair.

The women, as Henry Kavanagh saw, suffered most deeply. Often, returning to the Post Office garrison, he sensed that Agnes, his wife, was too lighthearted, too gay. "There, dear soul! You must be so tired and hungry, and I have cooked that horrid bit of beef so nicely for you." "But, dear wife," Kavanagh would ask, concerned, "have you eaten any?" Always Agnes made the same reply: she could never tell when his duties would end, she had eaten earlier. Much later Kavanagh confirmed his lingering suspicion—more often than not she had sacrificed her share.

At such times men seize eagerly on any prize fortune offers. Dr. Joseph Fayrer, espying a twittering flight of sparrows, loaded all four barrels of his sporting gun with No. 6 shot and bagged a hundred and fifty. All save Maria Germon, who pleaded lack of appetite, pronounced the sparrow curry delicious. Private Henry Metcalfe, on a hit-and-run sortie against the rebels, abandoned his musket to capture and truss two game fowl, but when he began to cram his turban with looted flour Corporal George King of the 32nd intervened. It was likely the flour was poisoned.

"Poison here, or poison there, George," Metcalfe rejoined, "I'll stick to it. I might as well die of poison as of hunger."

Now that rations were reduced again, Metcalfe realised he could no longer support the terrier, Bustle. Sadly he handed him back to the Rev. James Parker Harris, and somehow Harris contrived to keep the dog alive.

There was, at Brigadier John Inglis's post, a small white hen which ceased laying as soon as Inglis bought it early in the siege. At last Inglis decided to kill and eat it but on that day his small son Johnny rushed in crying, "Oh, Mama, the white hen has laid an egg!" This, the Inglises decided, must be given to Colonel Robert Campbell, of the 90th, who lay at their post gravely wounded; there were few such treats for the sick in these bitter days. To their astonishment the white hen, day after day, laid an egg for Colonel Campbell. On the 12th November, following a leg amputation, the Colonel died. Next day the small white hen did not lay. It never laid an egg again, but no one had the heart to kill it now.

Money had lost all meaning, thousand-rupee notes changed hands for a song, yet for the provisions of the dead, auctioned day by day, men bid with wild abandon. Brandy had soared to £5 a bottle. Coarse flour sold at 40s. a pound; a jar of honey was valued at £4 10s. Od. Hams were priced at £7 10s. Od. apiece.

Inside the Residency many, with desperate ingenuity, strove to cloak their nakedness. Within the trampled compounds was now a ragged grotesque assembly as if every man and woman sought as fancy dictated to express his own concept of Robinson Crusoe. Here was every variety of garment that could be won by barter, stolen or stripped from the dead: uniforms of billiard baize, pyjamas of embroidered curtain, red shell jackets smeared with offal, khaki, white drill dyed deepest sable with official ink, double-breasted coats of red, padded with cotton wool. Shakos, forage caps, leather helmets, helmets bound with turbans weighing three pounds apiece, wideawakes, tall silk hats. On snapping-cold nights many sentries wore, poncho fashion, native quilts stripped from the palaces. Ensign Hugh Pearson of the 84th was reduced to a shirt minus a sleeve, a backless flannel waistcoat, one red sock, one white, and a pair of odd shoes. One hard-pressed officer bound his elegant legs with red tape and Henry Kavanagh could not resist jesting, "It always tied one's *hands* before!" Mrs. Hamilton Forbes achieved a bizarre elegance with a skirt of green shot silk and her husband's black frogged alpaca jacket. When Manaton Ommaney, the Judicial Commissioner, died, one of Outram's aides bid successfully on his chief's behalf for a jacket of broadcloth. Just in time he stopped Outram wearing it on a visit of condolence to the widow.

Only the rich could dicker for tobacco at two shillings a leaf; the multitude resorted to nature. Smoke, rank and acrid-smelling, curled from meerschaum and cutty pipes, their bowls tamped with dried tea, chopped straw, withered neem and guava leaves, desiccated hops scraped from beer-barrels. All his life, to his doctor's despair, Sir James Outram had chain-smoked cheroots; now, wherever he went, he was stalked by Fusilier Arthur Owen, who scavenged the butts he cast aside. Often in compassion Outram must part with a cherished Manila and his stock was running low.

None set the keynote of true self-denial more than Outram himself. Did a gift of sherry come from Martin Gubbins, anxious to reinstate himself in his old chief's good graces? It was always, noted Outram's aide, Captain David Dodgson, passed on to the hospital. Was there a chance of despatching a line by messenger to Lady Outram in Agra Fort? If so, Outram never took it—"as all cannot send private notes, none shall." General Havelock accepted Gubbins's sherry, often a bottle a week, but "without it the doctors tell me I should not pull through." In truth the little general's battle had ended at the Baillie Guard Gate; only the innate sense of duty saw him struggling day after day into his faded uniform to trudge the two mile perimeter of his command. Browsing through Gubbins's library he had reverted to his first love, military history. It was as if he sought to cushion disappointment by re-living old battles whose outcome was known.

The resilience Katherine Bartrum had been first to evince was common to all women now. By mid-October, hardship had forged an indestructible tradition of relentless toil and simple heroism. They made chupattis for the sick from their meagre flour rations. They carried tea to the men at the ramparts through lancing shell-splinters. The bank manager's wife, Mrs. J. C. Parry, gave so freely of her rations to the wounded that ugly blotches and sores disfigured her face. When a surgeon gravely prescribed a change of diet, Mrs. Parry was tart: "I wonder you don't prescribe a change of air!"

The children, with true adaptability, saw it all as a glorious game. Adept in constructing mimic batteries, they fashioned balls of clay, hurling them against the walls to burst like shells. Grape-shot took the place of marbles; like experts they had learnt to cry "That's clean through his lungs" or "That wants more elevation." "You fire round shot," Captain Robert Anderson heard one small boy instruct his friend, "and I'll return shell from my battery."

Now the first exaltation had died courage was more conscious; no man or woman but was accustomed to living day and night under fire. Stories of hair's-breadth escapes were current, each vying with the other to induce a sense of pleasurable peril. Round shot bounded down a mess-table where officers sat at dinner; none was harmed as it ploughed through the opposite wall. Round shot tore the pillow from a man's head and left the sleeper unscathed. Buzzing bullets grazed the hair; a musket-ball tore away a corporal's stripes. Soon only spectacular near-misses merited comment. Sir James Outram was relaxing on Dr. Fayrer's verandah when a round shot struck the wall above his head, smothering him in a torrent of brick dust. Shaking the plaster from his coat, Outram neither rose nor relinquished his cheroot. Dispassionately he summed up: "Not a bad shot if it had been intended but they couldn't possibly know I was sitting here."

Stranger missiles than round shot made up the screaming barrage; the rebels' stocks of ammunition were running low. There was hammered and unsymmetrical shot, which howled, cooed, screeched and whistled like all the fiends of hell. "Holy Japers, the devils are firing cookhouses at us," an appalled private shouted as he raced for cover. There was shot fashioned from stone which cried like an owl through the dark night, *hoo, woo, woo, woo*. There was shot made from bullock horns and smoothing irons and grain-dealers' weight, and slugs made of telegraph wires, three-eighths of an inch thick, which could snatch the breath from a man as surely as bullets. Blocks of wood, two feet long, a foot thick, bound with iron, thundered like ninepins into the stockade— "here comes another beer-barrel," cried the troops lucky enough to dodge them.

"Bob the Nailer" was dead but still the sharpshooters harried them. Vainly the defenders beseeched the Rev. James Parker Harris to aid them; they had desperate need of the garrison's best shot. Quietly Harris declined—though he would keep lookout for snipers he had sworn never to take life save in self-defence. Near the Baillie Guard, Major Charles Napier North, chancing on a bullet-mould, set up a small factory, working an eight-hour day to turn out Enfield cartridges. Ensign Hugh Pearson was soon one of many who crouched at the parapets, Enfield jammed tight against his shoulder, alerted to fend off every sniper he saw. As the whiplash *crack* of the Enfield followed the dull *boom* of

"Brown Bess," sepoys came plummeting thirty feet from the tall trees to burst like rooks on the iron ground. From now until the final relief, the defenders would fire fully sixty thousand Enfield cartridges.

In the trees the sacred monkeys crouched petrified, jibbering with fear, scuttling from thick shade only to seek water.

In the hospital it was worse. All life, one officer noted, "seemed as tenuous as a spider's," for round shot screamed through the riddled walls two feet above the patients' heads. Here two hundred men lay in warm tainted twilight, waiting for death, behind barricaded windows, smelling of blood and vomit and broken wind, stark and cold and crying out in the night. All around lay heaps of dirty linen glazed and stiffened with blood, bottles of physic, pill boxes, blue powder papers, dirty wine glasses holding the remnants of drafts, plates choked with salt and blood in which leeches were disgorging. The lucky lay on blood-stained couches; others had only mattresses and cloaks. Beset by crippling shortages the surgeons were powerless. Tents were sliced up to serve as blankets. New patients found the shirts ripped cavalierly from their backs and torn up for bandages. One sponge served to cleanse the soiled buttocks of the dysenteric, to swab yellow-green gangrenous sores. Women stripped off their undergarments, scraping them with table-knives to serve as lint.

Surgical ignorance was abysmal; ten years would pass before Joseph Lister published his first findings on antiseptic surgery. Maggots writhed in open wounds. Doctors probed for bullets with unwashed fingers or unsterilised kitchen knives, while a comrade held the plunging patient's head. At Lucknow, such operations had an audience two hundred strong, men who had paid their entrance fee in the coin of mortal anguish, for the operating table was sited in their midst. Chloroform was long exhausted and often this audience heard men die by inches. "Eh, man, do I hurt ye?" Surgeon Charles Scott of the 32nd would enquire sharply, for to flinch was less than virile; a fat cigar rewarded the man who could live and stifle his whimpers.

Amputations were the commonest operations. If a bone

was splintered they were thought essential; a compound fracture of the femur demanded prompt amputation. All amputations were double-flap, to allow for shrinkage of skin and muscle; outward sloping cuts with long razor-edged knives could slice away the soft tissue within seconds. Complications were invariable. Following an amputation shoulder muscles often became anchylosed, or stiff and unusable. At Lucknow, up to 9th November all amputations had proved fatal. Often infection caused gangrene, pyœmia or necrosis of the bone.

These were the few who merited hospitalisation. More numerous by far were the hundreds who manned the seventeen garrisons, nursing their strength from day to day, redraw with scurvy, bowels lacerated by diarrhoea. Captain Charles Germon limped more painfully each time he visited Maria at Dr. Fayrer's house; slowly scurvy was knotting the cords of his legs. At night Maria confessed to him she was binding her hair in a lace cap, for fifteen women slept beneath one punkah and she was determined to keep her hair free from lice. Charlie sympathised; it was easier for a man, for most had now shaved their heads and were as bald as onions. An officer who claimed immunity risked being held down forcibly and worked over with a toothcomb, to lusty cries of "Let's draw his covert." All boasts were proven false. Next day he too would exhibit a shaven head like a monk's.

Uppermost in every mind was the question no man or woman would voice: How long can human beings survive like this?

It was a pertinent question. From 20th September to mid-November, the original garrison had lost 122 men, Outram's force a further 400 killed and wounded. The effective force was now 2,700 Europeans and Indians. The besiegers, it was thought, scarcely numbered less than sixty thousand rebels.

On the night of 9th October Martin Gubbins was roused by Outram's secretary with electric news: Delhi had fallen and the Flying Column was on its way. The garrison Outram had left at Alumbagh, four miles from the Residency, was in contact with Cawnpore and obtaining supplies and reinforcements from the surrounding countryside. To offset this was the knowledge that the bulk of the Residency's rations would be exhausted by the 6th November. And day by day, under the rebels' battering fire, defences were crumbling.

To the Reverend James Parker Harris, "every single building seemed to be marked with severe smallpox . . . so riddled with balls . . . you could scarcely put a pin's head between them." Maria Germon, paying a rare visit to Charlie at the Judicial Commissioner's post, marvelled that he was still alive: the building was a trembling ruin, protected only by a bamboo stockade. At Dr. Fayrer's house, the desperate defenders piled windows with boxes of earth to ward off snipers' bullets; even the mess silver of the 32nd Foot was plugging some breaches. Martin Gubbins, experimenting with books from his library, found *Gardners' Encylopædia* worth its weight in paper: no musket ball could penetrate beyond 120 pages.

By 7th October the insurgents' batteries were surrounded by trenches twenty feet deep and three feet wide and far beneath the earth, with the tenacity of moles, the rebels were working.

Later many survivors avowed that one sight above all others marked the Siege of Lucknow as unique: a sober conversation between two friends ending abruptly as one man hurled himself full length to the ground, his ear clapped to the sandy soil. Dimly, far below, he had heard the stealthy clink of a rebel pick-axe.

Above ground, this was a sport all could relish. Below in the dripping darkness, men who had proved dauntless in the open field often panicked like frightened children. One officer offered to place a bottle of brandy at the far end of a gallery: ten pounds would go to the man who made his first descent to bring it out. There were no takers. A soldier, scared out of his wits by a harmless fall of earth, was chided by his officer: "No one knows better than you that if you think the enemy are there you should go at them and not back from them."

"I didn't think at all," the soldier confessed. "Down below is very different from up above."

Ensign Hugh Pearson, who fought under Havelock at

Cawnpore, could sympathise personally: his initial venture underground was his last. For first a man must sway by a rope down a long dank shaft twelve feet deep, bumping and bruising himself against its sides. Blackness followed, a silence broken only by the thin whine of mosquitoes. Now began the eerie crawl forward on hands and knees. Was the gallery turning right or left? You knew only by butting your head against unyielding rock. Suddenly the roof of the gallery jarred your spine; this was the signal to wriggle snake-like on your belly. Sounds were minimal: the liquid sobbing of your own breath, the steady drip-drip-drip of water. At the far end of one such gallery Pearson had the chilling glimpse of a lone figure, sitting motionless, pistol in hand, listening. A few feet away behind the rock a rebel pick-axe tapped like a blind man's cane.

"At this point," Pearson confessed, "I scuttled out faster than I went in," but in one nightmare moment he saw all that needed to be seen: the sudden cascade of sandy earth, lantern-light glinting on the pick-axe blade, the searing thunderclap as the pistol fired and the light went out. He had recognised, too, the tall limber form of the man who kept this deadly vigil—Henry Kavanagh.

This was strange for Kavanagh had few natural qualifications. Unlike many privates of the 32nd Foot, ex-Cornish miners who tunnelled most of the listening galleries, he had never worked below ground. His lanky frame was ill-suited for worming through stifling passages. Yet by paradox he was finding in the darkness and danger the deep release from material problems that only terror and crisis seemed able to bring. Clad now in a suit of canvas dungarees he himself had made he was, to Sir James Outram and his staff, the Assistant Field Engineer. But to the Sikhs and all who worked alongside him he was "The Great Miner," *Burra Surungwala*.

Despite the light sandy soil both sides found they could dispense with casing and supports. This was fortunate for later Outram estimated Lucknow's mining operations as without parallel in modern war. Twenty times the rebels ran in their mine galleries towards the palaces and ramparts: in all but three instances these were detected. On the offensive the British hit back with twenty-one counter mines—a staggering total of 200 feet of shaft, 3,291 feet of gallery. To hamper them the rebels kept up a non-stop rain of squibs, rockets and brick-bats.

None of this troubled Kavanagh unduly. Hemmed in by darkness he consciously grappled fear, tempering himself for greater things. Would he ever claw his way free from this subterranean hell? Would the shaft collapse and bury him alive? The longer he stayed below, the more easily he could steel his body to obey the promptings of his will. Once, eager to achieve this more swiftly, he lay nine hours in a mine, wet, cramped and hungry, awaiting the rebels' advent.

For powder was short and it was accepted practice to break into the rebels' mines and drive the sepoys out rather than blow them up. Once, after mortally wounding two miners with a pistol shot, Kavanagh crept boldly into the enemy's gallery and taunted the sepoys aloft in the vernacular. But a hail of fire drove him back, choking with smoke, half blinded by fountains of earth.

Kavanagh was not giving up. Mining tools were in short supply and the Irishman had taken a fancy to those the wounded men had discarded. Within minutes, escorted by two Sikhs, Kavanagh had returned to his own gallery, calling boldly that he was a British officer. To his surprise the unseen sepoys listened in grave silence while he reproached them for their ingratitude.

"Why have you mutinied and what can you expect for the atrocities you have perpetrated?" Kavanagh harangued them.

"We are fighting for our religion which you meant to destroy," came a sepoy's disembodied voice.

"In what manner have we threatened your faith?"

"By giving us greased cartridges," the reply volleyed back.

But this, Kavanagh explained patiently, had been a mistake which the Government had tried most earnestly to rectify: never had there been any intention of disregarding religious beliefs. "Did you ever know the British Government to make false professions?" he exhorted them. "Has it not always spoken the truth?"

Then a silence fell upon this strange fraternisation, as if both sides for the first time found leisure to reflect on the futility of slaughter—a silence broken at length by a thoughtful voice remarking, "It is true!" Then the advent of an Indian officer put an end to the parley: sternly he ordered his men to fire, though at first they refused urging that they "wished to hear the Sahib speak." Kavanagh, seeing their attention diverted, could not resist a successful spring for the tools, but only two men, he noted, opened fire on him and their bullets, perhaps intentionally, went six feet wide.

Ever after, Sir James Outram would startle strangers by announcing poker-faced that Kavanagh was about to be hanged. The articles of war, he exclaimed, prescribed only death for a man who conferred with the enemy.

Above the damp twisting labyrinths, the bleak courage of the besiegers was still manifest: more and more the mould of confinement imposed on them all a single pattern of endurance. They moved in a lunar landscape of skeletal trees, of red earth humped and cratered, of walls gaping open to morning sun and cold night winds.

Once upon a time these buildings had resembled Italian villas, built of small flat bricks, with wide verandahs, flat roofs and gay shutters. Green gardens had encircled them, with pretty walls and tiny watercourses traced round each flower-bed. Once, at this time of year, blue passion-flowers had bloomed and scarlet cypress vine. The gardener sowed the early peas and re-potted the chrysanthemums. Afghan horse dealers brought muscat grapes packed in cotton wool and fluffy blue Persian kittens. Silks and challis and merino replaced muslin, and velvet bonnets were the fashion. Blue evening light lay beyond the mango groves where the sun dipped like a crimson ball; the punkah lay idle in the outhouse. The cookboys did not squat on damask stools to cook their master's dinner. Snipe was in demand, not gristly near-putrid meat. Once upon a time the Judge, the Commissioner, the Collector, were chosen dinner-table guests, not the importunate dead returning on waves of stench. Once, the ruined walls seemed to say, once upon a time.

XXXVII. LUCKNOW

9th November

Pale November sunlight flooded the Residency compound, the leaves still glistened with early dew, as Henry Kavanagh, wrapped in thought, left his quarters in the Post Office garrison. Normally the genial Irishman had a greeting for all comers, but today he was distrait, remote. Though his face was impassive, he trembled on the brink of a terrible decision.

It was now two days since young James May, an engineer's draughtsman in the same garrison, had given Kavanagh a preview of his current assignment: the plans which would aid the new Commander-in-Chief, Sir Colin Campbell, in his thrust for Lucknow. But Kavanagh, scanning them, knew a sudden disquiet. The plan offered Sir Colin but one approach-route—and even this would be hard to find for a man ignorant of the terrain.

Supposing a sudden rebel retreat opened up an easier route? What if their resistance along Havelock's earlier route was stiffer than in September? Could they, during Sir Colin's advance, overwhelm the small force he must leave at Cawnpore? The sheer weight of these imponderables cost Kavanagh precious sleep.

Then the logical solution burst from a blue sky to leave him weak and sick. For what Sir Colin needed was a man who knew the four miles of country that lay between the advance force and Lucknow as he might the rooms of his house. And the one man fully endowed with these qualifications seemed to be Henry Kavanagh.

Time was of the essence, Kavanagh knew. This morning, 9th November, the Siege of Lucknow had lasted 134 days. On 26th October, word had come that the Delhi Flying Column,

Brigadier Hope Grant commanding, had routed the rebels at Agra and must reach Cawnpore by 1st November. By 10th November, Cawnpore's garrison should number six thousand men.

But on the same day rations were again whittled down. Henceforth European troops must make do on eight ounces of leathery meat, the same of wheat, a handful of rice and salt.

At Outram's headquarters, Kavanagh contacted Kanauji Lal, the courier who in the night just past had brought current news of the Cawnpore force. A former courtroom bailiff, Kanauji Lal, a dark bantam-sized native of Oudh, had done good service as a spy.

Kavanagh came swiftly to the point. It was likely that Kanauji Lal would carry to the Commander-in-Chief the plans Kavanagh had scrutinised a few days previously. How would the spy react if Kavanagh donned a disguise and accompanied him?

Kanauji Lal was equally to the point. Nothing on earth would induce him to take the risk.

But Kavanagh, afire with zeal, went on pressing the point and at last the weary spy agreed to a compromise. Very well, the project had his blessing—but he and Kavanagh must leave the ramparts by different exits to meet at an agreed rendez-vous outside the native city. Kavanagh demurred. The city encompassed more than twelve miles of streets—these he could never penetrate unscathed. His Hindustani was good— yet scarcely fluent enough to survive a catechism by zealous sentries. Kanauji Lal shook a non-committal head.

Alone, in a secluded corner of the compound Kavanagh wrestled with the problem. If Kanauji Lal would not go with him could he find another guide as skilled? So little time remained. Then, abruptly, an icy chill of realisation invaded his body as a man who has charted his own destruction yet recognises with terror the point of no return. The dread of death stripped his feelings naked; his heart seemed to burst from his rib-cage, tears streamed down his cheeks, for this was an age when men wept readily. He fought against irresist-ible hysteria with everything he knew. Then the storm of terror was past, leaving him spent but wholly decided. At

2 p.m. he rapped resolutely on the door of Colonel Robert Napier, Outram's chief of staff.

At first the project seemed so impracticable Napier could not resist smiling. Then looking at Kavanagh's face he stopped short. When it came to mining operations the Irishman's intrepidity had astonished everyone. Five minutes later, closeted with Sir James Outram, Kavanagh was outlining his plan.

Florid, impassive, chewing thoughtfully on a cheroot, Outram heard him out in silence. And Kavanagh sensed the General was wavering. As to the value of the scheme—well, there Outram had no doubts. A European officer who knew the lie of the land as intimately as Kavanagh would be a godsend to the relieving force. Yet the chances of such a man sneaking undetected through the city were less than one in a million.

Reluctantly Outram shook his head. No officer could be ordered on such a misson—so had he the right to seek a volunteer? Earnestly he begged Kavanagh to withdraw.

Outram had good reasons. At thirty-six, Kavanagh touched five feet eleven and a half inches in his stockinged feet. Square shouldered and brawny with powerful freckled hands, his red-gold hair, beard and moustaches were in vivid contrast to his blue blazing eyes. Of the 2,396 Europeans with the Residency, few less resembled an Indian peasant.

But Kavanagh had an Irish turn to his tongue and at length Outram nodded. Kavanagh might go—but only if his disguise was so perfect as to defy detection. In Outram's voice Kavanaugh heard the undercurrent of doubt that this was possible.

Kavanagh went back to the Post Office garrison, but not to rest. He lay on his bed, scourged by indecision while Agnes, his wife, tried vainly to convince the children their meagre rations must suffice. Stubbornly he kept his back to the room. If he turned to face her, he was lost; all the years would lie in that glance and his secret would be out. He was tired and sleepy, he grumbled, when she coaxed him to come and eat—he needed to be left alone.

This was the worst of it, he knew. For thirteen years they had been man and wife and she had borne the brunt, the struggles and the debts, cheerfully uncomplaining. No father could be prouder of his children than he was now. Then why, Kavanagh tortured himself, why? What drove him on to seek glory, knowing that if he died the family he loved would face want and privation? Yet like a man in whose heart God implants a seed he knew this call could not be denied.

Much later, in his small ammunition factory near the Baillie Guard Gate, Major Charles Napier North was busy turning out Enfield cartridges when Kavanagh strolled in. The men chatted for a while of the coming relief: from tomorrow on, the Residency would be in active semaphore contact with Sir Colin's advance guard four miles distant. Again Martin Gubbins's library had proved invaluable; to find out how the system worked they had consulted the heading "Telegraph" in his *Penny Cyclopædia*.

Presently, with a cheery word, Kavanagh departed and North never knew that in the fifteen minutes of casual gossip Kavanagh had picked up the gage that Fate had tossed to him.

Now, seeking out servants and camp followers, Kavanagh passed swiftly from garrison to garrison. He wanted a short jacket of orange silk and a two-handled dagger and tight silk trousers fitting close to the skin. He wanted a cream-coloured turban and a tight-fitting muslin shirt and an embossed shield. He wanted a curved sabre, such as a badmash or Indian soldier of fortune carried, a white waistband, a yellow chintz cloth for his shoulders and narrow-toed Persian slippers.

There could be no more temporising; he knew that. To all intents and purposes, Lucknow's relief would be assured tonight, or he would die. Perhaps both, but this last possibility no longer frightened him. The chances were that he would fall on the return journey, but that *he* should guide the vast relief force within striking distance of the Residency was the important thing. The only thing.

If he worried it was over Agnes. Should she divine his secret, she alone would have power to dissuade him for the children's sake. But his natural calm, now the decision was made, helped to allay suspicion. The family did not question his kissing them all farewell at 6 p.m. for night duty at the mines was routine. The bundle containing his disguise went unquestioned.

Shouldering this, Kavanagh hastened through thickening darkness. Five hundred yards away near the Slaughterhouse Post stood a small outbuilding. This would serve as dressing-room. Here a young Eurasian, Francis Quieros, one of the few in the secret, already awaited him. Kavanagh now began the slow application of his make-up, while Quieros held the mirror. Lamp-black applied with a cork would be as effective as anything—thus must his face as far as the shoulders be tinted, and his hands as far as the wrists. Experimenting they now dipped the cork in oil—that would make the colour adhere. Scissors snipped ruthlessly at Kavanagh's red-gold curls.

At length Kavanagh straightened up, squinting at himself in the glass. Was that shade of black entirely natural? It scarcely seemed so but time was running out; it was too late to do better now. Perhaps the darkness of the night would aid him—yet this whole sortie hinged on Outram's inspection, carried out in a lighted room. At least Kanauji Lal, chuckling from the doorway, seemed satisfied. Now for Outram.

With Kanauji Lal following, Kavanagh stalked ahead, buffalo-hide shield slung behind him, sabre cocked rifle-wise over one shoulder, the turban's thick cream-coloured folds masking his red-gold hair. He heard a low murmur of voices from the room used by Outram's staff officers: Napier was there, no doubt, and Captain Frederick Sitwell, the A.D.C. But at this hour many servants and messengers came and went: would they accord him the second critical glance that was the true test? For his own safety that second glance must be hard and long.

To enter a house, Indian or European, wearing shoes, to take a seat uninvited, were then considered gross discourtesies. Still shod, Kavanagh now strode brashly in to Outram's officers and plumped comfortably on to a chair. At once an angry tumult of voices arose. Who was this stranger who was at such pains to be impudent? Kavanagh looked them squarely in the eye, trading sally for sally. What was that to them? Had they no welcome for an old friend? As their bewilderment mounted, he felt a small ember of confidence glow within him. Then Outram came in.

The General's glance was blank, void of recognition. He had hoodwinked them then—all of them. Not a man in the group had an eye keen enough to penetrate his disguise.

Suddenly—perhaps because of Kanauji Lal's rich chuckles—the realisation struck them. At once the atmosphere, heavy with distrust, took on the madcap mood of a charade. Everyone had a suggestion to make. Careful hands readjusted Kavanagh's turban. A pair of baggy purple-striped pyjama trousers, urged someone, would add the finishing touch and these Kavanagh donned. Then Outram, shaking with laughter, must apply the lamp-black all over again; broad smiles wreathed every face. At the last moment, Captain Frederick Sitwell pressed a loaded double-barrelled pistol on Kavanagh. If it came to the worst, this was a cleaner death than any the insurgents would offer.

This unobtrusive gesture was the sole token that Kavanagh embarked on any venture more hazardous than a schoolboy escapade.

But at 8.30 p.m., when it was time to leave, the laughter died. Both Outram and Napier, deeply moved, shook Kavanagh's hand. Guided by Captain George Hardinge, of the Oudh Irregular Cavalry, the Irishman and Kanauji Lal trod quietly through the darkened compounds. Four hundred yards ahead bulked the Water Gate picket; in the faint light of hiving stars, the river glistened. Kavanagh never forgot how fervently Hardinge squeezed his hand as they neared the water or his last words: "Noble fellow! You will never be forgotten." Then he had gone; in darkness and silence the two couriers began to undress.

At this point the river was a hundred yards wide, perhaps four and a half feet deep. Their clothes rolled into a bundle on their heads, the two now slipped as silently as otters down its bank. To Kavanagh it seemed then the shock of water knife-cold against his belly, the dark murmuring night, symbolised perils he was irresolute to face. To their right lay the enemy lines, extending past the palaces to the bridge of boats; to their left, the rebel strongpoints were bound around the graceful iron bridge they must soon cross, the stone bridge farther west which recrossed the river. Panic banished even fear of humiliation; he reached out to grasp Kanauji Lal. This final test had found him wanting; he lacked the spunk to go on.

But already the spy was out of reach, wading purposefully. His small dark silhouette had gained the opposite shore, slithering in shadow through a trench towards the shelter of a grove of trees. There was no going back: like it or no, Kavanagh was cast as a hero.

XXXVIII. LUCKNOW

9th to 10th November

Kavanagh was only half-dressed when a sound he could not identify made him stand very still. Craning into darkness he saw that the grove of trees in which he and Kanauji Lal crouched sloped to the edge of a pond. At the edge of this pond a man stood washing himself.

Kavanagh and Kanauji Lal lay prone, saying nothing, aware that if the intruder so much as glanced their way he would see them and this was the end. Presently the man went away.

The two spies moved forward. Ahead loomed a bee-hive cluster of mud huts; close by, the patrolling figure of a matchlockman. If they hailed him first, Kavanagh thought, would it disarm suspicion? Was it worth the risk?

"The night is cold," he called cheerfully.

"Very cold," grumbled the man with feeling. "It *is* a cold night."

"It will be colder by and by," rejoined Kavanagh carelessly. They walked on. The sentry had made no effort to halt them.

Seven hundred yards to go and there was the first checkpoint—the iron bridge spanning the river. Light glowed on the sleek coats of saddled Arabs—evidently a cavalry picket kept watch here. An officer, voicing a sharp challenge, was a black cut-out in a lighted upper window. Motionless, Kavanagh hung back as Kanauji Lal made for the light, a man with nothing to hide. They had come from the old cantonment— which the rebels held—and were making for their homes in the city. Eyes averted, Kavanagh heard the man's grunted dismissal.

Correctly he had reckoned that the worst of the journey lay ahead. Between the iron bridge, now safely cleared, and the stone bridge ahead lay nine hundred yards of river bank. At this hour the terrain swarmed with matchlockmen and sepoys, some escorting senior officers in palanquins. The lambent yellow flames of burning torches trembled on men's faces and the hands. Would the disguise stand up to scrutiny, Kavanagh wondered, at the moment when scrutiny came?

Then they were over the stone bridge, where the sentry, busy questioning a ragged peasant, did not even notice them, and into the *chowk*, the main street of the native city. Dim lights twinkled from high three-storeyed houses, their eaves seeming to lean together and shroud the stars. They tramped through the ooze and mire of an unkempt thoroughfare; there were fewer lights than formerly, Kavanagh noted, fewer people abroad. The soft clonking of camel bells mingled with the babel of tongues and a chill breeze brought the sweetness of burning spices. Several times Kanauji Lal proposed detours down dark curling streets but always Kavanagh restrained him: in loneliness lay danger. Here were swarms of armed men who yet jostled against them, incurious. A roistering guard of sepoys lolled and bantered with a group of harlots, whose noses were adorned with gold rings, their hands stained red with henna. Thankfully the spies hastened on.

At length the alleys fell behind. The stars glittered above silent fields. Kavanagh's spirits rose. Five months when only stench had clawed at the senses and now this—the sweet scents of grass and lime and jasmine. Happily munching a carrot he trudged on beside Kanauji Lal.

Two hours later the sudden knowledge that they were lost was like a slow chill of blood spreading upwards from the loins.

Kavanagh fought to keep control of himself. How far had they come? Four miles, perhaps five? Far from working south-east they had travelled almost due east for the lofty groves of old trees told him too plainly where they were—a green park where peacocks strutted, known as Dilkusha, or Heart's Delight. They had doubled back into the heart of the enemy's camp.

Now, at midnight on 9th November, Kavanagh knew that it was all going wrong and that neither disguise nor Dutch courage, or anything but the hand of God could deliver them. An old cultivator still labouring by starlight pleaded lameness. He could not show them the way. He knew only that parties of troops roamed everywhere. Kavanagh battled fear. Fear was a tortuous ally but in a few hours it would be dawn. How would his pigmentation look in the harsh light of morning? A second peasant loomed from the darkness and he caught his arm roughly: the man must set them on their way. But the peasant eluding him ran shouting for his village. Oil-lights came alive in dark huts and dogs were barking. Panting, cursing, the two men bolted for the canal nearby, hurtling headlong into the bed of a stream. How much farther could he go? Kavanagh wondered. The tight Indian slippers were chafing his toes and his heels were raw and blistered.

Through darkness, progress became agonisingly slow. They bruised their knees against garden walls, stumbling unsus-pecting down the scars of ravines. Another village huddled beneath the stars; if they could not find a guide here, what then? On hands and knees, Kavanagh crept forward into a thatched hut that stank like a byre. Then he recoiled; his fingers groping through blackness had encountered a woman's soft thigh. He lived an eternity, awaiting her first piercing scream.

Mercifully she heeded his earnest plea for silence, quietly awakening her mother, who set them on the right road again.

Now for Kavanagh each yard became a mortal effort of will. His feet, constricted by the tight slippers, held the sensation of walking on thorns. The long months of malnutrition were taking their toll. His weary body cried out for rest. Soon, very soon, he prayed, they must reach Alumbagh, the walled garden where the British advance guard lay.

It was then that Kanauji Lal, inexplicably, suffered a change of heart. He must confess it: he had never been within the walled garden housing the advance guard. His contact was with the Commander-in-Chief's main force, at the village of Bunnee, fully eighteen miles from Lucknow. Alumbagh was flanked on all sides by rebel rifle pits. To infiltrate it would be perilous, perhaps impossible.

Painfully Kavanagh recognised that his flayed feet must carry him many bitter miles yet. If Kanauji Lal lost confidence all was lost.

At 3 a.m. on 10th November, the truth of this came home with staggering impact. Ahead, from a mango grove, sounded the high reedy note of a man singing. A labourer preparing for the day's toil, thought Kavanagh idly—and heard in the same instant, the man's shout of alarm. Within seconds an armed picket of sepoys hemmed them in. Their voices mingled in an angry shout. Who were they that walked abroad at this hour? Whence had they come? Where were they bound?

A cold knot of despair lodged in Kavanagh's stomach for he was watching what the sepoys mercifully failed to see: the wadded tissue that was Outram's despatch to Sir Colin, written in a hodge-podge of French and Greek, flutter as gently as thistledown into thick grass. Kanauji Lal, fearful, was taking no chances.

But now, Kavanagh knew, he at least must get through for the only other sketch-plan of the British approach-route was lodged in his own turban.

Honey-tongued, Kavanagh cajoled the sepoys. They were poor travellers, unused to the presence of valorous soldiers. See how his friend was terrified by their martial aspect. This was true for little Kanauji Lal shook as if with ague. They were bound, Kavanagh explained, for Umroula, a village two miles east of the main British camp with sad news for a friend; his brother had "eaten" a British bullet at Lucknow. Immensely relieved, the rebels passed them on.

Kavanagh was limping in anguish; the pace seemed to crawl. He was less certain of direction; through anxiety to put distance between them and the last picket they had struck off into swampland. To know this was to know also it was too late to retrace their steps. As far as the eye could see the swamp sprawled in a boundless horizon of mud and sedge, dotted by islands of thorn-bushes and clumps of high spear-grass. Mud sucked at his tight slippers; the stink of marsh-gas caught at the pit of the stomach. Time and again small thorns tweaked the yellow scarf from his shoulders. Soon they waded waist high, moving more cautiously; in places they wallowed like buffaloes, the water up to their necks. Of necessity Kavanagh's powerful hands were grasping Kanauji Lal's neck; lacking this support, the little man would have sunk without trace. Kavanagh glanced again at his hands and for one moment the universe stood still.

The lamp-black had gone, washed clean by the waters of the swamp. The hands that held Kanauji Lal were European hands, bespotted by freckles.

There are times when only medieval oaths help a man clutch on to sanity. This, it burst upon Kavanagh now, was such a moment. He cursed and did not stop cursing. He cursed every rebel in Oudh. He cursed every strand of weed in the kingdom, each clod of mud, each drop of water. He wondered why Kanauji Lal was shaking, and was startled to find the little man consumed with laughter. Kavanagh's profanity had made him feel better.

Two hours had passed before they stumbled from the swamp, plastered with yellow-grey mud and weeds and now Kavanagh was adamant. Despite all Kanauji Lal's protests he must rest for fifteen minutes.

Where they paused now the trees had thinned to lone clumps. Beneath the moon the terrain was white desert, tes-sellated by dark shadows. Somewhere close at hand a vast army awaited them. Where, thought Kavanagh despairingly, where?

In the one village they could locate, a man shaken into wakefulness by Kanauji Lal greeted them only with bitterness. They were Rajah Maun Singh's men, were they, spying out the English strength? "Have you not heard that from the fel-lows who ran away from them?" he snarled. "Go away! and do not disturb our rest."

Unseen, they passed on, skirting the golden tongues of sepoy fires. No pickets were thrown out here. Time and again they stopped, listening for the subdued seashore murmur of a camp by night. Silence was absolute. Soon Kavanagh knew, would come the false dawn: the hushed moment, when early-rising peasants, oxen, ploughshares loomed like spectres through haze, dim, impalpable. A terrible lassitude seized him. Ignoring Kanauji Lal's entreaties he slumped to rest his bleeding feet.

"WHO COMES THERE?"

Galvanised, Kavanagh scrambled to his knees for this, though voiced in Indian accents, was the time-honoured British challenge. Miraculously, Kanauji Lal, traversing a mango grove in search of a guide, had stumbled on a British picket.

Dazed, Kavanagh, stumbling forward, found himself shaking hands with a Sikh officer. Guided by two troopers, he moved on towards the main force. Midway a horseman riding at full speed intercepted them; this was Lieutenant James Goldie, 9th Lancers, who at once led the bemused Irishman to his tent pressing on him dry stockings, trousers, a glass of brandy. Warmth and strength invaded Kavanagh's body; harsh chords of disquiet sundered his thoughts. Fear was still dormant within him. None of this could be quite real. He could not be safe, truly safe.

Mounted on a fine Burma pony, led by a staff officer, he presently jogged on to seek the Commander-in-Chief. It was 5 a.m. The sun grew higher in a blue metallic sky. Before him stretched two mighty lines of hill-tents, small canvas cones, each marked trimly with a blackboard showing the owner's designation.

From one tent there stepped now an elderly man of medium height. He stood poised on small well-made feet, one arm, the fist clenched, immobile at his side. From a lined face, its jaw hard and stubborn, blue eyes of a piercing shrewdness surveyed Kavanagh sternly.

"*I* am Sir Colin Campbell," came the reply in a strong Scots accent, to Kavanagh's query, "and who are you?"

At once, whipping off his turban, Kavanaugh produced Outram's note of introduction: "This, sir, will explain who I am, and from whence I came." As Sir Colin read, impetuously the Irishman was conscious of the General's face raised sharply to his after every line. "Is it true?" he queried brusquely.

"I hope, sir, you do not doubt the authenticity of this note?"

"No! I do not! But it is surprising—how did you do it?" Sir Colin shot at him.

But strangely in this ineluctable moment of triumph Kavanaugh was too tired to tell how it had been done. Indeed he scarcely knew. Reeling with fatigue, he begged a few hours rest—and then the whole incredible story of the night's venture should be told and plans finalised for the great advance. At once, his eyes compassionate, Sir Colin summoned an aide. In a tent whose dark-blue cotton lining shut out the sun, Kavanagh was left alone.

Nine hours earlier he had crept from the Residency at Lucknow into the deep soundlessness of this night, an obscure debt-ridden clerk haunted by dreams of destiny. He knelt now to thank his God, a figure in history.

XXXIX. LUCKNOW

10th to 12th November

Old Kharbardar, Hindustani for "walk warily," Auld Coudy, "Old Comfortable" in the dialect, Sir Crawling Camel: thus men called Sir Colin Campbell because he risked men's lives with reluctance and left nothing to chance.

At sixty-five, a Glasgow carpenter's son who had marched with bare bleeding feet in the great retreat of Corunna, Sir Colin was a firm believer that his troops should live to fight another day. But he was no man to spurn snap decisions when the need arose. "Tomorrow," was his rumored reply when asked how soon he could leave for India, and rumour said, too, that he had reached Calcutta on 13th August to replace Sir Patrick Grant armed only with a carpet bag.

This was the man on whom almost seven thousand men and women, from Brigadier Henry Havelock to Katherine Bartrum, depended for deliverance. An aide recalled him piquantly as "an odd little crumpled being with a bright eye and a face like a winter apple." At times his temper exploded like tinder, a weakness he sought in vain to master. "John Company's" officers ignited this spark as readily as Royal Artillery officers, another source of flashpoint. In these moments he would, as he cursed, scratch his head violently, leaving his curly grey hair standing bolt upright, "exactly like a portrait of Punch." Office work was anathema and so was formality. "Here he comes," he growled, sighting one officer addicted to documents, "hugging his papers as if they were a pretty woman."

This was a fighting soldier, whose fame, as creator of "the thin red line" at Balaclava, was assured: disdaining to form his troops in square, he faced the onslaught of Russian cavalry on a thin extended front and blew their squadron to smithereens. As a general he was at all times accessible for interview, even in the bath. A stickler for detail he had, before leaving Calcutta, personally inspected every boot-sole and buckle in his force. On his appointment as Commander-in-Chief, India, an officer wrote glowingly: "His presence is worth 10,000 troops." A ranker, more prosaic, rated him "a regular go-ahead fire-eating old cock."

This was the commander who, soon after 10 a.m. on 10th November, 1857, faced Henry Kavanagh across a breakfast-table that set the Irishman's mouth watering. Here was coffee with milk and sugar such as he had forgotten existed; here were platters piled with eggs and bacon and bread and butter and pots of chunky orange marmalade. Wolfing greedily at all that was set before him, Kavanagh struggled to reconcile bewildering contrasts: the tent with its soft blue and buff Persian carpet, the workaday appearance of a Commander-in-Chief, who wore only a blue patrol jacket, brown corduroy breeches and a pith helmet. Later Kavanagh would learn that this had been Sir Colin's garb all through the

Crimean campaign. In time of war he slept fully accoutred even to his boots.

To Kavanagh's delight, Sir Colin now revealed his plans to save Lucknow. One factor was paramount: no troops must manœuvre through the narrow streets of the native city. This could invite only the slaughter that had overtaken Havelock's force. The one alternative was to plan the relief in three defined stages. First the force would march as far as the walled garden called Alumbagh, where the British advance guard maintained semaphore communication with the Residency. Here tents and all heavy baggage would be left behind. Next, instead of striking for the city, as Havelock had done, the force would make a wide right-handed sweep over much of the ground Kavanagh had just covered—through the park called Dilkusha or Heart's Delight, past La Martinière College for Boys, through the Sikanderbagh (Garden of Alexander), which lay east of the Residency. Dilkusha marked the last staging post for all light carts, elephants, camels and bullock carriages.

The plan was hazardous. Against the absence of narrow streets, troops would contend for a series of isolated strongpoints, each one a fortress in itself. Moreover, to keep open communications at Alumbagh and Dilkusha, Campbell must employ close on a thousand men, over a four and a half mile line of retreat. To extricate the Residency's defenders he could match scarcely four thousand men, one strong brigade, against the enemy's fifty-three thousand, of whom thirty-two thousand were the armed retainers of feudal barons.

Meanwhile, Sir Colin cautioned Kavanagh to keep his counsel. The Irishman and he must work closely together, prospecting every inch of the terrain as they advanced, but young staff officers should know as little as possible—they gossiped irresponsibly. Kavanagh swelled with pride. *He*, Henry Kavanagh, would plan the advance with the Commander-in-Chief! He could scarcely credit his good fortune.

Next afternoon, 11th November, he could believe it still less, for here was he, an unknown Irish clerk, making one of the cavalcade of Sir Colin's staff officers as the Commander-in-Chief reviewed his troops for the first and last time. To Kavanagh the one drawback was his young untrained horse.

As Sir Colin, on a white charger, rode down the serried ranks, drawn up in quarter-distance columns in the centre of a vast plain, dark woods massed beyond, the Irishman's mount leapt and bucked as if a gadfly were on his back.

It was a breathtaking sight—and for Kavanagh, after the sombre years of drudgery, a moment crystallised in time. Before him stretched the force that would become a legend within its lifetime, the force that history textbooks have normally reduced to an obdurate mass, the relievers of Lucknow. Yet seen individually these were men as remarkable as Kavanagh himself, men whose differing hopes and aspirations have from the outset made part of our story.

Here, in the ranks of the 9th Lancers, resplendent with their blue uniforms and flagless lances, white turbans twisted round their forage caps, was Octavius Anson, whose yearning for Frances increased daily. A strange premonition of death haunted him: "It will last me ten years, if I live so long," he wrote of the warm flannel dressing gown he had bought at an auction. Within eighteen months the rigours of the campaign were to slay him as surely as any sabre. He was then forty-one.

And here, too, were other troops from Delhi, among them Lieutenant Arthur Lang, seasoned now in war, a harder and older man than the young engineer who watched with pain and foreboding the mass disarming of Mian Mir. "I have enjoyed this new life which I tried," he confessed. "I really chose aright when I thought a soldier's life was for me —exposure and fatigue, the music of ball and bullet . . . the blood danced in one's veins like mercury."

Of the newcomers, men of Lord Elgin's hastily diverted China Force, five thousand strong, many were part of units so singular as to be individuals in the mass. There was Captain William Peel's Naval Brigade from H.M.S. *Shannon*, who had begun their Indian campaign in the same unorthodox way as they meant to finish it—arriving in the largest ship (2,662 tons) ever to anchor in Calcutta, under a captain so high-spirited he and his officers sometimes pelted one another with oranges. "Who have you left your things to?" was the standing joke as they disembarked, for no man expected to come out of this alive, yet to the end the Naval

Brigade would maintain there was but one way to do things. Clad in loose open large-collared blue shirts worn outside loose blue trousers, broad-brimmed straw hats with white covers and black ribands, they refused to muster either in front of the camp, like infantrymen, or near their six 24-pounder siege guns, like artillerymen. The officers' lines astern, they persisted, formed their quarterdeck; it was here the boatswain piped all hands to grog.

Peel, third son of the late prime minister, a tall man with flashing blue-grey eyes and carefully-tended wavy hair, was a law unto himself. His two hundred sailors and marines, despite campaign crises, must shave daily; each man wore black well-polished shoes. At bath-time his sailors settled down to scrub themselves with a weird variety of pets—monkeys, goats, even squirrels. Infantry might march fourteen miles before breakfast; Peel's sailors, under Captain's orders, marched on full stomachs. To one observer, these "little men, four feet high, and four feet in the beam, always laughing and dragging about their guns," remained a mystery to the end. Already two army liaison officers had been seconded to their gun-teams; no Indian bullock-driver could fathom such directions as "starboard."

Above all there were the 93rd Highlanders, forming virtually a quarter of this force and Sir Colin's especial pride—"he showers his favours," wrote one soured Sassenach, "on the regiments which wear their knees bare." Among 1,070 men, 700 were Gaelic-speaking Highlanders, the bulk of them sturdy youngsters aged twenty-five. Virtually a military Highland parish, with ministers and elders selected from men of all ranks, they held, even in battle, regular services with communion plate. But these men, at Balaclava, made up the wavering line that stiffened to a red rampart at Sir Colin's snarled "Steady 93rd! Damn all that eagerness"—no men did he love or understand like these. No foe could disquiet them; so tough was little Johnny Ross that when a spent bullet smashed his front teeth he mistook it for a comrade's fist and knocked the man down. From Sergeant Michael Findlay, so cool he feared only sunstroke when his bonnet was shot off, to Sergeant Daniel White, who in battle recited Sir Walter Scott, the non-coms were as hardy. And to lead them through the battles ahead were officers of the same iron calibre: Captain "Wee Frenchie" Burroughs, who checked whether his troops had washed behind their ears, Lieutenant and Adjutant "Willie" MacBean, Inverness ploughboy, who rose to become a general. Yet, at an average height of five foot seven inches, all were overshadowed by champion caber-tosser George Bell, at six foot four inches the most powerful man in the regiment or the British Army.

In column, these men now wore not scarlet tunics but light brown holland blouses, faced with scarlet, designed for boat-work on the Canton River, rolled greatcoat slung across the right shoulder, Sutherland kilts. Equipment was the barest possible: sixty rounds of ammunition held in pouch, a hundred rounds in reserve, water-bottles and linen haversacks with three days' rations, rifle and bayonet. Every fifth man carried a three-gallon copper camp-kettle and a bill-hook. Other baggage was stacked in bullock-carts labelled "The Rattler," "Busy Bee" and "Kill the Darkie."

As Sir Colin, his face haggard and worn, drew rein before corps after corps, only solemn silence had greeted him, but as he halted before the 93rd, a thousand Scots who knew and loved him were cheering as one. His right arm rigid in salute, he hailed them: "Ninety-third! When I took leave of you in Portsmouth, I never thought I should see you again . . . but another commander has decreed it otherwise . . . There is work of danger and difficulty before us . . . the eyes of Europe and of the whole of Christendom are upon us, and we must relieve our countrymen, women and children, now shut up in the Residency of Lucknow. . . ."

But at the cheer which followed Henry Kavanagh's untractable mount snorted and kicked up his heels. Despite all the Irishman's efforts to check him, he bolted for base.

Before dawn on Thursday, 12th November, Kavanagh awoke. Despite darkness he sensed the camp had come alive: an invisible army took on new dimensions of activity and sound. Hastily, Highlanders roused themselves from feather bonnets that all night had served as pillows. Hobgoblin figures crouched above the flicker of blazing straw. Gulping at scalding coffee, men gagged back nausea at the unholy sulphurous smell of camels' breath. Then, as a bugle shrilled

"Strike tents!" the vast canvas city, as if powered by one rope, fell soundlessly. Caught unawares, Sir Colin himself leapt like Harlequin from beneath the folds of his tent. Swiftly, bedding was piled into large laced sacks called *saletahs,* loaded four to a camel.

The men now fell in. At attention, they presented arms; four thousand rifles and muskets jerked upwards. The right hands of four thousand men slapped smartly against the butts. At Sir Colin's side Kavanagh rode forward at a march; beyond, at the very head of the column, marched the 93rd, their pipes skirling "Castles in the Air." Soon the order passed along the column, "March at ease," "March easy." The men strode at a steady three miles an hour, muskets slung over their shoulders, puffing on cutty pipes. The camp-followers' cries of "March, march, very good plum cake," jarred with the bagpipes. From the darkness came mutters of *pani* from thirsty men who craved the water-carrier's four-gallon goatskin.

As the dust and clamour intensified, the landscape softened. The cavalcade wound through land like a green garden, as flat as an outspread palm. The air was as clear as glass. There now came in sight an open plain some eight hundred yards wide. Beyond lay the high walls of a garden, flanked by pretty summerhouses, enclosing a central palace. Above the tramp of marching feet, elephants trumpeting, the confused sound of many voices became audible. The column approached the first staging post for Lucknow's relief, where eleven hundred men of the advance guard anxiously awaited their coming: the wide-walled rectangle called Alumbagh, which means Garden of the World.

XL. LUCKNOW

14th November

By dawn on Saturday, 14th November, all within the Residency, Lucknow, had felt excitement banish the weariness of months. They tasted victory in advance and the taste was sweet. On the previous night a blazing tar-barrel on the Residency's roof had hopefully signalled their readiness and miraculously in answer a blue light had glowed from the roof of Alumbagh. This was the signal they had awaited. Henry Kavanagh had slipped safely through and for the second time within eight weeks a relief force was poised before the city. But with this final confirmation, Agnes Kavanagh's pride and anxiety diminished as one; she was now furious with her husband for running the risk at all.

As this day dawned, Kavanagh, at Sir Colin's side, watched in silence while the sharp-spoken old general, ivory-and-gilt spy-glass focussed, scanned the wide sweep of Dilkusha Park. Later Kavanagh would come to know this ritual well: the grave concentrated survey of earth and sky, while vital decisions were formulated. This, as young Arthur Lang later admitted, was "a very picturesque site for a battle." Beyond the lofty groves of trees, the browsing herds of deer, sprawled a green-shuttered summer palace like a French château. Ahead in the morning haze, sepoy skirmishers in white drill flitted eerily from tree-trunk to tree-trunk.

It was 9 a.m. Sir Colin lowered the spy-glass. With a wide sweep of his arm he indicated the green plain ahead. All men heard his command, as sharp as musketry. "There is your bed—take and lie on it!"

Those who fought at Dilkusha recalled this later as a battle where icy calm prevailed. As the British gun-carriages with infantry support jolted forward from the park's south-east corner, brief vignettes were imprisoned within memory: the vivid splashes of uniforms against sandy soil like daubs of colour on a palette; swarms of black buck and spotted deer bounding fearfully before them. Simultaneously from Dilkusha's palace, a masked battery of six guns opened fire: shells crashed about them. A round shot, smashing a private's musket barrel, drove it clean through his skull; the ranks of the 93rd shivered and broke. "Tell off again from the right," an officer screamed. The ranks tightened.

Now the shot flew thicker. Through the ranks of the 90th Light Infantry an elephant cannoned in berserk frenzy, the lower half of its trunk, almost severed by round shot, hanging by a strip. "Keep steady, men, close up the ranks," their officers shouted. The 90th tumbled aside then slogged on over broken ground. Against volleys of fire, men began to duck. "Don't, it's catching—I'll be doing it myself," Sir Colin's voice exhorted. Shell splinters broke about the naval brigade but Captain William Peel, though ultra-sensitive to shot, would admit no danger. "Nonsense, nonsense, it is only dust and dirt," he reproved the timid. Then he rallied his gunners. "One more broadside, if you please, gentlemen." The 24-pounders cracked as one; yellow-white smoke plumed amongst the trees. Calmly, the camp-followers of the 5th Fusiliers, espying a convenient tank, settled to wash their clothes. Rebel fire drenched them with vast geysers of water; unperturbed they scrubbed on.

Over low ditches and deep dykes the artillery bounded on, a gunner astride each horse, "as if the heavy field pieces and carriages were baby carts"—a pace so fast light cavalry could barely match it. Dismayed the rebels fell back down the hill to the shelter of La Martinière College. One hour had elapsed; Dilkusha Palace had fallen.

But Dilkusha, now taken, must be held; as garrison, Sir Colin would relinquish twelve hundred men. Barely three thousand men were left to relieve the Residency.

On down the hill towards the grey turreted pile of La Martinière College wound the artillery and the infantry skirmishers; the flagless lances of the cavalry dipped and glittered in the sun. Behind flowed the inexorable tide of the 93rd, bonnets crested by the gleaming skewers of bayonets.

Massed musketry fire from the sepoys crashed amongst the trees. Branches showered upon the surging figures, so thickly Lieutenant Jones-Parry thought irresistibly of the Babes in the Wood.

North-west, across the canal, scattered knots of scarlet and white were falling back, abandoning La Martinière—but too far away from where Sir Colin sat his white charger to determine whether the masonry bridge was entire. Again it was Henry Kavanagh who clinched the issue, spurring his horse under shelter of a ravine within a hundred yards of the bridge. Galloping back he brought word that the bridge seemed intact. But Sir Colin, eye glued to his spy-glass, shook his head. To him it seemed the bridge was broken.

At once Sir Colin's testy chief of staff, General William Mansfield, challenged him, "Why not assure yourself of it?" This was too much for Kavanagh; to doubt his courage was to touch exposed nerve-ends. "I can do that, too," he riposted and at once was urging his mount forward through volleys of rebel fire. Blood was flowing from his horse's flanks when he returned with vital intelligence: two arches of the bridge were broken, and in the direction which the rebels expected the British to advance the canal was so dammed up as to make it unfordable. By dusk on 14th November it was plain Sir Colin's tactics were working.

This night would be long and for most cheerless. All tents and baggage remained at Dilkusha; troops lay down in darkness, greatcoated, their arms by their sides. This night the defenders within the Residency saw the blue light coming closer: it glowed now from the roof of La Martinière. On this same roof Henry Kavanagh busied himself building a mammoth bonfire: this, as arranged by semaphore, was a signal to Sir James Outram. On the morrow his troops must fan out to occupy yet more buildings, facilitating relief.

Descending, Kavanagh found Sir Colin huddled, like any private, on the stone floor, asleep and dreaming of the bitter battle to come. Proudly the Irishman lay by the side of his newfound friend to dream too.

XLI. LUCKNOW

16th November

Often, in mid-November, the morning air drives chill across the plains of India. East of Lucknow the fields are warm with the vivid yellow of flowering mustard, the soft blue of flax, but there is no warmth in the breeze to temper the hours before sunrise. Afterwards the relievers of Lucknow recalled that on Monday, 16th November, 1857, dawn came like this at La Martinière College. A Scottish surgeon, William Munro, whom the men called "Kind Hearted Billy," would recall a colleague's quiet prophecy: "That is the last sunrise many will see."

Because of this, all who outlived the day held fast, sharp and indelible studies of the aching hour before battle. A chaplain recalled the vile monotonous oaths of troops aroused from sleep, men's breath foggy and nauseous with the sweet stink of rum. Others remembered huddling against old walls to catch the sun's faint rays, the braying of the washerman's jackasses. Surgeons treasured Sir Colin Campbell's concern for all who might soon be wounded. Over six hundred covered litters were available for a force four thousand strong and every one might be needed.

At Dilkusha, whose garrison saw no combat this day, they remembered the plain before sunrise pricked with golden darts of fire as the cooks crouched behind small cane screens, over glowing pits of charcoal or cowdung. Savoury smells tinged the raw mist of morning: chickens simmered in boiling water then swiftly curried, called "sudden death," roast peacock, prawn curry and moselle cup, beefsteak pie, parrot roasted with strips of bacon. This was food some had not tasted and now would never taste.

Already at La Martinière the men were falling in. Anxiously, like actors in the wings, Highlanders pressed their bonnets firmly on their heads, checked the tension of bayonet springs, loosened their ammunition. Those who could trap fireflies inserted them down their rifle-barrels, to illumine the least speck of rust between muzzle and breech. Troops were now issued a canteenful of tea and three days' rations: three pounds of salt beef, a dozen hard biscuits. In sober silence the officers of each corps heard Sir Colin's edict that ammunition should be used sparingly: in close fighting it was likely the men would wound each other as much as the enemy. In a few stark sentences he set the keynote of this day: "The enemy you are going to meet will stand and fire at you as long as you stand to fire at them. I must have none of that; there must be no hesitation, no halting . . . whenever you get within charging distance, *at* them with the bayonet."

Already, following a long earnest conference with Henry Kavanagh, Campbell had laid his plans. The rebels still anticipated the relievers would strike for the Residency through the heart of the native city—the dammed-up canal made that plain. On the roof of La Martinière College, staring out over the white temples and glittering domes, the two men debated the problem. Again Kavanagh's detailed knowledge of the terrain furnished the solution. The force should cross the canal as expected—then strike out in the opposite direction altogether, following the river bank for a mile then swinging sharply left along a road parallel to the fortified Sikanderbagh (Garden of Alexander). This, a vast pleasure garden a hundred and fifty yards square, circled by walls twenty feet high, was one of the two key strongpoints lying between Campbell's force and the Residency.

Readily Sir Colin had assented—and all the night past salvoes of balloon shells from Captain Peel's guns had burst over the decoy route, as if to herald the British advance.

By 9 a.m. the column, Kavanagh riding as scout, was defiling steadily through mist along the right bank of the river. Through mounting heat, men moved steadily, marching in fours, breathing hard, faces set with expectancy. Unchallenged, the force wended along narrow lanes, through thick mango plantations girdled by mud walls. Sir Colin, riding level, caught Kavanagh's eye and shook his head in silent

wonder. Only the rarest fortune had let natural barriers
like these go undefended.

Suddenly Kavanagh spurred forward; his eye had caught a
flash of white. A peasant trapped between the contesting armies was fleeing down a narrow lane. Checking the man,
the Irishman put salient questions. Yes, the Garden of Alexander was strongly occupied—perhaps by over two thousand
men. No, the insurgents had no suspicion that the British
were advancing in their rear. Kavanagh rode back to advise
Sir Colin. If the artillery advanced to mount the long low
plateau, running parallel to the building's south face, a
hundred yards from the wall, they would command the
main gateway of the garden.

This was pertinent advice. To launch troops against the
Sikanderbagh, which now sprang suddenly to view, would be
tantamount to murder. The high stone walls were flanked at
each corner by circular bastions; every yard of them was
pitted with loopholes. Within, a double storey of houses gave
the rebels a twin line of fire. In the garden's centre, on the
flat parapeted roof of a two-storied house, sharpshooters
were posted.

Nor was this all. The garden's southern entrance was
masked by a stout traverse of earth and masonry. To the north
a small wicket-gate was fortified as strongly. Not two hundred and fifty yards from the southern face, the rebels had
occupied and loop-holed a burnt-brick caravanserai. To the
south and east Alexander's Garden was lapped round by
rebel villages, each within musket range of the other.

Now the river bank came alive with colour: the skirmishers of the 53rd and 93rd were advancing. Bayonets held
splinters of morning light. Suddenly from the high walls there
burst a shattering crescendo of fire. Trumpets screamed,
Sir Colin was shouting, messengers doubled to and fro.
Checked by this fire the British could still seal off the rebels'
retreat to the river. The 53rd Foot, Sir Colin ordered, must
line a shallow trench close to its bank.

Transfixed, Kavanagh saw that one young officer had mis-
interpreted the order; a handsome white-faced youngster, he
spurred forward with drawn sword, rallying his men. Next
instant Sir Colin's voice cracked out: "Come back! Come

back, Lord Seymour! You have no business there! Consider yourself, my lord, as attached to my staff! I admire your noble spirit and must take care of you."

Sheepishly, the young officer rode back. The artillery passed him at a gallop, brass helmets gleaming, black horsehair plumes tossing. The main gateway, the rebels' one escape route, was now secure.

Concussion shattered the bright morning: the artillery's eighteen-pounders had opened fire. Beneath his feet Kavanagh felt the ground throb as if an earthquake threatened. Shells shrieked and shrieked; yellow-white claps of thundering flame split the dark pall of smoke.

In rear of the guns, the ranks of the 93rd stirred uneasily, as restless as colts in a stall; between each salvo silence yawned, for the artillery's gun-barrels must be allowed time to cool. Nor were these breech-loading days; riflemen needed time to re-load. A few, despite the showers of dirt and stones, settled patiently to play cards. Bullets whipped through their feather bonnets and the cooler hands joked sourly "Nae doot the niggers think our brains are higher up than ither men's." But forty minutes had passed and impatience was mounting; within each man the lust to kill grew like a small steady flame. Alert to this tension, Sir Colin admonished them: "Lie down, 93rd, lie down! Every man of you is worth his weight in gold in England today!"

Pandemonium reigned. The crash of cannon tore at the eardrums. Round shot screamed overhead like monster humming tops. Vast blocks of bricks and mortar were toppling; the smoke and heat pressed down like a curtain.

No longer could the infantry be restrained. From the ranks of the 53rd, Sergeant Joseph "Dobbin" Lee, as was his custom, gave his commander spirited advice: "Sir Colin, your Excellency, let the infantry storm . . . we'll soon make short work of the murdering villains."

"Do you think the breach is wide enough, Dobbin?" Sir Colin shouted back.

"Dobbin" Lee was sure of it. "Part of us can get through and hold it till the pioneers widen it with their crowbars to allow the rest to get in."

To Kavanagh, though no stranger to total war, the assault

seemed suicidal. This breach, despite drifting smoke, was visible to the right of the main gate—yet it seemed barely wide enough to admit one man. Grimly he watched the Sikhs of the 4th Punjab Infantry readying for the assault, a silent line of swarthy bearded men clutching tightly to their rifles. Sir Colin whipped the pith helmet from his head.

The Sikhs went over the low mud wall in a surging tide of khaki, haring for the breach. Musketry tore at them; two British officers fell dead; fractionally the Sikh ranks wavered. To Colonel John Ewart, commanding seven companies of the 93rd, Sir Colin roared: "Colonel Ewart, bring on the tartan!"

A chill of horror swept through Kavanagh's blood; no bugler had sounded the advance, Sir Colin's command was not repeated, but with a wild animal scream the Highlanders were over the wall, as if signalled by a starter's pistol, pounding for the breach, neck and neck with the Sikhs. Simultaneously two companies of Highlanders were pelting for the caravanserai. A dead wall stopped them.

"In at the roof! Tear off the tiles and go in through the roof, Highlanders!" Sir Colin yelled.

Breathlessly Kavanagh watched the flurry of black bonnets and Sutherland kilts swarming through smashed tiles, torn mats and broken bamboos. Grasping a hesitant ranker of the 53rd, Sir Colin stabbed a finger after the racing Highlanders: "Do you see that half-naked fellow? Follow him, he'll lead you to glory."

Already a Sikh had hurtled like a gymnast through the breach; fifty rebel bullets smashed into him as one. Behind him, a black bonnet hovered: then the Highlander, too, crashed forward dead. Bullets rattled like hail on the caravanserai's red-tiled roof. At this moment, Corporal William Forbes-Mitchell would always recall, Private Hope, a hard-drinking gentleman-ranker of the 93rd, died bloodily, his bowels bursting over his knees. Above him, his face distorted by frenzy, loomed James "Quaker" Wallace, who all along had dogged this man's footsteps. His cry was plainly audible above the skirling of "On wi' the Tartan": "Vengeance is mine, I will repay, saith the Lord! *I came to the Ninety-Third to see that man die!*"

What strange bond of hatred had linked these two, no man could say. Forbes-Mitchell knew only what every man in the regiment knew: that both were men of means who had enlisted under aliases, that Wallace had requested a posting to Hope's company, that both were mortal enemies already known to one another who never exchanged a word.

A rebel sabre crashed on the skull of one of the first officers in; swooning, he reeled helplessly; a curtain of flesh had fallen to blind him. Gasping and cursing, Lieutenant J. A. Woods, Madras Fusiliers, was wrenching at the stout double gateway: beside him Private Darby Cronley fell "stone dead like a dropped handkerchief." Within, the rebels tussled to bar the doors: grimly a subadar of the 4th Punjab Infantry wedged his left arm in the gap. A sabre slashed, almost severing his hand at the wrist. Crazed with pain, he withdrew his left arm, thrusting in his right. Again the sabre fell but the Sikh had won the precious time needed. A Fusilier jammed his Enfield against the rivet of the obstructing bar and blew his way in.

This was a hell on earth which no man who witnessed it ever forgot: the Highlanders, their faces blackened with gunpowder, pipeclay rubbed from their belts and gaiters, fighting shoulder to shoulder, tunics smeared with blood. They fought as they had been taught to fight, in groups of three, the central man lunging with the bayonet, two others supporting him from right and left. They clubbed and hacked and lunged amongst head-high grass, trampling the flowers which had adorned this pleasure-garden built for one of Wajid Ali's mistresses: purple bougainvillæa, yellow alamanda, scarlet convolvulus. They swayed amongst overturned string beds and through the drifting smoke of cooking fires, for the rebels, caught unawares, had been preparing breakfast.

"Look, chaps," a Highlander bawled, "here are fine hot scones." An officer waving a claymore screamed, "It's not hot scones we want, it's blood!"

No quarter was given and none was asked. Lieutenant William Gordon-Alexander of the 93rd was intrigued by the sepoys' attire: scarlet cloth coats dating from the Crimean war, high old-fashioned shakos, white crossbelts with portmanteau-like ammunition pouches, loose pink Turkish trousers and Turkish slippers. Yet these men, despite their un-wieldy garb, were courting death like Spartans. Private Allan Stewart of the 93rd, lunging with the bayonet, recoiled in the nick of time; with the bright steel barb deep inside him, the rebel still found strength to almost decapitate Stewart with his sword. Snarling, a Fusilier sought to jerk free his bayonet from a rebel's breastbone; the man's death blow severed the fingers of his left hand. Some, firing their mus-kets, next hurled them at the British, bayonet first, like javelins, then, drawing their sabres, rushed blindly on to destruction, ducking beneath the bayonets to slash at their adversaries' legs. Others, darting like salamanders through smoke and flame, smashed their spines leaping from the high roofs.

Shouts and screams, the wail of the bagpipes, merged into one nightmare symphony. In a kind of ecstasy, James "Quaker" Wallace, who single-handed killed twenty men, was chanting, as he lunged, the 116th Psalm, Scottish version:

> *I'll of salvation take the cup,*
> *On God's name will I call*
> *I'll pay my vows now to the Lord,*
> *Before His people all.*

Above the rebels' yells of *"Din, din"* and *"Chalo, bahadur"* (Come on, my brave one) rang the Sikh war-cry of *"Jai Kalsa Jee,"* the Highlanders' hoarse "Come on, men, for the honour of Scotland!" But more, as they stabbed, cried out, "Cawn-pore, you bloody murderers," for tales of the massacre had driven all mercy from their hearts. The one fitting retribution was a "Cawnpore dinner"—six inches of cold steel.

Even the officers, Kavanagh noted, seemed beyond con-trol; outside the Sikanderbagh, Colonel John Ewart, bleeding and near hysteria, stumbled up to Sir Colin, almost unhorsing him, with a vast crimson-covered regimental colour.

"I have killed the last four of the enemy with my own hand and here, sir, are their colours," he gabbled wildly. Sir Colin, severely practical, at once exploded: "Damn the colours, sir! Where is your regiment? Go back to your regiment, sir! I thank you for your zeal and gallantry, but go back to the regiment."

Sir Colin could not then know that Ewart, although a

brave soldier, had been appalled by this morning's slaughter and the realisation that he had personally killed eight men. "I earnestly pray that it may never again fall to my lot to take away the life of a human being," he wrote later. But young Arthur Lang felt no such pangs; the virus of hatred had long driven out the compassion of Mian Mir. "Didn't we get revenge!" he exulted, "the first good revenge I have seen. It was a glorious sight to see the mass of bodies, dead and wounded."

But to Kavanagh the sight within the Sikanderbagh after four hours of battle was one that could never be blotted out. The air was thick and scarcely breathable; the sweet fragrance of trampled flowers mingled with the reek of blood. Here was an insane litter of goblets and broken cooking pots and white statues reddened with blood; a drummer-boy of fourteen with tight golden curls lay like a crumpled doll in one corner. All over the courtyard the rebels lay in piles four feet high; the cotton clothing of many was on fire, literally roasting them in their own fat, and a pale stinking bluish vapour drifted from them to the branches of the pipal trees. To Kavanagh it seemed the dead, atop these piles, were breathing still; the dead heaved slowly in mass suspiration because the living piled far below were stifling to death. Lieutenant Sidney Jones-Parry, who cherished bizarre similes, thought suddenly of "a cheese alive with mites." And stricken men with their last breath cursed their victors: "If we could only stand we would kill you."

A future field-marshal, Lieutenant Garnet Wolseley, assigned to count the dead, found the total symbolic: exactly 1,857 had been slaughtered within Alexander's Garden. And suddenly the morning was so quiet that as the blood-stained smoke-blackened men fell in for the calling of the muster-roll, they could hear, far away in the Residency, the soft lament of the 78th Pipers.

Yet the rebels' mightiest strongpoint was still untaken. Two hundred and fifty yards from the Sikanderbagh, down a narrow defile, high garden walls enclosed the white mushroom dome of the Shah Najaf Mosque. Thick jungle and mud huts pressed close to these walls, making long-range assault impossible. Gravely Sir Colin communed with Kavanagh and his staff officers. Already it was early afternoon; somehow by dusk they must secure the mosque.

Tensely Kavanagh watched Captain Peel aligning the Naval Brigade's gun battery against the Shah Najaf, "very much as if he had been laying the *Shannon* alongside an enemy frigate." Within twenty yards of the wall, salvo after salvo blasted the Shah Najaf. The heat rippled in waves across the sandy soil; in silence men watched the shells strip grey-white flakes of mortar from the walls.

From beyond the river rebel cannon sent fire crashing back; on all sides the sailors fell dying. Corporal William Forbes-Mitchell never forgot one sailor, whose leg was carried off by round shot above the knee—"he sat bolt upright on the grass with the blood spouting from the stump of his leg like water from the hose of a fire-engine, and shouting, 'Here goes a shilling a day, a shilling a day! Go at them, my hearties!'" Then he fell back dead.

Soon one factor was plain; in pounding the walls Peel's artillery was achieving little more than creating further rebel loopholes. So harassing was the fire that poured from the Shah Najaf that Peel's sunny smile gave place to tight-lipped concern. In desperation Sir Colin now despatched a fire party under Lieutenant Sidney Jones-Parry to burn down the mud huts clustering the walls. But soon the young officer was forced to withdraw; his men, working with dire enthusiasm, had encircled themselves with fire. Sir Colin's impatience knew no bounds. He reproved Jones-Parry peremptorily: "You have not half burned the huts, sir."

Dismayed, Jones-Parry was stammering excuses about the intensity of the fire when Sir Colin, misinterpreting this as a slur on the troops' courage, turned on him "like a wild tiger." "Damn your eyes, sir, I will not allow you or any other man to tell me that the fire is too hot!" Hastily his Chief of Staff, General William Mansfield, interposed, "I think the officer means the fire of the burning huts." Mollified, Sir Colin growled, "All right, sir. It was my mistake."

Astride his white horse, Sir Colin sat as still as a statue, watching black wreathing banners of smoke blot out the battlefield, at times shifting to reveal the building sparkling all over with the bright flash of small arms. That the position could be little worse, he knew. The force could not turn back; its sole link with the Sikanderbagh and Dilkusha was a narrow lane already choked with the bullocks and camels of the rearguard. Yet three hours had passed and still Peel's guns firing at point-blank range could not breach the mosque's stout walls.

Sprinting under a storm of fire, a made-up battalion under Major Roger Barnston, 90th Light Infantry, made one vain attempt to scale the wall's pitted surface—but scaling-ladders were lacking, the parapets loomed twenty feet out of reach. By the light of burning torches the rebels swarmed above the assault-force, beating them back with a steady stream of missiles—brick-bats, grenades, burning wads of oil-soaked cotton, boiling water. Struck through the heart by a steel-headed arrow, a Highlander leapt six feet in the air then fell stone dead—one of many to fall lifeless beneath the walls. *"Allahu Akbar!"* the rebels screamed in triumph. *"Din! Din! Din!"*

By 5 p.m. Sir Colin saw there was no hope for it. Spurring up to Lieutenant-Colonel Alex Leith Hay, commanding the 93rd, he directed him to join the Highlanders up in close column. He had not, he apologised, intended to call on them again that day but the mosque must be carried and he himself would lead them. His last words were a clarion-call: "Remember, men, the lives at stake inside the Residency are those of women and children and they must be rescued. It is not will you take it or can you take it—*you must take it!*"

Then, ignoring the clamour of protest from the ranks that they must lead themselves since his life was too precious to risk, Sir Colin drew his sword, and cantered steadily towards the Shah Najaf.

To one officer the scene at this moment "more rivalled Dante's 'Inferno' than anything earthly." Darkness had fallen but still the Indian night was as bright as day; candent flames leapt from burning thatch. The bullets rattling on Peel's guns made "a noise like . . . a crowd of schoolboys . . . throwing stones at an empty saucepan." Shell and rockets screamed and splintered like an arsenal exploding; of all the mounted officers only Sir Colin and two others did not feel their horses crash beneath them before they reached the walls.

Suddenly, within the mosque, a rebel bugle blared the "advance," followed immediately by the "double." At once all firing ceased.

At this tense and mystifying moment, a lynx-eyed sergeant of the 93rd, John Paton, came running with news of a chance discovery that won him the Victoria Cross. In the north-west corner of the mosque's wall, only fifty yards from where the troops were massed, he had espied a practicable breach, half-screened by undergrowth.

Bayonets fixed, a party of fifty Highlanders crept noiselessly forward to explore. Penetrating the breach they found themselves on a flat roof, peering down sixteen feet into the dark gardens surrounding the mosque. It dawned on them now that the rebel bugle call had signified only retreat, for the gardens and the mosque itself were deserted. Fearful that Peel's shells would ignite five thousand pounds of gunpowder stored within, thousands of men had slipped silently through the river-gate on the northern wall.

Minutes later the joyous lilt of "The Campbells are Coming" pealed through the darkness. The 93rd had chosen a characteristic way to tell Sir Colin that the Shah Najaf was theirs.

Here inside the main gate on the mosque's south face, the old chief and his Highlanders bivouacked for the night. The men slept rolled in their greatcoats, fully accoutred, arms piled, loaded and capped, alert to fend off attack. Some kindled vast bonfires from stacks of dry wood for the night wind was bitter; small clay saucers of burning oil abandoned by rebel sentries flickered eerily on marble floors. Muffled drums pulsed and the pipes keened "The Flowers of the Forest" as a dead march, for this day's advance had cost the lives of many Highlanders. Through darkness came the soft voice of the chaplain reading the Ninetieth Psalm: "A thousand years in Thy sight are but as yesterday when it is past, and as a watch in the night . . . in the morning they are like grass which groweth up, in the morning it flourisheth and groweth up; in the evening it is cut down and withereth."

Silently Kavanagh, at Sir Colin's side, observed the old

general compose himself for sleep, and an aching affection swept through him to see "his stern puckered features, moving as if in deep thought." Some who settled to sleep recalled the Gaelic proverb, "The heart of one who can look death in the face will not start at a shadow." If this was true, few, after the day's carnage, could bear to face their dreams; they lay, their gaiters plastered with blood, crying out in nightmare. Thus one called: "Oh, mother forgive me, and I'll never leave you again," and another, re-living the bitter struggle, "Fire low, give them the bayonet!" So another voice, as if in response, took up the theme: "Charge, give them the bayonet!" a third cried, "Forward, forward"; others, like a threnody through this night of sorrow, "Cawnpore, you bloody murderers," "Cawnpore," "Cawnpore," "Cawnpore."

XLII. LUCKNOW

17th to 29th November

At dusk on 17th November Katherine Bartrum sensed the greatest perils were yet to come. For twenty-four hours she had known that Sir Colin's force was barely a thousand yards from the ramparts: the damp air seemed alive with the thunder of their guns. But now came momentous news: tomorrow night, 18th November, the defenders must evacuate the Residency without delay, taking no more baggage than they could carry. "My heart fails me at the thought of the terrible march," Katherine confessed in her diary, then with the strained dignity of one who had come to terms with sorrow she summoned fresh heart. At least she could carry Bobbie, and her wordly goods had dwindled now to a few old clothes. So "I must bid farewell to the little room where I seem to have lived a lifetime, so old in sorrow have I grown. . . ."

Despite this eleventh-hour liberation, many within the Residency felt a stifled irritation. Under fire, all had walked humbly with God; the advent of freedom brought material concerns to the fore. To leave behind clothes, books, silver, after five months of siege—it was *too* vexing! Hastily Mrs. Hamilton Forbes sorted out the best of her painted china. Mrs. Emily Polehampton elected to sacrifice everything but her late husband's harmonium. Few were as ingenious as the lively Maria Germon; beneath her plaid jacket she was attired in four flannel waistcoats, three chemises, one flannel and four white petticoats. As an afterthought she sewed "dear Mother's fish-knife and fork" into her pink flannel dressing-gown skirt; under this would be worn three pairs of stockings and three pairs of drawers.

As the hours passed, the discontent mounted; it was as if Sir Colin, like an untimely groom, had brought the carriage round too early. And surely Sir James Outram or Havelock could at least have given more notice of the withdrawal? At the very moment Sir Colin's Highlanders fought the bloody battle of Sikanderbagh, a twelve-hundred-strong force under Havelock had stormed out to secure a chain of rebel strongpoints between the Residency and the Shah Najaf Mosque.

In truth, Sir Colin's decision left both Outram and Havelock gasping. On the afternoon of 16th November, their advanced strong points were still half a mile from Sir Colin's; Outram's first intimation that succour was at hand was the sight of a tall man running fleetly towards them, doubling and twisting through a deluge of rebel fire. Dressed in a staff officer's cotton quilted tunic, a pair of Sir Colin's corduroy breeches and thigh-length jack-boots, his red-gold curls were hidden by a heavy pith helmet. Henry Kavanagh had effected one more vital link in Lucknow's relief.

The volatile Irishman felt tears spring to his eyes, for Outram, impulsively, had exclaimed in tribute, "Three cheers for Kavanagh! He is the first to relieve us." Oblivious to the snapping whine of bullets, he pressed forward to pump Kavanagh's hand and Havelock and Colonel Robert Napier and all the staff officers followed suit. "It was the proudest moment of my life," Kavanagh avowed later.

"Are you willing, Sir James, to join the Commander-in-Chief at once?" Kavanagh panted. "The road is clear, but there is that fire from the palace to be encountered."

But Outram, after the pent-up weeks, was seized by a wave of schoolboy impatience. "Never mind it!" he rejoined, and urging his staff-officers to follow, he jogged ponderously forward over the hummocky ground.

Now they realised, so clearly and so well, that bravado had supplanted common sense. A hail of rebel bullets burst about their feet; of the nine men who ran this deadly gauntlet, four, including Colonel Robert Napier, fell out to crawl wounded to the shelter of the Moti Mahal Palace. The blood was mounting to Havelock's pale cheeks; the asthmatic Outram was wheezing and purple; next Kavanagh, tripping headlong, gravel-rashed his nose. On they stumbled until at length, leaving Outram in the shelter of a mud hut, Kavanagh hastened on to find Sir Colin.

"Sir James Outram is waiting, sir, to see you," Kavanagh announced with a conjurer's bland air.

"The devil he is! Where is he? Where has he come from?"

"I have fetched him, Sir Colin, from the Residency, and he is standing yonder."

"Well done!" Sir Colin enthused. "Lead the way!"

Again Kavanagh swelled with pride, for it fell to his lot to introduce the three generals and to hear Sir Colin congratulate Havelock on the knighthood that the Queen, without his knowledge, had conferred on him. It was now that the old chief dropped his bombshell.

"Are you prepared, Sir James, to quit the Residency in two hours?" he urged. "Time is precious."

But when Outram, flabbergasted, blurted out, "It is impossible, Sir Colin," Campbell's temper again overmastered him. "Nothing is impossible, sir," he blazed back.

But Outram, though puzzled by Sir Colin's peremptory manner, stood his ground. "If you will permit me to explain the reasons for considering it impracticable, you will, Sir Colin, be well satisfied that it cannot be done," he answered firmly. In mellower mood, Sir Colin replied, "Very well, Sir James, we'll discuss this as early as possible."

At this hour, 4.30 p.m. on 16th November, Kavanagh was aware, as few men can ever be, of sharing a moment in history. The wreathing smoke, the throng of blue-coated staff officers, Sir Colin's stern lined face animated in discussion

—all these made part of the panorama. Suddenly, as news of this historic meeting passed from man to man, a deafening cheer rent the air. All along the line of retreat this cheering was taken up and redoubled until at last it was no more than a faint echo very far away. His eyes bright with tears, Havelock was greeting Brigadier Hope Grant and his men: "Soldiers, I am happy to see you. Soldiers, I am happy to think you have got into this place with a smaller loss than I had."

Quietly Hope Grant disillusioned him; their losses had not been eighty men as Havelock supposed. To date, the second relief of Lucknow had cost forty-three officers, four hundred and fifty men killed and wounded—and still the task of freeing the Residency's defenders lay ahead.

It was a mighty gamble. As Sir Colin planned it, each exterior line would pass one by one through its supports—as if, one expert wrote, "a gigantic sock, with its open top at the Dilkusha and its toe at the farthest corner of the Residency, were being pulled inside out." First all civilians, women and children and wounded must be escorted as far as Dilkusha. This accomplished, the old garrison, under Brigadier John Inglis, would withdraw from the Residency, followed closely by Havelock's men from the riverside palaces. Once both forces had passed through Sir Colin's advance posts at the Moti Mahal, these too would fall back, with the detachment at the Shah Najaf Mosque close behind. Meanwhile, at the Sikanderbagh, Sir Colin with the artillery and the last line of infantry would keep vigil until the last man had filed through, ready to strike with loaded guns if the rebels followed up. They would need speed, silence—and, above all, luck.

That Sir Colin's force had been guided thus far marked the peak of Kavanagh's triumph. From this moment, when he sprinted back to the Residency with Outram and Havelock through fresh volleys of fire, to 4th January, 1860, when Queen Victoria pinned the wine-red ribbon of the coveted Victoria Cross on his breast at Windsor Castle he would know no prouder day.

Others, like Katherine Bartrum, knew no such concrete satisfaction. At 6 p.m. on 19th November, after a day's delay, Katherine, along with scores of women, set out under cover of night on the first stage of the great retreat—passing in a covered litter, Bobbie in her arms, out through the shattered courtyards of the riverside palaces, on towards Sikanderbagh. To Katherine it seemed, despite the constant injunctions for silence, that only wild confusion reigned: the bawling of soldiers who had lost their regiments, the cries of camp followers, the stifled grunting of the litter-bearers, the crash and whine of bursting shells. At points along the route screens made from the canvas sides of tents had been set up to foil preying rebel scouts. Elsewhere trenches had been dug; temporarily abandoning their transport, the ladies filed silently along them until danger was past.

All along the route, lit by the livid glare of bursting shells, the fugitives' reactions varied—much depended on the transport they had been able to obtain. The Rev. James Parker Harris and his wife rode in a carriage drawn by two half-starved horses who stopped abruptly every five minutes—always at the point where the grapeshot was falling thickest. Eventually, abandoning it, they bolted for their lives. The Hon. Julia Inglis, refusing a litter that the sick might benefit, walked every step of the five-mile journey. Young Edward Hilton, also on foot, recalled it as a hair's-breadth passage; never would he forget the screaming volleys of grape, the cheery cries of the Naval Brigade, "What cheer, lads and lassies! Bend low and run as fast as you can!" And Maria Germon was now so weighted down with clothing her pony could barely support her; as an afterthought she had sewed her Honiton lace wedding-dress, her veil and two large shawls into her bustle and stuffed her inner pockets with jewellery. Each time she dismounted to creep along a trench it took the combined efforts of an officer, an Indian orderly, a tall soldier and a chair to boost her back into the saddle.

In these hours of danger, men gave themselves up to random thoughts. The Rev. James Parker Harris, absorbed in calculation, realised that throughout the siege he had conducted five hundred funerals. Financial Commissioner Martin Gubbins was still smarting at Sir Colin's trenchant rejection of his hospitality the previous evening. Arriving at Gubbins's house to dine, Sir Colin's eyes flashed fire to see the table laden with meat, vegetables, truffled sausages and champagne. His voice cut like a stockwhip: "How is it, Mr. Gubbins, that these things were not given to the starving garrison?" Arms folded he sat grimly throughout the meal, refusing so much as a crumb.

Sir Colin's indignation was fitting. At the Sikanderbagh, where two days back over eighteen hundred men had died in pain and torment, the simple provisions piled on trestle tables seemed to many the most wonderful sight they had ever seen. Fondly Katherine noted how Bobbie revelled in the tea and bread and butter an officer brought them: in five months, she reflected, life had offered him no greater treat. Wide-eyed one small girl assured her mother: "Mama, there is a loaf of bread upon the table. I'm certain of it; I saw it with my own eyes." Even adults felt the same; Maria Germon, weary with her exertions, ate a plate of cold mutton, bread and butter and a ham sandwich, finishing with a bottle of beer. One officer recorded in ecstasy: "For five months I had grubbed in dark corners and holes, amongst rats and mice and cobwebs; for five months had fed on tough beef and chupattis—and now a clean table-cloth, tea, milk and sugar. . . ."

Despite the aching anxiety of this night, Sir Colin, to all who saw him, seemed unquenchably jovial. When a private of the 93rd hastened up to ask whether he could fall out to assist an English nurse with a child, Sir Colin, poker-faced, queried, "Is she pretty, man?"

"Oh, Sir Colin, I told you that she wanted me to help her."

"Is she pretty, man?" Sir Colin twitted him. "For I thought that if she was pretty you would be all the better pleased to help her."

Taking this as assent, the Highlander still shook his head sadly: "There you are, Sir Colin, at your old nonsense again."

At 11 p.m., after many delays and false starts, the column moved on towards Dilkusha, the night's encampment. Huddled within her litter, Katherine Bartrum shivered; the night was chill, the noise and confusion too great for Bobbie to sleep. But suddenly she came bolt upright in the darkness, listening. Now the noise had died away. The night was a silent abyss pricked with stars; she was alone in boundless space. Her voice high with alarm she upbraided the litter-bearers: where were they taking her? Where were all the others? But the bearers, bewildered, could only shrug. They had strayed from the column and were quite lost.

But a hundred and forty punishing days of siege had momentarily proved too much for Katherine Bartrum. Overwrought, she was convinced the bearers had only malicious intent: all along they had planned this diversion to hand her over to the sepoys. With a wild scream, clutching Bobbie to her, she leapt from the litter, tripping and stumbling across the darkened plain. Presently, paralysed with terror, she stopped dead. Close by a voice had called. British pickets— or sepoys?

Stark terror was paramount. She blundered on through drifts of sand and dew-soaked grass, mud plastering the hem of her dress. Providence decreed that she ran full tilt into a party of British privates—but when Katherine, in tears, sobbed out her plight, one confessed: "We, too, have lost our way and only know that we are close to the enemy's pickets."

Later Katherine Bartrum was convinced that only the efforts of these men led her and Bobbie to safety. "We will do our best for you, poor girl," they reassured her; often she stumbled, fearful that she would let the child fall, but each time they guided her footsteps anew through the damp clinging sand. It was close to 2 a.m. when a sudden noise amongst the trees made all of them halt, listening. "Oh, God," one man burst out uncontrollably, "it is all up with us, we are done for now."

But in a moment their sense of responsibility for Katherine and the child had a sobering effect. "Don't scream," whispered one, "and we may be able to creep on." Presently, hearing no other sound, they glided forward. At 3 a.m., after three hours weary trek, they glimpsed the orange flicker of camp-fires. By rare fortune they had hit upon the main encampment in Dilkusha Park, where the famished survivors in one night were to demolish twenty days' rations.

And now that Katherine Bartrum was safe once more, the tension and solicitude for her child proved too much. She sank down on the wet grass, yearning for Robert's arms about her, and the tears flowed silently.

Two days later, at midnight on 22nd November, the old garrison began their own retreat. With Inglis and his staff officers, Outram stood in silence as the defenders of each garrison limped doggedly past in turn. Behind them as rearguard marched the men of the 78th Highlanders, at intervals breaking step; the regular tramp of feet might arouse rebel suspicions. Once they had gone the Residency seemed strangely lonely, for still the shells of ruined buildings glowed like Hallowe'en pumpkins with candle and lantern light, a ruse to incite volleys of rebel fire. Now, in silent tribute to the endurance that had been shown here, Outram and Inglis bared their heads to the Baillie Guard gateway.

Afterwards, rumour said, Inglis, as garrison commander, claimed the privilege of leaving last, until Outram, smiling, extended his hand and said, "Let us go out together." But George Couper, Lawrence's former secretary, recalled a salutation with a genuine ring of Outram: "Brigadier, you shall be the last man to leave the place which you have defended so well."

To the men who made up the rearguard along the route these last hours seemed the longest they had ever known. At first Lieutenant Sidney Jones-Parry had drawn comfort of a sort from the deafening symphony of the Naval Brigade's guns; to delude the rebels that he planned an immediate assault, Sir Colin had ordered Peel's guns to keep up a forty-eight hour barrage against the strongly-manned Kaisarbagh (Caesar's Garden) south-west of the Residency. Crouched five hundred yards from its walls, Jones-Parry and his men had watched with fascination as the brickwork toppled "like cheese under a slicer." But suddenly a staff officer galloped up with fresh orders; abruptly the guns grew silent. One by one they were limbered up to creak away towards Dilkusha. Jones-Parry now saw his men were near to cracking; in vain they urged that *they* formed the gun-guard. "Please sir," they begged, with mounting panic, "*please* let's march." Resolutely the subaltern shook his head; his orders were to hold on. A sweating half-hour had passed before an officer slipped through the darkness to bid them fall back.

Lieutenant-Colonel John Ewart and four companies of the 93rd Highlanders lay even closer to the rebels—in a ruined barracks only a hundred and fifty yards from the Kaisarbagh. Anticipating that his position might be rushed Ewart had lit two watchfires outside the barracks; towards midnight, to maintain the illusion of a tough force still on the alert, he ordered his men to heap fresh logs on the blaze. Then, withdrawing them one by one, he closed the ranks so tightly they could touch one another as they stole away.

It was a wise precaution; on this pitch-black night man after man kept his bearings only by a miracle. Few could have known the escape-route better than Lieutenant William Moorsom; as an engineer he himself had drawn up the final blueprint. Each time he tumbled headlong into an unseen ditch he reflected on the irony of this. Later, at Dilkusha Park, the rich oaths of Lieutenant Edward Carter, 90th Light Infantry, rent the darkness; "a beastly nigger," he avowed, had tried to place the legs of a string bed on his stomach. Sir Colin, he next day learned, had been seeking a resting-place for the night.

Not every aspect of this retreat was glorious, for human nature has as many facets as a diamond. At Dilkusha Park, the men of the 90th Light Infantry found closer acquaintance with some of Lucknow's ladies brought only disenchantment. When one soldier, who lay dying, beseeched a passing woman for water, she replied arrogantly: "There is the well, my man, and you can get the water yourself." Overhearing some malcontents criticise the inadequate transport, Sir Colin, turning in his saddle, rebuffed them: "Ladies— women, I mean—you ought to be thankful that you have got out with your lives for I do not know how it might have been in two hours more with you!"

Some were vexed and bewildered by the inexplicable delay. On 19th November, it had seemed, time was of the essence; they had been forced to quit the Residency with the minimum of baggage. Yet not until 11 a.m. on 27th November did Sir Colin give orders to resume the march on Cawnpore and despatch this triumphant message to Lord

Canning: "Last night I caused the garrison of Lucknow to execute its retreat from the Residency, covered only by the relieving force which then fell back on Dilkusha, in the presence of the whole force of Oudh. . . ." Within the hour Canning telegraphed back: "I congratulate you, my dear Sir Colin, with all my heart, on this great and joyful success."

But aside from his staff, few appreciated Sir Colin's current dilemma: at Cawnpore only five hundred men under Major-General Charles Windham, a Crimean hero, remained to guard the one bridge by which the Lucknow fugitives might cross the Ganges. Yet Sir Colin could not march for Cawnpore until Outram arrived at Alumbagh with the rear division—four thousand men of all arms, twenty-five guns, ten mortars. This force, thinly spread over a front three miles long and three miles deep, would hold Lucknow's rebels in check until Sir Colin returned to capture the city.

General Sir Henry Havelock did not live to share that triumph. The last mad scramble under fire along with Kavanagh and Outram proved too much for him; by 20th November, weak with dysentery, he was already passing blood. Three days later, though weaker still, he found strength to tell Outram: "For forty years I have endeavoured so to rule my life that when death came I might face it without fear."

At 9.30 a.m. on 24th November in a tent in Dilkusha Park, Havelock won this last battle. He died cradled in the arms of Harry, his son, and there was no fear in his eyes as he went to meet the God he had served a lifetime.

Two days after Sir Colin issued marching orders at Alumbagh, a chaplain named James Mackay was standing on the verandah of the General Hospital within the fortified entrenchment at Cawnpore. He had been less than eight months in India, his powers of observation were keen, and he looked on the world with a landscape-painter's eye. Thus he noted that the hospital's verandah was raised ten feet from the ground, affording a grandstand view, and that the two pillars of the verandah served as would a picture frame. It was 5.30 p.m., almost sunset, and the sky was flooded with golden-grey light, the backcloth to the most astonishing spectacle he had ever seen. A procession almost six miles long was approaching the bridge-of-boats, the dust so thick about the heads of horses and riders that those who made part of it could not see a man a yard away. But the chaplain could distinguish the dark faces of Indian servants, impassive beneath turbans of scarlet and gold, curvetting Arabs, lances dipping in the evening light, oxen, soldiers limping as if they walked on nails, palanquins, camels, children in bullock carts wailing lustily, litters bearing the wounded, red-curtained as always, "raw stumps hanging over the side like torn butcher's meat," ammunition tumbrils, elephants.

The chaplain knew many things that the column only dimly suspected. On the previous day General Windham's five hundred men, faced by three thousand rebels under Tantia Topee, had been forced to abandon Cawnpore city and retreat within this entrenchment. At dusk on the previous evening Sir Colin Campbell and his staff officers, precursors of this vast army, had clattered over the bridge-of-boats to ensure that it held secure. But the chaplain could not know that Katherine Bartrum and all the rest had on the previous day made a forced march of thirty-eight miles and that it would take thirty hours, most of them under fire, before the whole convoy was across. He did not know Katherine Bartrum or Henry Kavanagh or Maria Germon or Brigadier John Inglis or any of the participants so that while his eyes recorded faithfully, the true significance of this panorama escaped him.

What he saw was an epic interwoven with glory and horror and humour and agony that was just then passing into history. What he saw was the end of the siege of Lucknow.

XLIII. GANGES VALLEY

After 3rd December

Thus on 3rd December, 1857, before Sir Colin's army had vanquished Tantia Topee in the open field, the women and children and wounded of Lucknow left the entrenchment at Cawnpore and went out across the flatlands, south, toward the city of Allahabad.

With a hundred and forty days of siege behind them they were returning to a world which would perplex them for a long time. It would demand of the survivors of Lucknow an attitude they were incapable of striking. At Allahabad, on 7th December, the fort's password to honour their arrival was "Heroine." The fort's ladies, well-nourished on novels, knew exactly what to expect—a downcast mien, pale cheeks, sudden transports of grief. Within days Mrs. Matilda Spry, the fort chaplain's wife, was only one of many to wonder: was *this* how heroines conducted themselves with brisk matter-of-fact unconcern? "With few exceptions, you see no real sorrowing for husbands and children," she deplored. "They seemed a most cheerful party . . . it seemed so strange to see (them) walk off . . . to listen to the band. . . ." Then, a charitable soul, she excused them: "We must not blame them, poor creatures, for their apparent heartlessness . . . constant exposure to such fearful scenes caused their feelings to be blunted."

The abiding truth these women had learned was quite lost to her: the answer to death is life.

Of course, the public were kind—their efforts had swelled the Indian Mutiny Relief Fund to over £466,000. But they sought to interpret a riddle they had no power to understand. From Calcutta, where most survivors disembarked from the steamer *Madras* on 9th January, Lord Canning had already warned: "The best welcome which can be tendered . . . is one which shall break in as little as possible upon privacy and rest." Yet a royal salute boomed from Fort William's ramparts, the ships of war were dressed in honour, everyone who could took horse or carriage and rode down to Prinsep's Ghat to gape. Then the women began to file ashore and the first uncertain cheer trailed into silence. A lone gun booming a salute from the harbour seemed suddenly like a minute gun for the dead. The women's slow deliberate pace, the widows' weeds—these stopped the cheers in their throats. Something had gone awry with the celebrations—but exactly what the citizens could not tell.

They could not understand why the Hon. Julia Inglis found all letters from England too painful to read—surely she must crave news from home? And all the women were safe enough now—why did some start up from their beds in abject terror every half hour of the night? They had rejoiced to think of the defenders holding out grimly in their impregnable fort, and now people like the Rev. James Parker Harris persisted in setting them right: "We were in no fort at all: we occupied a few houses in a large garden with a low wall on one side and only an earthen parapet on the other in the middle of a large city . . . swarming with thousands of . . . foes."

In some ways Lucknow's survivors were supremely fortunate. For most, the Great Indian Mutiny was over. For Lord Canning and his commanders bloodier contests lay ahead. Not until March, 1858, did Sir Colin Campbell (now Lord Clyde) activate the mighty army that stormed Lucknow— twenty thousand men, almost a third of them Gurkhas, forty thousand camp-followers, "fourteen long miles of shot and shell." Yet this was only the first stage of the recapture of Oudh, which stretched on until December, 1858—the destruction of hundreds of forts, the capture of a hundred and fifty guns, the rounding up of a hundred and fifty thousand armed men. Ditches were filled in, jungles razed to allow patrols clear passage. By September, over six thousand newly-recruited Indian policemen manned sixty scattered outposts. Fifteen officers—among them Henry Kavanagh—rode from village to village collecting revenue.

This was a beginning, no more. By the spring of 1858,

only twenty-nine among four hundred and six leading rebels on the "Wanted" posters had been executed or even caught. At least three thousand rebels were hiding in the jungles of Bihar alone. In Central India, south of the Ganges, where the heat touched 115 degrees in the shade, it was worse. Under Major-General Sir Hugh Rose a force of four thousand five hundred men fought a crushing five-month campaign against the rebels—marching more than a thousand miles in heat so terrible that the dead lay mummified, capturing one hundred guns, two fortresses, two cities, twenty forts, fighting sixteen actions. When the elephants, their feet red-raw, gave up with tears of pain coursing down their cheeks, it was Rose's men who hauled the guns.

These were the red embers of a rebellion which, in the final reckoning, cost £40 million to suppress. By November, 1858, ten months after Lord Canning moved north to direct final operations from Allahabad, the government of India had passed from "John Company" to the Crown. A general amnesty was promised to all not guilty of murder, and Queen Victoria assured her new-found subjects, "It is our Royal will and pleasure that no one shall in any wise suffer for his opinions, or be disquieted by reason of his religious faith or observance." The last Governor-General, Canning, as first Viceroy, was determined not to yield up office until tranquillity reigned. *"You* shall have protection and security," he told the people, "but *I* will have peace." This above all they craved; vast areas of British India faced only ruin. The salt trade was at a standstill; no boats, while the rebels commanded the Ganges, could ply above Allahabad. The £500,000,000 invested in railways by Swiss and American bankers had paper value at most. Everywhere insurance companies clamoured for reimbursement; they had been forced to pay out on fully forty per cent of their policies.

Many Indians had scant sympathy with the mutiny. The Madras Army, made up largely of low-caste men, found no common cause with the rebels; their strength increased by fifteen thousand as the mutiny gathered adherents. Many sepoys of the Bombay Army had barely returned from Persia by the end of 1857. Among the princes, some, like the Nizam of Hyderabad, who held over three hundred thousand potential rebels in check, worked so doggedly to preserve the peace that only fifty thousand men took up arms among forty-eight millions.

Thus the stabilisation of India took less than five years. British troops were increased to sixty-five thousand. Sepoys were reduced to a hundred and forty thousand. All artillery passed under British control. The princes were confirmed in their territories. Army reorganisation was drastic: among seventy-three insurgent regiments of infantry and cavalry, only four commanding officers were re-appointed. To learn to withdraw from India gracefully and without dishonour was a harder lesson for the British: this took ninety years.

These were high-level concerns. For most the overriding factor was the mutiny's impact on their own way of life. To Amelia Horne it seemed, by the spring of 1858, that she had suffered a personality-change so radical nothing could ever be the same. She was not a Eurasian girl who had loved balls and fine clothes but a Moslem girl who had always worn a *coorta* and squatted on an earthen floor, scooping up curry with the shallow fried wholemeal bread called *parathas*. This woman was free of the virus of fear as Amelia Horne had never been. One day, shortly before the capture of Lucknow, Ahmad Ullah, *maulvi* of Fyzabad, summoned her to his presence. His followers, he told her, had grown so jealous he feared for her life. He had heard whispers of an attempt to poison her food. She must leave Ali Naqui Khan's palace now, while there was still time. The girl who had been Amelia Horne heard him with indifference. Often she yearned for death as for a lover.

That night, as she crept from the palace, she knew that only avarice had power to stir her. In the centre of the palace's courtyard stood a small one-storied building in which the Begum of Oudh at times held court. Beneath, in a damp stone cellar, the rebels had secreted over £450,000,000 of Wajid Ali's gold and jewels. It lay smothered from view beneath rubbish and an old green-painted wooden verandah blind. The knowledge that it lay there still obsessed Amelia Horne. This was the fierce dream she cherished: the thought of the power such wealth could bring.

If the *maulvi* had forsaken her, Trooper Mohammed Ismail Khan had no such intention. At dawn on 14th March, as Sir Colin's army once again hacked its way through Lucknow, Amelia was aroused hastily from her pallet. Outside a mettlesome horse was already saddled; panic-stricken, Amelia found herself hoisted into the saddle behind the trooper. From close at hand came a clamour of British voices; the trooper set spurs to the horse. Dizzy with terror Amelia saw a low archway loom ahead; as her head glanced against the stone a current of white-hot pain surged through her. Then she was falling and the horse, alarmed perhaps by the scream that burst from her, reared and trampled her foot. She felt the trooper lift her from the stones, knowing nothing in the world but pain.

Then she opened her eyes because Mohammed Khan was urging her, "Turn—turn and look back." Despite this command he had seized her hand tightly and was urging her forward but she looked back as she was bidden and saw, far away amongst the orange groves, the waving black bonnets of Highlanders. Then, seeing the light in the trooper's eyes, she forced herself to shrug indifferently. What were they to her? Many times she had professed her true faith to the *maulvis*.

But she could not disguise the wave of grief and disappointment that travelled through her. "You are cunning," the trooper taunted her. "Cunning like a monkey. All the British are like monkeys—they are cunning and they smell their food before they eat it."

Mohammed Ismail Khan had now tired of rebellion; he sought only the peace of his own village. Amelia Horne recalled only snatches of this journey. She remembered a road that was like a hard white spine beneath her bare bleeding feet. She recalled raw nights beneath the stars and crouching in feathery drifts of sugar cane while British troops tramped by, and the fever and ague that racked her frame. She remembered a four-day journey that in fact lasted three weeks, so ever-present were the British patrols. Then there was a damp dawn and dogs yelping outside mud huts and this was the village of Goorthree, near Allahabad, where the trooper lived.

A month passed, and little by little news trickled through. Rumour claimed the British were systematically searching village after village for captive Christians. Was it true that a man who released such a prisoner was granted a free pardon? Across the red glow of a cow-dung fire, Amelia, each evening, watched Mohammed Khan weighing his chances. If rumour lied, to escort her to Allahabad was to put his neck in a noose—yet suppose a column raided the village and found her here? Self-interest prompted a compromise solution. If Amelia would write a plea in his favour she was free to find her own way to Allahabad.

At this unforgettable moment, Amelia Horne felt her soul and her dreams and all that she had surrendered come alive again. "I thought my heart had been insensible to everything," she confessed later, for the violence of her own emotions startled her. Under the watchful eye of a village elder who understood English, her pen raced over the paper at Mohammed Khan's dictation. She wanted to leap for joy, to cry, to dance, to hug them all.

Then she was hastening alive and free down the white road to Allahabad. At last she reached a police outpost but the appearance of this small dark peasant girl announcing vehemently that she was a Christian, whose great-uncle lived in Allahabad, caused such astonishment that a large crowd collected. The officers heard her story, then summoned a litter to bear her on towards the city.

On 23rd April, 1858, this item appeared in the newspaper *Bengal Hurkaru*:

> *A correspondent at Allahabad, who writes on 8th April, states that a lady, whose name we do not give, of about sixteen or seventeen years of age, arrived at that station on the 7th. Her adventures have been great . . . she is in great distress of mind, often in tears, has forgotten much of the English language, and looks prematurely aged. . . .*

XLIV. LUCKNOW AND CALCUTTA

After 3rd December

No finite date has ever marked the Indian Mutiny's end. It did not peter out the day "John Company" died, 1st November, 1858, in a red-gold rain of fireworks on Calcutta's Maidan. As late as May, 1859, fifty thousand rebels still held out on the borders of Nepal. Thus for most men and women the mutiny ended on a day not of their own choosing —the day when Fate arbitrarily made plain what their roles in this drama had been.

For Jemadar Sita Ram Pande it ended on an afternoon in May, 1858, almost a month after Amelia Horne's deliverance. A supernumerary jemadar attached to the 2nd Punjab Infantry, which had fought under Sir Colin at the storming of Lucknow, he was seated at a trestle table in a shattered building questioning a long tatterdemalion line of rebel prisoners. Regiment? Village? Father's name? Caste?

These marked the cursory last rites of captured mutineers before a firing party commanded by Sita Ram exacted the price of rebellion in blood and fire.

Suddenly Sita Ram was galvanised. Among the long line before him one man was claiming to have served in the ranks of a regiment Sita Ram knew well. Knowing the answer, he yet asked, Had that not been Anunti Ram Pande's regiment? Almost indifferently the rebel replied: "I am Anunti Ram."

And now Sita Ram fought desperately not to credit it, knowing it was true. What village did this man come from? Of a certainty, Tilowee village. Long ago his father served with the 31st Native Infantry—Jemadar Sita Ram Pande. Then memory like a hæmorrhage broke through to flood the mind and it was as if the two men stood in privacy alone with their pain: the son, falling to his knees, begged his father not for absolution, only for condign punishment. He deserved no more, Anunti Ram stammered brokenly. He like all his regiment had mutinied without scruple, heading for Lucknow. All the time the British had been trapped inside the Residency, when Sita Ram was himself a rebel prisoner, Anunti Ram had been their sworn enemy.

And Sita Ram, hearing this, sprang up, for it was almost 4 p.m., the hour of execution. He hastened now to Major Browne, the commanding officer, and begged relief from duty. Let another officer command the firing squad this day. But Major Browne was a hot-tempered man; the sight of the stalwart old man moved him not to compassion but to insensate fury. Jemadar Sita Ram Pande was in sympathy with the rebels, he bellowed, and sought to shirk his duty. For this he would be courtmartialled.

Then the veteran's façade which Sita Ram had thought impregnable flawed like an eggshell, burst by the embryo of grief within. He stood at attention, the hot tears splashing down his cheeks and he cried: "If the Major orders it I will shoot every prisoner with my own hands—but one of them is my son."

This, Major Browne was loath to believe; he maintained that Sita Ram Pande had invented this cock-and-bull story to avoid shooting down his own kind. But at last, relenting, he sent for Anunti Ram.

"I shall never forget this terrible scene," Sita Ram wrote later, for he barely listened to Major Browne's relentless interlocution, confirming his every statement. Instead he heard a wily voice within him urge that his son still had a chance. A special plea for mercy, subtly stressing the father's long years of faithful service . . . Then he knew he could say nothing of this, even with the pain clenched inside him, for after long years the sense of duty was drawn tightly about him like a cloak. Because of Anunti and his comrades sorrow had fallen upon the land; women and children had died at Lucknow and Cawnpore and Meerut. His son deserved compassion but not his life.

So he stood silent, only snapping stiffly to attention when Major Browne ordered he be relieved from duty.

Sita Ram Pande went to his tent, hounded thither by the gibes of the regiment's Sikhs, for all had heard the story and abused him as one who had sired a renegade. He lay on his string bed waiting, and the silence seemed to stretch and tauten as men will stretch a hide. Then the volley shattered out, bursting like grapeshot into his nerves and belly and through the shoulders that would not stop shaking. They said afterwards that Anunti had died bravely—but why could he not have died in battle, as a soldier should?

On this day, the will to life that had borne him through countless affrays died in Sita Ram. No longer could he hold his head high before a company of troops. By 1860, though promoted subadar, the simplest drill movements were beyond him. They led him gently before Colin Campbell, Lord Clyde, and persuaded him to retire on pension. But back on his estate at Tilowee only old memories sustained him: a boy in scarlet and white riding south on a country pony from Agra, the stunned silence of an Afghan winter, a girl with eyes like a doe's, old and wrinkled now, to whom he lost his heart in blinding smoke.

Katherine Bartrum's mutiny ended on 11th February, 1858. It was as if the hand of God had snuffed out a taper, whirling her into a dark desert of eternity. Her plans were laid so carefully, in concert with the doctors, that even long afterwards she could not believe it to be true. These men, Calcutta physicians, had been at pains to warn her: Bobbie had grown so delicate that the journey to England by the overland route was now out of the question. "You must choose the four-month voyage by the Cape," one advised, "if you would save your child."

And Katherine had answered passionately, "Would I not save my child? God knows he is all I have to live for!"

This decision made, she had sought for compensations, as she had so sedulously taught herself to do. It would be longer now before she reached Bath and saw her parents, but the long sea voyage would quite restore Bobbie to health. And the *Himalaya* was such a graceful vessel, its cabins so trim and clean, and at least one friend would be aboard: Mrs. Emily Polehampton, the chaplain's widow, who was making the voyage to nurse the wounded troops.

Katherine knew that Bobbie was growing daily weaker. But the child looked so appealing in the clothes that his grandmother had sent from England that she could not bear to be parted from him for an instant. Each evening when the ladies of Lucknow set out for their evening drive from their quarters at No. 3 Harrington Street, Bobbie rode beside her.

On the morning of 10th February, Katherine and Mrs. Polehampton had already boarded the *Himalaya,* now at anchor in the river. This day, for the first time since reaching Calcutta, the child was too weak to take food. Quietly Mrs. Polehampton sought to brace Katherine for the shock: already the doctors had remarked how ill the child looked. And Katherine knew exactly what she meant. "But I *cannot* spare him . . . I have nothing else left."

That day Bobbie slept peacefully and her heart grew lighter. At evening, when she laid him on the bed, he was sleeping still but at 1 a.m. on 11th February, feral instinct brought her wide awake in the darkness. By a candle's guttering light she saw the child was tossing and restless: the tiny feet were like ice and her hands could not warm them. "Will you have some wine?" she whispered, as if Bobbie still had strength to answer: there was no other cordial to hand. Then she saw the child was choking and the wine had all dribbled down his chin. Her voice rising, she called to Mrs. Polehampton, "My child is dying." The elder woman, hastening from her cabin, advised cradling the baby in her lap; the candle-light rippled and the silence was urgent with the rasping of its breath. "Look," said Mrs. Polehampton, "how bright his eyes are growing. I am sure he sees something." But Katherine Bartrum had her eyes averted. She could not look at Bobbie then and she could not look again until the breathing stopped.

At 5 p.m. that day, Dr. Joseph Fayrer, who all along had followed the fortunes of the Lucknow garrison, came aboard to fasten down the tiny coffin in which the child lay, its hand encircling a white rosebud and a lock of Katherine's hair. It was Fayrer, too, who helped bear it down the long sanded path of the burial ground on the Lower Circular Road, Calcutta, to the plot in the south-west corner beneath a giant mango tree. Crows were raucous in the high branches, dry earth rattled on wood and again Katherine's face was turned away.

Afterwards the carriage jolted back towards the landing-stage, through broad silent streets, past white shuttered mansions, past the sprawling pile of Government House where Lord Canning all those Sundays ago had striven to avert the cataclysm which had overturned all their lives. Even now, from this dark pit of pain, Katherine Bartrum prepared to draw anew on the courage which had all along sustained her, which converts even the gentlest people into the earth's invincible inheritors. "I must find a work to do; I must work, work, or I shall go mad . . . during the voyage I am going to nurse our sick soldiers and work for them, making them clothes and helping them; my husband died a soldier's death and I love the soldiers now. . . ."

This courage, long after, led her to choose this epitaph to the memory of her dead: the question posed by Elisha, the Shunammite woman's reply:

Is it well with thy husband?
Is it well with the child?
And she answered, It is well.

S.S. *Viet Nam*
New Delhi
Lucknow
Allahabad
Calcutta
Worthing
Burgh Heath
June 1961-January 1963

POSTSCRIPT

Perhaps some readers are as curious as the writer as to what happened to many of the people in this book. Here, in no set order, is the little I have gleaned:

A few, enfeebled by the campaign's rigours, were cut down in the prime of life. Captain William Peel, of H.M.S. *Shannon,* died of smallpox in April 1858, six weeks after Lucknow's capture. He was thirty-three. Major Richard Baird-Smith, one of Delhi's few driving spirits, was "as weak as a child" by the siege's end; scurvy and diarrhoea combined to kill him at the age of forty-three. The Residency's chaplain, the Rev. James Parker Harris, was in his thirties when he died at sea on Good Friday, 1864.

Three of the key figures in the fight to relieve Lucknow were within eighteen months of one another. Charles John, Earl Canning, was first to go; in June, 1862, only two months after relinquishing office, the surgeons warned him that his liver was dangerously affected. "What! so soon!" were the impassive words with which Canning greeted death. His old commanders, Colin Campbell, Lord Clyde, and Sir James Outram were soon after buried within yards of his tomb in Westminster Abbey.

Tragedy marked Katherine Bartrum's life until her dying day—which came within nine years of her return to England. She bore her second husband, Dr. Benjamin Popham, a Nottingham physician, three children—Katherine, Bradshaw and Jane. In March, 1866, she died of pulmonary tuberculosis. Three years earlier Martin Gubbins went insane after failing to justify his anti-social conduct to the Government of India; he hanged himself at Leamington Spa.

But many more survivors went on to live full and contented lives. Colonel Arthur Lang was Chief Engineer of Public Works for the North-West Provinces when he retired in 1887. Young Hugh Gough was knighted and became a general. Dr. Joseph Fayrer became Honorary Physician to the Prince of Wales. Robert Tytler, promoted colonel, became first Governor of the Andamans Penal Colony in the Indian Ocean; Mount Harriet, the highest peak in that island chain, was named after his wife. Maria Germon succumbed to fashion and wrote her Lucknow memoirs—in common with twenty-six others who lived through the siege.

Young Edward Hilton, of La Martinière College, one of Lucknow's leading citizens, became author of that city's standard guide-book. Sergeant Joseph "Dobbin" Lee, who liked giving Sir Colin advice, ended his days as proprietor of Cawnpore's Railway Hotel. Private Henry Metcalfe, a drill instructor in Macclesfield, Cheshire, lived to see an army that dispensed with ramrods and greased cartridges; he was eighty when he died in 1915. Two years after the mutiny, on line duty at Aldershot, he had one brief touching reunion with the Harrises and Bustle.

Kavanagh lived a see-saw life to the end. Promoted to Civil Judge, with £2,000 a year salary, he was again, by 1876, weighed down by debt—perhaps because his family now totalled thirteen. Faced with compulsory retirement on a pension of £500 a year, Kavanagh refused in a fine fury and returned both his Victoria Cross and his Mutiny Medal to the man who first pondered his gallant offer—Lord Napier of Magdala, Outram's former chief of staff. The two resolved their differences finally; it was at Napier's house in Gibraltar that Kavanagh, returning to India, died in 1882.

Mohammed Bahadur Shah did not long survive the trial that exiled him for life. He died at Rangoon in 1862. Three months after Lucknow's capture, the dripping head of the *maulvi* of Fyzabad, betrayed by a treacherous Rajah, was laid before a district magistrate for a £5,000 reward. Until World War II it was a prized anatomical exhibit at the Royal College of Surgeons, London. Trooper Devi Din returned to soldiering with more distinction; by the century's end he was a general of the Kashmir Army.

The fate of Nana Sahib is an enigma even now. By 1858,

rumour claimed, his followers ranging the jungles south of Nepal, numbered a small army of doubles. Reports of his death were as regular as monsoon rain: he was stricken by epileptic paralysis, fever and diarrhoea, venereal disease. A notoriety-seeker, claiming to be the Nana, was gaoled for four years. But in death as in life the Nana remained a mystery; thirty years after the mutiny his "capture" was an infallible standby on All Fool's Day.

And Amelia Horne? Incredibly, at seventy-four she still lived on in the dingy riverside suburb of Howrah, Calcutta, giving piano lessons to a world that had forgotten all about the mutiny and Cawnpore. The men and women who had shared that life had passed into oblivion. William Bennett, the railway superintendent she married five months after her escape, was dead; General Mowbray Thomson had died peacefully in bed; *maulvi* Liaquat Ali, at whose trial she be-came a leading witness, died in penal servitude. Her sons and daughters had their own lives to lead. An old woman's ram-blings about gold and jewels tumbled beneath a broken verandah blind, the fortune the British recovered which she believed hers by right, met with kindly impatience. Her tragedy was to have outlived it all, even the hope of fortune. Only the dreams were hers.

The last survivor of the Indian Mutiny, Stanley Delhi-Force Tytler, ex-surveyor, died in Vancouver, British Co-lumbia, aged ninety-one.

ACKNOWLEDGMENTS

To present this story in the way that I sought to present it would have been impossible without the whole-hearted co-operation of the Central Government of India, the various state governments and the patient collaboration of many of their officials. I have to thank Professor Humayun Kabir, Minister for Scientific Research and Cultural Affairs, Government of India, who first gave the project his blessing, and, for the unending kindness they showed me in New Delhi, Dr. S. N. Roy and Shri V. C. Joshi, respectively Director and Assistant Director of the National Archives of India, and Miss E. David of their Research Room. In Delhi also I had invaluable practical help from Shri A. K. Ghosh, Director-General of Archæology, India, and Dr. Y. D. Sharma of that department; all through India the presence of their staff helped the landscape to spring to life. Mr. Balbir Singh, of the Archæological Survey, North-West Circle, tirelessly retraced with me every yard of the Ridge and the old walled city of Delhi and guided me through the maze of Meerut. Shri S. R. Rao and Mr. C. Joshi of the Northern Circle planned a fascinating trip through the Fort at Agra; Mr. A. W. Sadiq and Mr. Mohammed Shakur spent whole days by my side within the Residency and other Lucknow landmarks.

In Lucknow and Allahabad I owe especial debts of thanks to Mr. Mohammed Zaheer, Joint-Secretary for the Department of Cultural Affairs and Scientific Research, Government of Uttar Pradesh, to Dr. A. A. Rizvi and Dr. G. N. Saletore, State Archivist, for the research facilities they so freely granted. In Calcutta, Dr. Y. M. Mulay and Dr. A. D. Bannerjee, of the National Library of India, cut endless corners to save me the maximum of time. Miss Kanta Thakur, of the Government of India's Tourist Department, arranged every detail of my transport with streamlined efficiency. The whole project owes much to Sir Mortimer Wheeler, who generously provided me with many valuable introductions.

In Great Britain, the discovery of over thirty unpublished Mutiny diaries and collections of letters was in large measure due to the editors and columnists who gave space to my appeal—

notably Tony Arnold of *The Kent Messenger's* Dover office, A. L. Enfield, of *The Birmingham Mail,* and D. W. Partridge of *The Leicester Mercury.* My deepest thanks go also to Mr. S. C. Sutton and Miss V. Sugden of the India Office Library, to the Superintendent of Records, Commonwealth Relations Office, and to Lieut.-Col. Charles Appleby of the National Army Museum, Camberley. I have also to thank Lieut.-Col. O. G. White of the Dorset Military Museum; Major Bartlett of the Duke of Cornwall's Light Infantry Museum; Major J. F. Ainsworth of the Royal Sussex Regimental Museum; Colonel Hugh Cook of the North Staffordshire Regimental Museum, and Lieut.-Col. F. Clare of the 1st Greenjackets Regimental Museum.

Much of the detail here incorporated is of so personal a nature that I must remain eternally grateful to the descendants of those concerned. Peter C. Bartrum, Squadron-Leader Christopher Bartrum and Peter Pagan, Director of Bath's Municipal Libraries, all provided material otherwise unobtainable concerning Katherine Bartrum. For valuable clues on Harriet Tytler I am indebted to Mrs. Hesther Tytler, Mrs. John Drolet, Sir Kerr Fraser-Tytler, Mrs. Norah Rayner and Cedric Titler. Mrs. Sylvia Kavanagh furnished some intriguing sidelights on T. Henry Kavanagh. Details on Amelia Bennett (née Horne) proved harder to come by; that I ran them to earth was due to the unstinted help of Douglas Harris and Lindsay Emmerson of *The Statesman,* Calcutta, Mrs. Vera Roberts, Mr. Noel Roberts and Mr. Denzil Luxor.

Apart from those noted in the manuscript bibliography, so many other people loaned books and data that could not be traced elsewhere or gave valuable advice and help that I hope they will accept the bare mention of their names in token of my gratitude: Mrs. Alfreda Bean; Mrs. L. Bechley; Mr. Christian Brann; Mrs. Mary Clements; Mr. R. S. Cockburn; Mrs. B. A. Cole; Miss Anna Dodgson; Mr. C. H. Forbes; Major A. E. Galloway; Mr. George Gates-Reed; Mr. P. B. Gomes; Secretary to the Christian Burial Board, Calcutta; Mr. Norman Hamilton; Brigadier D. S. Hoysted; Mr. James Leasor; Mr. and Mrs. R. F. Leonard; Major Lawrence L'Estrange; Major E. W. Manners; Mrs. E. M. Morgan; Miss Evelyn Martin-Atkins; Mrs. Mabel Newell; Mr. James K. Peer; Mr. Leslie Periton; Mr. F. H. Ponting; Mr. John Prebble; Miss N. G. Ray; Dr. Violet Reade; Mrs. P. M. Rutter; Mr. Frederick Smith; Mr. Robert Songhurst; Mr. Kenneth Cromb Urquhart; Mr. Peter Walne, County Archivist for Berkshire; Mr. John Webster, Deputy Chief Constable for Leicestershire; Mr. and Mrs. H. O. Young.

For the illustrations I am grateful to the Parker Gallery, London, and to Paul Popper Ltd., and for the remainder of the Radio Times Hulton Picture Library.

Finally, those who worked alongside me through every stage of the project deserve special mention. My wife, besides contributing much valuable research, once again proved the only typist brave enough to face my handwriting. Miss Mabel Eyles valiantly saw the final draft through its every stage. My heartfelt thanks go also to Joan St. George Saunders and her researchers for the mountain of meticulous detail they amassed and to my own chief researcher, Jemima Williams, an inspiration to the team that rallied round her.

A NOTE ON SOURCES

No writer on the Indian Mutiny can help but break fresh ground —and for this reason, while dispensing with a source apparatus, it seems important to indicate all material derived from unpublished sources. Colonel Charles Stuart's journal, kept while Military Secretary to the Governor-General (India Office Home Misc. 726) proved not only the best guide to Lord Canning's working habits (Sections I, II, VI, XIV) but a mine of information on such diverse subjects as the Emperor Bahadur Shah's diet and living conditions in Cawnpore entrenchment. Additional data on the greased-cartridge question (Section II) crops up in Sir John Hearsey's papers (British Museum Add MSS 41489) and Captain Edward Martineau's letters (I.O. Home Misc. 725).

The complex question of Henry Kavanagh's debts (Sections X, XXVII) are fully detailed in Foreign Consultations, 200-203, Jan. 11, 1856 (National Archives of India). Amelia Horne's narrative (Sections VII, XII, XIII, XV, XXIX, XXX, XXXI, XLIII) is taken substantially from the narrative account she prepared just after the Mutiny. (B.M. Add. MSS 41488). Katherine Bartrum's published account of her experiences at Lucknow (Sections VII, XXVII, XXVIII, XXXIV, XXXV, XXXVI, XLII, XLIV) has in every instance been supplemented by the privately-owned Bartrum letters and journal. Captain David Dodgson's manuscript account gives further details on Robert Bartrum's death (Section XXXV).

Henry Lawrence's warning to Canning concerning the sepoys (Section II) comes from Secret Consultations, 564, Dec. 18, 1857 (N.A.I.). Vivid accounts of the Meerut disaster (Section II) occur in the merchant Abrahams's account (B.M. Add MSS. 41996) and in the draft Divisional Narrative of Events, Meerut Division, File 42/1858 (Uttar Pradesh Archives). F.C. 468-70, Apr. 15, 1859, reveals the presence (Section V) of a tenth man inside the Delhi Magazine. The transfer of the main Magazine was authorised by Dalhousie in F.C. 341-7, Dec. 27, 1850 (both N.A.I.).

Most of the decisions concerning the Cawnpore entrenchment, including its cost (Section VII) are taken from the Cawnpore Collectorate Mutiny Records, Files 36 and 55 (U.P. Arch.) and these same records (Files 43, 736) are my main sources for the men who worked alongside Nana Sahib and how the siege affected the city (Section XIII). The Mutiny services of Rajab Ali on the Ridge at Delhi (Sections VIII, XV, XXXIII) are outlined in F.C. 539-45 Aug. 6, 1858 (N.A.I.). Facts on the conduct of Delhi's sepoys are drawn from diverse sources—among them Kedernath's diary (I.O. Home Misc. 725), F.C. 18, Oct. 22, 1858, S.C. 5-8, Sept. 25, 1857 (N.A.I.).

The anarchy sweeping the countryside as the Mutiny gathered pace (Section IX) is well documented by the Daily Reports for Saharanpur District, File 1858, the Bolandshahur Collectorate Mutiny Records and File 84 of the Bareilly Commissioner's Office Mutiny Records (all U.P. Arch.). Colonel Stuart's journal (I.O. Home Misc. 726) quotes John Lawrence on the irregular cavalry's debts. File 23 of the N.W. Provinces Foreign Dept. Proceedings, 1858 (Secretariat Room, Lucknow), and the Trial of Government versus Nawab of Farrukhabad (U.P. Arch.) throw light on this bizarre story. A good eye-witness account of the Allahabad rising features in the Rev. Thomas Moore's diary (B.M. Add. MSS. 37151-3).

Anna Madeleine Jackson's privately-owned narrative is probably the most vivid account of life (Section X) as the jungle fugitives lived it: I have drawn principally from this. The sepoys' taste for indulging in lengthy law-suits is touched on in F.C. 86-8, Oct. 29, 1852.

General Wheeler's gloomy letter to Henry Lawrence on the eve of the Cawnpore rising (Section XII) forms Folio 12 of B. M. Add. MSS. 39922. Brigadier Neill's views on the Mutiny (Section XIV, XXVI) are mostly taken verbatim from his diary and letters (I.O. Home Misc. 726). These throw some light on his relations with Havelock (Sections XIV, XXVIII, XXXIV). The best source for Havelock's order of march (Section XIV) and for the conditions pertaining *en route* to Cawnpore (Section XIX) is the order Book of the 64th Foot.

Medical conditions prevailing at Delhi (Section XXIII) are made horribly real by Surgeon Edward Hare in his memorandum on the Siege (I.O. Home Misc. 726) and there are useful hints on this subject in File 65, Foreign Dept. Procs., N.W. Provinces, 1857-9 (S.R. Lucknow). Surgeon Hare was equally an informed source on General Wilson's mental malaise (Sections XXXIV, XXV), early disaffection at Ambala (Section II), Commissioner Barnes's colossal bluff of the Maharajah of Patiala (Section XXIII), the Emperor Bahadur Shah's appearance after the Siege and Sir Theo Metcalfe's ruthless unconcern for rebel prisoners (Section XXXIII).

Much material concerning Richard Baird-Smith has appeared elsewhere (Sections XXIII, XXIV, XXV, XXXII), but in working over the family papers I unearthed a few additional pointers. The salient facts on Hodson's insurance premiums (Section XXIII) are in F.C. 3699-3702, Dec. 31, 1858 (N.A.I.). Bahadur Shah's first overtures to the British (Section XXIII) are described by General Thomas Reed, who also depicts the rebel cavalry's surprise onslaught, in his letters to John Lawrence (I.O. Home Misc. 726). Similarly the narrative of Ahsanullah Khan (I.O. Home Misc. 725) details Bukht Khan's sudden promotion (Section XXIII).

Much of the unpalatable truth concerning Martin Gubbins, from his costly defences to his conduct throughout the Siege of Lucknow (Sections XXVII, XXVIII) is drawn from two main sources—F.C. 104-5, Feb. 26, 1858, and F.C. 104-8, July 15, 1859 (N.A.I.). The same archives contain Lord Canning's own summary of Gubbins— S.C. 564, Dec. 18, 1857.

The efforts of some magistrates to preserve the peace (Section XVI) find a place in File 41/58, Dept. XVII, narrative of events at Aligarh (U.P. Arch.) and F.C. 1352-3, Dec. 30, 1859 (N.A.I). Colonel Sherer's recipe for keeping his regiment tranquil (Section XVI) is as he himself gives it (I.O. Home Misc. 727). The sepoy Koodru's bewilderment is mirrored in his report, S.C. 81-2, July 31, 1857 (N.A.I.).

Two subalterns who marched with Havelock, Hugh Pearson and William Moorsom, proved lively correspondents and from their letters, privately owned, I have drawn much background material for the battle of Cawnpore (Sections XIX, XXI), the weeks of waiting at that station (Sections XXVIII, XXXIV), the first abortive relief of Lucknow (Section XXXIV) and life in the Residency with Havelock up to the second relief (Section XXXVI). Moorsom also records (Sections XIV, XXVIII) the doubts held by some of Havelock's officers regarding his fitness to command.

Henry Lawrence's wish to transfer Nicholson to Lucknow is no idle fancy (Section XXV); he expresses it to Lord Canning in S.C. 564, Dec. 18, 1857. Bahadur Shah's poem, one of the few preserved for posterity, is Folio 10, Bundle 19, of the Persian and Urdu Mutiny Papers (both N.A.I.). Numerous sources testify to the peasants' increasing resistance (Section XXVI) to the sepoys' depredations—notably Narrative of Events attending the restoration of authorities in Benares District (I.O. Home Misc. 724A), (I.O. Home Misc. 725, Folios 457-82,) and Colonel Stuart's journal (I.O. Home Misc. 726). Some idea of the rebels' monthly expenses can be gleaned from S.C. 7, March 26, 1857 (N.A.I.), and File 84, Bareilly Commissioner's Mutiny Records (U.P. Arch.).

What the Mutiny cost in terms of hard cash (Section XXVI) is evidenced by F.C. 21-9, Sept. 11, 1857, F.C. 25-32, Sept. 4, 1857, F.C. 30-3, Sept. 3, 1858, and F.C. 41, Nov. 12, 1858. Some glimpses of the human suffering involved occur in File 26, Cawnpore Collectorate Mutiny Records (U.P. Arch.) and in the privately-owned diary of Samuel Carrington. Canning's guidance to civil officers when dealing with rebels is found in S.C. 114, Aug. 28, 1857 (N.A.I.).

Concerning Lucknow, Inglis's offer to evacuate the Residency (Section XXVIII) and Canning's fear of a second Cawnpore are detailed in S.C. 218-25 Sept. 25, 1857, and the identically-dated F.C.

231 (N.A.I.). Captain David Dodgson's privately-owned account points up the differences between Outram and Havelock (Section XXXIV). Pipe-Major Alexander M'Kellar has the last word on the pipes of Lucknow in B.M. Add. MSS. 37151, Fol. 68.

Lord Canning's message to the loyal Princes (Section XXXIII) after the fall of Delhi can be found in F.C. 98-106, Oct. 9, 1857. The responsibility for sparing Bahadur Shah's life is argued at length in F.C. 51-78, Dec. 31, 1857 (both N.A.I.). Edward Vibart's letters are a franker source on the reign of terror that was post-siege Delhi than the book he later published, John Lawrence's protests against looting (Section XXXIII) are on record in S.C. 28-30, Jan. 29, 1858 (N.A.I.), and in File 12, Meerut Commissioner's Mutiny Records (U.P. Arch.). A typical case that shocked Lord Canning appears in S.C. 519-22, Jan. 29, 1858 (N.A.I.).

The file S.C. 531, Oct. 30, 1857 (N.A.I.), contains Outram's frank statement of the Lucknow garrison's plight. Apart from sources mentioned earlier, my account of their hardships (Section XXXVI) is drawn from several privately-owned manuscripts: the diary of Mrs. C. M. Brydon, the letters of Captains John Spurgin and David Dodgson, those written by Lieut. John Edmondstone and Captain Edward Lowe (D.C.L.I. Museum) and the letters of Assistant Surgeon Francis Collins. The doctor also proved an unrivalled source on campaign diet (Section XLI), the battle of Dilkusha (Section XL) and Campbell's relief of Lucknow (Section XLII). Another sharp-eyed observer with the relieving force was Private William Wilkie, whose diary records, among other gems, Sir Colin's acid comment to the ladies of Lucknow (Section XLII). The letters of Arthur Browne Spry and Samuel Carrington's diary give piquant views of the survivors' arrival at Allahabad (Section XLIII).

Post-Mutiny records are, of course, legion. Measures involved in the pacification of Oudh (Section XLIII) are listed in F.C. 139-42, Oct. 1, 1858 (N.A.I.) and File 688, Cawnpore Collectorate Mutiny Records (U.P. Arch.). Estimated rebel strengths occur in F.C. 355-62, April 30, 1858, and Military Consultations, 437, 470, June 25, 1858 (N.A.I.). Detailed instructions for dealing with surrendered mutineers are given in F.C. 3589-94, Dec. 31, 1858 (N.A.I.). The Cawnpore Pardons Register (U.P. Arch.) lists many such instances. The documents that above all sum up the plight of the insurance companies are F.C. 3699-3702, Dec. 31, 1858, and F.C. 468-70, Feb. 25, 1859.

BIBLIOGRAPHY

MANUSCRIPT SOURCES

INDIA

New Delhi—National Archives of India

Foreign Consultations, Political; Foreign Consultations, Secret; Military Consultations, 1850-9.

Mutiny Papers (Persian and Urdu) taken from the Palace after the Fall of Delhi—Box 59; Bundles 17, 19.

Lucknow—Secretariat Record Room

Proceedings, Foreign and Criminal Depts., N.W. Provinces, Political Imperial Record Dept., 1857-9.

Foreign Dept., N.W. Provinces Narratives, 1858.

Original Daily Bulletins issued by E. A. Reade, Agra, May-July, 1858.

Foreign Dept.—Oudh Abstract Proceedings General, February-December, 1856.

Original Telegrams sent to and by E. A. Reade, 1858-9.

Foreign Dept.—N.W. Provinces—Proceedings of Government, 1858.

Allahabad—State Archives, Government of Uttar Pradesh

Meerut Commissioner's Office Mutiny Records, File No. 10: Mutiny in Muzaffarnagur; File No. 12: Fall of Delhi.

Bareilly Commissioner's Office Mutiny Records, File No. 84.

Agra Division Post-Mutiny Records, 1858-74: Files No. 4, 9, 15, 41, 42.

Kanpur Collectorate Mutiny Records, Dept. XIII—Files No. 13, 26, 36, 43, 55, 62, 70, 112, 146, 633, 635, 637, 688, 736; Kanpur Collectorate Pardons Register.

GREAT BRITAIN

London—Commonwealth Relations Office (India Office)

Home Miscellaneous 724 A—727—Sir John Kaye's Papers, including:—724 A:—Demi-official correspondence connected with the Mutiny and disbandment of the 19th N.I.; Memoranda of General Sir Patrick Grant; Report of Brigadier Thomas Polwhele on events at Agra, 1857; Reports of Inspector-General of Ordnance on Powder, Harness and Tents.

725: Narrative of Ahsanullah Khan, Physician to the Emperor

Bahadur Shah; Correspondence of Beni Madho; Delhi diary of Kedernath; Munshi Mohan Lal's account of the Mutiny; letters from Lord Elphinstone to General Jacob; correspondence of Captain E. M. Martineau; notes on the Fatehpur district, May-June, 1857.

726: Correspondence and Diary of Brig.-General James Neill; Delhi letters of General Thomas Reed; Ensign Stanley Mortimer's account of the storming of Delhi; Journal of Colonel Charles Stuart, military secretary to the Governor-General; Surgeon Edward Hare's memorandum of the siege of Delhi; narrative of Colonel Edward Greathed H.M. 8th Foot, on storming of Water Bastion, Delhi.

727: Private diary of Colonel George Sherer, commanding at Jalpaiguri, June, 1857-September 1858.

MSS. European C—94—C. B. Saunders' MSS. on Delhi and life at Meerut.

MSS. European B—188—City of Delhi during the Siege.

MSS. D 533 1-2—Mutiny at Azimgarh.

London—British Museum—Department of Manuscripts

Add. MSS. 41488—Correspondence of Major James Garner Holmes, commanding 12th Irregular Cavalry, Sigauli—Narrative of Miss Amy Horne.

Add. MSS. 37151-3—Diary of the Rev. Thomas Moore, Chaplain to the Forces at Lucknow.

Add. MSS. 38985-6, 38989—The Layard Papers.

Add. MSS. 39922, fol. 12—Sir Hugh Wheeler to Sir Henry Lawrence, June 4, 1857.

Add. MSS. 41489—Letters of General Sir John Hearsey.

Add. MSS. 41996—Miscellaneous Mutiny Papers.

Add. MSS. 40027, fols. 175-86—The Napier Papers.

Add. MSS. 43818-25—3 vols.—Diary and Letters of Lieutenant Arthur Lang (part-printed in Army Historical Research Journal, Vols. 8-11, 1930-2).

Add. MSS. 41925—Letters to General Sir John Hope Grant serving in India.

Camberley, Surrey—National Army Museum

Fairweather, Surgeon-General James, *Through the Mutiny with the 4th Punjab Infantry:* narrative account.

Hall, Colonel Montagu, *Reminiscences of the Indian Mutiny, 1857-8:* narrative account.

Smith, Lieutenant O. Ludlow, 48th N.I. *Letters from Lucknow, May, 1857-March, 1858.*

Reading, Berks.—Berkshire County Archives

Ewen, Ensign Arthur, 38th Foot: *Letters from India, 1857-8* (Ref.: D/EE/C/ 2/12).

Dorchester, Dorset—Dorset Military Museum

MSS. *Digest of H.M. 54th Foot, 1775-1881.*

Bodmin, Cornwall—Duke of Cornwall's Light Infantry Museum
Edmondstone, Lieutenant John, and Lowe, Captain Edward, 32nd
   Light Infantry: *Letters written from Lucknow, January, 1858,
   and October-November, 1857.*
Chichester, Sussex—Royal Sussex Regimental Museum
   Record of the Services of the 35th Royal Sussex Regiment.
   Record of the 3rd Bengal European Fusiliers.
Lichfield, Staffs.—North Staffordshire Regimental Museum
   Letters and Reports of Incidents During the Indian Mutiny.
   Order Book of H.M. 64th Foot, January, 1857-June, 1860
   Record of Services, the 64th Regiment.

PRIVATELY-OWNED
The manuscripts listed here are in all cases the property of their
owners to whom I am deeply indebted for so generously making
them available.

Major Richard Baird-Smith, Bengal Engineers: letters written to
   his wife from the Siege of Delhi, 1857. (Miss Claire Craig,
   Dorchester, Dorset).

Mrs. Katherine Bartrum: an original diary of the Siege of Lucknow. (Mrs. Dulcie Boyle, Weymouth, Dorset).

Mrs. Katherine Bartrum: letters from Lucknow, Allahabad and
   Calcutta, 1857-8. (Peter C. Bartrum, Berkhamsted, Herts.).

Lieutenant Robert Biddulph, Royal Artillery: mutiny letters,
   September, 1857-November, 1858. (Mrs. Jean Dryland, Aldershot, Hants.).

Major John Brooks, 1st Bengal Light Cavalry: letters from Allahabad and Lucknow, 1858-62. (J. E. H. Brooks, Oadby, Leicester).

Mrs. C. M. Brydon: diary of the Siege of Lucknow, May-
   December, 1857. (Mrs. Rachel Blackburn, Criccieth, North
   Wales).

Samuel Carrington, railway engineer: letters from Calcutta and
   Allahabad, June, 1857-March, 1859. (Noel Carrington, Lam-
   bourn, Berks.).

Mrs. Louisa Chalwin: letters from Calcutta, Meerut and Cawnpore,
   1856-May, 1857. (Mrs. M. M. Nicholl, Topsham, Devon).

Robert Clifford, H.E.I.C.S.: mutiny journal of the United Provinces, November, 1856-December, 1859 (Lady Lloyd, Fresh-
   water, Isle of Wight).

Major George Clowes, 8th Hussars: Indian Mutiny letters, 1857-9.
   (Robert Poore-Saurin-Watts, Ledbury, Herefordshire).

Assistant Surgeon Francis Collins, 5th Fusiliers: extracts from
   letters from Dinapore and Lucknow, 1857-8. (Commander Francis Collins, R.N. (retd.), Winchester, Hants.).

Cornet Charles Combe, 3rd Bombay Light Cavalry: Persian campaign and Indian Mutiny letters, 1856-9. (Edmond Combe, Richmond, Surrey).

Lieut.-Colonel Edmund Cornwall Legh: letters from Lucknow, June-October, 1858. (J. E. H. Brooks, Oadby, Leicester).

Lieutenant Charles Crump, Madras Artillery: Indian Mutiny letters, 1857. (H. E. Humphreys, Wellington, Somerset).

Captain David Dodgson, 30th N.I. : a narrative of the 1st relief and Siege of Lucknow. (Lt.-Commander C. V. Dodgson, R.N., Alcester, Warwickshire).

Lieutenant Charles Stephen Fowle, 22nd N.I.: narrative of the Fyzabad Mutiny. (Mrs. G. E. Clayton, Salisbury, Wilts.).

Mrs. Philip Goldney: narrative of the escape from Sultanpore. Miss Amy Goldney, Edinburgh).

Lieutenant J. McLeod Innes, Bengal Engineers: letters concerning the Siege of Lucknow. (Mrs. Christina Morley, Beaconsfield, Bucks.).

Mrs. Lucy Innes: narrative of the Siege of Agra Fort. (Mrs. Christina Morley, Beaconsfield, Bucks.).

Anna Madeleine Jackson: a personal narrative of the Indian Mutiny and the flight from Seetapore. (Mrs. Constance Jackson, Tenterden, Kent).

Charles Jenkins, Joint-Magistrate and Collector: letters from Shahjehanpore, 1857. (Lieut.-Colonel James Vans Agnew, London, W.I.).

Judge Arthur Littledale: letter (August, 1857) describing the Siege of Arrah. (A. J. Littledale, Thatcham, Berks.).

Assistant Surgeon Thomas Mawe: letters written from Naogon, May, 1857. (Mrs. M. K. Minns, Manchester, Lancs.).

Lieutenant William Moorsom, 52nd Light Infantry: letters and diary of Havelock's campaign and the Siege of Lucknow. (H. F. Longmore, Lymington, Hants.).

Ensign Hugh Pearson, 84th Foot: letters from India, 1856-9. (F./Lieut. R. M. Pearson, R.A.F., Reading, Berks.).

Captain Robert Poore, 8th Hussars: Indian Mutiny letters, December, 1857-December, 1858. (Robert Poore-Saurin-Watts, Ledbury, Herefordshire).

Lieutenant Charles Gilbert Robinson, Bengal Artillery: letters from Meerut and Delhi, 1857-9. (Miss L. Robinson, Folkestone, Kent).

Miss Edith Sharpley: memories of Agra Fort during the Mutiny. (Miss Daisy Ashton, London, W.II).

Mrs. Elizabeth Sneyd: Indian Mutiny reminiscences of Shahjehanpore and Calcutta. (Author's collection).

The Rev. Arthur Browne Spry: Allahabad Mutiny letters. (Mrs. F. E. Hume-Spry, Hastings, Sussex).

Captain John Spurgin, 1st Madras Fusiliers: letters written during the Siege of Lucknow, October-November, 1857. (Mrs. Muriel Cameron, Edinburgh).

Assistant Surgeon John H. Sylvester: diary of the Persian campaign and the Indian Mutiny, 1854-61. (Miss Beryl Sylvester Hodder, Worthing, Sussex).

Miss Agnes Timbrell: Nusseerabad Mutiny narrative. (Rear-Admiral J. S. Powell, D.S.O., R.N., Twyford, Hants.).

Lieutenant Edward Vibart, 54th N.I.: mutiny letters from Delhi, Meerut, Cawnpore and Lucknow, April, 1857-March, 1858. (Mrs. Audrey Farmiloe, London, W.8).

Private William Wilkie, 79th Highlanders: Crimean and Indian Mutiny Diary, 1854-9. (Mrs. M. J. Plant, London, S.E.16).

Lieutenant Douglas Wimberley, 79th Highlanders: diary of the 79th in the Mutiny. (Major-General Douglas Wimberley, Coupar Angus, Perthshire).

NEWSPAPERS AND PERIODICALS

The Times
Allen's Indian Mail
Army and Navy Gazette
Bengal Hurkaru and India Gazette
Bombay Calendar and Almanac
Calcutta Weekly Chronicle
Delhi Gazette
Delhi Sketch Book
The Englishman
The Friend of India
The Hindu Patriot
Illustrated London News
Indian Planters' Gazette
Indian Sporting Review
Lahore Chronicle
Madras Church Missionary Record
The Moffusilite
Phoenix
Punch
Saunders' Monthly Magazine for All India
Tait's Edinburgh Magazine
The Witness in the East

PUBLISHED SOURCES

ADYE, SIR JOHN. *Recollections of a Military Life*. London: Smith, Elder, 1895.

ADYE, SIR JOHN. *The Defence of Cawnpore*. London: Longman, 1858.

AITCHISON, SIR CHARLES. *Lord Lawrence*. Oxford: Clarendon Press, 1892.

ALISON, ARCHIBALD. *Lord Clyde's Campaign in India*, in Blackwood's Magazine, October, 1858.

ANDERSON, ROBERT P. *Personal Journal of the Siege of Lucknow*. London: William Thacker, 1858.

ANSON, BREVET-MAJOR OCTAVIUS. *With H.M. 9th Lancers During the Indian Mutiny*. London: W. H. Allen, 1896.

At the Front: A Soldier's Experiences in the Crimean War and Indian Mutiny, Paisley: Alexander Gardner, 1916.

ATKINS, J. B. *Life of Sir W. H. Russell* (2 vols.). London: John Murray. 1911.

ATKINSON, G. F. *Curry and Rice on Forty Plates*. London: Day and Son, 1856.

ATKINSON, G. F. *The Campaign in India, 1857-8*. London: Day and Son, 1858.

BAGLEY, F. R. *A Small Boy in the Indian Mutiny*, in Blackwood's Magazine, Vol. 227, 1930.

BALDWIN, REV. J. R. *Indian Gup: Untold Stories of the Indian Mutiny*. London: Neville Beeman, 1897.

BALL, CHARLES. *History of the Indian Mutiny* (2 vols.). London: London Printing and Publishing Co., 1858.

BANNERJEA, B. N. *The Last Days of Nana Sahib* in Indian Historical Records Commission Proceedings, Vol. XII, 1932.

BARKER, GENERAL G. D. *Letters from Persia and India*. London: Bell and Sons, 1915.

BARTRUM, MRS. KATHERINE. *A Widow's Reminiscences of the Siege of Lucknow*. London: James Nisbet, 1858.

BASU, MAJOR B. D. *Rise of the Christian Power in India*. Calcutta: R. Chatterjee, 1931.

BAYLEY, JOHN. *The Assault of Delhi*. London: William Ridgway, 1876.

BAYLEY, JOHN. *Reminiscences of School and Army Life*. London: privately printed, 1875.

BEAMES, JOHN. *Memoirs of a Bengal Civilian*. London: Chatto and Windus, 1961.

BECHER, MRS. AUGUSTA. *Personal Reminiscences in India and Europe, 1830-88*. London: Constable, 1930.

BECHER, MAJOR EVANS. *The English in India: letters from Nagpore, 1857-8*. London: Chapman, 1859.

BELLASIS, MARGARET. *Honourable Company*. London: Hollis and Carter, 1952.

The Bengal Mutiny, in Blackwood's Magazine, September, 1857.

BENNETT, MRS. AMELIA. *Ten Months' Captivity after the Massacre at Cawnpore*, in The Nineteenth Century, June, 1913.

BENSON, A. C. (*ed.*). *The Letters of Queen Victoria, 1837-61*, Vol. III. London: John Murray, 1907.

BERNCASTLE, DR. JULIUS. *The Revolt of the Bengal Sepoys*. Sydney: J. Clarke, 1857.

BHARGAVA, K. D. *A Note on Tantia Topee*, in Indian Historical Records Commission Proceedings, Vol. XXIV, 1948.

BIDDULPH, H. *The Capture of Lucknow*, in Soc. Army Hist. Research Journal, Autumn, 1936.

BILLOT, FREDERIC. *L'Inde, l'Angleterre et La France*. Paris: Dantin, 1857.

BLANCHARD, SIDNEY. *Yesterday and To-Day in India*. London: W. H. Allen, 1867.

BONHAM, JOHN. *Oudh in 1857: Some Memories of the Indian Mutiny*. London: Williams and Norgate, 1928.

BOST, ISABELLA. *Incidents in the Life of.* Glasgow: McNaughton and Sinclair, 1913.

BOURCHIER, COLONEL GEORGE. *Eight Months' Campaign Against the Bengal Sepoy Army.* London: Smith, Elder, 1858.

BRADSHAW, LIEUTENANT J. H. *Letters on the Delhi Campaign* in The Oxfordshire and Buckinghamshire Light Infantry Chronicle, Vol. XVIII, 1909.

BROCK, REV. WILLIAM. *A Biographical Sketch of Sir Henry Havelock.* London: James Nisbet, 1858.

BROWN, J. *The Capture of Lucknow,* in The Calcutta Review, June, 1860.

BROWN, J. *Havelock's Indian Campaign,* in The Calcutta Review, March, 1859.

BROWNE, JOHN. *Cawnpore and the Nana of Bithur.* Cawnpore: Victoria Press, 1890.

BROWNE, JOHN. *The Lucknow Guide.* Lucknow: American Mission Press, 1874.

BRUCE, J. F. *The Mutiny at Cawnpore,* in Punjab University Hist. Soc. Journal, April, 1934.

BUCHANAN, C. *Christian Researches in India.* London: G. Routledge, 1858.

BUCKLER, F. W. *The Political Theory of the Indian Mutiny,* in Royal Hist. Soc. Transactions, Series 4, Vol. V, 1922.

BURNE, SIR OWEN, *Clyde and Strathnairn.* Oxford: Clarendon Press, 1891.

BURTON, R. G. *Indian Military Leaders* in The United Service Magazine, Vol. 174, 1916.

BURTON, R. G. *Women Warriors in India,* in The United Service Magazine, Vol. 175, 1916.

BUTLER, LT.-COLONEL LEWIS. *Annals of the King's Royal Rifle Corps,* Vol. III. London: John Murray, 1926.

BUTLER, REV. WILLIAM. *The Land of the Veda.* New York: Carlton and Lanchan, 1872.

CAMPBELL, SIR COLIN. *A Narrative of the Indian Revolt from its Outbreak to the Capture of Lucknow.* London: W. Clowes, 1858.

CAMPBELL, SIR GEORGE. *Memories of My Indian Career* (2 vols.). London: Macmillan, 1893.

CAMPBELL, ROBERT. *The Indian Mutiny: its causes and remedies.* London: Charles Evans, 1857.

CAMPBELL, ROBERT. *India: its government, misgovernment and future considered.* London: Effingham Wilson, 1858.

CARDEW, MAJOR F. G. *Hodson's Horse, 1857-1922.* Edinburgh: William Blackwood, 1922.

CAREY, W. H. (ed.). *The Good Old Days of Honourable John Company.* Calcutta: R. Cambray, 1907.

CASE, MRS. ADELAIDE. *Day by Day at Lucknow*. London: Richard Bentley, 1858.

CAVE-BROWNE, JOHN. *The Punjab and Delhi in 1857* (2 vols.) Edinburgh: William Blackwood, 1861.

CAVE-BROWNE, JOHN. *Incidents of Indian Life*. Maidstone: W Dickinson, 1895.

Cave-Browne's 'The Punjab and Delhi', in The Calcutta Review Vol. 38, 1863.

CAVENAGH, SIR ORFEUR. *Reminiscences of an Indian Official*. London: W. H. Allen, 1884.

The Cawnpore Outbreak and Massacre:. Calcutta: J. F. Bellamy 1857.

CHALMERS, COLONEL JOHN. *Letters Written from India During the Mutiny and Wazir Campaigns*. Edinburgh: T. and A. Constable 1904.

CHAMBERLAIN, GENERAL SIR CRAUFORD. *Remarks on Captain Trotter's Biography of Major W. S. R. Hodson*. Edinburgh: R. and R. Clark, 1901.

CHAND, BOOL. *Urdu Journalism in the Punjab,* in Punjab University Hist. Soc. Journal, April, 1933.

CHATTOPADHYAYA, H. B. *Mutiny in Bihar,* in Bengal Past and Present, Vols. 74-5, 1955-6.

CHATTOPADHYAYA, H. B. *The Sepoy Army, its strength, composition and recruitment* in The Calcutta Review, May, July-September 1956.

CHAUDHURI, S. B. *Civil Rebellion in the Indian Mutinies*. Calcutta: World Press, 1957.

CHICK, NOAH (ed.). *Annals of the Indian Rebellion*. Calcutta: Sanders, Cones and Co., 1859.

CHUNDER, BOLANAUTH. *Travels of a Hindu* (2 vols.). London: N Trubner, 1869.

CHURCHER, EMERY. *Some Reminiscences of Three-Quarters of a Century in India*. London: Luzac and Co., 1909.

COLVIN, SIR AUCKLAND. *Life of John Russell Colvin*. Oxford: Clarendon Press, 1895.

The Company's Raj, in Blackwood's Magazine, November, 1857

COOPER, FREDERICK. *The Crisis in the Punjab*. London: Smith Elder, 1858.

COOPLAND, MRS. RUTH. *A Lady's Escape from Gwalior*. London: Smith, Elder, 1859.

CORK, BARRY J. *Rider on a Grey Horse*. London: Cassell, 1958

COSENS, LT.-COLONEL F. R. and WALLACE, C. L. *Fatehgarh and the Mutiny*. Lucknow: Newul Kishore Press, 1933.

COTTON, SIR EVAN. *Calcutta Old and New*. Calcutta: W. Newman 1907.

CRAWSHAY, GEORGE. *The Immediate Cause of the Indian Mutiny.* London: Effingham Wilson, 1858.

CRAWSHAY, GEORGE. *The Catastrophe of the East India Company.* London: privately printed, 1858.

The Crisis in India: the causes and proposed remedies by a retired officer.

CROMB, JAMES. *The Highland Brigade.* London: Simpkin, Marshall, 1886.

CROMMELIN, W. A. *Memorandum on Three Passages of the River Ganges in the Rainy Season of 1857.* Calcutta: Gazette Office, 1858.

CROOKE, WILLIAM. *Songs of the Mutiny,* in The Indian Antiquary, April and June, 1911.

CROSSE, LT.-COLONEL CHARLES. *The Punjab Movable Column Under Nicholson,* in The United Service Magazine, June, 1896.

CRUMP, LIEUTENANT C. W. *A Pictorial Record of the Cawnpore Massacre.* London: Henry Graves, 1858.

CULROSS, JAMES. *The Missionary Martyr of Delhi.* London: J. Heaton, 1860.

CUNNINGHAM, SIR HENRY. *Earl Canning.* Oxford: Clarendon Press, 1891.

CUST, R. N. *Pictures of Indian Life.* London: Trubner, 1881.

CUST, R. N. *A District during the Rebellion,* in The Calcutta Review, September, 1858.

CUTHELL, EDITH. *My Garden in the City of Gardens.* London: John Lane, 1905.

DALHOUSIE, LORD. *Private Letters (ed. J. G. Baird).* Edinburgh: William Blackwood, 1910.

DALY, MAJOR H. *Memoirs of General Sir Henry Dermot Daly.* London: John Murray, 1905.

DANGERFIELD, GEORGE. *Bengal Mutiny.* London: Hutchinson, 1933.

DANVERS, R. W. *Letters from India and China During the Years 1857-8.* London: Hazell, Watson and Viney, 1898.

DAS, MANMATHA NATH. *Western Innovations and the Rising of 1857,* in Bengal Past and Present, Vol. 76, 1957.

DASHWOOD, A. F. *Untimely Arrival at the Siege of Lucknow,* in The Listener, 2nd December, 1936.

DATTA, K. K. *Some unpublished papers relating to the Mutiny,* in Indian Historical Quarterly, March, 1936.

DATTA, K. K. *Nature of the Indian Revolt of 1857-9,* in Bengal Past and Present, Vol. 73, 1954.

DATTA, K. K. *Some newly discovered Records relating to the Bihar phase of the Indian movement,* in Patna University Journal, Vol. 8, 1954.

DATTA, K. K. *Popular Discontent in Bihar,* in Bengal Past and Present, Vol. 74, 1955.

DATTA, K. K. *Some Original Documents Relating to the Indian Mutiny*, in Indian Historical Records Commission Proceedings, Vol. 30, 1954.

DATTA, K. K. *Contemporary Account of the Indian Movement of 1857*, in Journal of the Bihar Record Society, Vol. 36, 1950.

DATTA, K. K. *Biography of Kunwar Singh and Amar Singh*. Patna: K. P. Jayaswal Research Institute, 1957.

DE KANTZOW, COLONEL C. A. *Record of Services in India, 1853-86*. Brighton: T. Phillips, 1898.

DE WATTEVILLE, COLONEL H. *The British Soldier*. London: Dent, 1954.

DEWAR, DOUGLAS. *In the Days of the Company*. Calcutta: Thacker, Spink and Co., 1920.

DEWAR, DOUGLAS. *Bygone Days in India*. London: John Lane, 1922.

DEWAR, DOUGLAS, *and* GARRETT, H. L. O. *Reply to Mr. F. W. Buckler's Political Theory of the Indian Mutiny*, in Royal Hist. Soc. Transactions, Vol. 7, 1924.

DICKINSON, JOHN. *Last Counsels of an Unknown Counsellor*. London: Whiting and Co., 1883.

DIGBY, W. *A Friend in Need*. London: Indian Political Agency, 1890.

DIVER, MAUD. *Honoria Lawrence*. London: John Murray, 1936.

DODD, G. *History of the Indian Revolt and of the Expeditions to Persia, China and Japan*. London: Chambers, 1860.

DODGSON, LT.-COLONEL DAVID. *General Views and Special Points of Interest of the City of Lucknow*. London: Day and Son, 1860.

DUBERLEY, MRS. FRANCES. *Campaigning in Rajputana and Central India*. London: Smith, Elder, 1859.

DUFF, DR. A. *The Indian Rebellion: its causes and results*. London: James Nisbet, 1858.

DUNLOP, ROBERT H. *Service and Adventure with the Khakee Ressalah*. London: Richard Bentley, 1858.

DURAND, H. M. *The Life of Major-General Sir Henry Durand* (2 vols.) London: W. H. Allen, 1883.

DUTT, ROMESH. *India in the Victorian Age*. London: Kegan Paul, Trench, Trubner, 1904.

EDWARDES, LADY EMMA. *Memoirs of the Life of Sir H. B. Edwardes* (2 vols.). London: Kegan Paul, Trench, 1886.

EDWARDES, H. B. *and* MERIVALE, H. *Life of Sir Henry Lawrence*. London: Smith, Elder, 1873.

EDWARDES, MICHAEL. *The Necessary Hell*. London: Constable, 1958.

EDWARDES, MICHAEL. *The Orchid House*. London: Constable, 1960.

EDWARDS, WILLIAM. *Personal Adventures during the Indian Rebellion.* London: Smith, Elder, 1858.

EGERTON, CAPTAIN FRANCIS, R.N. *Journal of a Winter's Tour in India* (2 vols.). London: John Murray, 1852.

The Electric Telegraph, in The Calcutta Review, March, 1858.

ERSKINE, W. C. *Chapter of the Bengal Mutiny.* Edinburgh: William Blackwood, 1871.

The European Soldier in India, in The Calcutta Review, March, 1858.

EWART, LT.-GENERAL J. A. *Story of a Soldier's Life* (2 vols.). London: Sampson Low, Marston, Searle and Rivington, 1881.

FAYRER, SIR JOSEPH. *Recollections of My Life.* Edinburgh: William Blackwood, 1900.

The First Bengal European Fusiliers in the Delhi Campaign, in Blackwood's Magazine, January, 1858.

The First Bengal European Fusiliers after the Fall of Delhi, in Blackwood's Magazine, June, 1858.

The First Bengal European Fusiliers at Lucknow, in Blackwood's Magazine, July, 1858.

FITCHETT, REV. WILLIAM. *The Tale of the Great Mutiny* (3rd edn.). London: Smith, Elder, 1903.

FORBES, ARCHIBALD. *Colin Campbell, Lord Clyde.* London: Macmillan, 1895.

FORBES, ARCHIBALD. *Havelock.* London: Macmillan, 1891.

FORBES, ARCHIBALD. *Glimpses Through the Cannon Smoke.* London: George Routledge, 1880.

FORBES, MRS. HAMILTON. *Some Recollections of the Siege of Lucknow.* Axminster: Edwin Snell, 1905.

FORBES-MITCHELL, WILLIAM. *Reminiscences of the Great Mutiny.* London: Macmillan, 1893.

FORGNES, E. M. *La Révolte des Cipayes.* Paris: Hachette, 1861.

FORJETT, CHARLES. *Our Real Danger in India.* London: Cassell, Petter and Galpin, 1877.

FORREST, SIR GEORGE. *History of the Indian Mutiny* (3 vols.). Edinburgh: William Blackwood, 1904.

FORREST, SIR GEORGE. *Life of Field Marshal Sir Neville Chamberlain.* Edinburgh: William Blackwood, 1909.

FORREST, SIR GEORGE (ed.). *Selections from the State Papers of the Military Dept. of the Government of India* (4 vols.). Calcutta: Military Dept. Press, 1902.

FORSYTH, SIR DOUGLAS. *Autobiography and Reminiscences.* London: Richard Bentley, 1887.

FORTESCUE, HON. J. W. *History of the British Army,* Vol. XIII. London: Macmillan, 1930.

FOSTER, SIR WILLIAM. *John Company.* London: John Case, 1926.

FRASER, E. *The Pearl's Brigade in the Indian Mutiny*, in Mariner's Mirror, Vol. XII, 1926.

FRASER, CAPTAIN HASTINGS. *Our Faithful Ally, the Nizam.* London: Smith, Elder, 1865.

FRITH, WALTER. *A Private of the Mutiny*, in The Cornhill Magazine, new series, Vol. XXI.

FROST, THOMAS. *A Complete Narrative of the Mutiny in India.* London: Read and Co., 1857.

GARDINER, SIR ROBERT. *A Military Analysis of the Remote and Proximate Causes of the Indian Rebellion.* London: Byfield, Hawkesworth, 1858.

GARRETT, H. L. O. *The Trial of Bahadur Shah II*, in Punjab University Hist. Soc. Journal, April, 1932.

GERMON, MARIA. *Journal of the Siege of Lucknow (ed. Michael Edwardes).* London: Constable, 1958.

GIBNEY, ROBERT D. *My Escape from the Mutineers in Oudh.* London: Richard Bentley, 1858.

GILBERT, HENRY. *The Story of the Indian Mutiny.* London: George Harrap, 1916.

GILLIATT, EDWARD. *Daring Deeds of the Indian Mutiny.* London: Seeley Service Co., 1918.

GIMLETTE, LT.-COLONEL GEORGE. *Postcript to the Records of the Indian Mutiny.* London: Witherby, 1927.

A Glance at the East, by a Retired Bengal Civilian. London: L. Booth, 1857.

GOLDSMID, F. J. *James Outram* (2 vols.). London: Smith, Elder, 1880.

GORDON-ALEXANDER, LT.-COLONEL W. *Recollections of a Highland Subaltern under Sir Colin Campbell.* London: Edward Arnold, 1898.

GOUGH, SIR HUGH. *Old Memories.* Edinburgh: William Blackwood, 1897.

GOWING, THOMAS. *A Soldier's Experience, or a Voice from the Ranks.* Nottingham: Thomas Forman, 1905.

GRAHAM, G. F. *Life and Work of Sir Syed Ahmed Khan.* London: Hodder and Stoughton, 1909.

GRANT, ALEXANDER. *Physician and Friend.* London: John Murray, 1902.

GRANT, SIR J. H. *and* KNOLLYS, SIR H. *Incidents in the Sepoy War.* Edinburgh: William Blackwood, 1875.

GRANT, SIR J. H. *Life and Selections from his Correspondence* (2 vols.). Edinburgh: William Blackwood, 1894.

GRAY, ROBERT. *Reminiscences of India and North Queensland.* London: Constable, 1913.

GRAY, LIEUTENANT W. J. *Journal of the Siege Train from Feroze-*

pore to Delhi, in Soc. Army Hist. Research Journal, Vol. x, 1931.

GREATHED, HARVEY. *Letters Written During the Siege of Delhi.* London: Longman, 1857.

GRETTON, LT.-COLONEL G. LE M. *Campaigns and History of the Royal Irish Regiment.* Edinburgh: William Blackwood, 1911.

GREY, COLONEL L. J. *Tales of Our Grandfather.* London: Smith, Elder, 1912.

GRIFFITHS, CHARLES. *A Narrative of the Siege of Delhi.* London: John Murray, 1910.

GROOM, WILLIAM TATE. *With Havelock from Allahabad to Lucknow.* London: Sampson Low, 1894.

GUBBINS, MARTIN. *An Account of the Mutinies in Oudh and of the Siege of the Lucknow Residency.* London: Richard Bentley, 1858.

GUPTA, P. C. *Nana Sahib at Bithur,* in Bengal Past and Present, Vol. 77, 1958.

GURNEY, REV. J. H. *The Moral of a Sad Story.* London: Rivington, 1857.

HALLS, JOHN. *Arrah in 1857: its defence and relief.* Dover: George W. Grigg, 1893.

HALLS, JOHN. *Two Months in Arrah in 1857.* London: Longman, Green, Longman and Roberts, 1860.

HANDCOCK, COLONEL A. G. *A Short Account of the Siege of Delhi.* Simla: Government Central Printing Office, 1892.

HARCOURT, H. M. *Delhi: a Man Hunt,* in Blackwood's Magazine, November, 1930.

HARE, AUGUSTUS. *The Story of Two Noble Lives,* Vol. II. London: George Allen, 1893.

Harington, Captain Hastings: a Memoir. London: Nisbet, 1862.

HARRIS, MRS. G. *A Lady's Diary of the Siege of Lucknow.* London: John Murray, 1858.

HEARSEY, CAPTAIN J. B. *Narrative of the Outbreak at Seetapore.* Seetapore: privately printed, 1858.

HEDAYAT ALI. *A Few Words Relative to the Late Mutiny of the Bengal Army.* Calcutta: privately printed, 1858.

HEELY, WILFRED. *Letters from India,* in The National Review, 1934.

HERBERT, DAVID. *Great Historical Mutinies.* London: Nimmo's National Library, 1875.

HERFORD, IVAN. *Stirring Times Under Canvas.* London: Richard Bentley, 1862.

HILTON, EDWARD. *The Tourist's Guide to Lucknow, 9th edn.* Lucknow: F. W. Perry, 1916.

HODSON, WILLIAM. *Twelve Years of a Soldier's Life in India.* London: John W. Parker, 1859.

HOLLOWAY, JOHN. *Essays on the Indian Mutiny*. London: Dean and Son, 1863.

HOLMES, F. M. *Four Heroes of India*. London: S. W. Partridge, 1892.

HOLMES, T. R. *The Mutiny*, in Cambridge History of India, Vol. VI. Cambridge: University Press, 1932.

HOLMES, T. R. *History of the Indian Mutiny, 5th edn.* London: Macmillan, 1898.

HOLMES, T. R. *Four Famous Soldiers*. London: W. H. Allen, 1889.

HOSEASON, COMMANDER JOHN, R. N. *Remarks on the Rapid Transmission of Troops to India*. London: Edward Stanford, 1858.

HUNTER, CHARLES. *Personal Reminiscences of an Indian Mutiny Veteran*. Brighton: A. Horton Stephens, 1911.

HUNTER, SIR WILLIAM. *The Marquess of Dalhousie*. Oxford: Clarendon Press, 1890.

HUTCHINSON, MAJOR-GENERAL GEORGE. *Narrative of the Mutiny in Oudh*. London: Smith, Elder, 1859.

India: its dangers considered in 1856 by a Retired Officer. Jersey: Joshua Coutance, 1858.

Indian Domestic Economy and Receipt Book, 5th edn. London: G. P. Meaden, 1860.

The Indian Mutiny, by a Former Editor of The Delhi Gazette. London: George Routledge, 1858.

The Indian Mutiny: the last phase, in Blackwood's Magazine, Vol. 191, 1912.

INGE, LT.-COLONEL D. M. *A Subaltern's Diary*. London: Rait, Henderson, 1894.

INGLIS, HON. JULIA. *The Siege of Lucknow, a diary*. London: James R. Osgood, McIlvaine and Co., 1892.

INGLIS, HON. JULIA. *Letter containing extracts from a journal kept during the Siege of Lucknow*. London: privately printed, 1858.

INNES, COLONEL. *The Campaign of 1857-8*, in The Calcutta Review, March, 1859.

INNES, LT.-GENERAL JAMES. *Lucknow and Oudh in the Mutiny*. London: A. D. Innes, 1895.

INNES, LT.-GENERAL JAMES. *The Sepoy Revolt*. London: A. D. Innes, 1897.

IRELAND, WILLIAM. *A History of the Siege of Delhi, by an officer who served there*. Edinburgh: A. and C. Black, 1861.

JACOB, SIR GEORGE LE G. *Western India Before and During the Mutinies*. London: Henry S. King, 1871.

JAMES, DAVID. *Life of Lord Roberts*. London: Hollis and Carter, 1954.

JASON, DR. KURT. (*ed.*). *Letters of the Prince Consort, 1813-61*. London: John Murray, 1938.

JOCELYN, JULIAN. *History of the Royal and Indian Artillery, 1857.* London: Royal Artillery Institution, 1915.

JOHNSON, W. T. *Twelve Years of a Soldier's Life.* London: A. D. Innes, 1897.

JONES, GAVIN. *My Escape from Fatehgarh.* Cawnpore: Pioneer Press, 1913.

JONES, CAPTAIN OLIVER, R.N. *Recollections of a Winter's Campaign in India.* London: Saunders and Otley, 1859.

JOYCE, MICHAEL. *Ordeal at Lucknow.* London: John Murray, 1938.

A Judicial Trial During the Indian Mutiny, in The Calcutta Review, Vol. 115, 1902.

JWALA, SAHAI. *The Loyal Rajputana.* Allahabad: Indian Press, 1902.

KAVANAGH, T. HENRY. *How I Won the V.C.* London: Ward and Lock, 1860.

KAYE, SIR JOHN. *History of the Sepoy War* (3 vols.). London: W. H. Allen, 1864-7.

KAYE, SIR JOHN. *Lives of Indian Officers* (2 vols.). London: W. H. Allen, 1867.

KAYE, SIR JOHN. *Peregrine Pulteney.* London: John Mortimer, 1844.

Kaye's Sepoy War, in The Calcutta Review, Vol. 41, 1865.

KEENE, H. G. *Fifty Seven.* London: W. H. Allen, 1883.

KEENE, H. G. *Handbook for Visitors to Allahabad, Cawnpore and Lucknow, 2nd edn.* Calcutta: Thacker Spink, 1896.

KEENE, H. G. *A Servant of John Company.* London: W. Thacker, 1897.

KEENE, H. G. *The Literature of the Rebellion,* in The Calcutta Review, March, 1859.

KENNEDY, REV. JAMES. *Life and Work in Benares and Kumaon, 1839-77.* London: T. Fisher Unwin, 1884.

KILLOUGH, LE COMTE H. RUSSELL. *16,000 lieues à travers l'Asie et l'Océanie* (2 vols.). Paris: Hachette, 1864.

KNIGHT, A. E. *The Romance of Colonisation,* Vol. III. London: S. W. Partridge, 1897.

KRISHAN LAL. *The Sack of Delhi as Witnessed by Ghalib,* in Bengal Past and Present, Vol. 74, 1955.

LANDON, PERCEVAL. *'1857'.* London: W. H. Smith, 1907.

LANG, LIEUTENANT ARTHUR. *Diary and Letters, 1857-8,* in Soc. Army Hist. Research Journal, Vols. 9-11, 1930-2.

LANG, JOHN. *Wanderings in India.* London: Routledge, Warne and Routhorpe, 1859.

LAURENCE, T. B. *Six Years in the North-West.* Calcutta: G. C. Hay, 1861.

LAVERACK, SERGEANT ALFRED. *A Methodist Soldier in the Indian Army*. London: T. Woolmer, n.d.

LAWRENCE, LT.-GENERAL SIR GEORGE. *Forty Years' Service in India*. London: John Murray, 1874.

LAWRENCE, SIR HENRY. *Essays Military and Political*. London: W. H. Allen, 1859.

LEASOR, JAMES. *The Red Fort*. London: Werner Laurie, 1956.

LECKEY, EDWARD. *Fictions Connected with the Indian Outbreak of 1857*. Bombay: Chesson and Woodhall, 1859.

LEE, J. F. *and* RADCLIFF, F. W. *The Indian Mutiny up to the Relief of Lucknow*. Rawalpindi: privately printed, 1918.

LEE, JOSEPH "DOBBIN". *The Indian Mutiny: a narrative of the events at Cawnpore*. Cawnpore: Victoria Press, 1893.

LEE-WARNER, SIR WILLIAM. *The Life of the Marquis of Dalhousie*. London: Macmillan, 1904.

Letters from Delhi, 1857 (*ed.* George C. Barnes). London: Monthly Review, n.d.

LEWIN, MALCOLM. *The Way to Lose India*. London: James Ridgway, 1857.

LEWIN, MALCOLM. *The Government of the East India Company and its Monopolies*. London: James Ridgway, 1857.

LEWIN, LT.-COLONEL THOMAS. *A Fly on the Wheel, or How I Helped to Govern India*. London: Constable, 1912.

Life in the North-West, in The Calcutta Review, March, 1857.

LOCKWOOD, EDWARD. *The Early Days of Marlborough College*. London: Simpkin, Marshall, Hamilton, Kent and Co., 1893.

LOW, C. R. *A Memoir of Lieut.-General Sir Garnet Wolseley*. London: Richard Bentley, 1878.

LOW, URSULA. *Fifty Years with John Company*. London: John Murray, 1936.

LOWE, THOMAS. *Central India During the Rebellion of 1857-8*. London: Longman Green, 1860.

LUDLOW, J. M. *British India, its Races and its History* (2 vols.). Cambridge: Macmillan, 1858.

MCKEE, REV. JAMES. *Obstacles to the Progress of Christianity in India*. Belfast: News-Letter Office, 1858.

MACCREA, R. *The Tablets in the Memorial Church, Cawnpore*. Calcutta: Thacker Spink, 1894.

MACGREGOR, SIR CHARLES. *Life and Opinions*. Edinburgh: William Blackwood, 1888.

MACKAY, REV. JAMES. *From London to Lucknow* (2 vols.). London: James Nisbet, 1860.

MACKENZIE, COLONEL ALFRED. *Mutiny Memories*. Allahabad: Pioneer Press, 1891.

MACKENZIE, MRS. COLIN. *Life in the Mission, the Camp and the*

Zenana, or Six Years in India (3 vols.). London: Richard Bentley, 1853, 1872.

MACKENZIE, MRS. COLIN. *English Women in the Rebellion,* in The Calcutta Review, September, 1859.

MACLAGAN, MICHAEL. *'Clemency' Canning.* London: Macmillan, 1962.

MACMULLEN, J. *Camp and Barrack-Room.* London: Chapman and Hall, 1846.

MACMUNN, LT.-GENERAL SIR GEORGE. *The Indian Mutiny in Perspective.* London: G. Bell, 1931.

MACMUNN, LT.-GENERAL SIR GEORGE. *Behind the Scenes in Many Wars.* London: John Murray, 1930.

MACMUNN, LT.-GENERAL SIR GEORGE. *Jan Compani Kee Jai,* in The Cornhill Magazine, January-June, 1910.

MACMUNN, LT.-GENERAL SIR GEORGE. *Dawn at Delhi,* in The Cornhill Magazine, July-December, 1913.

MACMUNN, LT.-GENERAL SIR GEORGE. *Devi Din, Mutineer,* in Blackwood's Magazine, April, 1928.

MACMUNN, LT.-GENERAL SIR GEORGE. *Some New Light on the Indian Mutiny,* in Blackwood's Magazine, Vol. 224, 1928.

MACPHERSON, A. G. *The Siege of Lucknow,* in The Calcutta Review, September, 1858.

MAJENDIE, LIEUTENANT VIVIAN. *Up Among the Pandies, or A Year's Service in India.* London: Routledge, Warne and Routledge, 1859.

MALET, H. P. *Lost Links in the Indian Mutiny.* London: T. Cautley Newby, 1867.

MALLESON, COLONEL GEORGE. *History of the Indian Mutiny* (6 vols.). London: W. H. Allen, 1878-80.

MALLESON, COLONEL GEORGE. *The Indian Mutiny.* London: Seeley, 1891.

MALLESON, COLONEL GEORGE. *The Mutiny of the Bengal Army* (2 parts). London: Bosworth and Harrison, 1857-8.

MALLESON, COLONEL GEORGE. *Recreations of an Indian Official.* London: Longman, Green, 1872.

MALLESON, COLONEL GEORGE. *Havelock,* in The Calcutta Review, September, 1860.

MANCHESTER, MAN, A. *A Voice from India to the Men of Manchester.* Manchester: Joseph Pratt, 1858.

MANGIN, A. (*ed.*). *La Révolte au Bengale.* Tours: Mame et Cie, 1862.

MARRYAT, FLORENCE. *'Gup': sketches of Anglo-Indian Life.* London: Richard Bentley, 1868.

MARSHMAN, J. C. *Memoir of Major-General Sir Henry Havelock.* Longman, Green, Longman, Richards, 1860.

MARTIN, CHARLES. *La Puissance Militaire des Anglais dans l'Inde et l'insurrection des Cipayes.* Paris: Hachette, 1859.

MARTIN, R. MONTGOMERY. *The Indian Empire* (3 vols.). London: London Printing and Publishing Co., 1858-61.

MAUDE, COLONEL EDWIN. *Oriental Campaigns and European Furloughs.* London: T. Fisher Unwin, 1908.

MAUDE, COLONEL F. C. *and* SHERER, J. W. *Memories of the Mutiny* (2 vols.). London: Remington, 1894.

MAUNSELL, F. R. *The Siege of Delhi.* London: Simpkin, Marshall, Hamilton, Kent, 1912.

MEAD, HENRY. *The Sepoy Revolt.* London: John Murray, 1857.

MECHAM, C. H. *and* COUPER, G. *Sketches and Incidents of the Siege of Lucknow.* London: Day and Son, 1858.

MEDLEY, JULIUS. *A Year's Campaigning in India.* London: W. Thacker, 1858.

MEEK, REV. ROBERT. *The Martyr of Allahabad.* London: James Nisbet, 1857.

MERCER, MAJOR E. S. *A Letter to Rt. Hon. the Earl of Ellenborough.* London: Edward T. Whitfield, 1861.

METCALFE, CHARLES (*ed.*). *Two Native Narratives of the Mutiny of Delhi.* London: Archibald Constable, 1890.

METCALFE, PRIVATE HENRY. *Chronicle of the 32nd Foot* (*ed. Lt.-General Sir Francis Tucker*). London: Cassell, 1953.

MILES, A. H. *and* POTTLE, A. J. *Fifty-Two Stories of the Indian Mutiny.* London: Hutchinson, 1895.

Military Hygiene in India, in The Calcutta Review, December, 1859.

MINTURN, ROBERT B. JR. *From New York to Delhi.* London: Longman, Brown, Green, Longman and Roberts, 1858.

Mister Wilberforce's Mutiny Story, in The Oxfordshire Light Infantry Chronicle, Vol. IV, 1895.

MOEGLING, T. *The Indian Crisis of 1857,* in The Calcutta Review, December, 1857.

MONTALAMBERT, LE COMTE DE. *Un débat sur l'Inde au Parlement Anglais.* London: W. Jeffs, 1858.

MONYPENNY, W. F. *and* BUCKLE, G. E. *The Life of Benjamin Disraeli,* Vol. IV. London: John Murray, 1916.

MORRIS, MALCOLM. *The Progress of Medicine During the Queen's Reign,* in The Nineteenth Century, June, 1897.

MORRISON, J. L. *Lawrence of Lucknow.* London: G. Bell and Co., 1934.

MOTTRAM, R. H. *Trader's Dream: the romance of the East India Company.* New York: Appleton Century Co., 1939.

MUIR, SIR WILLIAM. *Reports of the Intelligence Departments of the North-West Provinces* (2 vols.). Edinburgh: T. and T. Clark, 1902.

MUNRO, SURGEON WILLIAM. *Reminiscences of Military Service with the 93rd Sutherland Highlanders.* London: Hurst and Blackett, 1883.

MUNRO, SURGEON WILLIAM. *Records of Service and Campaigning in Many Lands* (2 vols.). London: Hurst and Blackett, 1887.

MUTER, MRS. DUNBAR. *My Recollections of the Sepoy Revolt.* London: John Long, 1911.

MUTER, MRS. DUNBAR. *Travels and Adventures of an Officer's Wife in India, China and New Zealand* (2 vols.). London: Hurst and Blackett, 1864.

The Mutinies, the Government and the People. Calcutta: D'Rozario and Co., 1858.

The Mutinies and the People. Calcutta: I. and C. Bose, 1859.

Mutinies in India: extracts of Letters from an Assistant Surgeon in the Infantry of the Hyderabad Contingent. Privately printed, 1857.

NAPIER, COLONEL ROBERT. *Report on Engineering Operations at the Siege of Lucknow.* Calcutta: Government Works Press, 1859.

Narrative of the Indian Mutinies of 1857 compiled for the Madras Military Male Orphan Asylum. Madras: Asylum Press, 1858.

NASH, J. T. *Volunteering in India.* London: George Philip, 1893.

NEWBOULT, A. W. *Padre Elliott of Fyzabad.* London: Charles Kelly, 1906.

NICHOLL, LT.-GENERAL T. *Saugor, A Story of 1857.* Woolwich: Royal Artillery Institution, 1894.

NORGATE, LT.-COLONEL T. *and* PHILLOTT, LT.-COLONEL D. C. *From Sepoy to Subadar.* Calcutta: Baptist Mission Press, 1911.

NORMAN, SIR HENRY. *Lecture on the Relief of Lucknow.* Simla: Station Press, 1867.

NORMAN, SIR HENRY. *Narrative of the Campaign of the Delhi Army.* London: W. H. Dalton, 1858.

NORTH, MAJOR CHARLES. *Journal of an English Officer in India.* London: Hurst and Blackett, 1858.

NORTON, JOHN BRUCE. *The Rebellion in India: how to prevent another.* London: Richardson Bros., 1857.

O'CALLAGHAN, DANIEL. *Scattered Chapters: the fatal falter at Meerut.* Calcutta: privately printed, 1861.

ORLICH, LEOPOLD VON. *The Military Mutiny in India.* London: T. and W. Boone, 1858.

Oudh, in Blackwood's Magazine, May, 1858.

Our Indian Empire, in Blackwood's Magazine, December, 1857.

OUTRAM, SIR JAMES. *The Campaign in India, 1857-8.* London: Smith, Elder, 1860.

Outram at Alumbagh, in The Calcutta Review, March, 1860.

OUVRY, HENRY. *Cavalry Experiences and Leaves from My Journal.* Lymington: C. T. King, 1892.

OUVRY, MRS. MATILDA. *A Lady's Diary Before and During the Indian Mutiny.* Lymington: C. T. King, 1892.

OWEN, ARTHUR. *Reminiscences of a Veteran of the Days of the Great Indian Mutiny.* Lucknow: Murray's London Printing Press, 1916.

OWEN, REV. WILLIAM. *Memorials of Christian Martyrs.* London: Simpkin, Marshall, 1858.

PAGET, MRS. LEOPOLD. *Camp and Cantonment.* London: Longman, Green, Longman, Roberts and Green, 1865.

PANCKRIDGE, H. A. *A Short History of the Bengal Club.* Calcutta: Art Press, 1927.

PANDIT, V. P. *Trial of an Impostor of Nana Sahib,* in Indian Historical Records Commission Proceedings, Vol. xxx.

Parliamentary Reports: Mutiny in the East Indies. 1857: Vols. 29, 30. 1857-8: Vols. 42, 43, 44. 1859: Vols. 11, 23, 25, 37. 1860: Vol. 50.

PARRY, S. H. J. *An Old Soldier's Memories.* London: Hurst and Blackett, 1897.

PARSONS, LIEUTENANT RICHARD. *A Story of Jugdespore.* London: Army and Navy Co-Operative Society, 1904.

PASKE, SURGEON-GENERAL. *A Link in the Chain of the Mutiny,* in The English Illustrated Magazine, September, 1894.

PEARSE, HUGH. *The Hearseys.* Edinburgh: William Blackwood, 1905.

PEARSON, HESKETH. *The Hero of Delhi: John Nicholson and his Wars.* London: William Collins, 1939.

PEILE, MRS. FANNY. *The Delhi Massacre: a narrative by a lady.* Calcutta: Indian Daily News Press, 1870.

PHILLIPPS, ALFRED. *Anecdotes and Reminiscences of Service in Bengal.* Inverness: Courier Office, 1878.

PITT, F. W. *Incidents in India and Memories of the Mutiny.* London: Kegan Paul, Trench, Trubner, 1896.

POLEHAMPTON, REV. HENRY. *A Memoir, Letters and Diary.* Ed. E. and T. S. Polehampton. London: Richard Bentley, 1858.

POLLOCK, J. C. *Way to Glory: the Life of Havelock of Lucknow.* London: John Murray, 1957.

The Post Office in the Mutiny, in Journal of the Punjab Historical Society, Vol. IV, 1916.

PRITCHARD, ILTUDUS. *The Mutinies in Rajputana.* London: John W. Parker, 1860.

Punjab Government: Mutiny Records, Correspondence and Reports, Vols. VII and VIII. Lahore: Punjab Government Press, 1911.

RAIKES, CHARLES. *Notes on the Revolt in the North-West Prov-*

inces. London: Longman, Brown, Green, Longman and Roberts, 1858.

RAMSAY, LT.-COLONEL BALCARRES. *Rough Recollections of Military Service and Society* (2 vols.). Edinburgh: Blanchard, 1882.

RAWLINSON, H. G. *Two Captures of Gwalior Fort,* in Indian Historical Records Commission Proceedings, Vol. 12, 1929.

Red, White and Blue: sketches of Military Life (3 vols.). London: Hurst and Blackett, 1862.

REES, L. R. *A Personal Narrative of the Siege of Lucknow.* London: Longman, Brown, Green, Longman and Roberts, 1858.

Revolt in Central India, 1857-9. Simla: Government Press, 1908.

REYNOLDS, REGINALD. *The White Sahibs in India.* London: Martin Secker and Warburg, 1937.

RICH, CAPTAIN GREGORY. *The Mutiny in Sialkot.* Sialkot: Hande Printing Press, 1924.

RICKETTS, GEORGE H. *Extracts from the Diary of a Bengal Civilian, 1857-9.* Privately printed, 1893.

A Ride for Life, in Blackwood's Magazine, January-June, 1878.

RIVETT-CARNAC, COLONEL H. *Many Memories of Life in India, at Home and Abroad.* Edinburgh: William Blackwood, 1910.

RIZVI, A. A. (*ed.*). *Freedom Struggle in Uttar Pradesh* (6 vols.). Lucknow: Information Department, 1957-61.

ROBERTS, FIELD-MARSHAL LORD. *Letters Written During the Indian Mutiny.* London: Macmillan, 1924.

ROBERTS, FIELD-MARSHAL LORD. *Forty-One Years in India* (2 vols.). London: Macmillan, 1897.

ROBERTSON, LT.-GENERAL SIR ALEXANDER. *Memoirs of General Sir Edward Harris.* London: Harrison and Sons, 1858.

ROBERTSON, H. D. *District Duties during the Revolt in the North-West Provinces.* London: Smith, Elder, 1859.

ROTTON, REV. JOHN. *The Chaplain's Narrative of the Siege of Delhi.* London: Smith, Elder, 1858.

ROWBOTHAM, WILLIAM (*ed.*). *The Naval Brigades in the Indian Mutiny.* London: Navy Records Society, 1947.

RUGGLES, JOHN. *Recollections of a Lucknow Veteran.* London: Longman's, 1906.

RUSSELL, WILLIAM HOWARD. *My Diary in India, 1858-9.* London: Routledge, Warne and Routledge, 1860.

SALMOND, ALBERT. *Salmond of Waterfoot.* London: Walter Eyre, 1887.

SAMADDAR, J. N. *Two Forgotten Mutiny Heroes,* in Indian Historical Records Commission Proceedings, Vol. x, 1927.

SAVARKAR, VINAYAK. *The Indian War of Independence of 1857.* Calcutta: R. Bhattacharaya, 1930.

SAYYID AHMED KHAN. *Rissalah Asbab-e-Bhgwat-i-Hind* (trans. Graham and Colvin). Benares: privately printed, n.d.

SCOT, CAPTAIN PATRICK. *Personal Narrative of the Escape from Naogon to Banda.* Dumfries: Herald Office, 1857.

SEATON, MAJOR GENERAL SIR THOMAS. *From Cadet to Colonel* (2 vols.). London: Hurst and Blackett, 1866.

SEDGWICK, FRANCIS. *The Indian Mutiny of 1857.* London: Forster, Green and Co., 1909.

SEN, SURENDRA NATH. *Eighteen Fifty-Seven.* Delhi: Ministry of Information, Government of India, 1957.

SETON, CAPTAIN SIR JAMES. *Outram's Division Watching Alumbagh,* in Journal of the Royal United Services Institution, Vol. 28, 1885.

SEYMOUR, CHARLES CROSSLEY. *How I Won the Indian Mutiny Medal.* Benares: Medical Hall Press, 1888.

SHACKLETON, ROBERT. *A Soldier of Delhi,* in Harper's Magazine, October, 1909.

SHADWELL, LT.-GENERAL L. *Life of Colin Campbell, Lord Clyde* (2 vols.). Edinburgh: William Blackwood, 1881.

SHEPHERD, J. W. *A Personal Narrative of the Outbreak and Massacre at Cawnpore (3rd edn.).* Lucknow: Methodist Publishing House, 1886.

SHERER, JOHN. *Daily Life During the Indian Mutiny.* London: Swan Sonnenschein, 1898.

SHERER, JOHN. *At Home and in India.* London: W. H. Allen, 1883.

SHERRING, REV. MATTHEW. *The Indian Church During the Great Rebellion.* London: James Nisbet, 1859.

SIEVEKING, I. G. *A Turning Point in the Indian Mutiny.* London: David Nutt, 1910.

Sir Hugh Rose, in The Calcutta Review, Vol. 41, 1865.

SMITH, G. *The Poetry of the Rebellion,* in The Calcutta Review, December, 1858.

SMITH, LT.-COLONEL RICHARD BAIRD. *Baird-Smith Papers During the Indian Mutiny,* in Journal of the Royal United Services Institution, Vol. XIX, 1914.

SMITH, R. BOSWORTH. *Life of Lord Lawrence.* London: Smith, Elder, 1883.

SMITH, VINCENT. *The Oxford History of India.* Oxford: Clarendon Press, 1919.

SOMERVILLE, E. *Wheel-Tracks.* London: Longman's, 1923.

SPEAR, PERCIVAL. *The Twilight of the Mughuls.* Cambridge: University Press, 1951.

STARK, HERBERT. *The Call of the Blood.* Rangoon: British Burma Press, 1932.

Statements of Regiments of Cavalry, Infantry and Artillery Embarked for India from 1st July, 1857, to 18th February, 1858.

STEEL, MRS. FLORA. *On the Face of the Waters.* London: Heinemann, 1897.

STEEL, MRS. FLORA. *The Garden of Fidelity.* London: Macmillan, 1929.

STEWART, COLONEL CHARLES. *Through Persia in Disguise.* London: Routledge, 1911.

STEWART, LT.-COLONEL RUPERT. *The Victoria Cross.* London: Hugh Rees, 1916.

STOCQUELER, J. H. *Handbook of India* (3rd edn.). London: W. H. Allen, 1854.

STRANGE, THOMAS BLAND. *Gunner Jingo's Jubilee.* London: Remington, 1893.

SUMNER, PERCY (ed.). *Indian Mutiny Recollections of Bugler Johnson,* in Soc. Army Hist. Research Journal, Autumn, 1941.

SURI, V. S. *Rajab Ali Manuscripts in the Punjab Government Record Office,* in Indian Historical Records Commission Proceedings, Vol. 29, 1953.

SWANSTON, W. O. *My Journal, by a Volunteer.* Calcutta: Baptist Mission Press, 1858.

SWINEY, G. C. *Historical Records of the 32nd (Cornwall) Light Infantry.* London: Simpkin, Marshall, 1893.

SYLVESTER, JOHN. *Recollections of the Campaign in Malwa and Central India.* Bombay: Smith, Taylor, 1860.

TAIMURI, M. H. R. *Some Unpublished Documents on the Death of the Rani of Jhansi,* in Indian Historical Records Commission Proceedings, Vol. 29, 1953.

TAYLOR, ALICIA CAMERON. *Life of General Sir Alex Taylor.* London: Williams and Norgate, 1913.

TAYLOR, BAYARD. *A Visit to India, China and Japan in the Year 1858.* Edinburgh: William Blackwood, 1859.

TAYLOR, MEADOWS. *Letters During the Indian Rebellion.* London: John E. Taylor, 1857.

TEMPLE, SIR RICHARD. *In the Century Before the Mutiny.* Bombay: privately printed, n.d.

TEMPLE, SIR RICHARD. *Men and Events of My Time in India.* London: John Murray, 1882.

THACKERAY, C. B. *A Dark and Fateful Sunday,* in Royal Artillery Journal, Vol. LXI, 1934.

THACKERAY, C. B. *Four Men on a Ridge,* in The Army Quarterly, October, 1933-July, 1934.

THACKERAY, COLONEL SIR EDWARD. *Two Indian Campaigns, 1857-8.* Chatham: Royal Engineer's Institute, 1896.

THACKERAY, COLONEL SIR EDWARD. *A Subaltern in the Indian Mutiny,* in The Royal Engineer's Journal, 1930.

THACKERAY, COLONEL SIR EDWARD. *Recollections of the Siege of Delhi,* in The Cornhill Magazine, July-December, 1913.

THICKNESSE, H. J. A. *The Indian Mutiny at Mhow and Indore*, in The Royal Artillery Journal, Vol. LXI, 1934.

THOMPSON, EDWARD. *The Other Side of the Medal*. London: Hogarth Press, 1925.

THOMPSON, EDWARD. *Suttee*. London: Allen and Unwin, 1928.

THOMPSON, EDWARD, *and* GARRATT, G. T. *Rise and Fulfilment of British Rule in India*. London: Macmillan, 1934.

THOMSON, CAPTAIN MOWBRAY. *The Story of Cawnpore*. London: Richard Bentley, 1859.

THORNHILL, MARK. *Personal Adventures of a Magistrate During the Indian Mutiny*. London: John Murray, 1884.

THORNTON, LIEUT.-COLONEL L. H. *Some Lucknow Memories*, in The Army Quarterly, Vol. 25, 1932.

Thoughts of a Native of Northern India on the Rebellion. London: W. H. Dalton, 1858.

THURBURN, E. A. *Reminiscences of the Indian Rebellion, by a Staff Officer*. London: Army and Navy Co-Operative Society, 1889.

Tourist's Guide to the Principal Stations between Calcutta and Multan and Allahabad and Bombay. Calcutta: W. Newman, 1875.

TRACY, LOUIS. *Red Year*. London: F. V. White, 1908.

TREVELYAN, RT. HON. SIR GEORGE. *Cawnpore*. London: Macmillan, 1865.

TREVELYAN, RT. HON. SIR GEORGE. *The 'Competition Wallah'*. London: Macmillan, 1864.

Trial of Mohammed Bahadur Shah for Rebellion, 1857. Lahore: Punjab Printing Co., 1870.

TROTTER, CAPTAIN LIONEL. *Life of John Nicholson*. London: John Murray, 1898.

TROTTER, CAPTAIN LIONEL. *Life of Hodson of Hodson's Horse*. London: Everyman's Library, 1910.

TROTTER, CAPTAIN LIONEL. *The Bayard of India*. London: Everyman's Library, 1910.

TUCKER, HENRY. *A Letter to an Official Concerned in the Education of India*. London: W. H. Dalton, 1858.

TURNBULL, LT.-COLONEL JOHN. *Letters Written During the Siege of Delhi*. Torquay: Directory Printing Works, 1886.

TURNBULL, LT.-COLONEL JOHN. *Sketches of Delhi*. London: T. Maclean, 1850.

TWEEDALE, LORD (ed.). *Letters from the Field During the Indian Rebellion*. London: Waterlow and Sons, 1907.

TWEEDIE, MAJOR-GENERAL W. *A Memory and A Study of the Indian Mutiny*, in Blackwood's Magazine, December, 1904.

Two Unpublished Proclamations of Nana Sahib, in Indian Historical Records Commission Proceedings, Vol. XXV, 1948.

TYRRELL, LT.-GENERAL F. H. *The Services of the Madras Native*

Troops in the Mutiny, in The Asiatic Quarterly Review, Vol. 26, 1908.

TYRRELL, ISAAC. *From England to the Antipodes and India.* Madras: Thompson and Co., 1902.

TYTLER, HARRIET C. *Through the Sepoy Mutiny and Siege of Delhi*, in Chambers' Journal, Vol. XXI, 1931.

URQUHART, DAVID. *The Rebellion in India: the wondrous tale of the greased cartridges.* London: D. Bryce, 1857.

URQUHART, DAVID. *The Rebellion in India: the illegality of the acts abolishing native customs.* London: D. Bryce, 1857.

VALBEZEN, EUGENE DE. *Les Anglais et l'Inde.* London: W. H. Allen, 1883.

VANDEVELDE, LOUIS J. *Etude sur les Indes Anglaises.* Brussels: Guyot, 1857.

VAUGHAN, SIR J. L. *My Service in the Indian Army and After.* London: Archibald Constable, 1904.

VERNEY, LIEUTENANT EDMUND, R.N. *The Shannon's Brigade in India.* London: Saunders, Otley, 1862.

VIBART, COLONEL EDWARD. *The Sepoy Mutiny.* London: Smith, Elder, 1898.

VIBART, COLONEL HENRY. *Addiscombe: its heroes and men of note.* London: Archibald Constable, 1894.

VIBART, COLONEL HENRY. *Richard Baird-Smith, Leader of the Delhi Heroes.* London: Archibald Constable, 1897.

WAGENTREIBER, MISS. *The Story of Our Escape from Delhi.* Delhi: Imperial Hall Press, 1894.

WAINE, HARRY (*ed.*). *Extracts from the Diary of Sergeant Thomas Anderson, R.H.A.*, in The Army Quarterly, July and October, 1936.

WALKER, T. N. *Through the Mutiny.* London: Gibbings and Co., 1907.

WALLACE, C. L. *Fatehgarh Camp, 1777-1857.* Lucknow: R. D. Seth, 1934.

WALLACE-DUNLOP, M. A. *and* R. *The Timely Retreat* (2 vols.). London: Richard Bentley, 1858.

WALSH, REV. J. J. *A Memorial of the Fatehgarh Mission.* Philadelphia: Joseph M. Wilson, 1859.

WARREN, LE COMTE E. DE L. *L'Inde Anglais Avant et après l'Insurrection.* Paris: Hachette, 1862.

WATERFIELD, ARTHUR. *Children of the Mutiny.* Worthing: Caxton Printing, 1935.

WATSON, EDMUND S. *Journal with H.M.S. Shannon's Naval Brigade.* Kettering: W. E. and J. Goss, 1858.

WHEELER, EDMUND H. *What Shall We Do at Delhi?* London: Daniel F. Oakey, 1857.

WHITE, S. DEWE. *Indian Reminiscences*. London: W. H. Allen, 1880.

WHITTON, F. E. *The Last of the Paladins: Sir Hugh Rose and the Indian Mutiny*, in Blackwood's Magazine, June, 1934.

WICKINS, PRIVATE CHARLES. *Journal of the 90th Light Infantry*, in Soc. Army Hist. Research Journal, 1957-60.

WILBERFORCE, REGINALD. *An Unrecorded Chapter of the Indian Mutiny*. London: John Murray, 1894.

WILLIAMS, REV. EDWARD. *Cruise of the Pearl Round the World*. London: Richard Bentley, 1859.

WILLIAMS, G. W. *Memorandum and Depositions on the Outbreak at Meerut*. Allahabad: Government Press, 1858.

WILLIAMSON, DR. GEORGE. *Notes on the Wounded from the Mutiny in India*. London: John Churchill, 1859.

WILSON, GENERAL ARCHDALE. *Letters*, in Journal of United Services Institution of India, 1923.

WILSON, JAMES. *Letter to John Bright, Esq., on the India Question*. London: Edward Stanford, 1854.

WILSON, MINDEN. *History of Bihar Indigo Factories*. Calcutta: General Printing Co., 1908.

WILSON, MAJOR THOMAS F. *The Defence of Lucknow*. London: Smith, Elder, 1858.

WIMBERLEY, CAPTAIN DOUGLAS. *The 79th Highlanders in the Indian Mutiny*.

WINDHAM, GENERAL SIR CHARLES. *Crimean Diary and Letters*. London: Kegan Paul, Trench, Trubner, 1897.

WINGFIELD, ENSIGN. *Indian Mutiny Letters*, in The Oxfordshire Light Infantry Chronicle, Vol. v, 1896.

WINTRINGHAM, THOMAS. *Mutiny*. London: Stanley North, 1936.

WISE, JAMES. *Diary of a Medical Officer*. Cork: Guy and Co., 1894.

WOLSELEY, FIELD MARSHAL VISCOUNT. *The Story of a Soldier's Life*. London: Archibald Constable, 1903.

WOOD, SIR EVELYN. *From Midshipman to Field Marshal*. London: Methuen, 1906.

WOOD, SIR EVELYN. *The Revolt in Hindustan*. London: Methuen, 1908.

WOOD, SIR EVELYN. *Winnowed Memories*. London: Cassell, 1918.

WOODRUFF, PHILIP. *The Men Who Ruled India*. London: Jonathan Cape, 1953.

WYLIE, MACLEOD. *The English Captives in Oudh*. London: W. H. Dalton, 1858.

WYLLY, H. C. *Neill's Blue Caps*. Aldershot: Gale and Polden, 1925.

WYNTER, PHILIP. *On the Queen's Errands*. London: Sir Isaac Pitman, 1906.

YEOWARD, GEORGE. *An Episode of the Rebellion and Mutiny in Oudh.* Lucknow: American Methodist Mission Press, 1871.

YOUNG, COLONEL KEITH. *Delhi, 1857.* London: Ward R. Chambers, 1902.

YULE, H. (*ed.*). *Life and Service of Major-General W. H. Greathed.* London: privately printed, 1879.

COMING SOON FROM BALLANTINE...

THE DESTRUCTION OF DRESDEN

by

David Irving

"The destruction of Dresden remains a serious query against the conduct of Allied bombing."
—*Winston Churchill*

On February 13, 1945, in a series of three bombing raids, the beautiful city of Dresden, Germany was obliterated. The reasoning behind the most successful and indiscriminate annihilation in human history—the devastating destruction of countless art treasures, 175,000 homes, and approximately 135,000 human lives (almost twice the toll at Hiroshima)—has never been clearly defined.

In "one of the finest and most memorable and valuable documentaries concerning the last war" (John Pudney—London Evening Standard), David Irving lifts the veil from what may well prove to be one of the most controversial episodes in the history of warfare.

"We should be grateful to Mr. Irving for having devoted long study to this question and for having now provided us with as accurate an account of what actually happened as we are likely to obtain . . ."
—Sir Harold Nicholson *The London Observer*

U6026   *16 pages of photographs*   75c

OUTSTANDING WORLD WAR I BOOKS
AVAILABLE FROM BALLANTINE

1918: THE LAST ACT   Barrie Pitt (U6017-75c)

"His purely military exposition is brilliant, his battle reports are as vivid as any novelist's and his understanding of the whole scene—as it might appear to an omniscient observer with a critical eye but no blinding commitment to either side . . . is very nearly without parallel."
Photographs and Maps.   —THE NEW YORKER

GALLIPOLI   Alan Moorehead (S416-75c)

"An account of that WW I campaign written as Bruce Catton might write of the Civil War . . . . It adds up to one of the great tragedies of our tragic times, both softened and made more poignant by the naivete and humanity that went into it."
Photographs.   —Walter Millis

IN FLANDERS FIELDS   Leon Wolff (U6001-75c)

A factual account of one of the most insane and brutal blood baths in the history of the Great War. The battle raged for eight months and took a total of 500,000 allied troops to gain just 4½ miles of blood-soaked land.

Leonard Mosley's fascinating account of the little known East African Campaign

DUEL FOR KILIMANJARO

In German East Africa during World War I—thousands of miles from the trenches of France—11,000 native troops under the command of General von Lettow-Vorbeck fought a British army of 200,000 men!

The only German General who was *not* defeated during the conflict, von Lettow-Vorbeck was a man of daring, imagination and courage who scrupulously observed the rules of civilized warfare.

ILLUSTRATED

U5016   60c